ALBUERA 1811

For my favourite daughters –
Katie, Elizabeth and Laura

ALBUERA 1811

THE BLOODIEST BATTLE
OF THE PENINSULAR WAR

Guy Dempsey

Foreword by
Donald E. Graves

FRONTLINE BOOKS, LONDON

Albuera 1811

This edition published in 2008 by Frontline Books,
an imprint of Pen and Sword Books Ltd,
47 Church Street, Barnsley, S. Yorkshire, S70 2AS
www.frontline-books.com

ISBN: 978-184832-499-2

British Library Cataloguing in Publication Data
Dempsey, Guy C.
Albuera, 1811 : the bloodiest battle of the Peninsular War
1. Albuera, Battle of, Albuera, Spain, 1811
I. Title
940.2'742'0946

Library of Congress Cataloging-in Publication Data available

For more information on our books, please visit
www.frontline-books.com, email info@frontline-books.com
or write to us at the above address.

Printed and bound in Great Britain by Biddles Ltd, King's Lynn

Contents

6 **Contents**

Illustrations

Maps

Cartographic Note

The maps in this book are based on the terrain depicted in Spanish National Topographical Map No. 802-III. All unit placements and movement timings represent reasoned conclusions based on analysis of primary source information.

KEY TO MAP SYMBOLS

☐	British	☰	Artillery	——	Road
☐	Portuguese	✳	Skirmishers	——	River
☐	Spanish	→	Allied advance	·······	Seasonal river
☐	French	→	French advance	∴	Buildings
◢	Cavalry	☐	Woods		

ARMY ABBREVIATIONS

CH	Chasseurs	**D**	Dragoons
VL	Vistula Legion Lancers	**LM**	Latour-Maubourg
KGL	King's German Legion	**CG**	Combined Grenadiers
LD	Light Dragoons	**PV**	Penne-Villemur
DG	Dragoon Guards	**HUS**	Hussars

Chronology

Peninsular War Events Before Albuera

1807

27 October Treaty of Fontainbleau allies Spain with France

30 November French occupy Lisbon

1808

February French troops occupy key fortresses in Spain

19 March Charles IV agrees to abdicate in favor of Ferdinand VII

April Napoleon summons Charles and Ferdinand to Bayonne

2 May Popular uprising in Madrid

5 May Charles cedes rights to the Spanish throne to Napoleon

6 May Ferdinand cedes rights to the throne to Charles

June Joseph Bonaparte accepts crown of Spain

18 July Dupont surrenders French force to Spanish at Bailen

1 August British forces under Wellesley land in Portugal

21 August Wellington defeats Junot's army at Vimeiro

30 August Junot agrees to evacuate Portugal pursuant to the Convention of Cintra

November Napoleon defeats Spanish armies at Gamonal, Espinosa and Tudela

4 December Madrid surrenders to French

1809

16 January British forces under Moore defeat Soult at Corunna

20 February Saragossa falls to the French

28 March French forces crush a Spanish army at Medellin

29 March Soult captures Oporto

12 May British forces drive Soult out of Oporto

28 July British and Spanish defeat French forces at Talavera

19 November French forces rout Spanish at the Battle of Ocaña

11 December Girona falls to the French

1810

1 February Seville falls to the French

5 February French begin siege of Cadiz

14 May Lerida falls to the French

9 July Ciudad Rodrigo falls to the French

28 July Almeida falls to the French

27 September Wellington rebuffs Masséna at the Battle of Bussaco

11 October Masséna reaches the Lines of Torres Vedras (Portugal)

1811

2 January Tortosa falls to the French

21 January Olivenza falls to the French

19 February French rout Spanish forces at the Battle of the Gevora

4 March Masséna begins retreat from Lisbon

5 March British forces prevail at the Battle of Barrosa

10 March Badajoz falls to the French

21 March Campo Mayor falls to French

25 March Campo Mayor abandoned by the French

15 April Olivenza falls to the British

3–5 May Wellington prevails at Battle of Fuentes de Onor

4 May British start siege of Badajoz

16 May Battle of Albuera

Acknowledgements

The research for this book was conducted over a very long period of time and I consequently owe innumerable debts of gratitude to helpful historians, archivists, librarians and Napoleonic researchers (professional and amateur) all over the world who provided assistance along the way. I would like to start by naming the most significant institutions that contributed to my research: The Badminton Archives, Badminton House, South Gloucestershire, England; Bedfordshire Record Office; The British Library, London; Derbyshire Record Office; Durham Record Office; Central Library, Royal Military Academy, Sandhurst; the Musée de l'Armée, Paris; The Museum of the Royal Welch Fusiliers, Caernarfon Castle, Gwynedd, Wales; The Museum of the Duke of Edinburgh's Royal Regiment, Salisbury, England; The National Archives and Library of Scotland, Edinburgh; The National Army Museum, London; The National Archives/Public Records Office, Kew, England; The Newberry Library, Chicago; Sterling Memorial Library, Yale University, New Haven, CT; The New York Public Library; The Anne Brown Military Collection, Brown University, Providence, RI; Archives et Centre Culturel d'Arenberg, Enghien, Belgium; Arquivos Nacionais de Torre de Tombo, Lisbon; The Royal Artillery Institution, Woolwich, England; Musée Pyrénéen, Lourdes, France; and The Rye Free Reading Room, Rye, NY.

One of the most enjoyable aspects of historical research is that it brings one into contact with generous and helpful people all over the world. With apologies to anyone I have overlooked, I wish to thank the following individuals for their contributions to this work: Peter Harrington and Tony Broughton for assistance with illustrations; Luis Sorando Muzás and José Luis Arcon Dominguez for help with Spanish questions; Dr J. Q. C. Mackrell; Nigel Lutt; Page Life for introducing me to Major Wilson's Journal; Joy Austria for verifying the content of Wilson's Journal; Michael Taenzer for help with German sources; Geert van Uythoven; Rory Muir; Philip Haythornthwaite; Mark Urban; Bob Burnham, Steve Smith, Tom Holmberg, Ron McGuigan, Oliver Schmidt and other assorted contributors who responded to Albuera questions on the Napoleon Series Discussion Forum; Desmond Vigors for sharing his unique research concerning the Guelphic Archives; Alan Lagdon for sharing Lieutenant Bayley's letter; Jean Sarramon; Antonio Henrique Afonso; Markus Gärtner; J.-P. Loriot for transcribing the French order of battle from the SHAT; and Vivien Burgess for tracking down an obscure article. I also received important help with sources from an array of translators: Manfred Ernst (German); Simone Meiseles,

Alejandro Millan Seeber and João Centeno (Portuguese); and Barbara Gazdik and Witold Lawrynowicz (Polish).

Two people qualify for special mention because of the extraordinary help they have given me. Mark Thompson is the modern pioneer of serious research concerning the battle and his book, *The Fatal Hill – The Allied Campaign under Beresford in Southern Spain in 1811*, showed the way for my work. I am grateful to him both for his reprints of rare pamphlets relating to the campaign and his willingness to share sources and discuss complex points of detail. Don Graves, who has written the best short history of the battle in *Fix Bayonets! A Royal Welch Fusilier at War, 1796–1815*, his fascinating biography of Major Thomas Pearson of the 23rd Foot, graciously shared with me his vast knowledge of the battle and, equally importantly, his practical experiences as a professional historian.

I would also like to thank Michael Leventhal of Frontline Books for allowing me scope to write the comprehensive study that lies before you. I am grateful to Henry Alban Davies and Donald Sommerville for saving me from many small errors and inconsistencies. Any errors left are my fault, not theirs. The maps were prepared by Jonathan Young of Red Lion Mapping, who did a superb job with the complex raw material presented to him.

As has been the case with all my books, the most important assistance I received was from my family. I therefore also also want to express my gratitude and love to Nancy, Katie, Elizabeth and Laura for their support of my unusual and lengthy research project. Also deserving of mention are Will, Sam, Connor and Cary Sullivan and Emily, Sarah and Teddy Stubbs.

Notes for Readers

This book has been written in accordance with the Duke of Wellington's views on writing about battles: 'If it is to be history it must be the truth, and the whole truth, or it will do more harm than good, and will give as many false notions of what a battle is, as other romances of the same description have.'[1] I have consequently tried to make sure that everything the reader finds in this book will be the 'truth' (or will, at least, be information obtained from critical examination of primary sources), which is why this book is heavily annotated. With very few exceptions, simplified author and title references are used for each work cited in the notes, but these simplified references can be used to find the full details of the work in the Bibliography.

In addition, the following abbreviations are used in the notes for the purpose of saving space:

B. = Beresford
EP = Edward Pakenham
N. = Napoleon
W. = Wellington
NA/PRO = National Archives/Public Records Office, Kew
NAM = National Army Museum, London
SHAT = Service Historique de l'Armée de Terre, Paris
AN = Archives Nationales, Paris
Correspondance = The edition of Napoleon I's *Correspondance* published by
   Napoleon III
Dispatches = The 1838 edition of the Duke of Wellington's *Dispatches*
Supp. Despatches = Wellington's *Supplementary Despatches*, as published 1858–72

All British officer names have been verified against the War Office *Army List* for 1811. Every British officer who joined the Portuguese Army to serve under Beresford kept his British rank as well as receiving a Portuguese rank that was at least one step higher. When such an officer is mentioned in this work, his higher Portuguese rank is

---

1. W. to Earl of Mulgrave, 21 December 1815, quoted in Duncan, *History of the Royal Regiment of Artillery*, Vol. 2, pp. 447–8.

used. Since the French did not have an official army list after 1805 due to Napoleon's concerns about military secrecy, the spelling of all French officer names has been conformed to the extent possible to that used in Martinien's *Tableaux* and the biographical dictionaries compiled by Six and Quintin.

All place names have been conformed to Spanish usage.

Foreword

I am very pleased to contribute a foreword to *Albuera 1811*, Guy Dempsey's new study of that notorious but somewhat neglected engagement that has always deserved closer examination from historians than it has received. This is not only because – as the subtitle states – Albuera was the bloodiest single battle, in terms of losses suffered by the number of troops engaged, of the Peninsular War but also because it has been the subject of controversy from the time the last shot was fired nearly two centuries ago. It is therefore a matter of celebration that, at long last, 'Red Albuera' has finally been accorded the attention it merits.

I am also pleased that Guy Dempsey has rendered his acknowledgement to Mark Thompson whose pioneer work, *Fatal Hill*, on the 1811 campaign in Extremadura, marks the beginning of modern re-examination of Albuera. In addition, I am gratified that he has acknowledged *Fix Bayonets!*, my biography of Lieutenant General Sir Thomas Pearson which contains a shorter account of Albuera that concentrates on the role of the Fusilier Brigade in the battle, particularly the 23rd Foot, or Royal Welch Fusiliers. The three of us have long corresponded about Albuera, exchanging information and research discoveries.

Guy Dempsey, however, has gone beyond these earlier examinations and extended his research, both broadly and deeply, into hitherto untouched sources – notably in French and Spanish archives. He not only provides a succinct but complete background context for the engagement by examining the campaigns of 1810 and 1811 which led its being fought but his analysis and narrative of the actual battle is complete, dispassionate and objective. Noteworthy is the fact that although Albuera saw the soldiers of six nations (Britain, France, the German states, Poland, Portugal and Spain) fight and fight hard, it is almost impossible to detect national bias in Dempsey's work.

Albuera 1811 emphasises the stress of combat, from the highest levels of leadership to the lowest. We follow Marshal William Beresford, personally brave but perhaps too sensitive for the command he held, as control of the engagement slips inexorably out of his hands and we march or ride with the soldiers of six nations at the unit level, as they try to do their duty in a terrible and confusing battle. The author, however, always keeps a tight grip on his emotions, as one must while writing about such a subject and states the facts, but does *not* underline them. Indeed, as becomes clear below, the bare facts of Albuera are terrible in themselves.

A notable attribute of this book is Dempsey's careful analysis of the tactical methods used by the opposing armies during the battle. As Dempsey quite rightly points out, for the British army Albuera witnessed a departure from its standard infantry tactics in the Peninsula – with cruel results. In doing so, Dempsey has discovered and, more importantly, corrected a very serious error made by Sir Charles Oman concerning the deployment of the French army at Albuera in his account of the battle. This error, repeated by almost every historian who has come after Oman, including John Fortescue and the present author (who faces some revision if my biography of Pearson is reprinted), has coloured our perception of the battle since 1911 when it first appeared in print. This is revisionism of the highest order – going back to the original source and seeing if it says what others have stated it does – and it is also the essence of scholarship.

Albuera 1811, however, is more than just a dry analytical discourse on the leadership, strategy, operations and tactics of the opposing armies in a sanguinary Peninsular battle. Guy Dempsey has provided considerable information on its human cost. The chapters on the treatment of the wounded, the burying of the dead, the fate of prisoners on both sides, the notification of fatal casualties and the postwar life of some of the principal characters of the engagement emphasize that, among the victims of war, are often its survivors. Particularly touching are the postwar stories of Lieutenant Matthew Latham of the 3rd Foot, dreadfully mutilated in the face while defending his regiment's colours and Général de brigade Jean-Pierre Maransin, shot through the abdomen at the battle and who, not expected to live, did so but with great difficulty.

The author completes his account with some very useful appendices. These include detailed orders of battle, an analysis of casualties, the uniforms of the opposing forces and an examination of some of the myths that have grown up around Albuera including the loss of British colours and the origins of 'The Die Hards', the regimental nickname of the 57th Foot, at the battle. Nor does he neglect the postwar pamphlet battle waged by Beresford and his detractors, which has provided so much primary source material about the battle and the campaign of which it forms a part.

In sum, *Albuera 1811* is an excellent, detailed and exciting account – based on much new research and told with a remarkable economy of prose – of an important but long-neglected battle of the Napoleonic wars. In my opinion, it will be accorded the accolade of being the definitive study of its subject for a long time to come and it belongs in the library of not only scholars and serious students of the Napoleonic wars but also the general reader interested in the nature and cost of combat in the early nineteenth century. At one and the same time, readable, comprehensive and compelling, *Albuera 1811* is an exercise in military history at its best.

Donald E. Graves
2008

ALBUERA 1811

Oh, Albuera! glorious field of grief!
As o'er thy plain the pilgrim prick'd his steed,
Who could foresee thee, in a space so brief,
A scene where mingling foes should boast and bleed!
Peace to the perish'd! may the warrior's meed
And tears of triumph their reward prolong!
Till others fall where other chieftains lead
Thy name shall circle round the gaping throng;
And shine in worthless lays, the theme of transient song!

from 'Childe Harold's Pilgrimage, A Romaunt',
by Lord George Byron

Introduction

The solitary rider who entered the gates of the Portuguese fortress of Elvas on the evening of Monday, 20 May 1811, had made good time on his journey, but his pace probably slowed as he started the long winding climb to the centre of town. Portuguese Lieutenant Colonel Robert Arbuthnot, the Military Secretary to Field Marshal Sir William Carr Beresford, Commander-in-Chief of the Portuguese Army, had been a soldier for fourteen years, but it is doubtful that he had ever previously had an assignment to equal the one he was discharging that day. For he was riding to meet Lieutenant General Viscount Wellington of Talavera (the former Sir Arthur Wellesley), commander of the British forces in Portugal, and in his pocket he carried a dispatch for Wellington from Beresford describing a battle fought against the French by a combined Spanish, Portuguese and British army at the village of Albuera in Spain on Thursday, 16 May 1811.[1]

As might be expected given Wellington's disregard for military pomp and circumstance, there was little evidence in the Elvas town square to indicate the presence of his temporary headquarters other than a few officers and men in jackets of various hues of red. There was also little formality as Lieutenant Colonel Arbuthnot presented himself to one of Lord Wellington's aides and was immediately ushered into the general's presence despite the fact that Wellington and his staff were engaged in their dinner. There was a brief greeting and then the dispatch was handed over. Wellington cleared space at the table, opened the letter and began to read.

When he arrived at Elvas on the afternoon of the previous day, Wellington had found waiting for him a short, private letter written by Beresford on the 17th. The letter reported that a French army under Marshal Jean-de-Dieu Soult had been repulsed by Beresford's forces, but the action was described in terms better suited to a valiant defeat than a decisive triumph:

---

1. The name of the village appears as 'La Albuera' on modern maps prepared by the Geographic Service of the Spanish Army and that version of the name was also used in some contemporary accounts of the battle. However, for the sake of convenience and consistency with the usage of most participants and historians, this book omits the prefatory article in referring to both the village and the battle. As to the precise spelling of the place name, even contemporary Spanish sources seem split on whether the village was known as 'Albuera' or 'Albuhera', with the latter spelling being perpetuated through history primarily because it was used by the British Army in awarding battle honours to the units that participated in the action. Once again, convenience and consistency have led to the use of the more familiar spelling without the 'h' in this book.

... tho' against my own most decided opinion ... I consented to oppose Soult ... We have by beating him escaped total destruction ... and I am very, very far from feeling happy after our triumph.[2]

Wellington responded immediately with a short, encouraging word to his subordinate:

Your loss, by all accounts, has been very large; but I hope that it will not prove so large as was at first supposed. You could not be successful in such an action without a large loss; we must make up our minds to affairs of this kind sometimes, or give up the game.[3]

Now Beresford's official report gave the stunning details: the Allied position had been outflanked by a surprise manoeuvre, one entire brigade of precious British troops had been annihilated in a cavalry charge, another had literally been shot to pieces in an unprecedented musket duel with enemy infantry, and a third had suffered grievous casualties in a final desperate charge against superior numbers which had at least enabled Beresford to retain final possession of the corpse-strewn field of battle. The French had held their original position through the 17th and had only retired (without any pursuit) on the 18th. As if the facts alone were not bad enough, Wellington was appalled to find that the dispatch was written in a completely despondent tone. Although the original dispatch has been lost to history, something of its flavour can be imagined from Beresford's covering letter, which has survived:

Arbuthnot with the dispatch will set out for you this evening, and reach you before you go to bed ... I feel much for the number we have lost and I thank you for what you state; but I freely confess to you I can scarcely forgive myself for risking this battle, and I as freely confess that it was very unwise, and I am convinced that I ought not to have done it.[4]

Wellington was a politician as well as a military man; he knew that a 'whining report ... would drive the people in England mad'.[5] As he recalled years later, his response to the problem was refreshingly forthright: 'I said directly, this won't do, write me down a victory. The dispatch was altered accordingly. Afterwards, they grew very proud of the battle, and with full reason.'[6] A British pen thus resolved the ambiguities left over from the clash of swords on the battlefield.

The reaction of Wellington was the most decisive aspect of the Battle of Albuera. On 21 May, Wellington accompanied Lieutenant Colonel Arbuthnot back to Allied headquarters at Albuera itself and a revised dispatch was quickly drafted (albeit one which still bore the date of 18 May).[7] The tone of Beresford's opening paragraph now left nothing to doubt:

2. B. to W., 17 May 1811, Wellington Papers 1/330, Southampton University, quoted in Woolgar, 'Writing the Dispatch', p. 8. Numerous sources incorrectly state that Soult's first name was Nicolas, but that name is nowhere to be found on his baptismal certificate, which is reproduced in Hayman, *Maligned Marshal*, opposite p. 96.
3. W. to B., Elvas, 19 May 1811 (4:30 p.m.), *Dispatches*, Vol. 7, p. 573.
4. B. to W., Albuera, 20 May 1811 (10:30 a.m.), *Supp. Despatches*, Vol. 7, pp. 133–4.
5. W. to William Wellesley-Pole, 2 July 1811, *Supp. Despatches*, Vol. 7, pp. 175–7, at 176.
6. Stanhope, *Notes of Conversations*, p. 90.
7. The exact changes made are unknown, but they were probably extensive since the surviving manuscript copy of the dispatch signed by Beresford is in the handwriting of Lord Fitzroy Somerset,

I have infinite satisfaction in communicating to your Lordship that the allied army, united here under my orders, obtained, on the 16th instant, after a most sanguinary contest, a complete victory over that of the enemy, commanded by Marshal Soult.[8]

Arbuthnot carried the report on to London, and on 3 June 1811, the day before the 73rd birthday of King George III, it was published in the *London Gazette*. Its reception was unequivocal. As custom demanded, Arbuthnot, as the bearer of dispatches announcing a major victory, received an immediate promotion. On 7 June, the Lords and Commons adopted unanimous votes of thanks to recognise '. . . the merits of the general, the officers and the gallant army engaged in the glorious battle of Albuera'.[9]

The Battle of Albuera thus became a French defeat and a British, Portuguese and Spanish victory, but, despite the many significant outcomes that were possible when the battle began, it never became a significant event in history (except, most certainly, for the individuals who fought there). If Marshal Beresford had been routed, another French invasion of Portugal might have become possible; if he had merely been forced to retreat, the result might have been a dramatic weakening of the British commitment to support the struggle of the Spanish and Portuguese against Napoleon. If, on the other hand, Marshal Soult's small army had been destroyed, the fall of Badajoz to the allies would have certainly ensued and allied reconquest of Andalucia would have become a realistic possibility for 1811. As the battle ebbed and flowed, any of these outcomes could have occurred, but in the end neither army was able to achieve a decisive enough triumph to bring about any such results.

The Battle of Albuera is, nevertheless, a worthy subject for study. The military history of this period is so overshadowed by the colossal figures of Napoleon and Wellington that a major battle fought without either present provides a unique opportunity for investigating and understanding the elements of Napoleonic warfare as it was actually practised on the battlefield by 'ordinary' commanders. The demands of siege warfare, the complexity of coalition command, the opportunistic employment of cavalry, the use of pontoon bridges, the relative merits of line and column tactical formations, the power of massed artillery – all these topics and more form part of the Albuera story. The pages that follow constitute an attempt to tell that story in fine detail, using primary source material from all the contending armies to dispel long-standing confusion and correct long-standing misconceptions (engendered in many cases by nationalistic bias) about the events of that distant spring day. The story of Albuera is, however, more than a mere tale of drums and guns and serried ranks. It is also, to paraphrase Lord Byron, an epic narrative of grief and glory, so this book also tries to describe the experiences of individual soldiers during the battle and the effects of the battle on men who survived the action, whether wounded or not, captured or free, and on the families and friends of the men who were killed.

Wellington's military secretary, not that of Arbuthnot, Beresford's own staff officer. There is even one manuscript change in Wellington's own hand (adding a favourable reference to Brigadier Carlos d'España). Woolgar, 'Writing the Dispatch', pp. 8–9.

8. The full text of Beresford's final report was published in *The London Gazette Extraordinary* of 3 June 1811, and is reproduced as an enclosure to W. to Lord Liverpool, 22 May 1811, *Dispatches,* Vol. 7, pp. 588–93.

9. Hansard, *Parliamentary Debates*, Vol. XX, Cols. 511–17 and 519–32.

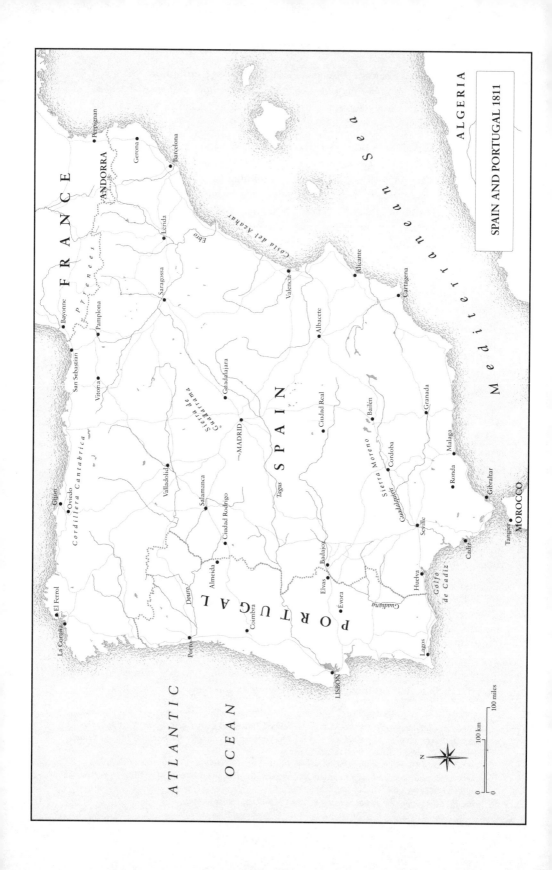

SPAIN AND PORTUGAL 1811

Chapter 1

The French Invasion
of Portugal

The story of Albuera perhaps starts most logically, albeit somewhat remotely, with Napoleon's overthrow of the Spanish monarchy in 1808.[1] In theory, at least, the replacement of the old Bourbon dynasty by Napoleon's brother, King Joseph, was achieved with sufficient legal formality to make Joseph the legitimate new monarch to whom all Spain should have been subservient. In reality, of course, the Spaniards took exception to the change and forced Napoleon to establish his brother's position by right of conquest rather than by acquiescence of the governed. The French armies were triumphant everywhere they found an organised foe to fight, but the new Bonapartist state which came into being in their wake was clearly an artificial creation. Moreover, its existence was compromised from its inception by the need to pay an extraordinarily heavy price in money, supplies and even territory for Napoleon's support.

By 1810, after two years of near-constant strife, the size of Joseph's kingdom looked respectable enough on paper, but the only territory he truly controlled was that actually occupied by the French and their allies and by his own small army. On all sides, military threats presented themselves. Indeed, the French armies in Spain in 1810 were essentially fighting a five-front war. To the north and west, Galicia had liberated itself in 1809 and the French occupation of the Asturias was continually being challenged. In the west, a large French force was required to face the combined armies of Britain and Portugal. In the south, Marshal Soult had conquered Andalucia and Granada with three army corps, but these proved to be only just sufficient for the subsequent tasks of besieging the temporary Spanish capital of Cadiz, screening the surviving Spanish field armies in the neighbouring regions of Extremadura and Murcia and reacting to the forays of regional guerilla bands and Spanish regular forces supported from a variety of bases, including Gibraltar. On the eastern side of the Peninsula, the forces of General Louis-Gabriel Suchet had their hands full contending with the Spanish forces in Catalonia and Valencia. Finally, the French were engaged throughout the country in a protracted and debilitating struggle against the guerilla

---

1. For more detailed information about the overthrow of the Bourbon monarchy, see this author's chapter, 'The Peninsular War: A Reputation Tarnished', in *Napoleon: The Final Verdict*, London, 1996, pp. 83–110, a collection of essays edited by Philip Haythornthwaite.

forces which, fed by a mixture of religious zealotry and national indignation over Napoleon's treatment of their country, had sprung up to pose a nearly insoluble problem for the occupying armies.

From Napoleon's strategic perspective, however, the situation was much simpler. England was his implacable foe and therefore the British Army in Portugal had to be his primary target. Given the ease with which the French forces were able to defeat regular Spanish armies, it seemed logical to conclude that, once the British were disposed of, the rest of Spain would fall easily under French control. Moreover, the British forces in the Peninsula seemed vulnerable as a practical matter. The British Army was small and it had been quiescent since the Talavera campaign in the summer of 1809. Furthermore, the only support it could call upon was a Portuguese Army which could hardly be very impressive given that the French had carried off the best Portuguese officers and men in 1807 to form the Portuguese Legion serving with the French Army.

As a result, the centrepiece of the French plan of campaign for 1810 was to be an invasion of Portugal which would rid the Iberian Peninsula once and for all of the British forces which simultaneously supported the Portuguese monarchy and posed a threat to Napoleon's Spanish puppet state. Although Marshal Soult had been appointed in October 1809 as the senior field officer of all the French and allied military forces under King Joseph's command, it was obvious by the start of the new year that he would be much too preoccupied in Andalucia to oversee that key task. For a while, it appeared the Napoleon might take advantage of peace with Austria to come to the Peninsula himself, but he was ultimately distracted by the demands of arranging his divorce from Josephine and remarriage to Marie Louise of Austria. He finally decided in April 1810 that he would call upon Marshal André Masséna, one of his most capable and experienced commanders, to serve in his stead as commander of the newly formed, and aptly named, Army of Portugal. Masséna, now aged fifty-two, had recently received the title of Prince of Essling in recognition of his brilliant service in the battles outside Vienna in 1809, and he was reputedly unhappy with having drawn such a difficult assignment instead of an easier ceremonial command in some pleasant city. Napoleon, however, used a combination of flattery and challenge which left the marshal little practical choice in the matter: 'Who else can I send to Portugal to restore my affairs there, which have been compromised by bunglers, if not the man who has always saved the day for me in the past.'[2] Masséna therefore reluctantly accepted the challenge, perhaps trusting in the combination of skill and luck which had gained him a reputation as the 'Cherished Child of Victory'.[3]

The first task for the marshal was to decide on his line of advance with due consideration of the deceptive military geography of the Iberian Peninsula. On paper, the best route for an invader heading from Madrid to Lisbon would appear to be the direct one following the valley of the Tagus River. But, as General Jean-Andoche Junot and his men discovered during the first French invasion of Portugal in 1807, that approach is in fact impractical for artillery, wheeled transport and horsemen in any

2. Masséna, *Mémoires,* Vol. VII, p. 20.
3. For the origins of this sobriquet in 1797 during the first Italian campaign of Bonaparte, see Marshall-Cornwall, *Marshal Masséna,* p. 48.

significant numbers. Instead, the two recognised invasion routes between Portugal and Spain are more oblique, one situated north of the Tagus and the other well to the south of that river. Each route is marked at the frontier between the two countries by a matched pair of border fortresses, one Spanish and one Portuguese, in recognition of the fact that they are two-way thoroughfares. In the north, the fortresses are Ciudad Rodrigo on the Spanish side of the frontier and Almeida on the Portuguese side. In the south, the pair is Badajoz in Spain and Elvas in Portugal. Given logistical limitations, an invader desiring to proceed on either of these routes had to control or neutralise both fortresses of the relevant pair. At the start of 1810, all these towns were held by France's enemies.

In theory, Masséna was free to choose whichever of the two routes he preferred, but the fact that the bulk of his army was situated in Old Castile made an advance on Lisbon from the north more likely. In addition, what freedom he did have was eliminated at the end of May when Napoleon dictated instructions setting both objectives and a timetable for the marshal:

> [I]nform the Prince of Essling that ... he will first besiege Ciudad Rodrigo and then Almeida, all the while preparing for a methodical advance into Portugal, which I do not wish to enter before September, after the heat and, above all, after the harvest.[4]

Accordingly, once Masséna had assembled his invasion force, he began work to secure both components of the northern gateway. The Spanish garrison of Ciudad Rodrigo mounted an unexpectedly stubborn defence, but the fortress nevertheless surrendered on 10 July.[5] Both Masséna and Soult believed that Badajoz should then have been secured as well before the invasion of Portugal was attempted, with Soult putting the case most bluntly (and prophetically) in a June letter to Marshal Louis-Alexandre Berthier, the titular major general of all the French armies in Spain:

> As soon as the siege of Ciudad Rodrigo is over, it makes sense to attack Badajoz even before attacking Almeida and entangling ourselves in Portugal. If we enter Portugal before taking Badajoz, we will perhaps be obliged to reverse course and besiege that town. If we capture Badajoz at once, the success of the expedition against Portugal is assured; if we do not, then the expedition will remain a risky business.[6]

The emperor, however, dismissed that idea on 29 July as a waste of effort which would divert attention from the primary objective of defeating the British:

> The Emperor does not believe that it is necessary to take Badajoz, an undertaking which itself would involve a significant siege and which would as well lead inevitably to a siege of Elvas, which is an even stronger fortress; once

---

4. N. to Berthier, 29 May 1810, *Correspondance*, No. 16519, Vol. 20, p. 385.
5. For details of the siege of Ciudad Rodrigo, see Horward, *Napoleon and Iberia*, pp. 80–185.
6. Soult, *Mémoires*, p. 207. Baron Antoine Jomini, the military theorist who actually participated in the invasion as a staff officer serving under Marshal Michel Ney, held the same view: 'It is clear that the invasion would have had more chances for success if Soult had captured Badajoz at the same time as Masséna took Almeida and if the two armies advanced in concert against Lisbon on both banks of the Tagus.' Jomini, *Guerre d'Espagne*, p. 161.

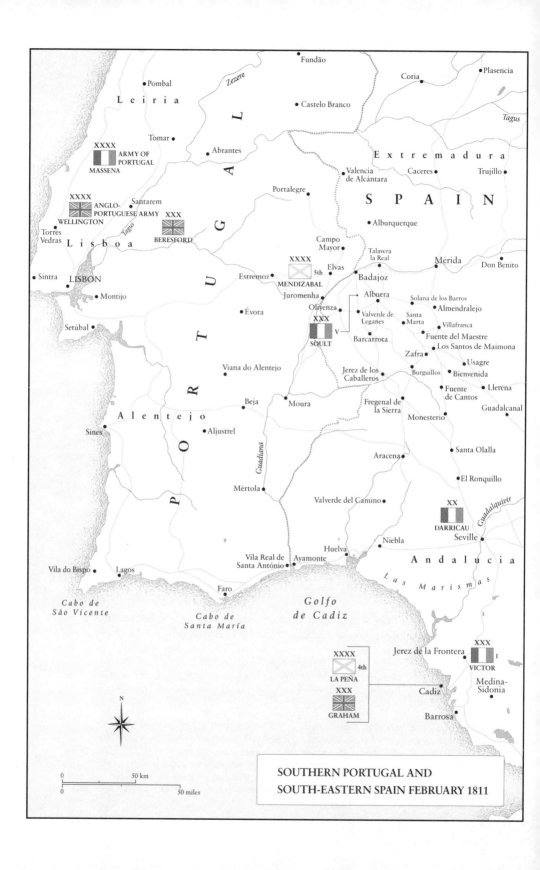

SOUTHERN PORTUGAL AND
SOUTH-EASTERN SPAIN FEBRUARY 1811

the English have been beaten and forced to re-embark, Badajoz and Elvas will fall easily.[7]

What Napoleon failed to consider, however, was that the possibility that he might need Soult to cooperate with Masséna via the southern invasion route in order to ensure that victory over the British was achieved.

Masséna therefore proceeded instead to attack Almeida. This time the fortunes of war favoured the French because a single artillery shot from the besiegers touched off a massive explosion in the main ammunition storage room of the fortress. With the town in ruins, the garrison decimated and gunpowder supplies nearly exhausted, the governor of the fortress was forced to surrender on 28 August.[8] Masséna was now free to march on Lisbon. Wellington and his Anglo-Portuguese army inflicted a sharp repulse on the French at the Battle of Bussaco on 27 September, but they were not strong enough to halt Masséna's progress for long. By early October, the Army of Portugal was swiftly approaching Lisbon and seemed poised to accomplish Napoleon's objective of driving the British into the sea.

Unfortunately for the French, however, Masséna was not successful, and the primary reason for his failure was one of the most remarkable 'secret' weapons in all of history – the agglomeration of fortifications and field works which is known collectively as the Lines of Torres Vedras.[9] Conceived by Wellington in a memo dated 20 October 1809 and built by thousands of Portuguese labourers working under the direction of British engineers commanded by Lieutenant Colonel Richard Fletcher, the Lines reached from the shores of the Atlantic Ocean to the banks of the Tagus River north of Lisbon, and thus covered the approaches both to the Portuguese capital and to possible embarkation points for a defeated British army. Even given the sometimes primitive state of early nineteenth-century communications, it is almost inconceivable that the French could have been unaware of such an immense project. In fact, however, they were, and this intelligence failure made the effect of the Lines all the more stunning. The recollections of Jean-Jacques Pelet, Masséna's senior aide-de-camp, are perhaps typical of French reaction to this unexpected development:

> The Lines were of such an extraordinary nature that I daresay there was no other position in the world that could be compared to them. In effect, it was not enough to encounter this formidable wall of rocks, supported on the one side by the sea and the other by an immense river. Behind it was a great capital with its arsenals, workshops, magazines to furnish all need, workers of every description, artillery depots and numerous batteries where large calibre guns were concentrated. Moreover, the population was deluded and influenced enough to construct and defend all those fortifications; there was sufficient time to prepare them in advance, an open sea to feed everyone and a large unencumbered fleet.[10]

Masséna probed and prodded, but soon concluded that any attempt to break through the Lines would at best lead to a pyrrhic victory. He was, however, stubborn

---

7. Berthier to Masséna, 29 July 1810, *Correspondance*, No. 16732, Vol. 20, pp. 552–3.
8. For the siege of Almeida, see Horward, *Napoleon and Iberia*, pp. 249–317.
9. See generally, Norris & Bremner, *The Lines of Torres Vedras*.
10. Pelet, *Campaign in Portugal*, p. 234.

as well as skillful, as he had proved in holding off the forces of the Second Coalition at Zurich in 1799 and in clinging tenaciously to the besieged city of Genoa in 1800 while Napoleon executed the alpine crossing that led to the victory of Marengo. The marshal therefore decided to play a waiting game in the hope that future events might resurrect the possibility of a successful conclusion to his campaign. He summarised the situation for the emperor:

> I will hold my position with the hope that the Portuguese refugees in Lisbon will turn against the English, who have reduced them to the most horrific misery, or that Lord Wellington will leave his fortifications to offer or receive battle. If my efforts to establish a bridge across the Tagus are successful, I will be able to manoeuvre on both banks and live off the resources of the Alemtejo [*sic*], which is the most fertile and richest province of Portugal. I will also be able in this position to await the reinforcements which Your Majesty will not have failed to have sent me.[11]

This message was entrusted to Division General Maximilien-Sebastien Foy, who left the Army of Portugal on 31 October with an entire infantry battalion as his escort. He arrived at Ciudad Rodrigo on 8 November and then immediately set out for Paris, which he reached on 21 November. On 14 November, Masséna pulled back to a more defensible position based on Santarem, but otherwise his situation remained unchanged.

By this point, it was clear that the original French invasion plan for 1810 had failed. The only hope for the imperial forces was the creation of a new, alternate plan which could use the achievements of Masséna as a building block for success. One such plan would have been to collect an army of reinforcements and send it directly to Masséna so that the marshal would have enough troops either to batter through the British fortifications or to open up a realistic second front on the other bank of the Tagus River. Another would have been to open that second front with a strong force advancing out of Andalucia under Marshal Soult. With General Foy in Paris to provide eyewitness testimony concerning Masséna's situation, Napoleon for once had relatively fresh information to act on and there were no other foreign or domestic problems to distract his attention. Despite these favourable circumstances, the greatest captain of his age failed to apply the elementary principle of concentration of effort which was normally the hallmark of his military thinking. He settled for trying both plans simultaneously, but neither decisively.

The direct reinforcements took the form of the newly-organised IX Corps under the command of General Jean-Baptiste Drouet d'Erlon.[12] In fact, as early as 3 November, Napoleon had ordered him to move to Almeida and to re-open communications with the Army of Portugal.[13] After his briefing from Foy, Napoleon apparently took steps to hasten Drouet d'Erlon's movements, but the new formation was so lacking in staff and transport that its progress was excruciatingly slow and it had still not made contact with Masséna by the end of the year. More importantly, the size of the force was

---

11. Masséna, *Mémoires*, Vol. 7, pp. 249–50.
12. The IX Corps was formed from assorted detached battalions and provisional regiments by orders initiated on 28 September. N. to Berthier, *Correspondance,* Nos. 16962 and 16963, Vol. 21, pp. 154–6.
13. N. to Berthier, 3 November 1810, *Correspondance*, No. 17097, Vol. 21, pp. 250–1.

unlikely to lead to any decisive result since it had an original paper strength of less than 20,000 men and Drouet d'Erlon had been ordered to leave substantial garrisons along his lines of communications as he moved through Portugal.[14] Even more remarkable is the fact that Napoleon never formally made IX Corps part of the Army of Portugal, so it was not actually subject to Masséna's orders. As a last irony, Drouet d'Erlon's force was made up in significant part of battalions originally destined to reinforce parent units in the Army of the South, so their use in Portugal meant that Soult was correspondingly deprived of their services.[15]

The plan of opening a second front from Andalucia depended entirely on the talents of Marshal Soult (b. 1769), a complex man who was one of only a very few French generals with sufficient confidence to stand up to the emperor if he felt such a stance was warranted. He had learned his craft as a general under the tutelage of none other than Masséna in fighting in Switzerland in 1799 and Genoa in 1800. Elevated to the marshalate in 1804, he had led IV Corps of the Grande Armée to triumph after triumph at Austerlitz, Jena and even Eylau. His performance earned him the title of Duc de Dalmatie (Dalmatia, often wryly translated as the 'Duke of Damnation' by his British opponents). According to Wellington, who had governmental dealings with him after the Restoration, Soult 'was a very large man – very tall and large, like Marshal Beresford – a harsh voice, and not a very pleasant countenance or manner'.[16] During his time in Spain, he was constantly embroiled in controversy. He failed to defeat Moore at Corunna, was associated with an abortive effort to be recognised as sovereign of northern Portugal, and was soundly defeated at Oporto in 1809. He feuded frequently with King Joseph and his fellow marshals, but he always managed to avoid complete disgrace because Napoleon valued his abilities as an administrator and commander. He also became noticeably rapacious in the Peninsula, amassing great wealth and a huge collection of valuable paintings and, despite his devotion to his wife, Louise, keeping a mistress (known to the troops as '*la Maréchale*') in lavish style at Seville.[17] By 1811, one of his senior aides-de-camp, Colonel Alfred-Armand-Robert de Saint-Chamans, thought that Soult had become more cautious in battle as he became more wealthy.[18]

The decision to use Soult's forces to break Masséna's stalemate was a remarkable about-face for the emperor, given that Napoleon had made no effort at all during early 1810 to coordinate Soult's and Masséna's activities and thus anticipate the situation he now faced. In fact, the emperor's only relevant actions earlier in the year seem almost to have had the opposite effect. First, as noted above, he affirmatively rejected Soult's proposal for joint action against Badajoz. Second, in July, Napoleon redesignated all of Soult's troops south of the Sierra Moreno mountains as an autonomous force called the Armée du Midi (Army of the South) reporting direct to the emperor in Paris.[19] Soult

14. Oman estimates that at most 8,000 men of IX Corps ultimately came into contact with the Army of Portugal. Oman, *History*, Vol. 4, p. 20.
15. Compare the list of constituent battalions of IX Corps given in Oman, *History*, Vol. 4, App. XII, with the French Orders of Battle for V Corps (in App. II) and for I Corps (in App. V).
16. Stanhope, *Notes of Conversations*, p. 19. In fact, Soult was only 5 ft 6 in. tall. Gotteri, *Soult*, p. 26.
17. D'Héralde, *Mémoires*, p. 144.
18. Saint-Chamans, *Mémoires*, p. 35.
19. N. to Berthier, 'Instructions for the Duke of Dalmatia', 14 July 1810, *Confidential Correspondence*, No. 629, Vol. 2, p. 129. This communication does not appear in Napoleon's official *Correspondance*, but a version in French appears in Soult, *Mémoires*, at pp. 193–4.

had been made, in effect, the viceroy of a significant portion of King Joseph's kingdom, but he was not accountable to that monarch. The impetus for this development was ostensibly more economic than military in that the emperor hoped that Soult would thereby be empowered to do a better job of exploiting the resources of Andalucia to maintain his forces and thus of making 'war support war'. In the long run, however, its military significance was pre-eminent because it confirmed Napoleon's decision to make do without a central military authority in the Peninsula. Soult's and Masséna's commands (and all the others except for the Army of the Centre) were independent of King Joseph and, equally importantly, of each other.

This decentralisation of command and control within the Peninsula itself set the scene for future difficulties because coordination could now be achieved, if at all, only by way of Paris. The probability of such difficulties coming to pass was, moreover, enhanced by the extraordinary communication problems which faced the French. Due primarily to the unremitting hostility of the Spanish and Portuguese peoples, it was almost impossible for the French forces to communicate efficiently and effectively with either the emperor or with each other. For instance, Masséna's lines of communication were cut almost as soon as he advanced into Portugal, so that not even his own rear echelons, far less the other commanders in Spain, had any information as to his whereabouts and progress from 18 September to 8 November.[20] Under such circumstances, and especially given the weeks necessary for the transmission of even a high priority communication to Paris and back, Napoleon often lacked the necessary intelligence on which to base good instructions. (Ironically, most of his best information came from British newspapers.[21]) The creation of a true central military command in Spain with full decision-making authority would have mitigated the problem, but, given the personalities and personal agendas of King Joseph and of Napoleon's Peninsular marshals, such a development was not a realistic possibility in the absence of the emperor himself.

Soult was not idle while Ciudad Rodrigo and Almeida were being besieged, but he was very much pursuing his own parochial goals rather than seeking to give intentional support to Masséna's invasion. In fact, the only way in which his activities were linked to those of Masséna was, ironically, through the actions of the Spanish General Pedro Caro y Sureda, the Marquis de la Romana, a man whom Wellington called the 'brightest ornament' of the Spanish Army.[22] When Division General Jean Reynier's II Corps, which had been based on Mérida and Medellin, marched north of the Tagus to join the Army of Portugal, la Romana's Army of Extremadura at Badajoz was set free to menace Andalucia's north-western boundary. In August, la Romana pushed forward nearly to Llerena in the Sierra Moreno range separating the valley of the Guadalquivir River from that of the Guadiana, but he was repulsed there by Division General Jean-Baptiste Girard's division of Marshal Édouard Mortier's French

20. Oman, *History*, Vol. 3, p. 447.
21. See, e.g., N. to Berthier, 20 November 1810, *Correspondance*, No. 17146, Vol. 21, pp. 280–1, at 280: 'My Cousin, you will find enclosed extracts from the latest English newspapers.' Wellington was aware of, and frustrated by, this information flow: ' . . . it is a fact come to the attention of the Commander of the Forces, that plans of the enemy have been founded on information . . . extracted from the English newspapers, which information must have been obtained through private letters from officers of the army.' General Order, 10 August 1810.
22. W. to Liverpool, 26 January 1811, *Dispatches,* Vol. 7, pp. 196–8, at 196.

V Corps. This incursion was, remarkably, as worrisome for Wellington as for the French, because he was counting on la Romana's support when he retired within the Lines, and he was consequently anxious that the Army of Extremadura should avoid unnecessary risks in the meanwhile:

> I did arrange a plan of operations with the Marques [*sic*] de la Romana, applicable to his own corps when this country [Portugal] should be attacked; but, although I entertain a high opinion, and great regard, for the Marques de la Romana, I cannot feel confident that he will carry the plan into execution. Indeed, I am apprehensive that he has already put it out of his power to be of much use to us, and the enemy may certainly cut him off from us. However, I have written to urge him to fall back, and secure his communications with us under any event.[23]

Since the Army of Extremadura was particularly weak in mounted troops, Wellington also sent la Romana the Portuguese cavalry brigade of General George Madden as a reinforcement so that the Spaniard would have a better chance for survival if the French ventured out of the mountains. Instead of falling back, however, la Romana made another offensive move towards Seville in mid-September, reaching Monesterio on the main road, but he retreated precipitately when Soult concentrated the entire V Corps against him. Mortier's force pursued, cutting up the Spanish rear-guard at Fuente de Cantos on 15 September, and ultimately reached Fuente del Maestre, a mere thirty miles from Badajoz. However, when la Romana withdrew across the Guadiana, V Corps was simply not strong enough on its own either to follow or to take advantage of the retreat by besieging Badajoz or one of the other satellite fortresses in the area, and Soult apparently did not feel there was enough urgency to the situation to find reinforcements for Mortier elsewhere within his command. Mortier remained in Extremadura for some time, then pulled back towards Andalucia in early October just as Masséna was approaching Lisbon.

Although Soult and Mortier could not have known it at the time, this withdrawal was contrary to the emperor's express wishes. On 29 September, the emperor, perhaps becoming concerned that he might have skimped on the forces allotted to the Army of Portugal, initiated his belated effort to use the Army of the South to assist Masséna. Specifically, he instructed Marshal Berthier to have Soult use Marshal Mortier's force to prevent la Romana's Spaniards from giving assistance to the British:

> ... order the Duke of Dalmatia to press La Romana's force constantly with the V Corps so as to foil any attempt by him to cross the Tagus or march on the rear of the Army of Portugal. Let him know that the English have weakened themselves in Cadiz to reinforce their army in Portugal ... [and that] his primary goal should be to create a diversion and to be a support to the Army of Portugal.[24]

This order demonstrates Napoleon's capacity for strategic insight by its anticipation of the plans actually agreed between Wellington and la Romana, but its value was compromised by the all-too-normal delay in its delivery. By the time this

---

23. W. to Liverpool, 29 August 1810, *Dispatches*, Vol. 6, pp. 392–3, at 392.
24. N. to Berthier, 29 September 1810, *Correspondance*, No. 16967, Vol. 21, p. 158.

communication reached Soult at the end of October, it was certain that the British had not reduced the Cadiz garrison at all and that la Romana was already well on the way to joining Wellington within the Lines with part of his army in accordance with the arrangements they had made during the summer.[25] The order was thus obviously out of date, but it still forced Soult to make a decision as to how he should interpret the emperor's intent. Either a more daring or a more subservient general might have responded by marching Mortier immediately towards the Tagus on the trail of la Romana. Soult, however, was a realist. He had no direct information which would cause him to believe that Masséna was not in full control of his own destiny, while he had very good reason to believe that detaching V Corps alone out of the mountains across the Guadiana and into the Alentejo region of Portugal would be very risky indeed, both for V Corps itself and for the security of the entire province of Andalucia.[26] He eventually chose to treat the order as one he had the discretionary authority to disregard because of changed circumstances and consequently made no immediate move to send V Corps back into Extremadura.

At the same time, however, Soult was astute enough as both a general and a courtier to know that he needed strong grounds for disputing a direct order from the emperor beyond the fact that it was arguably based on stale information. He had therefore developed and was in the process of executing an alternate plan which, in his opinion, was likely to benefit both the Army of the South and the Army of Portugal with much less risk than the initiative proposed by Napoleon. That alternate plan was an attack on the Spanish fortress of Badajoz, an expedition which, as evidenced by the letter cited earlier, had apparently been on Soult's mind since the summer. From a strictly military point of view, securing the gateway to the southern invasion route was an eminently intelligent objective to aim for, because success would simultaneously create a credible southern threat against Wellington and provide enhanced protection for Andalucia. Unfortunately, a campaign involving a siege required more preparation than a straightforward push to the Tagus. There were plenty of cannon and siege materiels in the immense arsenals of Seville, but it took time to organise them into a proper siege train. It was only on 1 December that Soult felt confident enough about his preparations to reveal his planned offensive against Badajoz officially in a letter to Berthier: 'The enterprise is a big one, but ought to succeed – at least it will produce a happy diversion in favour of the imperial army in Portugal.'[27] One might have expected this letter to herald the start of the offensive, but it was followed only by the collection of more supplies and equipment.

While Soult's preparations proceeded methodically, Masséna's situation was deteriorating day by day. Masséna's personal resolve to hold his position never wavered, but his ability to do so ultimately depended on the stamina and resourcefulness of his men. They displayed these qualities to a degree that even inspired professional admiration from their opponent, Wellington:

25. Soult, *Mémoires*, p. 205 specifies that the 29 September order (which Soult refers to by the date of 30 September) did not reach him until one month after it was sent.
26. King Joseph himself told Soult that no news must be good news because, he reasoned, Masséna would surely have found a way to communicate if he was really in need of assistance. Soult, *Mémoires*, pp. 205–6.
27. There is no reference to this letter in Soult's memoirs or any published French sources. This quoted passage comes from Oman, *History*, Vol. 4, p. 26, who apparently had access to a copy.

It is certainly astonishing that the enemy have been able to remain in this country so long; and it is an extraordinary instance of what a French army can do ... With all our money, and having in our favour the good inclinations of the country, I assure you that I could not maintain one division in the district in which they have maintained not less than 60,000 men and 20,000 animals for more than 2 months.[28]

While he waited, Masséna pushed forward with preparations for laying a temporary bridge over the Tagus near its confluence with the Zezere River.[29] To develop his plans, he had men such as Colonel Pelet, who had worked on the crossing of the Danube in 1809; to carry them out, he had men such as General Jean-Baptiste Eblé, who would go on to build bridges over the Beresina River in Russia in 1812. The project was definitely feasible, but Masséna knew he needed Soult's cooperation to have a realistic chance for success and, if Pelet is to be believed, the Prince of Essling personally and presciently doubted whether such cooperation would ever be forthcoming: 'The V Corps will not come, or Soult will accompany it and use it for some personal operation.'[30] There was, in fact, one further negative possibility – Soult might come, but arrive too late to save Masséna. Speed, as always in war, would be important. Unfortunately, as French preparations for the attack on Badajoz dragged on, that third possibility became by far the most likely one. Soult must have come to this realisation himself, because on 31 December he sent another self-serving letter emphasising how difficult it was for him to accomplish anything he was asked to do because he had received almost no financial and material support from France since his conquest of southern Spain.[31] He did not, however, abandon his plan for a diversionary attack against Badajoz.

28. W. to Liverpool, 21 December 1810, *Dispatches,* Vol. 7, pp. 51–5, at 54.
29. See generally, Pelet, *The French Campaign*, Chapter 9, 'Preparations to Cross the Tagus'.
30. Pelet, *The French Campaign*, p. 329.
31. Soult to Berthier, 31 December 1810, quoted in part in Soult, *Mémoires*, p. 209.

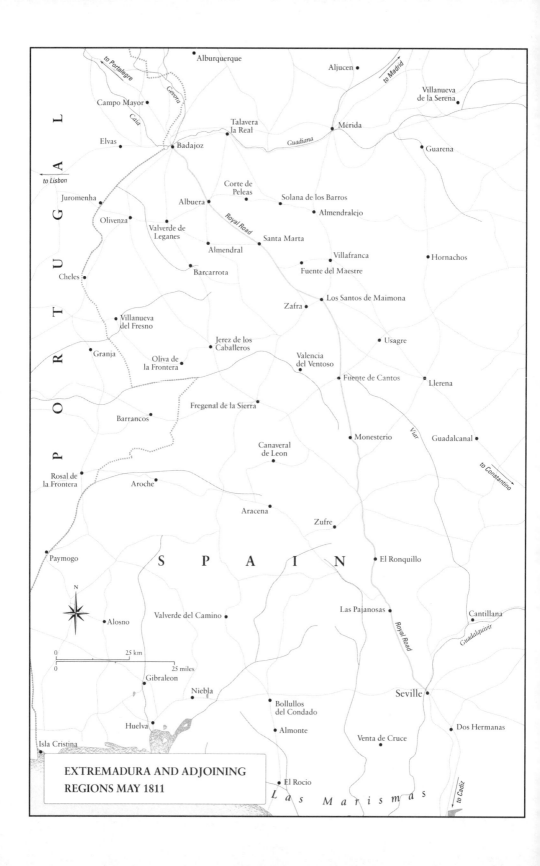

EXTREMADURA AND ADJOINING
REGIONS MAY 1811

Chapter 2

Soult's Capture of Badajoz

The long-awaited French offensive into Extremadura left Seville on 2 January 1811. Soult's oddly proportioned force (consisting of 14,000 infantry, 4,000 cavalry, 2,000 engineers and gunners and 34 guns) was formed by combining Marshal Mortier's V Corps with cavalry and support troops detached from other commands within Andalucia. Travelling in two parallel columns using the two primary passes over the Sierra Moreno mountains, the French ran into delays almost immediately after setting out.[1] First, they encountered heavy rain. The right-hand column, moving by way of Guadalcanal, Llerena and Usagre, was not greatly affected, but the left-hand column, which included the siege train of over 300 wagons and which was advancing via Ronquillo to Santa Ollala and Monesterio, became strung out as draught animals struggled in the muddy conditions.[2] Next, cavalry patrols from the left column discovered a force of 5,000 Spanish infantry under Teniente General Francisco Ballasteros, who was coincidentally moving south from Extremadura on a parallel route with orders to threaten Seville. On 4 January 1811, Soult detached the infantry division of Division General Honoré-Théodore-Maxime Gazan to drive Ballasteros away from both the main invasion route and from Seville. When Ballasteros continued to head south and west, Gazan made the mistake of allowing himself to be drawn away from the decisive theatre of action in an over-zealous pursuit which ultimately lasted three weeks. When Gazan finally caught up with his foe on 25 January, the clash was inconclusive and Ballasteros was able to ferry the bulk of his force safely across the lower Guadiana River into the Algarve province of Portugal.[3]

The rest of Soult's force meanwhile pressed on into Extremadura. The Spanish defenders, weakened by the recall of Ballasteros to the south, retired before him, intending to make Badajoz, the provincial capital, the focal point of resistance. However, the local Spanish commander, General Gabriel Mendizabal, took two questionable actions in carrying out his withdrawal. First, he threw a large garrison into the second-rate fortress of Olivenza. Second, on 8 January, he hurriedly evacuated the town of Mérida and allowed its bridge over the Guadiana to fall intact into French hands despite orders to destroy all crossings. This latter development was particularly problematic for Wellington because it opened up so many strategic alternatives for the

1. Lapène, *Conquête*, pp. 70–1.
2. Lamare, *Relation*, p. 3.
3. The details of Gazan's detour are given in Lamare, *Relation*, pp. 5–9.

French that it became difficult for him to guess what they might do next. At first Wellington was sure that the French would take advantage of the capture of the intact bridge to advance into the Alentejo towards Lisbon even if that meant cutting loose from their communications with Andalucia.[4] Shortly thereafter, however, he received reports which suggested that the French were moving north from Mérida to link up with Masséna via the French-controlled bridge over the Tagus at Almaraz.[5] Wellington thought this move might well lead to a general action in front of Lisbon:

> I reckon that Mortier, supposing him to march by Almaraz, can be [with Masséna] on the Zezere in the first days of February, and I think it probable that the battle for the possession of this country, and probably the fate of the Peninsula, will be fought in less than a month from this time.[6]

Further information soon proved that both his conclusions were wrong and that the French were, in fact, remaining on the left bank of the Guadiana. This meant that the Alentejo was safe for the moment, but that Olivenza, a town of some 5,000 inhabitants situated four leagues (approximately twelve miles) to the south and west of Badajoz, was not.[7] Olivenza had been ceded by the Portuguese to the Spanish following the short war between those two countries which took place in 1801, and had never been properly repaired or maintained by its new owners. There was so little prospect for a successful defence that la Romana specifically ordered his deputy to abandon the position in the face of any French advance.[8] Mendizabal's contrary decision to reinforce that garrison inspired Wellington to exasperated sarcasm in a letter to his brother, Henry Wellesley, the British ambassador to the Spanish government in Cadiz:

> ... no arrangement was ever more completely Spanish than to have sent between 3000 and 4000 of their best men into Olivenza, a place without artillery, ammunition, or provisions, under circumstances in which it was impossible, if they should be attacked, that they could be relieved![9]

An attack was not long in coming. With his siege train delayed by adverse weather conditions and Gazan's division chasing after Ballasteros, Soult decided it would be rash to attack Badajoz without first having established a base in the province, so Olivenza immediately became the interim objective of the French.[10] The first trenches for the siege of Olivenza were opened on 13 January, and there was so little interference from the defenders that work proceeded very swiftly. Within ten days a practicable breach had been achieved and, rather than face an assault, General Manuel Herck unconditionally surrendered his garrison on 23 January.[11] Probably the only uncomfortable moment for Soult during the entire siege was provided by the

4. W. to B., 12 January 1811, *Dispatches*, Vol. 7, pp. 124–6, at 124.
5. W. to B., 15 January 1811, *Dispatches*, Vol. 7, p. 139.
6. W. to Stuart, 16 January 1811, *Dispatches*, Vol. 7, pp. 141–2, at 142.
7. Lamare, *Relation*, pp. 23–4.
8. W. to Liverpool, 2 February 1811, *Dispatches*, Vol. 7, pp. 221–4, at 222.
9. W. to Henry Wellesley, 20 January 1811, *Dispatches*, Vol. 7, pp. 158–9, at 158.
10. Soult, *Mémoires*, p. 210.
11. For some, surrender to the French was far from a novelty. One Spanish soldier filing out of the fortress was heard to say: 'This is the seventh time I have been made prisoner by the French. I am confident that I will find a way to escape again.' Petiet, *Souvenirs Historiques*, p. 336.

belated arrival on 20 January of three separate dispatches from Berthier (dated 28 November and 4 and 10 December) reiterating Napoleon's desire to have V Corps sent to support Masséna.[12] That of 4 December in particular was couched in terms which must have reminded Soult that his Badajoz plan constituted direct disobedience of an imperial order:

> His Majesty is unhappy that, when it comes to dispositions as important as those relating to the safety of his army in Portugal, you have let General La Romana slip away to the Tagus without pursuing him. If the army of the Prince of Essling is defeated, you, duke, will have occasion to find out how important that will be for the emperor's armies in Andalucia and how much they will be compromised thereby. The movement of La Romana proves that the situation in Portugal is the most important thing for the affairs of Spain.
>
>   . . . It is indispensable for a corps of ten thousand men, taken from the Army of Andalucia . . . to make contact with the Prince of Essling and General Drouet [d'Erlon].
>
>   . . . By my letters of 30 September, 26 October and 14, 21 and 28 November, I have reiterated to you the wishes of the Emperor in this regard, and His Majesty has no doubt that a corps of all arms of the Army of Andalucia, equal in force to that of La Romana, is at this moment already on the Tagus and in communication with the Prince of Essling because, as I have said before, no movement in Andalucia can have any result if the Prince of Essling does not succeed, a point which has been well understood by La Romana. His Majesty therefore orders you to send a corps to the Tagus to join in the principal operation, which is the destruction of the English.[13]

As if these words were not emphatic enough, the order also specified that 'All other considerations must give way before the movement prescribed.'

Astonishingly, despite the pressure exerted by this communication, Soult never wavered from his chosen course of action. The new order was certainly clearer and more emphatic than the emperor's earlier instructions, but, as Soult saw the matter, it was still unrealistic in terms of its stated objectives and the force assigned to achieve them. In the first place, he felt he did not have 10,000 men to spare for Masséna if he was simultaneously responsible for maintaining control over Andalucia – there were simply not enough troops to go around.[14] Second, even if the troops were available, Soult still had grave doubts that an expedition to the Tagus was anything other than an invitation to another disastrous defeat like Bailén, doubts he expressed in the reply he immediately sent back to Paris while reminding the emperor that control of the border fortresses was an acceptable alternate course of action:

> It is clear to me that if I were to thrust a corps of 10,000 men forward to the Tagus, as was His Majesty's intention before Your Highness [Berthier] wrote me on 10 December, it would never reach its destination and would be cut off and surrounded before I could go to its aid. It thus seems to me that, under the

---

12. The date of arrival of these orders is specified in Soult, *Mémoires*, p. 208.
13. Berthier to Soult, 4 December 1810, in Jones, *Journals of Sieges*, Vol. 3, Appendix A, pp. 193–4. This order is summarised with a short quote in Masséna, *Mémoires*, Vol. 7, p. 302.
14. Soult, *Mémoires*, p. 208.

prevailing circumstances, I can best fulfill the intentions of His Majesty, and be of use to the Army of Portugal, by taking Olivenza, Badajoz and Campo-Mayor, from where I should be able to communicate with Marshal the Prince of Essling.[15]

A mere two days after this reply had been dispatched to Paris, yet another letter arrived from Berthier, this one dated 22 December 1810, reiterating the same orders. Soult was forced once again to write to the emperor and dig an even deeper potential hole for his career: 'This order is impossible to execute – it will cause us to lose V Corps and ruin the Emperor's affairs in Andalucia without being any help to the imperial Army of Portugal.'[16] The marshal also reiterated his view that the attack he was about to make on Badajoz was the only reasonable course of action under the then prevailing circumstances: 'I declare on my honour ... that I do not think it is possible to do more without compromising the fate of the imperial troops that I left behind in Andalucia.'[17]

This last caveat is especially telling because, particularly with the benefit of hindsight, one can recognise that it was concern for the retention of Andalucia that deprived the French of whatever small chance they might have had to defeat Wellington. Napoleon should have ordered Soult to support Masséna not just with 10,000 men, but with the whole of his army, thus subordinating all other objectives to the greater purpose of defeating the British. The value of such a radical move can be judged by the fact that its mere possibility was cited by Wellington as grounds for keeping a full complement of transport vessels on station at Lisbon after Masséna's withdrawal to Santarem:

> I am also certain that, if the British army should not be obliged to evacuate Portugal, the French army must withdraw from Andalusia. I think it not improbable, therefore, that a large part of it, if not the whole of the French army in Andalusia will be introduced into the southern parts of this kingdom.
>
> I do not despair of holding my ground against this accumulation of force, and I have taken measures to prevent the only inconvenience which it can produce, viz., a deficiency of supplies. But as these troops are all within a few marches of me, and an order from Paris would not only put them in motion, but they could be in this country almost before the transports could arrive in England, I cannot think it advisable, in the existing situation of affairs, to send them out of my reach.[18]

Such a concentration of manpower by the French would, however, have entailed abandoning the siege of Cadiz and all but the largest towns in Andalucia, and Napoleon, the greatest practitioner in history of concentration of force in military operations, apparently could not bring himself to abandon the gains which had been made in that province. As a result, the type of order Wellington feared was never given and Soult was left in practice with discretionary authority to determine just what assistance the Army of Portugal would receive from him.

15. Soult to Berthier, 22 January 1811, in Belmas, *Journaux*, Vol. 1, pp. 470–3, at 472.
16. Soult to Berthier, 25 January 1811, *Ibid.*, p. 474–5.
17. *Ibid.*
18. W. to Liverpool, 21 December 1810, *Dispatches*, Vol. 7, pp. 51–5, at 52.

Though it in no way diminishes the moral fortitude shown by Soult, his spirited defence of his actions turned out to be moot because Napoleon had, even as the defence was being composed, already acquiesced to Soult's proposed offensive against Badajoz. When Napoleon received the messages sent by Soult in December, one might have expected an explosion of imperial wrath. Instead, the emperor implicitly validated his marshal's decisions by modifying the timetable of his original instructions to begin only after the capture of Badajoz had been effected:

> It is necessary to write immediately to the Duke of Dalmatia to inform him that after the capture of Badajoz, he is to advance immediately to the Tagus with his siege train to give the Prince of Essling the means to besiege Abrantes.[19]

This reference to Abrantes corroborates the recollections of General Foy that Napoleon was focused on that town during their meetings in November: 'Masséna must take Abrantes ... The only way to get Wellington to make a forward move will be to force him to try to raise the siege of Abrantes.'[20] There is reason to believe, however, that the emperor expected at the time he gave this new order that Badajoz would be French no later than the end of January.

Perhaps the only direct result of the arrival of Berthier's 4 December dispatch was that Soult moved on to his next objective without delay after the capture of Olivenza even though Gazan's division had still not rejoined the expedition. As the French arrived before Badajoz on 26 January, however, only an extreme optimist would have fancied their chances of making any headway against this powerful fortress. First, Badajoz was a well-fortified town with a population of 16,000–17,000 souls and a garrison of at least 9,000 with 170 cannon, while the French besieging force numbered barely 17,000 soldiers with only 34 siege guns.[21] Second, although the town itself was situated on the left bank of the Guadiana River, the garrison had easy access to the other bank of the Guadiana by way of a spectacular Roman bridge protected by a fortified bridgehead and a significant outwork named the Fort of San Cristoval.[22] Third, it had a courageous and resourceful governor in the person of General Rafael Menacho. Fourth, and most importantly, the garrison was in touch with General Mendizabal's covering force and was aware that significant additional forces had been dispatched to the aid of the fortress as soon as Wellington learned of Soult's incursion. These reinforcements were an infantry brigade commanded by Brigadier Carlos d'España, followed five days later on 20 January by the rest of General la Romana's force from within the Lines of Torres Vedras.

On 20 January, after it had become clear that the French were not pushing on across the Guadiana, Wellington wrote a memorandum to la Romana to express his views of the strategic situation then facing the allies. In that document, he specified to his Spanish colleague that 'The relief of the battalions in Olivenza is the first subject for consideration', but he also cautioned that:

> The Spanish Generals should bear in mind, however, that the last body of troops which their country possesses is that under the command of the Marquis de la

19. N. to Berthier, 25 January 1811, *Correspondance*, No. 17295, Vol. 21, pp. 367–8.
20. Quoted in Oman, *History*, Vol. 3, p. 457.
21. Lapène, *Conquête*, p. 81.
22. Lamare, *Relation*, pp. 113–15.

Romana, and that it should not be risked in operations of difficult or doubtful result.[23]

In light of that reality, Wellington had four concrete recommendations for his allies: firstly, destruction of the bridges at Mérida and Medellin to deny the French easy access to the right bank of the Guadiana; secondly, formation of an entrenched camp across the Guadiana from Badajoz; thirdly, reinforcement of the garrison defending Badajoz with troops from Cadiz led by General Ballasteros; and finally, relocation to Elvas of bridging equipment (including boats) then assembled at Badajoz.

Allied plans immediately received a severe and unexpected blow. On 21 January, la Romana was stricken by chest spasms. He recuperated for a day, but when he took steps to return to work, the effort brought on a fatal heart attack and he died suddenly on the 23rd.[24] General Mendizabal, as the next most senior officer in the region, assumed command of the whole of la Romana's corps, but the void left by la Romana's passing was a large one. Back in December, Wellington had revealed his views on Spanish leadership in a letter to his brother prompted by the rumour that la Romana was going to be re-assigned to a new command:

> Mendizabel [*sic*], who now commands in that province under the Marquis, is a valuable officer. He will, I am convinced, do his duty in every situation in which he is placed; but a very erroneous estimate is formed of the services rendered by the Marquis de la Romana, and of the abilities of Mendizabel, or of any other officer under the command of the Marquis de la Romana, if it is supposed that he or any of them can at all supply his [la Romana's] place.[25]

One imagines that Wellington's assessment of Mendizabal had already changed for the worse in light of the Spaniard's bungled defence of Olivenza, but the British commander nonetheless tried to make the best of the situation by sending a cordial letter to Mendizabal (whose name he now spelled correctly) promising cooperation and reminding him of the points made in his memorandum to la Romana.[26] Even without la Romana, however, the prospects for a successful defence of Badajoz seemed so bright that Wellington continued to believe that it was unnecessary to send any British or Portuguese troops to its assistance other than the cavalry of General Madden already detached for that purpose.

The reinforcements headed for Badajoz would pose a significant challenge to Soult, but, ironically, this development meant that the French had already achieved the precise diversion of forces away from Masséna that Napoleon desired. Nevertheless, Soult had never intended his offensive to be a mere feint, so despite the disadvantages they faced, the French calmly set about besieging Badajoz. The French attack was directed by 56-year-old Engineer General François-Joseph d'Éstienne, baron de Léry, an expert at classic, Vauban-style siege craft, who, after examining the walls of the town and the three significant outer fortifications, chose a line of approach running through the Pardaleras hornwork lying south-west of the fortress.[27] Trenches were

23. Memorandum of W. to la Romana, 20 January 1811, *Dispatches*, Vol. 7, pp. 163–5, at 163.
24. W. to Henry Wellesley, 28 January 1811, *Dispatches,* Vol. 7, p. 205.
25. W. to Henry Wellesley, 13 December 1810, *Dispatches,* Vol. 7, pp. 43–4, at 43.
26. W. to Mendizabal, 24 January 1811, *Dispatches,* Vol. 7, pp. 183–4.
27. The best source for the story of the French attack against Badajoz is the *Relation* by General

dug, batteries established and Division General Marie-Victor-Nicolas de Fay, vicomte de Latour-Maubourg, and six regiments of cavalry were dispatched to the right bank (Portuguese side) of the Guadiana to cut off (at least temporarily) communications between the town and any relief forces. Just upriver from Badajoz, the French even established a ferry protected by a simple bridgehead fortification on the Spanish bank.[28] The real work was done each night under the cover of darkness, with engineers, artillerymen and infantry soldiers transformed into labourers digging new approaches (or saps) towards the town and establishing new batteries.

The garrison displayed equal energy in blasting away with their superior number of artillery pieces and periodically executing sorties from their fortifications to disrupt the work of the French attackers. These raids were generally the work of only two or three hundred soldiers who had the limited aim of inflicting casualties, capturing equipment and destroying supplies and earthworks, but occasionally they involved sufficient forces to qualify as pitched battles. For instance, on 31 January, Governor Menacho launched an attack involving four battalions of infantry, two squadrons of cavalry and two guns. It was only beaten back when the troops on duty in the siege trenches were reinforced by an extra battalion of the 88th Line, the 1st, 3rd and 5th Companies of Sappers and a company of Sappers from the Grand Duchy of Warsaw. The Spanish cavalry came from a different direction than the infantry and surprised a group of workers supervised by two senior French engineer officers. In the intense fight that followed, Battalion Chief Cazin was killed by multiple lance and sabre strokes. Captain Vainsot managed to kill two of his attackers with his sword, but he was ultimately overwhelmed and left more dead than alive suffering from ten or eleven wounds. Overall, the French suffered sixty-five casualties on the day.[29]

Like any siege, this one had a horrifying routine. Each night, despite frequent rain and frigid temperatures, the French infantry assigned to the trenches traded their guns for shovels and under the direction of engineer and artillery officers dug new saps towards the town in precisely measured segments and established new batteries to cover the work in progress. Knowing what was happening, the defenders responded with sorties and fierce bombardments that attempted to halt the work of the besiegers or, literally, blow it away with multiple cannon shots. Each day, the French batteries, one of them named for the slain Battalion Chief Cazin, hammered away at the city defences or lobbed in mortar and howitzer shells to panic the civilian population (a practice which disgusted the artillery professionals in the French army).[30] Even on a day without a sortie, each side was bound to suffer a number of casualties.

This routine continued even after 5 February when General Mendizabal arrived at Badajoz with an army of nearly 12,000 men. The quality of this force was debatable – General Madden, for instance, observed that they were 'a fine body of men, but possessing few experienced officers, and but little general system or regularity of

Lamare, who was a chef de bataillon of engineers employed at the siege. (Authorship of the rare first edition of 1825 was attributed only to 'Colonel L****', but Lamare's name was used for the second edition.) Belmas, *Journaux*, provides copies of official correspondence and reports that complement Lamare's narrative.

28. Lamare, *Relation*, Map No. 2. The ferry was created using three vessels brought in pieces by wagon from Seville. Belmas, *Journaux*, Vol. 3, p. 665.
29. Lamare, *Relation*, p. 23; Belmas, *Journaux*, Vol. 3, p. 672.
30. Lamare, *Relation*, pp. 28–9.

discipline; individually brave, but very incompetent to act embodied'.[31] The kinds of problems such soldiers could encounter were all too apparent on 6 February when misbehaviour by a Spanish cavalry brigade allowed General Latour-Maubourg to inflict a sharp reverse on Madden's men before the French cavalry was temporarily forced to pull back across the Guadiana.[32] The sheer numbers of new Spanish troops alone exacerbated the already difficult situation of the besiegers, however, and many, including Colonel de Saint-Chamans assumed that the French would be forced to abandon the siege:

> I expected, when Soult called me the day after the arrival of this Spanish army, that he would be dictating an order of retreat, but I realised that I still did not know him very well when I saw how strongly he responded in this circumstance to the challenge of all the obstacles facing him. The orders he issued demonstrated instead his firm resolve to continue the siege even though it was no longer possible to maintain a blockade on both sides of the Guadiana.[33]

The Spanish reinforcements quickly made their presence felt on 7 February by way of a sortie involving 6,000–7,000 of the city's defenders (including 300 cavalry). The four Spanish columns succeeded in capturing three of the French redoubts (although they failed to spike the French guns because the engineer officer carrying the nails was wounded), but then Marshal Mortier personally led the reserves of V Corps in a counter-attack that routed the enemy after some stiff fighting.[34] The Spaniards lost nearly a thousand men, while the French suffered some 400 casualties.[35] After this repulse, however, the relieving force took up a passive position on the right bank of the Guadiana on the heights of Santa Engracia near the Fort of San Cristoval, but neglected to entrench their camp as had been suggested by Wellington. On the basis of what he had observed of Mendizabal thus far, Wellington was decidedly pessimistic about the outcome of the siege:

> The Spaniards have done exactly what I recommended them not to do, and have omitted that which I recommended them to do; and that has happened as I foretold. If the French have 2000 or 3000 infantry on the right bank of the Guadiana to support the[ir] cavalry, the Army of the Left and Badajoz will both be lost.[36]

For their part, the French responded to the distractions posed by the relief force with a single-minded focus on the progress of their siege works, which moved forward relentlessly night after night despite copious amounts of rain that made life miserable for all the soldiers involved. On the night of 11/12 February, a storming

31. Madden, 'Narrative of Operations', p. 66.
32. Madden, 'Narrative of Operations', pp. 72–4. Madden was so disgusted by the pusillanimous behaviour of the Spanish cavalry that he lodged a formal complaint with Mendizabal.
33. Saint-Chamans, *Mémoires*, p. 193.
34. The cause of the Spanish failure to spike the guns they captured is mentioned in Madden, 'Narrative of Operations', p. 73.
35. Belmas, *Journaux*, Vol. 3, pp. 681–2. During the fierce fighting, General Gazan was hit in the arm and Colonel Jean Pierre Vigent of the 64th Regiment was hit in the knee, a wound that proved mortal when he rejected the amputation recommended by his surgeon. D'Héralde, *Mémoires*, p. 149.
36. W. to Beresford, 10 February 1811, *Dispatches*, Vol. 7, pp. 249–50 at 250.

party consisting of 60 sappers and 400 grenadiers and voltigeurs from the 21st and 28th Light Regiments and the 100th and 103rd Line Regiments seized the Pardaleras outwork, which was quickly incorporated into the web of batteries and trenches stretching towards the fortress.[37] By 18 February, the French had built a total of sixteen batteries, although not all of them were in use at the same time since, as work progressed, older batteries were shut down and their cannon were moved to newer positions closer to the city walls.[38] Despite the robust progress made by the besiegers, however, Soult was worried that siege craft alone was insufficient to make him master of the city. He concluded that he first needed to defeat Mendizabal in the field and he set in motion a bold plan to do so as soon as the rain-swollen waters of both the Guadiana and its tributary, the Gevora, subsided.

The Battle of the Gevora, fought on 19 February, was one of the most remarkable fights of the Napoleonic Wars and it demonstrates emphatically the mastery of the French Army in the Peninsula over its Spanish regular opponents. It is not possible to determine how much of the planning and execution of the battle was attributable to Marshal Soult and how much was attributable to Marshal Mortier, but, however it worked, the combination was a felicitous one.[39] The preliminary step they took was to drive the Spaniards away from the support of Fort of San Cristoval by means of an artillery barrage from a siege battery unveiled dramatically on the left bank of the Guadiana on 17 February:

> A battery had expressly been constructed, and they had succeeded in gaining its exact range; the consequence was an immediate fall of tents, and a precipitate departure from the present ground to another out of range . . . It was not possible that any regularity could be observed, as every one shifted for himself.[40]

Latour-Maubourg's cavalry was then moved up to the banks of the Gevora River and, during the night of 18/19 February, nine battalions of General Girard's division of V Corps, accompanied by twelve cannon and both marshals, crossed the Guadiana at the ferry and joined the cavalry.[41] At dawn the next morning, with their movements favoured by a thick fog, the French crossed the Gevora and attacked the Spanish army, a total of no more than 6,000 men assaulting a force of at least 10,000 occupying higher ground. The stunning result was a complete victory for the French.

Despite their inferior numbers, the French had an elaborate plan for a double envelopment that they executed flawlessly. Latour-Maubourg's horsemen crossed the Gevora at a ford, dispersed some Spanish cavalry to their front and then made a great sweep to the right that brought them up behind the Spanish left flank. Meanwhile, Girard's foot soldiers repaired a bridge in front of them and crossed there. The three

37. Lamare, *Relation*, pp. 39–41.
38. Belmas, *Journaux*, Vol. 3, p. 695.
39. A French medical officer observed that two marshals was an extravagant number of senior commanders for such a small force, but the extravagance paid dividends in this instance. D'Héralde, *Mémoires*, p. 144.
40. Madden, 'Narrative of Operations', p. 80.
41. The French force consisted of the 34th, 88th and 100th Line Infantry Regiments, the 21st Chasseurs, the 4th Spanish Chasseurs, the 2nd and 10th Hussars, the 14th and 26th Dragoons, the elite company of the 27th Chasseurs and twelve guns. Lamare, *Relation*, pp. 55–6.

battalions of the 100th Line, led by General Girard himself, were dispatched on a sweep to the left, climbed the heights exactly where the Spanish camp had been before it was chased away by the French artillery and then advanced along the ridge, collapsing the Spanish right flank. The French centre was maintained by General Armand Philippon's brigade consisting of the 34th and 88th Line Regiments with the support of the 2nd Company of the 4th Horse Artillery Regiment. These two infantry units adopted the kind of mixed tactical formation that is often discussed by modern experts in Napoleonic tactics but that is rarely documented in primary sources. In this case, each regiment consisted of three battalions and advanced with the middle battalion deployed while the battalions on either side remained in column.[42] This formation fired as it advanced, then pushed forward with the bayonet when the Spanish line began to collapse as a result of the French flank attacks.

General Mendizabal may have been a 'sincere and disinterested patriot' as well as a 'gallant and brave soldier', but he did not on this occasion demonstrate any skills as a commander.[43] He was aware of French movements that should have led him to suspect that Soult was planning to attack, but he failed to cover the line of the Gevora and surrendered the tactical initiative to the French. Captain John Squire of the Royal Engineers expressed a common view of the Spanish commander in very colourful language:

> Mendizabel [*sic*] was an idiot. On the 18th February, the enemy threw a bridge over the Guadiana above Badajoz. Don Carlos de España, an active officer, whom I know very well, reconnoitred the bridge, and made his report to Mendizabel, who was playing at cards. Very well, said the chief, we'll go and look at it tomorrow! At daybreak the Spanish army was surprised.[44]

The thick morning fog on the 19th was obviously not Mendizabal's fault, but he misinterpreted the reports he received early in the morning and concluded that the French were merely probing the Spanish position. Even when it became clear to the Spanish general that a significant attack was underway, he could still have foiled Soult's design by retreating precipitately into the fortress or towards Elvas, thus preserving his army as a threat to the French. Instead, Mendizabal gallantly but recklessly led his troops in a counter-attack, but he had wasted so much time that the Spanish position had already been unalterably compromised as the first troops routed by the French panicked the rest:

> ... the sudden irruption of so many dispersed individuals – the firm advance, and well-supported fire of the enemy – the appalling shout – the cries, lamentations, and confusion excited by the admixture of conquered friends, and conquering foes, and more than all, the want of discipline so absolutely necessary on such trying occasions ... caused such a panic in this last division, that scarcely firing more than one discharge, or waiting the near approach of their adversaries ... it suddenly gave way ... and fell back in total disorder![45]

---

42. This detail comes from Soult's Order of the Day announcing the victory on 20 February 1811. Belmas, *Journaux*, Vol. 3, p. 759.
43. Madden, 'Narrative of Operations', p. 92.
44. Letter from Captain Squire, 1 March 1811, quoted in W. Napier, *History*, Vol. 3, p. 648.
45. Madden, 'Narrative of Operations', p. 85.

Assailed on all sides, the Spanish force disintegrated and became easy prey for the French cavalry:

> Such was the destruction dealt among this dispersed multitude that the French hussars became at length tired of killing, and with horrid imprecations, ordered the frighted [*sic*] and imploring Spaniards to strike the stock[s] of their muskets forcibly on the ground, so as to break them, and repair to a rendezvous they pointed out near Badajoz, which order was gladly obeyed.[46]

Only some steadiness in retreat from the troops led by Brigadier Carlos de España enabled a few units to reach Elvas. When the tally was taken over the next few days, the Spaniards were found to have lost approximately 1,100 killed and wounded plus over 7,000 prisoners (including 350 officers). They also lost 6 standards and 17 guns. The total casualties of the French were some 400 men.[47] A disgusted Wellington summed up the performance of his allies in two letters written to his brother the same day he learned of the defeat:

> This is the greatest misfortune which has fallen upon the allies since the battle of Ocaña, and in the existing state of the war more likely than that event to affect their interests vitally; and it was not to be expected. I could not imagine that an army having two rivers between it and the enemy, and knowing that the enemy was endeavouring to pass one of them, could have been surprised in such a strong position … it [the defeat] would certainly have been avoided if the Spaniards had been anything but Spaniards.[48]

One of Soult's aides had a decidedly more favourable view of the situation: 'The exploits of Marshal Soult do not have to be exaggerated in the papers like those of many other commanders; at the same time no one believes them because they seem incredible.'[49]

With the destruction of Mendizabal's army, the calculus of the siege of Badajoz once again became very simple – the city was bound to fall to its besiegers unless some external event occurred that could deprive the French of the fruits of their victory. Within this calculus, the critical variable was time – time for developments in Portugal and back in Andalucia to affect the ability and willingness of the French to press their attack. Soult tried to control that variable as much as he could by pressing the siege vigorously to conclusion in the aftermath of his victory, but once again the Spanish proved that they were a much tougher opponent behind walls than they were in the field. The garrison of Badajoz may have been shocked by the debacle at the Gevora, but, amazingly, it was not demoralised and every new effort by the French was met with an unflagging resistance guided by General Menacho.

The first place the garrison looked to for external help was Portugal but, although Wellington exhorted the defenders of Badajoz to 'hold out to the last extremity', he did not provide any more tangible assistance.[50] This response was driven mainly by

---

46. Madden, 'Narrative of Operations', p. 90.
47. Lamare, *Relation*, pp. 53–4.
48. Two letters from W. to H. Wellesley, 23 February 1811, *Dispatches*, Vol. 7, pp. 285–7.
49. Bory de Saint-Vincent to Léon Dufour, 26 March 1811, in Lauzun, 'Épisodes', pp. 421–557 at 437.
50. W. to Mendizabal, 22 February 1811, *Supp. Despatches*, Vol. 7, p. 71.

the fact that Wellington felt he did not have sufficient troops to spare for another relief attempt until either reinforcements arrived from London or Masséna's army retired back to Spain, but it also reflected his disillusionment about providing more assistance to the Spanish. Wellington was so discouraged by the fact that his allies could not avoid trouble even when he pointed it out to them that he in some sense wrote off the possibility that Badajoz could be saved:

> Although experience has taught me to place no reliance upon the effect of the exertions of the Spanish troops, notwithstanding the frequent instances of their bravery, I acknowledge that this recent disaster has disappointed and grieved me very much. The loss of this army, and its probable consequence, the fall of Badajoz, have materially altered the situation of the allies in this part of the Peninsula; and it will not be an easy task to place them in the situation which they were, much less in that in which they should have been, if this misfortune had not occurred.[51]

What Wellington did instead was concentrate on the task immediately in front of him – the defeat of Masséna. He did not give serious consideration again to the relief of Badajoz until that goal was achieved.

Even in the absence of action by Wellington, however, the French siege of Badajoz could have been severely compromised by a vigorous diversion against the French forces left behind by Soult in Andalucia. They were certainly vulnerable because of the number of men who had been diverted to the Badajoz expedition and because Soult had failed to appoint a single commander for all the troops left behind (consisting primarily of I Corps at Cadiz under Marshal Victor, the garrison of Seville under Division General Augustin Darricau, the remains of IV Corps at Granada under Division General Sebastiani and Division General Godinot's depleted division at Cordova). Unfortunately, in one of the great strategic failures of the whole war, the British and Spanish tried twice but were ultimately unable to create a single effective diversion.

The first diversionary effort was the campaign leading to the Battle of Barrosa that had been conceived by the Spanish regency shortly after Soult departed for Extremadura. It did not involve any coordination with Wellington and it apparently assumed that Badajoz would not need any assistance beyond that which would be provided by la Romana and Mendizabal because it began with the transfer of the allied attack force to Tarifa, far away from Cadiz and even farther away from Seville and Extremadura. Perhaps the regency would have changed its plans if news of the defeat at the Gevora had arrived before Sir Thomas Graham and the British portion of the chosen troops sailed away on 21 February but, even with that information in hand, it sent the rest of the expeditionary force off on 24 February under the command of General Manuel La Peña.

Once Graham and La Peña rendezvoused at Tarifa on 27 February, the combined force began the long march back to Cadiz to assault the French siege lines from the rear. Graham had graciously conceded command of the expedition to La Peña, but he almost immediately had reason to regret that decision as the Spaniard made some questionable choices about the route and speed of the advance. Nevertheless, the

51. W. to Liverpool, 23 February 1811, *Dispatches*, Vol. 7, pp. 288–90 at 289.

combined force ultimately arrived back at Cadiz in position to inflict a monumental setback on the French, but at the crucial moment La Peña lost the will to act decisively and he stood by while Graham and his men fought alone at Barrosa on 5 March and single-handedly defeated two divisions of Marshal Victor's force. A vigorous pursuit would almost certainly have lifted the siege of Cadiz and saved Badajoz as well, but Graham correctly concluded he could no longer trust La Peña, so he revoked his command concession and marched his battered troops back onto the island on which Cadiz is located, followed shortly thereafter by the Spaniards, who were reluctant to act alone and may have even been so paranoid as to fear that the British might seize possession of Cadiz in their absence.[52] As the allied campaign collapsed into an exchange of accusations and recriminations, a much-surprised Victor called up what few reinforcements remained to be had from other French forces and quickly re-established the breached portion of his siege lines.

The second diversion involved General Ballasteros and his division, last seen being chased into Portugal at the end of January. If Ballasteros had joined forces with Mendizabal outside Badajoz before the Battle of the Gevora or returned to Cadiz to participate in the advance against Victor, his relatively small but experienced force of some 4,000 men might have affected the outcome of some very significant events. Instead, he maintained the independence of his command and made an advance on Seville in late February. This might have diverted Soult's attention from Badajoz if it had been pressed home boldly, but Ballasteros allowed himself to be distracted by the manoeuvrings of a small French force under Adjutant-Commandant (Staff Colonel) Victor Rémond.[53] Ballasteros finally inflicted a sharp reverse on Rémond on 2 March, whereupon Darricau, the commander of Seville, was forced to leave the French base virtually undefended as he collected every spare French soldier in the vicinity and advanced to rescue Rémond on 5 March. Darricau put up such a confident front that Ballasteros came to believe that another French force from Soult's field army was approaching his flank and he consequently retreated to the Tinto River despite the fact that he outnumbered the combined Darricau/Rémond force.

While all these events were taking place in Andalucia, the French at Badajoz anxiously persevered in the task before them. Having put himself in a position to win the prize, Soult was determined that he would never abandon the siege unless the arrival of bad news from Portugal or Andalucia forced him to do so and he accordingly called for more sacrifices from his men. The French soldiers were exhausted, wet and hungry, but fortunately they were sustained by a spirit of professionalism that gave human form to Soult's resolve. Captain Édouard Lapène, a young artillery officer attached to the second division of V Corps, later wrote a history of the 1811 campaign that includes a vivid anecdote of French life on campaign before Badajoz:

> I will never forget what happened in bivouac on one of the many stormy nights we had during the winter of 1811. I was awakened suddenly by a massive thunderstorm that soaked through my clothing within seconds ... My unit was already on its feet arranged in a circle around an enormous fire fed by thick wooden beams whose intensity was only slightly diminished by the ubiquitous

---

52. Von Schepeler, *Histoire*, Vol. 3, p. 157.
53. This episode is covered in von Schepeler, *Histoire*, Vol. 3, p. 134. Oman refers to Rémond as a general, but he did not achieve that rank until August. Oman, *History*, Vol. 4, p. 129.

water. Drenched with rain, the soldiers seemed less preoccupied with the storm and their miserable situation than they were in listening in respectful silence to one of their old comrades recounting, with a remarkable recall of places and dates, the series of victories and defeats, and disasters and triumphs experienced by the French Army over the prior twenty years ... captivated as I was by the charm of that story retracing the successes and glories of France, I regretted only slightly my lost sleep.[54]

Despite this attitude, the French were still measuring daily progress only in terms of yards in the days following their great victory. Then, on 3 March, the thirty-second day of the siege, a lucky shot changed their fortunes. Just before sunset on that day, the Spaniards staged a minor sortie that caught the besiegers unawares and resulted in the spiking of twelve or thirteen guns, a development that would have been a significant blow to the French except that the spiking was inexpertly done and the French were able to repair the damage. More importantly, however, General Menacho had positioned himself on the ramparts to observe the progress of the attack and in the course of the action he was struck by a stray cannon shot and killed.[55] The news of his death soon reached the French and, on the evidence of a letter written that same day by Captain Sigismund de Pouget, the Marquis de Nadaillac and an ADC to Latour-Maubourg, it seems to have been common knowledge that this development was very favourable to them: '[Governor Menacho] a very brave and stubborn man, has, fortunately for us, been killed by a cannonball; his death should advance the capture of the city.'[56]

Menacho's successor, Brigadier José de Imaz, had a good reputation but he was certainly not as strong a personality as his predecessor, although that was not immediately apparent as a practical matter. What was apparent was that the final moments of the siege were fast approaching as the French trenches reached the edge of the ditch surrounding the fortress and the besiegers began to make preparations to establish a final breaching battery consisting of six 24-pounder cannon. They also dug mines under the ditch that were packed with explosives to be detonated in an effort to destroy the inner wall of the ditch. Before either the breaching battery or the mines were completed, however, Marshal Soult's resolve was once again put to the test. On 8 March, he finally received the triple-barrelled bad news that Masséna had begun his retreat from Lisbon, that the allies at Cadiz had sent out an expedition that was marching to attack Marshal Victor's siege force from the rear and that Ballasteros was threatening Seville.[57] Any one of these unfavourable developments might have been reason enough to abandon the siege, but all three together suggested that his offensive was bound to end in failure. Soult refused to panic, however, and gambled that he still had a few days left to bring the siege to a successful conclusion before his situation became truly untenable. When his siege experts expressed a litany of time-consuming difficulties that the French still faced, Soult decided to make things very simple – he announced that he wanted to be inside Badajoz within forty-eight hours and that he would find other men who could

54. Lapène, *Conquête*, p.104
55. Lamare, *Relation*, p.66. According to Belmas, this was the 35th, not the 32nd, day of the siege.
56. Nadaillac, 'Lettres et Notes', p.473.
57. Belmas, *Journaux*, Vol.3, p.714.

meet that challenge if they were not up to the task.[58] His simple message had its intended effect and by 9:00 a.m. on 10 March, the French had opened a practicable breach in the city walls. Soult ordered a cease-fire and dispatched an officer to summon the Spanish governor to surrender and to spare his men and the inhabitants of the town from the consequences of a French assault.

It was now that the death of General Menacho was truly felt. Brigadier Imaz promptly called a council of war to discuss the French proposition rather than rejecting it summarily and, as one commentator has pointed out, that act is the universal symbol of a desire to capitulate rather than a desire to resist.[59] Speaking first, the senior engineer, Julian Alvo, outlined a gloomy prognosis and the majority of his fellow officers agreed with his conclusions. The final decision was still up to Imaz, however, and the council ended with him surprisingly endorsing the remarks of his second-in-command that the fortress should be 'defended to the last drop of blood'.[60] That declaration was apparently for public relations purposes only, however, because the governor immediately began surrender negotiations with the French that dragged on into the afternoon. Ever mindful of the passage of time, Soult finally decided to force the issue of surrender by massing an assault force in front of the breach. This bold action entirely intimidated Imaz and he hurriedly signed a formal capitulation at 3:00 p.m. Three elite companies of the 103rd Line Regiment were quickly admitted to the fortress and occupied the Trinity Gate, the Fort of San Cristoval and the bridgehead on the left bank of the Guadiana. At 10:00 a.m. on 11 March, the remaining 7,880 able-bodied men of the garrison marched out and piled their arms on the glacis of the fortress. Another 1,100 sick and wounded, 170 artillery pieces of various calibres, vast quantities of gunpowder and food for the garrison for a month also fell into French hands.[61]

The abrupt end of the siege of Badajoz was a spectacular victory for Soult that more than amply rewarded his brave gamble to see the siege to a conclusion. It was also, ironically, the sole concrete success achieved by the French as a result of Masséna's tenacious maintenance of his position before Lisbon, although from a strategic point of view the capture of the fortress could never compensate for the failure of the Army of Portugal. Masséna's aide, Colonel Pelet, expressed this thought succinctly when he told Napoleon that Soult had 'exchanged an entire kingdom for a single town'.[62] The loss of Badajoz was simultaneously a huge disappointment for the allies, particularly in light of the remarkable fact that, at the time of the surrender, Imaz was in possession of the critical information that Masséna had retreated and that a relief force would soon be on its way to him. This news was transmitted on Wellington's orders by means of semaphore flags displayed in the Portuguese fortress of Elvas that were clearly visible to the garrison at Badajoz:

> ... send an express to General Leite [the Portuguese commander at Elvas], and
> desire him to tell the Governor of Badajoz by telegraph that he must hold out

58. Lamare, *Relation*, p. 73.
59. Von Schepeler, *Histoire*, Vol. 3, p. 145.
60. The details of the council of war are given in an appendix to Gómez de Arteche y Moro, *Guerra*, Vol. 7, pp. 544–7.
61. Belmas, *Journaux*, Vol. 3, pp. 718–21.
62. Pelet, *Mémoires*, pp. 537–8.

to the last extremity, that Masséna has begun to retire, and that he may expect
assistance as soon as it is in my power to give it to him. Desire Leite to warn
him to keep that communication secret.[63]

Given that receipt of that message was explicitly acknowledged by Imaz and that
Badajoz was still well-supplied with ammunition and food when it surrendered,
Wellington was certain that treachery had played a role in the denouement of the
siege:

Nobody entertains a doubt that Imaz sold Badajoz. He appears to have
surrendered as soon as he could after he knew that relief was coming to him,
lest his garrison should prevent the surrender when they should be certain of
the truth of the intelligence of Masséna's retreat.[64]

This judgment is undoubtedly too harsh, since the promised relief was still many
days away and Soult was definitely prepared to launch an immediate assault on the
breach. There is even an ironical possibility that Wellington's injunction to keep the
news sent by telegraph a secret may have inadvertently contributed to the surrender
by causing Imaz to withhold that information from his own commanders. Imaz was
nevertheless court-martialed when he returned from captivity in France in 1814, but
no evidence of wrong-doing was ever found. Whatever the cause of Imaz's behaviour,
it was simply one further piece of evidence for Wellington that the Spanish
government was doing a terrible job of conducting their war effort:

The Spanish nation have lost Tortosa, Olivenza, and Badajoz, in the course of
two months, without sufficient cause; and in the same period, Marshal Soult,
with a corps never supposed to be more than 20,000 men, has taken, besides
the last two places, or destroyed above 22,000 Spanish troops.[65]

63. W. to B., 6 March 1811, *Dispatches*, Vol. 7, pp. 344–5. The distance between Elvas and Badajoz is
    nine miles, but Elvas is situated on high ground and the intervening terrain is flat, so there was line-
    of-sight visibility between the two towns.
64. W. to Henry Wellesley, 20 March 1811, *Dispatches*, Vol. 7, pp. 380–1 at 380; W. to Henry Wellesley,
    16 March 1811, *Dispatches*, Vol. 7, pp. 366–7 at 367.
65. W. to Liverpool, 14 March 1811, *Dispatches*, Vol. 7, pp. 354–61 at 361.

Chapter 3

The First British Siege
of Badajoz

The capture of Badajoz by the French might have led to immediate decisive consequences if it had occurred when Masséna first arrived before the lines of Torres Vedras in September 1810, but by March 1811 it was a development devoid of its original intended strategic significance because the French no longer had any chance of achieving their primary objective of driving the British out of Portugal. It did, however, have the collateral effect of barring the invasion route to Andalucia to the allies until the fortress could be retaken, a situation that annoyed Wellington almost as much as the manner in which the town had fallen: 'It ... [is] impossible to do anything to the south till Badajoz should be again in our hands.'[1] Once Wellington drove Masséna out of Portugal, the need to rectify that situation determined his strategic priorities: 'The first object of our attention must be to regain Badajoz.'[2] Because Badajoz had changed partners in the odd minuet of Peninsular warfare, it was now up to the allies to recapture the town and re-establish the strategic balance in their favour.

The man Wellington selected to lead the Badajoz expedition was Marshal William Carr Beresford (b. 1768), the Commander-in-Chief of the Portuguese Army. Beresford was the acknowledged (though illegitimate) son of Lord Waterford, one of the most prominent peers of the Anglo-Irish aristocracy of which Wellington himself was a member, so he had important connections in his favour, but his military career could have ended abruptly just after it began in 1785 due to a hunting accident that deprived him of sight in his left eye.[3] Beresford surmounted that handicap, however, and went on to serve in India, Egypt, the Cape Colony, South America and Madeira. Although he was viewed as a good officer, at the start of the Peninsular War he was better known for his defeats than his successes, since his most prominent command had involved an attack on Buenos Aires in 1806 that had ended with his surrender and then his escape from captivity in Argentina. Beresford had therefore been something of a surprise choice for the Portuguese command in 1809, but he had performed well at the task of

---

1. W. to Lord Burghersh, 8 July 1811, Westmoreland, *Correspondence*, p. 46–51 at 47.
2. W. to Liverpool, 7 May 1811, *Dispatches*, Vol. 7, pp. 521–5 at 522.
3. Beresford was shot by Ensign Molyneux, a fellow officer of the 6th Foot, while they were hunting partridge in Nova Scotia. Clarke, *The Georgian Era*, Vol. 2, p. 111.

reorganising the Portuguese military and Wellington had genuine respect for his abilities: 'All that I can tell you is that the ablest man I have yet seen with the army, and the one having the largest views, is Beresford.'[4] Wellington had consequently called upon Beresford to replace Lieutenant General Rowland Hill in command of the allied forces south of the Tagus River when the latter officer went back to England on sick leave at the end of 1810. Given that Hill was still absent in March 1811, Beresford was the logical choice for command of this important expedition.

Marshal Beresford was a memorable and unusual person. His sightless eye gave his face a forbidding aspect that was compounded by his large size and fierce temper: 'He was a man of herculean strength, and as a soldier [was] terrible to look upon at all times.'[5] His manners also left much to be desired according to one gentleman who hosted the marshal for several days, although the fellow ultimately concluded that Beresford was nonetheless blunt good company:

> I can safely say that in my life I never took so strong a prejudice against a man [Beresford]. Such a low-looking ruffian in his air, with damned bad manners, or rather none at all, and a vulgarity in his expressions and pronunciation that made me at once believe he was as ignorant, stupid and illiterate as he was ill-looking. Yet somehow or other he almost wiped away all of these notches before we parted. In the first place, it is an invaluable property in any man to have him call a spade a spade ... Then ... you ... find out that he has been in every part of the world and in all the most interesting scenes of it.[6]

The soldiers who served under him took a more positive view of the man. One private thought '[A] braver or better man I never served.'[7] William Warre, a long-time member of the marshal's military family, acknowledged that Beresford had some rough edges to his personality, but thought that without them he would never have succeeded in his efforts to reorganise the Portuguese Army in 1810:

> There exists not a more honourable firm man or a more zealous Patriot. His failings are mere foibles of a temper naturally warm and hasty, and great zeal to have everything right, without much patience. Those who accuse him of severity are either those who have felt it because they deserved it, their friends, or people wilfully ignorant of the state in which he found the army. And of how much he has foreborne, as to myself, I declare I do not know one instance of severity, and [do know] numberless ones of his mercy, and goodness of heart, where others would have been less lenient.[8]

On a very simplistic level, it was obvious that the faster the allies moved on Badajoz, the more successful they would be because their speed would limit the amount of time available for the French to re-stock supplies and repair the damage they had caused to the fortifications during their own siege of the fortress. Things started off well enough, since some troops actually started for Badajoz on 8 March in

4. W. to Bathurst, 2 December 1812, *Supp. Despatches*, Vol. 7, p. 484. The extraordinary story of Beresford's reorganisation of the Portuguese Army is well told in Vichness, 'Marshal of Portugal'.
5. Pearson, *The Soldier Who Walked Away*, p. 97.
6. T. Creevey to Miss Ord, 24 August 1827 in Creevey, *The Creevey Papers*, Vol. 2, pp. 126–7.
7. Pearson, *The Soldier Who Walked Away*, p. 9.
8. Warre to Mother, 6 February 1810, in Warre, *Letters*, pp. 104–8 at 105.

an effort to relieve the fortress before it fell, but that fast start proved to be illusory. Major Alexander Dickson, commander of Marshal Beresford's Portuguese artillery, recalled that Wellington soon changed his mind and called back both Beresford and some of the troops designated for his corps in anticipation of a major battle against Masséna's army:

> Almost immediately after they [the French] commenced their retreat, Marshall [sic] Beresford's corps was ordered to march towards Portalegre [on the way to Badajoz]. I marched from Chamusca on the 9th, reached Gafete on the 11th, where I was ordered to halt, as well as the rest of the corps marching up, in consequence of the Marshall [sic] being sent for by Lord Wellington.[9]

That potential crisis quickly passed, but by the time it did Badajoz had surrendered. As a result, Beresford's mission changed from relief of Badajoz to recapture of the fortress and this development made his progress significantly more vulnerable to three looming problems: bad weather, supply shortages and the complexities of coordinating his movements with those of three different auxiliary Spanish forces. The combination of those three problems ultimately prevented Beresford from generating and sustaining the kind of urgency of movement necessary to optimise his chances for success and set him on a direct (although not yet inevitable) course towards a rendezvous with Soult at Albuera.

The French, on the other hand, were very quick to exploit their victory at Badajoz. Although Soult and a significant portion of Gazan's division started back to Seville at full speed on 14 March, Marshal Mortier and the remainder of V Corps expanded on the French success by crossing the Guadiana in force and attacking some of the lesser border fortresses still in allied hands – Campo Mayor, Alburquerque and Valencia de Alcántara. This last town was abandoned by its Spanish defenders and, in a performance worthy of the Prussian Army in 1806, the Spanish commander at Albuquerque surrendered his men and a near-impregnable castle to a few hundred horsemen under Latour-Maubourg on 15 March.

Campo Mayor proved to be a tougher proposition. Its commander, an ornery Portuguese officer named Major José Joaquim Tallaya, inspired his outnumbered garrison of militiamen and home guards to hold out until the French breached the town's walls and, even then, he exacted favourable surrender terms that included the right of everyone in the garrison except a few regular soldiers to go home on parole.[10] The French, however, had no intention of retaining Campo Mayor and their other conquests – they merely wanted to relieve them of useful artillery and supplies and to make them unusable as bases for Beresford.

While the French were picking this low-hanging fortress fruit, Beresford was assembling his formidable attack force consisting of the 2nd and 4th British Divisions, a full Portuguese infantry division, another independent Portuguese infantry brigade, four brigades of British and Portuguese cavalry and assorted artillery and engineer contingents. These were all sound troops, but the quality of their commanding officers was more variable. With Hill away, Major General William Stewart (b. 1774) had command of the 2nd Division. Stewart was in his prime as a military officer and had a

9. Dickson to MacLeod, 21 March 1811 in Dickson, *Manuscripts*, Vol. 3, pp. 362–4 at 363.
10. The terms of surrender dated 21 March are reproduced in Belmas, *Journaux*, Vol. 1, pp. 795–6.

service record that was second to none in its depth and breadth.[11] His first commission in the army had been purchased when he was aged twelve and he eventually served in such disparate locations as the West Indies, Sicily, Egypt, Denmark and Walcheren Island in addition to the Peninsula. He had been attached to the Austrian Army in 1799 and was present at the Battle of Zurich, became one of the co-founders, along with Colonel Coote Manningham, of the original Rifle Brigade in 1800 and had even fought with Nelson at the Battle of Copenhagen in 1801. As evidenced by the innovative regulations he formulated for the Rifles, he was very much a student of his craft as a soldier and he expected as much from his subordinates:

> Stewart makes it a rule to strike at the heads. With him the field officers must first be steady, and then he goes downwards: hence the privates say, we had better look sharp if he is so strict with the officers.[12]

He also had another much-valued quality – courage:

> I have often heard Colonel Colborne (Lord Seaton) affirm that if he were asked to name the bravest man he had ever seen (and *no one* was a better judge), he should name Sir William Stewart.[13]

With Stewart replacing Hill, his own brigade, the first of the division, also had an interim commander. Perhaps not surprisingly given the admiration expressed by Colborne for Stewart in the prior paragraph, Lieutenant Colonel John Colborne (b. 1778) of the 66th Foot was Stewart's choice, a fact that must have rankled with Lieutenant Colonel George Duckworth of the 2nd/48th Foot, who was senior to Colborne and had commanded the brigade for parts of 1810 before Stewart arrived on the scene. Major General Daniel Hoghton (b. 1770), the commander of the third brigade, resented Stewart's advancement and made so many complaints to Beresford on the subject that the marshal was compelled to share them with Wellington:

> Hoghton is really so importunate to be removed from his situation under Stewart that, however I dislike pestering you on these subjects, I can only say that I would be most glad if you would get him from Stewart, as it will save me an hour per diem hearing what is no ways amusing.[14]

No one had anything especially bad to say about the other brigadier of the 2nd Division, Major General William Lumley (b. 1769), but that may be simply because little was expected of him. When Wellington questioned the Horse Guards in 1810 as to whether there were any better general officers who might be sent to the Peninsula instead of Lumley, the Military Secretary (Henry Torrens) sent Wellington a reply that perhaps did not paint as positive a picture as the sender may have intended:

> I never thought him [Lumley] a clever man, but he is zealous, active, obedient, and brave as a lion. He is not intended by nature for anything bigger than a brigade; but that, it is generally thought, he will do well.[15]

11. Stewart's early career is conveniently summarised in Verner, *Rifle Brigade*, pp. 47–50.
12. W. Napier, *Sir Charles Napier*, p. 19.
13. Smith, *Autobiography*, Vol. 1, pp. 170–1.
14. B. to W., April 29, 1811, Wellington Papers WP1/328/72, University of Southampton.
15. Torrens to W., 19 September 1810, quoted in Fortescue, *British Army*, Vol. 7, p. 419.

Against this backdrop, Beresford must have been pleased when he learned that Brigadier Robert Long (b. 1771) had been appointed to command his cavalry because he was known to be 'an active and most intelligent officer, and possessed of no ordinary share of talents'.[16] Long in turn formed a favourable first impression of Beresford after three days in his company: 'I am inclined to like him exceedingly. I find him unreserved, affable, open, sociable and obliging.'[17] As will be seen, however, each man soon formed a very different opinion about the other. There was also an incipient issue in the fact that Long was junior to General Madden, the commander of the Portuguese cavalry brigade that had been operating with Mendizabal.

Major General Sir Galbraith Lowry Cole (b. 1772) was technically only the provisional commander of the 4th Division, but he had held that command since February 1810 and had not been replaced while he was on sick leave in England early in 1811, so his position was apparently secure.[18] In matters non-military he was the antithesis of Marshal Beresford: 'General Cole is a young man ... with very polished manners and great charm.' Another officer expressed the difference between the two men in very practical terms – Cole gave the best dinners among Wellington's officers, and Beresford the worst. It also did not help matters that Cole was friendly with Hoghton. Beresford and Cole may not have got along well socially, but they probably had more in common on the field of battle: 'And though a hot-tempered and passionate man, he [Cole] is as kind and generous as he is brave, and a more truly gallant and enterprising soldier never breathed.'[19]

The senior brigade of the 4th Division had been commanded by Cole, but was now in the hands of Brigadier James Kemmis (b. 1751). Kemmis, who was significantly older than most of his colleagues, is the mystery man of the Peninsular army – there is almost nothing known about him except for the barebones facts of a service career which began in the American Revolutionary War.[20] An officer who served under him did record, however, that Kemmis was 'generally very much disliked'.[21]

The second brigade had only become the fusilier brigade through a reorganisation of its component units in December 1810 under the auspices of Colonel Edward Pakenham, but he was soon detached for service with Wellington's headquarters leaving the very young but well-regarded Lieutenant Colonel Sir William Myers (b. 1783) of the 7th Fusiliers in command instead. The Portuguese brigade attached to the 4th Division had been commanded by Brigadier General William Harvey (b. 17??, formerly a lieutenant colonel of the British 70th Foot) for over a year. On 14 March, just as the campaign was beginning, the brigade received an addition to its strength in the form of the 1st Battalion of the Loyal Lusitanian Legion.[22]

---

16. Description by Henry Torrens quoted in McGuffie, *Peninsular Cavalry General*, p. 47.
17. Long to Brother, 21 March 1811, quoted in McGuffie, *Peninsular Cavalry General*, p. 69.
18. General Order for 22 February 1810: 'Major General Cole is to command the fourth division until further orders.' Quoted in Smythies, *Historical Records*, p. 117.
19. Cole, *Memoirs*, pp. 59, 65, 69 and 75. The first quote is a description of Cole in 1805 by Roverea. The second was written by George Napier in 1828.
20. Smythies, *Historical Records of the 40th*, pp. 515–16.
21. Fryer, *'Our Young Soldier'*, p. 115.
22. Ward, 'Portuguese Infantry Brigades', pp. 103–12.

Since Beresford was the Portuguese Commander-in-Chief, it was particularly important for him to have a strong Portuguese contingent in his force.[23] This was provided first and foremost by a full Portuguese division commanded by Marechal de Campo [Lieutenant General] John Hamilton (b. 1755), the senior British officer in Portuguese service aside from Beresford. One of his brigades was commanded by Brigadier General Agostinho Luiz da Fonseca (b. 1751) and the other by Colonel Archibald Campbell (b. 1769, formerly a lieutenant colonel of the British 71st Foot), who was formally promoted to brigadier on 8 May. On 23 March, the 5th Caçadores were removed from Hamilton's Division and combined with the 5th Portuguese Line to form another, independent Portuguese brigade commanded by Brigadier General Richard Collins (b. 1775, formerly a lieutenant colonel of the 83rd Foot), an officer who was fluent in French, German, Spanish and Portuguese as well as English.[24] Beresford also had two Portuguese cavalry brigades, the one under Madden already in action and one under Colonel Loftus William Otway (b. 1775, formerly a lieutenant colonel of the 18th Hussars). Beresford also brought along many of his senior Portuguese Army staff officers, including Colonel Benjamin D'Urban (b. 1777), the Quartermaster-General, who functioned in many ways as Beresford's chief of staff.

Beresford's force was supported by four field artillery units, but that force lacked a unified command structure. There were two Portuguese batteries commanded by Major Dickson (b. 1777, formerly a captain in the Royal Artillery) and two batteries of the King's German Legion commanded by Major Julius Hartmann (b. 1774) of the KGL. The two men fortunately had great respect for each other and were able to work together easily.

The Anglo-Portuguese troops assembled in a leisurely fashion at Portalegre and enjoyed the benefits of weather that 'was warm and delightful as an English May'.[25] Beresford himself did not arrive until 20 March and the 4th Division only appeared two days later. To the marshal's consternation, he found that Cole's men were badly worn out and in desperate need of shoes because of hard marching described by Sergeant John Cooper of the 7th Fusiliers:

> Off we started and made a forced march … over hilly stony roads without a mouthful of bread. Great numbers of men unable to keep up; remained on the roads or in the fields during a wet night. I hobbled on with the column; but I suffered dreadfully from hunger, thirst, little shoes and blistered feet.[26]

They had covered over a hundred miles in six days, but it is nevertheless odd to find the troops so destitute less than a month after leaving their comfortable winter quarters near Lisbon. Beresford was even more amazed to find that many of the men of the 2nd Division were also shoeless, since they had started off south of the Tagus and done comparatively little marching.

Despite these unpromising circumstances, Beresford was spurred to immediate action by one of the many communications that arrived with great regularity from Wellington:

23. Most of the information about the officers commanding Portuguese units comes from the article by Ward cited in the preceding note and from Halliday, *Observations*.
24. Haythornthwaite, *Armies of Wellington*, p. 30.
25. Sherer, *Recollections*, p. 140.
26. Cooper, *Rough Notes*, p. 53

You had better lose no time in moving up to Portalegre, and attack Soult, if you can, at Campo Mayor. I will come to you if I can; but if I cannot, do not wait for me. Get Castaños to join you, from Estremoz, with any Spanish troops he can bring with him. You must be two days marching from Portalegre to Campo Mayor, I believe.[27]

As is illustrated by this message, Beresford's force may have been geographically separated from the main army, but it was most definitely not an 'independent' command in any true sense of that term. Although the marshal had some discretion, it was eminently clear that Wellington expected his subordinate to follow the path laid out for him with minimal variation. Such an approach could in theory have led to the same kind of problems Soult had with stale instructions from Paris, but it did not in practice because of the relatively short distance between Beresford and Wellington and the efficiency of the British courier system that delivered most messages between them within forty-eight hours of dispatch. What it did lead to, however, was a stifling of Beresford's initiative that was to have some significant consequences in the days and weeks ahead.

Whether the men were ready or not, Beresford's whole Anglo-Portuguese force began to advance towards Campo Mayor on 24 March. By the morning of the 25th, he was close enough to Campo Mayor to send Brigadier Long to circle around the north side of the town while the main force came in from the south. The security arrangements of the French seem to have been somewhat lax since they did not detect the advancing enemy, but that may be because they were already in the process of withdrawing and had sent their own artillery plus a wagon train of captured guns and supplies off to Badajoz at the break of dawn. All that remained was a rear-guard under General Latour-Maubourg consisting of several battalions of the 100th Line and three regiments of cavalry – the 26th Dragoons and the 2nd and 10th Hussars – plus 80 men from the 4th Chasseurs from King Joseph's Spanish Army, perhaps 2,400 men in all. The French were veteran soldiers and would not be an easy prize, but the stage seemed to be set for Beresford's vastly superior force to inflict some significant damage on their opponents.

The action began brilliantly with Long's men, spearheaded by the 13th Light Dragoons, routing the French cavalry and then conducting a relentless pursuit that led to 'the killing of the Colonel of the 26th Regiment of Cavalry ... [and the] taking [of] 15 pieces of artillery and several ammunition wagons' and ended only at the fortifications of Badajoz, just over eight miles from where they started.[28] Unfortunately, after the 13th Light Dragoons had disappeared from the scene in pursuit of the enemy cavalry, Beresford was informed that the regiment had in fact been captured *en masse* and, based on that erroneous information, he immediately halted the rest of his troops (including the heavy cavalry brigade under Long's command) until the situation could be clarified even though he appeared to have the

---

27. W. to B., 18 March 1811, *Dispatches*, Vol. 7, p. 372.
28. Long to Brother, 28 May 1811, quoted in McGuffie, *Peninsular Cavalry General*, pp. 73–81 at 80. Vital-Joachim Chamorin, commander of the 26th Dragoons, was killed by Corporal Logan of the 13th Light Dragoons in single combat. Chamorin, who was esteemed by Soult as one of the best advance guard officers in the French Army, had actually been promoted to the rank of brigade general a scant twenty days before his death. Lievyns, *Fastes*, Vol. 3, pp. 68–9.

rest of the French column at his mercy.[29] At the same time, General Girard, some cavalry and a large portion of his brigade (the 34th and 40th Line Regiments) sallied forth from Badajoz and forced the 13th Light Dragoons to withdraw away from the main road.[30] Taking fullest advantage of these two developments, a resourceful (if astonished) Colonel Joachim-Jérôme Quiot (b. 1775) calmly led his own 100th Line and the rest of the column safely back to Badajoz, recovering all the missing artillery pieces along the way.

That shocking outcome to the day's action was universally deplored and led to a dramatic deterioration in the relationship between Beresford and his cavalry commander. Long thought it was a 'disgrace' for the British to have allowed the French to retreat in safety and blamed Beresford's interference for preventing him from having achieved a better result.[31] Beresford in turn felt Long was to blame for faulty execution of his orders and for not being able to provide accurate information as to the whereabouts of his men.[32] As between the two, Beresford was probably guilty of the greater error in curtailing any further offensive action after he received the erroneous report about the 13th Light Dragoons, but in that regard the real culprit was Wellington, who on 20 March had sent a stern admonition to Beresford to avoid putting his cavalry at risk, an instruction that must have been ringing in the marshal's head when he thought the 13th Light Dragoons had been lost:

> I have always considered the cavalry to be the most delicate arm we possess. We have few Officers who have practical knowledge of the mode of using it, or who have ever seen more than two regiments together; and all our troops, cavalry as well as infantry, are a little inclined to get out of order in battle. To these circumstances add, that the defeat of, or any great loss sustained by, our cavalry, in these open grounds, would be a misfortune amounting almost to a defeat of the whole; and you will see the necessity of keeping the cavalry as much as possible *en masse*, and in reserve, to be thrown in at the moment when an opportunity may offer of striking a decisive blow.[33]

In light of this communication, it is thoroughly understandable why Beresford may not have wanted to put any more troops at risk until the fate of the missing cavalry was determined. His hesitation, however, quickly became a topic of conversation and correspondence among the senior officers of the British Army, and most of the opinions were unfavourable to the marshal. A typical comment is this one from a letter written by Colonel Pakenham, Wellington's adjutant-general:

> Beresford is a clever man but no General; his Anxiety is too great, and he cannot allow an Operation to go through by its first impulse without interference, which generally on such occasions mars every thing ... He brought 20,000 men close to the Enemy not above 2000 strong, and yet by some mismanagement

29. The source of the misinformation was apparently one Baron Tripp, a Dutch émigré serving on Long's staff whose first name is not given in any source. Tripp must have been a volunteer with no official status as there is no trace of a staff officer with that surname in the *Army List* for 1811.
30. D'Héralde, *Mémoires*, pp. 149–50.
31. Long to Brother, 28 May 1811, quoted in McGuffie, *Peninsular Cavalry General*, pp. 73–81 at 79.
32. Beresford, *Letter to C. E. Long*, pp. 19–27.
33. W. to B., 20 March 1811, *Dispatches*, Vol. 7, pp. 374–6 at 374–5.

... he not only let them escape, but allowed them to recover fifteen Guns which the 13th L.D. took from them.[34]

As the campaign continued, Beresford and Long would each be under close scrutiny for signs as to whether his performance at Campo Mayor was an aberration or evidence of serious command deficiencies.

The inadvertent victim of this acrimony was the 13th Light Dragoons. Based on Long's and Beresford's first incomplete reports about the combat at Campo Mayor, Wellington formed the view that the failure to capture the French rear-guard had in fact resulted from irresponsible behaviour on the part of the regiment during its pursuit and he composed a blistering rebuke that he ordered read to the unit:

> I wish you [Beresford] to call together the Officers of the [13th Light] Dragoons, and point out to them the mischiefs which must result from the disorder of the troops in action. The undisciplined ardour of the 13th Dragoons, and the 1st regiment of Portuguese cavalry, is not of the description of the determined bravery and steadiness of soldiers confident in their discipline and in their Officers. Their conduct was that of a rabble, galloping as fast as their horses could carry them over a plain, after an enemy to whom they could do no mischief when they were broken ... If the 13th Dragoons are again guilty of this conduct I shall take their horses from them, and send the Officers and men to do duty in Lisbon.[35]

Later additional information would reveal that Wellington's view was incorrect, but the British commander was never one to apologise publicly for a mistaken judgment. He is, however, reputed to have told some officers of the regiment that he would not have sent the letter if he had known the true facts.[36] To their personal credit, both Long and Beresford made special efforts to mitigate the effects of Wellington's criticism and vindicate the performance of the regiment. The men of the 13th Light Dragoons may have been less concerned with this controversy than their officers because they had the consolation of having taken immense plunder from the enemy: 'Several of our men got great sums of money, watches, plate, &c.; and among the rest I have got a fine young blood mare, a silver-mounted sword, saddle, bridle, &c.'[37]

With the French chased from the right bank of the Guadiana, the next thing Beresford had to accomplish was to move his forces to the left bank. Since the bridge at Badajoz was unavailable to the British, the Guadiana could only be crossed above Badajoz at Mérida or below the town at Juromenha, and Beresford chose the latter crossing point because of its proximity to Elvas, the strongest fortification in Portugal. When the water was low, the Guadiana was fordable at that location, but this being early spring, the river was 'four feet deep and about 180 yards wide', so the British were forced to construct a bridge using pontoons to span the deepest part of the river and wooden trestles in the shallows. It took until 4 April to assemble the necessary bridging materials and improvisation was called for as soon as the bridge building began because the river unexpectedly rose another three feet, a change 'supposed to

---

34. EP to 'Tom', 15 April 1811, and EP to Longford, 16 April 1811, in Pakenham, *Letters*, pp. 87–8.
35. W. to B., 30 March 1811, *Dispatches*, Vol. 7, pp. 412–13 at 412
36. Barrett, *XIII Hussars*, Vol. 1, p. 136.
37. Bennett, 'Memoirs', p. 89.

be occasioned by the melting of the snow in the mountains' since the weather at Juromenha was 'fine'.[38] The crossing of the whole Anglo-Portuguese force ultimately took some seventy-two hours and while it was in progress there was another incident that further soured Beresford's attitude towards General Long. Early on the morning of 7 April, a large French force (including the 2nd Hussars and the voltigeurs of the 88th Line) managed to penetrate the British perimeter, caused nocturnal alarms in the village where Beresford had his headquarters, and surprised and captured an entire squadron of the 13th Light Dragoons under Major Redmond Morres without a struggle.[39]

Beresford may have been surprised that the French did not make a stronger effort to disrupt his crossing, but he could not have known the full extent to which French offensive capabilities had been compromised by some significant changes in the command and composition of his immediate opponent, the French V Corps. First, Brigade General Armand Philippon (b. 1761), a resourceful veteran who commanded the first brigade of the first division of V Corps, was appointed governor of Badajoz with a garrison composed of six infantry battalions, five of which were also taken from V Corps.[40] Then, Soult took the second division of V Corps back to Seville with him. Finally, at the end of March, Marshal Mortier received long-awaited orders to return to Paris and, overjoyed to be leaving Spain, he departed with alacrity, taking his chief of staff and several other staff officers with him.[41] His recall was a huge loss for the French, at once depriving them of an eminent battlefield leader and unsettling the command structure and morale of the corps he had led since 1808, and it must be attributed entirely to Napoleon, who had no real pressing need for Mortier's services at that time.[42]

Mortier's unexpected successor at the head of V Corps was Division General Latour-Maubourg (b. 1768), an ex-émigré and life-long cavalryman who was Soult's choice for the job.[43] Unlike the many parvenu barons in the Grande Armée, holding titles earned on the field of battle, Latour-Maubourg was a genuine aristocrat with a reputation for honesty and probity who had reached the rank of colonel in the army of Louis XVI before he emigrated.[44] That appointment could hardly have pleased Division General Girard (b. 1773), the commander of the first division, who had been

38. Dickson, *Manuscripts*, Vol. 3, pp. 373–5.
39. *Ibid.*, p. 382; the circumstances of the loss of the squadron are discussed in detail in Long to Brother, 12 April 1811, quoted in McGuffie, *Peninsular Cavalry General*, pp. 83–90, at 85–6. Beresford said this incident was 'one of the most singularly neglectful cases I ever heard of in my military experience and is really incredible.' B. to W., 7 April 1811, Wellington Papers WP1/327/27, University of Southampton.
40. There is no record of the composition of the Badajoz garrison during April, May and June, but according to a return dated 11 July 1811, the six battalions in the fortress belonged to the 40th, 88th, 58th, 100th and 103rd Line Regiments and the 21st Light Regiment. Lamare, *Relation*, p. 161.
41. Lapène, *Conquête*, p. 138, records the date of his departure as being 26 March, but von Schepeler says he did not leave until 7 April, while Soult states that Mortier stayed with his command until it reached Llerena. Von Schepeler, *Histoire*, Vol. 3, p. 264; Soult, *Mémoires*, p. 229. Soult says he made a strong but ultimately unsuccessful effort to convince Mortier to stay.
42. According to Soult's ADC, Colonel Louis-Bertrand-Pierre Brun de Villeret, who visited Paris at the beginning of May on a mission for Soult, Napoleon was actually surprised and upset when he learned that Mortier had returned to France, so there may have been some confusion between the emperor and Berthier as to exactly when Mortier should have been ordered to leave his command. Gotteri, *Soult*, p. 418.
43. Soult, *Mémoires*, p. 229.
44. Thoumas, *Grands Cavaliers*, Series 2, p. 339.

one of the fabled 'Volunteers of '93' who answered the first call of *la patrie en danger* during the French Revolution and who had served with V Corps since 1806, but he was two years junior to Latour-Maubourg as a division general. Division General Gazan (b. 1765), who had commanded the second division of V Corps for many years and was senior to both the other two generals, was apparently not considered as a replacement because he had been serving as chief of staff for Soult's Armée du Midi since early February.[45] Since that time, his former division had been commanded on a provisional basis by Brigade General Joseph Pépin (b. 1765), a veteran of Napoleon's Egyptian campaign and the commander of its first brigade, although the second brigade under Brigade General Jean-Pierre Maransin (b. 1770) had been detached at the beginning of the month to face the Spanish troops under Ballasteros operating near the mouth of the Guadiana River.

Even if Mortier had remained in command, there is little doubt that the V Corps would still have been forced to retreat because the French had barely 9,000 men available for action after deducting Gazan's division with Soult and the battalions detached to garrison Badajoz. Beresford, on the other hand, had nearly 20,000 men under his own direct command and, in a meeting on 30 March, he made arrangements with Capitán General Francisco Xavier Castaños (b. 1758) that ensured the participation of the remnants of Mendizabal's army in the next phase of the campaign. Castaños was viewed by many as a man who had been extremely lucky to triumph over the French in the Battle of Bailén and who thereafter lived off the reputation he gained by that victory:

> General Castaños was with me yesterday; he seems a perfect old woman, whose sole occupation is powdering his hair, and patrolling about the country with a suite of servants and soldiers from 50 to 60 in number, at which the common people gaze with admiration and cry out 'Viva!'[46]

Be that as it may, Castaños was a zealous promoter of cooperation with the British and that attitude was to exert a significant influence over the outcome of the campaign. After the disaster at the Gevora, his so-called 5th Army was a mere shadow force of no more than 3,500 men, but it did have able commanders. The two weak infantry divisions were led by Brigadier Pablo Morillo (b. 1778), who played only a minor role in the campaign, and Brigadier Carlos de España (b. 1775), a Frenchman by birth who had joined the Spanish Army in 1792 and was esteemed as 'an active, intelligent and brave' officer.[47] The weak cavalry division with six accompanying cannon was in the hands of Brigadier Conde [Count] Louis de Penne-Villemur (b. 1761), another Frenchman, but this time one who had been raised in Spain.[48] Castaños commenced his cooperation by ordering General Morillo to occupy Mérida and detaching all his cavalry (about 650 men) to cooperate with Brigadier Long's cavalry force.[49]

45. Pépin de Bonnerive, 'Général Pépin', p. 283.
46. Long to Brother, 24 April 1811, McGuffie, *Peninsular General*, pp. 95–7, at 96.
47. Hay, *Narrative*, p. 137. De España was a real favourite with the British because he spoke English.
48. The count's first name is one of the best-kept secrets of the Peninsular War. AN File 240 AP (Fonds Villemur).
49. Dutton, *Founder of a City*, p. 53. The Spaniard even allowed the appointment of Lieutenant William Light of the 4th Dragoons as a liaison officer attached to Spanish cavalry headquarters.

Given the size of the combined forces arrayed against him, Latour-Maubourg began a speedy retirement, but not before making the questionable decision to leave behind at Olivenza a garrison of some 400 men under Colonel Jean Niboyet, a force large enough for the loss to be felt but small enough to have absolutely no chance of causing material disruption to the Anglo-Portuguese advance.[50] Since the 4th Division under General Cole was still suffering from lack of shoes, Beresford assigned it the sedentary task of recapturing Olivenza. The French garrison put up a surprisingly bold front that discouraged the attacking force from trying an immediate assault on the under-manned fortifications, so Cole decided to approach the capture in a classical manner instead and sent Major Dickson to fetch siege guns from Elvas. As soon as these were in place, the surrender followed quickly and on 15 April the Anglo-Portuguese took possession of the town.[51] (The unnecessary sacrifice of the Olivenza garrison even called forth an expression of disgust from Napoleon himself when he learned of it from the British papers, although his criticism was mistakenly directed at Soult instead of Latour-Maubourg.[52]) In the meanwhile, Beresford had continued on with the bulk of his force. Some of these men were sent north to link up with the Spanish forces at Mérida and thus effect a loose blockade of Badajoz while Beresford led the rest after Latour-Maubourg. This pursuit had multiple objectives – Beresford wanted 'to clear Extremadura altogether of the [V] corps … to give confidence to the people, and thus secure the resources of the province during the siege of Badajoz.'[53]

In pursuit of these objectives, the 2nd Division and Beresford's cavalry bivouacked at Albuera on 12 April, the first time that the name of the village appears in British narratives of 1811 (although the French had visited there during their approach to Badajoz in January). On 16 April, Long's cavalry, reinforced with two mule-drawn Spanish artillery pieces, engaged the French at Los Santos and routed the 2nd and 10th Hussars in an exchange of charges, capturing over a hundred prisoners.[54] This time, however, good order prevailed in the pursuit of the defeated enemy, a circumstance that gave Beresford an opportunity to repair some of the damage done to the reputation of the cavalry at Campo Mayor:

> I am happy to inform your lordship that though visibly with the utmost anxiety to overtake the enemy, and going at a very smart rate, our cavalry kept the most regular order, the 13th Light Dragoons deserving my best commendation.[55]

When Beresford reached Zafra he thought he might have a chance to defeat General Maransin's brigade, which had unwittingly come within striking distance while chasing General Ballasteros's division away from Seville, but the French were

50. The full composition of the garrison is unknown, but it definitely included one under-strength company (50 men) of the 1st Battalion of the 21st Light, which itself was part of the Badajoz garrison. Bouvier, *Historique du 96e Régiment*, p. 217.
51. Cole, Report to B., 16 April 1811, reproduced in *Supp. Despatches*, Vol. 13, pp. 614–15. Interestingly, Cole attributes his 'trifling' loss in large part to the suppressing 'fire kept up by the British light companies, and the rifle companies of the 60th and the Brunswick Regiments, under Majors Pearson and Birmingham, and the flank companies of Colonel Harvey's Portuguese brigade.'
52. N. to Berthier, 7 May 1811, *Correspondance*, No. 17701, Vol. 22, p. 146. Oman mistakenly cites this letter as being in 'Vol. XXI' of Napoleon's *Correspondance*.)
53. D'Urban, *Report of Operations*, p. 14.
54. Long to Brother, 17 April 1811, quoted in McGuffie, *Peninsular Cavalry General*, pp. 90–3, at 91.
55. B. to W., 18 April 1811, Wellington Papers WP1/327/81, University of Southampton.

informed about Beresford's presence in time to retreat safely and avoid entrapment. Latour-Maubourg thought briefly about making a stand at Llerena, but quickly concluded it would be safer to retire all the way to Guadalcanal, covering the road to Cordova but leaving open the direct route to Seville via the Royal Road.

Viewed in the most positive light, Beresford's achievements since the action at Campo Mayor were not inconsiderable:

> [He had] in a fortnight, and certainly under no trifling difficulties, passed the Guadiana, reduced Olivenza, cleared Estremadura of the enemy, obtained disposal of all its resources, and shut in Badajoz.[56]

From another perspective, however, Beresford had made no concrete progress towards achieving his primary objective of capturing Badajoz and, in fact, the absence of such progress had afforded the French garrison sufficient time to repair the damage inflicted during the French capture of the fortress and lay in sufficient supplies to be prepared for a major siege. Brigadier Long, who was now much inclined to find fault with the actions of his superior, thought that Beresford's performance had been dismal:

> The consequence is we … [have been] parading about since 25th *ult.* [March] with 20,000 men doing nothing … I know not where the fault lies, nor is it my business to enquire. But one cannot help seeing with regret the army detained on the banks of the Guadiana for days wanting a bridge to pass it … that same army calling out in vain for bread … and an insignificant Town garrisoned by 300 men detaining 5,000 men before it for days in consequence of the want of Artillery.[57]

More importantly, the lack of progress by Beresford was also troubling to Wellington. He consequently decided to make a flying visit to the south to meet Beresford and find out exactly what could be done to put the British offensive back on track. Major Hercules Pakenham of the 7th West India Regiment, serving as an assistant adjutant-general to his brother Edward, perhaps expressed the common view of the situation when he wrote: 'His [Beresford's] conduct has been dilatory in the extreme, – so much so that Ld. W., who has not rest at any time, set off yesterday to put matters in some train.'[58]

The news that Wellington was on the way stimulated some important activity on the part of Beresford as he came to grips with the odd circumstance that his expeditionary force lacked sufficient heavy artillery to mount the formal siege of Badajoz that was now required to achieve his strategic objective. The fault for this omission must belong in large part to a combination of the British government and Wellington, since they had plenty of time during the winter of 1810/11 to address this weakness in Wellington's army, but did nothing about it. As a result, when Beresford's mission changed after the fall of Badajoz to Soult, the only plan Wellington was able to articulate for making good the necessary ordnance was distinctly unsophisticated – he told the marshal to take the artillery he needed from the armaments available at

56. D'Urban, *Report of Operations*, p. 15.
57. Long to Brother, 12 April 1811, quoted in McGuffie, *Peninsular Cavalry General*, pp. 83–90, at 88.
58. Hercules Pakenham to Lord Longford, 16 April 1811, Pakenham, *Letters*, p. 88.

the nearby Portuguese fortress of Elvas: 'Elvas must supply the means, if possible [for the siege]; if it has them not, I must send them there.'[59]

This weak plan was made even worse through lack of execution – no one did anything to put it into action. During all the delays in late March and early April, and even when Major Dickson went back to Elvas to obtain the guns necessary to besiege Olivenza, no one thought to start gathering materiel at Elvas for the larger task ahead at Badajoz. It was not until 17 April that Dickson was charged with the task: '. . . on the 17th . . . Captain Squire and myself went forward . . . to see the Marshall [sic] and receive his orders. He directed us to return to Elvas and make preparation for the siege of Badajoz'.[60]

Once he got started, however, Dickson wasted no time and by 19 April he had chosen 34 artillery pieces for the job – sixteen brass 24-pound cannon, eight brass 16-pounders, two 10-inch howitzers and eight 8-inch howitzers. He also arranged for 150 Portuguese artillerymen from the Elvas garrison to accompany the guns forward. In the meanwhile, two battalions of light troops of the King's German Legion commanded by Major General Charles von Alten (b. 1764) arrived at Elvas from Lisbon to reinforce Beresford. They were veteran troops with a skilled leader, but they had not seen action since the Walcheren fiasco and still suffered from some of the adverse medical after-effects of that campaign.[61]

Wellington arrived at Elvas on 20 April, but Beresford only returned from Zafra on the 21st. That same day, they set off together to conduct their own reconnaissance of the allied objective, travelling by way of Juromenha with Colonel Richard Fletcher, Wellington's chief engineer, and bringing Alten's brigade along as an escort.[62] This precaution proved to be important, because they approached Badajoz on 22 April while a party from the garrison was out cutting wood. Thinking that the British were making an effort to capture that detachment, General Philippon responded by ordering a major sortie by the garrison. Three battalions of French troops poured out of the fortress and Captain Bösewiel's company of the 2nd KGL Light Battalion was caught between that force and the returning woodcutters with predictably bad results for the Germans.[63] The sortie did not, however, prevent Wellington and Beresford from completing a full examination of the fortifications on the left (or eastern) bank of the Guadiana. Unfortunately, they were not able to reconnoitre the defensive works of the right bank of the river, including the formidable Fort of San Cristoval, nor is there any evidence that the two generals visited Albuera, either on the way to or from Badajoz.

By the time that they returned to Elvas on the 23rd, Wellington was clear on how he wanted the campaign against Badajoz to proceed and he outlined his plans in a series of three memoranda, all dated 23 April 1811, that provide the strongest possible evidence that Wellington, not Beresford, was responsible for most of the allied strategic decisions made in the early spring of 1811. The first memorandum, addressed to Marshal Beresford, Colonel Fletcher and Major Dickson, laid out detailed

59. W. to B., 27 March 1811, *Dispatches*, Vol. 7, pp. 407–8, at 408.
60. Dickson to MacLeod, 23 April 1811, *Manuscripts*, Vol. 3, pp. 381–5, at 384.
61. Beamish, *History of the KGL*, Vol. 1, p. 331.
62. Jones, *Journals of Sieges*, Vol. 1, p. 15.
63. Beamish, *History of the KGL*, Vol. 1, pp. 332–3. The captain was wounded and his company overall had 13 men killed or wounded and 36 taken prisoner.

specifications for the siege of Badajoz.[64] The document refers to breaking ground initially in front of all three outworks, but in fact Wellington had already agreed with his engineers to concentrate on the relatively weak walls of the castle at the north-east corner of the fortress because it was thought to be the one plan of attack that could lead to a victory fast enough to thwart any plans Soult might have for relieving the garrison:

> Lord Wellington … determined to lay immediate siege to Badajos [sic], if any plan of attack could be offered which should not require more than sixteen days' open trenches, as in that period … it was calculated that Marshal Soult would be able to collect a force equal to its relief.[65]

Concentration on the castle meant as a practical matter that the Fort of San Cristoval on the right bank of the Guadiana had to be the first point of attack since it outflanked any direct approach to the castle walls. Once the fort was taken, the allies would be able to fire down into the town at will and assault the castle without interference.

The second memorandum, addressed to Marshal Beresford alone, set forth the actions Beresford should take in the event the French attempted to relieve the besieged city.[66] Much of the detail had to do with caring for the guns and stores assembled for the siege, but it also outlined how the Spanish forces of Castaños and Ballasteros should be used to create a screen of allied troops between Soult and the siege. The most important point of the memo is that Wellington gave Beresford in writing full and absolute discretion to decide how to respond to a French advance depending on the circumstances then prevailing: 'All this must be left to the discretion of Sir William Beresford. I authorise him to fight the action if he should think it proper, or to retire if he should not.'[67] If, however, Beresford ultimately decided to fight, Wellington was in no doubt as to where the marshal should meet the enemy: 'I believe that, upon the whole, the most central and advantageous place [for Beresford] to collect his troops will be at Albuera.' He gave no specific reason for that choice, but the Albuera position was athwart one of the few river crossings on the road from Seville and it met two important strategic needs of the allies. First, it was served by secondary roads which provided direct communication through Valverde and Olivenza to the bridge over the Guadiana at Juromenha and, ultimately, the fortress of Elvas in Portugal some sixteen miles away. Second, it was accessible to Spanish troops coming north from the coast by means of a series of roads parallel to those typically used by the French. Both the Spanish and Anglo-Portuguese elements of the allied force thus had lines of retreat from Albuera back to their own respective bases.

The last memorandum, addressed to the 'Officers in Command of Corps in Estremadura', outlined the roles that Wellington wanted his Spanish allies to play in the coming campaign:

> The corps of allied British and Portuguese troops, under Marshal Sir William Beresford, being about to be employed in the siege of Badajoz, it is desirable

64. 'Siege' Memorandum, 23 April 1811, *Dispatches*, Vol. 7, pp. 493–4.
65. Jones, *Journals of Sieges*, Vol. 1, pp. 12–13. The time frame of sixteen days is also mentioned in Toreno, *Histoire*, Vol. 4, p. 53.
66. 'Beresford' Memorandum, 23 April 1811, *Dispatches*, Vol. 7, pp. 490–2.
67. 'Beresford' Memorandum, *Dispatches*, Vol. 7, p. 491.

that the Spanish troops in Estremadura, the Condado de Niebla, and Andalusia, should cooperate in and protect that operation ... and the following plan is proposed for the consideration of the Spanish General Officers.[68]

The plan proposed by Wellington was very simple even though it involved three separate Spanish forces – the remains of the 5th Army under Castaños and two corps from the 4th Army under Generals Blake and Ballasteros.[69] Capitán General Castaños was to continue supporting Beresford as he had for the past month and was also to provide three battalions of the 5th Army to serve directly with the force investing Badajoz when the siege finally began. Teniente General Ballasteros, who had been chased into Extremadura with a division of troops from the 4th Army in the middle of April, was asked to remain where he was and cover the main routes between Seville and Badajoz. The last force, another one from the 4th Army under the command of Teniente General Joaquin Blake (b. 1759), had only landed on 18 April at the mouth of the Tinto River and was still making its way slowly to Extremadura at the time the memo was being written.[70] This was the most significant Spanish contingent in terms of strength and Blake was reckoned to be one of the most accomplished Spanish general officers:

> General Blake, the descendant of an Irish family, had, previous to the revolution, been a colonel of infantry ... from which rank he rose to the command in chief ... [He was] soldierlike in his person and address, with a manner that indicated firmness and resolution.[71]

He had founded the Spanish general staff in 1810 and had been chosen to be one of the three regents ruling on behalf of Ferdinand VII, so he was also a man with considerable political clout. It was consequently essential that he should be willing to cooperate with Beresford by watching the westernmost roads that might be used by Soult in an advance to save Badajoz and by joining forces with the corps under Ballasteros if and when the French went on the offensive.

The fact that Wellington was willing to solicit Spanish help is quite remarkable given the disastrous results of all prior instances of Anglo-Spanish military cooperation during the Peninsular War. In 1808, Sir John Moore's army had put itself in harm's way to buy time for Spain to organise resistance to Napoleon, but found the promised support of Spanish armies in Galicia and the Asturias to be illusory. In 1809, Wellington actually joined forces with a Spanish army commanded by General Gregorio Cuesta, but it proved useless in the Battle of Talavera and abandoned him in the subsequent retreat. Finally, in 1811 itself, Wellington had been sorely frustrated by the abysmal

---

68. 'Cooperation' Memorandum, *Dispatches*, Vol. 7, pp. 494–6, at 494.
69. The Spanish government changed the designation of its armies in early 1811. Their forces in Catalonia were designated the 1st Army, those at Valencia became the 2nd Army, and those in Murcia became the 3rd. Patriot forces in Andalucia, including the garrison of Cadiz, were transformed into the 4th Army; those in Extremadura became the 5th while the soldiers in Galicia and the Asturias became the 6th and 7th Armies, respectively. See generally, Gómez Ruiz, *El Ejército*, pp. 341–352.
70. Benavides Moro, *Blake*, p.335. The Spanish government's willingness to detach such a large portion of the 4th Army for service away from Cadiz may represent an effort on the part of the Spaniards to make amends for the Barrosa fiasco.
71. Hay, *Narrative*, pp. 21–2.

performance of General Mendizabal and the incompetence of General La Peña had almost led to the destruction of General Graham's force at Barrosa. Wellington realised, however, that Beresford would have no chance for a successful siege without the assistance of substantial Spanish forces, so he intentionally chose to ignore all these prior unfavourable experiences and to conduct himself as if nothing had ever gone wrong in the relationship. That decision was a stroke of pragmatic genius.

The memo ended with yet another surprise. Given the polyglot nature of the allied forces in Extremadura, Wellington realised that it was essential to establish a clear understanding of who would command whom when all the allied forces were assembled for action. Wellington, of course, wanted Beresford to be in charge, but although the Portuguese marshal out-ranked Blake and Ballasteros, he was out-ranked in turn by Castaños. However, Wellington was aware of the sensitivity of his allies concerning questions of command and, moreover, he believed that Castaños did not actually intend to take the field with the much-reduced 5th Army since he also had responsibilities in Galicia. Taking all these factors into consideration, Wellington hit upon an approach that was almost too clever by half. He proposed on his own initiative that command of any joint force be determined exclusively on the neutral principles of rank and seniority so that he would get credit for being gracious while at the same time attaining his desired command result so long as Castaños stayed away:

> It is proposed that the troops of the several nations shall carry on these operations under the command of their several chiefs, of course communicating with each other constantly … but in case of joining for the purpose of giving battle to the enemy, it will be necessary that the whole should be under the orders of the Officer of the highest military rank.[72]

The memo further stipulated that: 'The Spanish General Officers are requested to state to Sir William Beresford whether they will, or not, cooperate with him in the manner above proposed.' Although the cooperation memorandum was written in English, it was conveyed to its Spanish recipients with a covering letter in French, the language commonly used for communications between the British and their Spanish allies.[73] Separately, Wellington made it clear to Beresford that he should not proceed with the siege unless and until he had received affirmative responses from all the Spanish commanders.[74]

Before he left Elvas on 24 April, Wellington dealt with one last piece of business raised by Beresford. The marshal had continued to be unhappy with the performance of General Long as his cavalry commander and he finally asked Wellington for a replacement on the pretext that he needed a commander who was senior to both Long and General Madden in order to retain the latter officer's services. Beresford's first choice, General Henry Fane, was unavailable since that officer was on leave in England. Wellington offered him instead Sir William Erskine, a controversial figure to say the least: 'You [Beresford] will find him more intelligent and useful than anybody you have. He is blind, which is against him at the head of cavalry, but very cautious.'[75]

72. 'Cooperation' Memorandum, *Dispatches*, Vol. 7, p. 496.
73. W. to Castaños, 24 April 1811, *Dispatches*, Vol. 7, pp. 500–2.
74. W. to B., 6 May 1811, *Dispatches*, Vol. 7, p. 518.
75. W. To B., 24 April 1811, *Dispatches*, Vol. 7, p. 503.

In a decision that reveals the extraordinary extent to which he was disenchanted with Long, Beresford chose Erskine and Wellington himself wrote to Long to confirm the news that he was being replaced:

> You will have observed by the General Order of the day, that I have altered the arrangements which I had made for the command of the cavalry on the left of the Tagus … I have not yet determined in what manner it will be most advantageous to the service to employ you. I request you, therefore, to remain with the troops under Sir William Beresford till you hear further from me.[76]

Whether General Long received this letter before the battle is unknown, but in any event, since Erskine did not come south until later in the month, Long temporarily retained his command.

Armed with Wellington's three memoranda, Beresford probably wanted to set about his assigned tasks with a renewed vigour, but he immediately ran into a problem beyond his or Wellington's control. During the night of 24 April, the Guadiana rose seven feet and swept away the temporary bridges at Juromenha, thus cutting the most direct route for moving siege guns and supplies to Badajoz and postponing progress indefinitely.[77]

On the positive side, however, the allied forces continued to grow stronger both in terms of numbers and the solidarity of the bonds between Beresford and the Spaniards. First, two new batteries of British artillery arrived from Lisbon: one was Captain George Lefebure's Royal Horse Artillery troop equipped with three 6-pounder guns and one 5½-inch howitzer and the other was Captain James Hawker's Royal Artillery company equipped with five 9-pounders and one 5½-inch howitzer.[78] Next, General Blake and his force made their way north from the coast and reached the frontier of Extremadura. Finally, General Castaños met Beresford in person on 30 April to fine-tune arrangements for the participation of his troops in the imminent siege. In the meanwhile, Beresford kept the French V Corps in check by launching Colborne's brigade (with some attached cavalry and guns) on a limited offensive:

> The object of this movement is to check the inroads of the enemy's parties of pillage, to give confidence to the people of Estremadura, and to cover the collection of our own supplies, while it will announce in Andalusia the neighbourhood of a British force by showing troops on the frontier.[79]

Even when communications via Juromenha were restored on the 29th, the process of bringing siege guns and supplies forward across the river was still exceedingly

---

76. W. to Long, 11 May 1811, *Dispatches*, Vol. 7, pp. 543–4. Curiously, there is no mention of this letter in McGuffie's biography of Long.
77. D'Urban, *Journal*, p. 204; Jones, *Engineer Officer*, p. 99.
78. Dickson, *Manuscripts*, Vol. 3, p. 389. British batteries normally had six guns in total, so these two were under-strength. No explanation has been found for this unusual circumstance. Duncan, *History*, Vol. 2, p. 296.
79. D'Urban, Memorandum for Colonel Colborne, 29 April 1811, a copy of which was kindly provided by Dr J. Q. C. Mackrell, a descendant of Col. Colborne. Colborne described his expedition in the following terms: '[D]uring the siege of Badajoz I was sent into the Sierra Moreno as a moveable column to attract the enemy's attention, and we performed a march of about 260 miles in a very short time.' Colborne, Letter to Rev. Yonge, 18 May 1811.

slow and it was not until 4 May that Colonel Fletcher, the engineer in charge of the siege, told Beresford that everything was in readiness at Olivenza for a final approach to Badajoz. Beresford then set his siege troops in motion and, on 4 May, two brigades of Stewart's 2nd Division invested Badajoz on the left bank of the Guadiana. They were reinforced a day later by Hamilton's Division and one brigade of Cole's 4th Division. General Lumley was put in charge of the siege forces on the right bank of the river, and on 8 May he closed the circle around Badajoz by deploying Kemmis's brigade of the 4th Division and the 17th Portuguese Regiment from Elvas against the bridgehead and the Fort of San Cristoval. There was, however, still one last important piece of preliminary business to be settled in accordance with Wellington's instructions before the siege could begin in earnest. Although Beresford had met General Castaños after the Spaniard had received Wellington's cooperation memorandum, he had not received an official Spanish acceptance of Wellington's proposals and the marshal accordingly pressed Castaños dutifully for an answer. A negative response would have forced a reconsideration of the plans for the siege but, since Castaños showed no inclination to leave Extremadura, an affirmative reply could make Castaños the commander-in-chief for any joint action. Castaños broke his official silence on 8 May in a letter in which he accepted Wellington's plan of operation on behalf of himself and General Blake, albeit with one astonishingly gracious alteration.[80] Whether Castaños was trying to save Wellington from the dilemma he had created for himself or whether the Spaniard simply believed that there was a better way to split responsibility for the allied war effort, he countered with his own proposal that command of all joint forces should fall to the general who brought the most troops to the field of battle. As Wellington confessed to Lord Liverpool, this unselfish offer by Castaños saved Wellington from a very awkward position:

> I have to mention to your Lordship that, when I proposed that plan to General Castaños, it was understood that the general, having been appointed to command the army in Galicia, as well as that in Estremadura, was aiming to establish his headquarters near mine; and Marshal Sir William Beresford would of course, as the senior to General Blake, have had the command in the action, for which it was the object to provide; and this delicate question would thus have been settled in a manner satisfactory to all parties ... General Castaños, however, remained in Estremadura, contrary to my expectations, and he settled the question in a much more satisfactory manner; but in one which I could not with propriety have proposed; and if I had proposed it, it would in all probability have been rejected.[81]

Needless to say, Castaños's offer was immediately accepted by Wellington.

Informed of the Spanish consent the day it was sent, Beresford was able to let the siege work commence and, by the end of 8 May, trenches had been opened against all three points of attack identified by Wellington in the siege memorandum and

---

80. An English translation of Castaños's letter was published in *The Times*, 12 June 1811, p. 3, col. C. It is not clear whether General Blake was aware of Castaños's counter-proposal concerning joint command before it was made.
81. W. to Liverpool, 22 May 1811, *Dispatches*, Vol. 7, pp. 594–5.

Badajoz was once again under siege. Like the French attackers before them, the allied forces participating in the siege understood that they did not have an easy task ahead of them:

> A siege is one of the most arduous undertakings on which troops can be employed, – an undertaking in which fatigue, hardships, and personal risk, are the greatest, – one in which the prize can only be obtained by complete victory, and where failure is usually attended with severe loss or dire disaster.[82]

The physical labour of digging trenches and approaches was performed primarily by working parties of soldiers who resented the hard work and the limited opportunities for distinction:

> ... the duties of a besieging force are both harassing and severe; and ... death in the trenches never carries with it that stamp of glory, which seals the memory of those, who perish in a well-fought field.[83]

Things went badly for the besiegers from the start. As planned, the British concentrated first on attacking the Fort of San Cristoval:

> ... the intention was to breach the castle, while batteries were established on the right bank of the Guadiana to take in flank and in reverse its defences. With this view it was necessary to take Fort Cristoval, a small work having a stone revetment immediately opposite the castle and on the right bank of the Guadiana. The whole was intended to be a simultaneous operation, so as to have divided the attention of the enemy.[84]

The first problem encountered by Captain John Squire, the Engineer officer in charge of the attack on San Cristoval, was that the ground surrounding the fort was more difficult to work than expected: 'The soil was hard and rocky and our own tools infamous.' It was therefore impossible to dig normal trenches and instead the British were forced to create their siege works using above-ground gabions (large baskets filled with earth dug elsewhere). On the 10th, the French staged a sortie on the right bank that was easily repulsed, but an over-zealous pursuit led to heavy casualties for the besiegers:

> ... our loss on this occasion was very severe, owing to the gallant but imprudent advance of the troops quite to the glacis of San Cristoval, and to a situation in which they were exposed to the fire of musketry and grape from that outwork, as well as from the body of the place.[85]

When the British finally established a full battery within range of the fort on 11 May and opened fire, four out of the five guns were disabled on the first day:

> The Battery against San Cristoval opened at daylight this morning; the Portuguese Artillery directing the fire were inexperienced and made very bad

82. Jones, *Journals of Sieges*, Vol. 1, p. ix.
83. Sherer, *Recollections*, p. 152.
84. Squire, Letter to Bunbury, 17 May 1811, in Squire, Letters.
85. W. to Liverpool, 15 May 1811, *Dispatches*, Vol. 7, pp. 562–5 at 564. The total loss was more than 400 officers and men killed or wounded. Jones, *Journals*, Vol. 1, p. 24.

practice; whilst the enemy kept up a very hot fire, and completely silenced it before night.[86]

Although it was not entirely clear at the time, the first British siege of Badajoz effectively ended with the destruction of this first battery because on that same day Beresford received a report that Soult had assembled a 'considerable corps' for the relief of the fortress, although there was no definitive word that it had actually marched from Seville. That confirmation came the next day when 'an aide-de-camp who had been sent to General Blake at Barcarrota, returned with the information' that Soult's force had reached Santa Olalla.[87] The cumulative effect of all the delays caused by weather, indecision and inadequate siege materials was now glaringly obvious. Far from having the sixteen days necessary (by Wellington's calculation) to capture Badajoz, Beresford had had only four. Under the circumstances, the marshal realised he had no option but call off the siege until Soult's advance was thwarted: 'We can return to the Siege afterwards, meanwhile the operation must be to a certain degree suspended and the Stores as far as is practicable put in safety during the Contest.'[88]

Beresford did, however, try one last bluff to achieve his objective and sent a formal summons of surrender to Governor Philippon at noon on Sunday, 12 May. After mendaciously telling the French commander that he had no expectation of being relieved, Beresford offered him the honours of war and a chance 'to spare the unfortunate inhabitants of the town' the effusion of bloodshed 'without object or utility' that would inevitably occur and be his responsibility if he persisted in 'a useless defence'. This mixture of cajolery and threat might have worked on an Imaz, but Philippon had a clearer sense of his responsibilities: 'Sir, I am like you very concerned about unnecessary bloodshed, but since the defence of Badajoz has been entrusted to me, I am obliged to oppose your troops with all possible resistance.'[89] The town was safe for the moment, but an 'effusion of bloodshed' elsewhere was now very much a possibility.

---

86. Jones, *Engineer Officer*, p. 101.
87. D'Urban, *Report of Operations*, p. 20.
88. Entry for 12 May 1811 in D'Urban, *Journal*, p. 213.
89. The details of Beresford's summons and the French reply are in Lamare, *Relation*, pp. 120–2.

Chapter 4

The French Advance
to Albuera

At the start of May 1811, Marshal Soult was in a very familiar position – he was threatened from all sides by enemy forces, he had no direct news of the other French armies in the Peninsula and he was receiving periodic missives from Paris containing fanciful orders based on inaccurate information. The only thing Soult was sure of was that Badajoz would soon be under attack again and that he would have to organise a relief expedition if he wanted to preserve the gains he had made during the winter and avoid a pointless sacrifice of the garrison. The marshal was also aware of two important considerations that could affect his plans. First, he had been informed that IX Corps, commanded by General Drouet d'Erlon and composed primarily of detached battalions belonging to regiments serving with the Armée du Midi, had been ordered by Napoleon to leave Portugal and make its way immediately to join up with him.[1] Second, he knew that Teniente General Blake had landed on the coast west of Seville with a large force, but he was uncertain of that officer's ultimate destination.

On 4 May, Soult decided that the preservation of Badajoz was the main priority and he wrote to Berthier stating that he would be leaving for Extremadura on 9 May with 20,000 infantry, 3,000 cavalry and 30 cannon, but that he did not expect to fight a battle until he had been joined by Drouet d'Erlon's force.[2] On the very day of his departure, however, Soult wrote again and, since he had not had any news about Drouet d'Erlon in the interim, he clarified that his plans for battle were no longer dependent on the arrival of reinforcements.[3] He described instead his intention to fight using a combination of V Corps, a contingent requisitioned from troops in eastern Andalucia (including Division General Sebastiani's IV Corps) and another contingent taken from the Seville garrison and Marshal Victor's I Corps besieging Cadiz:

> I propose to leave tonight with the reserve units I have assembled to advance
> into Estremadura with the objects of relieving Badajoz, obliging the enemy to

---

1. Soult, *Mémoires*, p. 231.
2. Soult to Berthier, 4 May 1811, transcribed in W. Napier, French Documents.
3. As it turns out, Soult made the right decision when he decided not to count on d'Erlon's arrival. The orders from Napoleon had reached d'Erlon on 23 April, but they were countermanded by Masséna who kept d'Erlon with the Army of Portugal until after the battle of Fuentes de Oñoro. Masséna, *Mémoires*, Vol. 7, p. 502–3.

retreat across the Guadiana, and facilitating the arrival of the corps commanded by General Count d'Erlon ... I am leading the left column [the troops from Seville and Cadiz] personally and once all three groups have joined forces, I will give battle to the enemy no matter what his force may be.[4]

The composition of the French relief force (which is detailed in Appendix A: Part 3) had a number of unusual aspects. Since Soult was in command, he brought along the senior technical and administrative officers of the Armée du Midi, which made the force remarkably top-heavy given the number of troops involved and the simultaneous presence of the full staff of V Corps. For instance, Soult had two senior commanders for his artillery: Brigade General Charles-Étienne-François Ruty (b. 1774), the artillery commander of the Armée du Midi, and Brigade General Jean-Dominique Bourgeat (b. 1760), in command of the artillery of V Corps. Ruty was esteemed as a technician and had even invented a new type of howitzer that was used in Spain.[5] Bourgeat had seen more active service than his younger colleague and was widely recognised as a zealous, intelligent and active officer, but his career had nearly foundered in 1810 when he was placed in command of Marshal Ney's artillery instead of the officer Ney had asked for and became a target of the marshal's anger. Ney called for his dismissal, but the Minister of War recognised the injustice of the situation and transferred Bourgeat instead to V Corps, where he had already distinguished himself at the French siege of Badajoz by devising the artillery crossfire that served as a key preliminary to the Battle of the Gevora.[6]

The force was also inordinately strong in cavalry since it was easier for Soult to free up mounted units rather than infantry units for the expedition. As a result, Soult decided to pull General Latour-Maubourg away from V Corps and put him in charge of this large cavalry contingent even though this move had the ripple effect of shaking up the command structure of V Corps once again. Division General Girard became the provisional commander of the corps and the senior brigadier, Brigade General Michel-Sylvestre Brayer (b. 1769), replaced him at the head of the corps' first division. Division General Gazan was present in his capacity as Chief of Staff to Soult, but there was uncertainty as to whether he would again take field command of the second division in place of Brigade General Pépin. Soult tried to mitigate some of the obvious problems arising from the improvised nature of the two independent infantry brigades (called 'divisions' in some sources) he created for the expedition by appointing two old and trusted subordinates to command them: Brigade General François-Jean Werlé (b. 1763), who had joined the French Army as a private in 1781 and had fought for Soult in 1799 and 1800, and Division General Deo-Gratias-Nicolas Godinot (b. 1765), a dragoon in the pre-Revolution army and a favourite of Soult.[7] The cavalry, too, had some impromptu formations so overall most French commanders had unfamiliar subordinates and colleagues.

The strength of Soult's force can be established with reasonable certainty in terms

4. Soult to Berthier, 9 May 1811, in J. Bonaparte, *Mémoires*, Vol. 8, pp. 4–8.
5. It is possible that this is the same type of howitzer discussed in Note 12 overleaf.
6. Rey & Remy, *Bourgeat*, pp. 74–7 and 84–6.
7. Godinot's rank was brand new, since he had only been promoted from Brigade General on 10 March (10 May according to some sources, but that does not seem right since he was already on his way to Albuera that day).

of the number of men who marched to Albuera, but not in terms of the number of artillery pieces the marshal may have had available. Lapène says the French had '18,000 bayonets and 4,000 horses' but does not mention artillery and staff troops, while Soult himself estimates he had 24,000 available men.[8] These estimates line up well with the total of 920 officers and 23,340 men given in Oman's Appendix, which he says is based on a strength return dated 1 May in the French Archives Nationales.[9] (Surprisingly, about half of the regimental strength totals in Oman are higher or lower than those in a strength return of the same date in the SHAT, but the differences roughly cancel out in terms of the overall total.[10]) Oman's total, however, includes 65 officers and 2,186 men for three battalions of the 51st Line whereas in fact only the 2nd Battalion of the 51st took part in the expedition.[11] Assuming that the three battalions were of equal strength, 1,500 officers and men must therefore be deducted from Oman's numbers, leaving Soult with a total strength of just under 23,000.

Estimates of the number of artillery pieces that accompanied the expedition range from a low of 30 to a high of 50. The most significant source of confusion on this subject is undoubtedly the fact that there were elements of ten different French artillery companies (batteries) present at Albuera. However, almost all of these were represented by under-strength detachments that lacked their regulation complement of guns (6 cannon and 2 howitzers per foot battery and 4 guns and 2 howitzers per mounted battery) so Soult did not have anywhere near the amount of artillery which that number of units would normally imply. Instead, the 1 May report indicates that the 9 artillery companies belonging to V Corps and the reserve artillery had only 29 guns combined, of which 13 were howitzers.[12] (Unfortunately, it does not indicate how the guns were distributed among the companies.) Since the official Spanish report on the battle states that the other company present, a horse artillery company assigned to support Brigade General André-Louis Briche's brigade, was equipped with its full complement of 6 artillery pieces, the total number of French guns was most likely 35.[13]

Soult left Seville in the middle of the night of 9/10 May, perhaps in an attempt to hide the fact of his departure. However, since the preparations for the march had been very noticeable and since the French were operating in the midst of a large hostile population, it was inevitable that the news of the relief force would be passed quickly to his enemies. Soult therefore realised his best hope for success lay in moving so quickly that Beresford would have little time to react before the French arrived. A normal march covering the 134 miles from Seville to Badajoz was reckoned to have

8. Lapène, *Conquête*, p. 150; Soult, *Mémoires*, p. 231.
9. Oman, *History*, Vol. 4, pp. 634–5.
10. 'Situation des Troupes composant l'Armée Impériale du Midi a l'époque du 1er Mai 1811', SHAT, Carton C8/356.
11. The hitherto unrecognised fact that there was only a single battalion of the 51st with the expedition comes from Soult's Unpublished Report and from the regimental history, which specifies that the unit in question was the 2nd Battalion. Painvin, *Historique de 51e*, p. 310.
12. The 29 guns were composed of two 12-pounders, nine 8-pounders, five 4-pounders, seven 6-inch [*6 pouces*] howitzers and six 4½-inch [*4 pouces, 6 lignes*] howitzers. The size of these last howitzers is unusual and it may be that these are the same guns referred to in a recent article that states (based on an 1827 report) that so-called 'Spanish' howitzers [*obusiers espagnol* or *obusiers de 12 cm*] with modified carriages that could be transported by pack mule were used to good effect at Albuera. Morillon, 'L'Artillerie de Montagne', p. 32.
13. Burriel, *Albuhera*, p. 13

ten stages of varying lengths, each of which would constitute a day's journey. Soult led his force forward at double that pace:

> Soult himself . . . left Seville at midnight on the 10th and bivouacked late that same day at Venta. His force occupied Santa-Ollala on the 11th; Monesterio on the 12th; and Fuente de Cantos on the 13th, where they made contact in the evening with the troops of V Corps brought forward by Generals Latour-Maubourg and Girard. These forces, reinforced with Godinot's brigade, pushed immediately forward to Los Santos; the rest of the army, including headquarters, moved obliquely to the left [right?] and occupied Bienvenida. On the 14th, the marshal made his headquarters at Villa Franca and gave orders to Colonel [François Louis] Bouchu [b. 1771], commander of the reserve artillery, to fire several rounds from his 12-pounder cannon to alert the garrison at Badajoz of the imminent arrival of help.[14]

Unfortunately, the signal was not heard by General Philippon.

If Soult travelled fast, the news of his advance travelled faster and, as noted earlier, by 12 May, Beresford already had confirmation of the French advance and preliminary information about the size and composition of Soult's relief force. Napier later accused Beresford of having been in ignorance of Soult's movements until then, but that is another exaggeration brought on by the historian's efforts to depict Beresford in as negative a way as possible. Beresford certainly did not know exactly when Soult would advance, but he was kept well informed of French preparations along the way.

The existence of this information was no accident – it was the product of an intelligence-gathering network put together by both Wellington and his brother, Henry Wellesley, the British envoy to the Spanish Cortes in Cadiz, who took two specific steps to ensure that they received a steady stream of reliable intelligence about French movements from confidential agents operating within Spain.[15] First, Wellington posted Major John Austin of the 58th Foot to the frontier of Extremadura as one of his so-called 'exploring officers' to make contact with Spanish patriots and guerillas in Andalucia. Second, from his ambassadorial residence in Cadiz, Henry Wellesley maintained a web of spies within Andalucia who reported to him via an operative in Puerto Santa Maria on the Spanish mainland across the bay from the besieged city. Between these two sources, there was little or nothing about French troop movements leading up to Soult's departure that escaped detection. There is no clearer example of the advantage gained by the British through fighting a war in the home territory of their ally.

As planned, the allies on the frontier between Extremadura and Andalucia retired as the French advanced and sought to avoid any serious action. The withdrawal was uneventful except for a flare-up of the friction between Beresford and his cavalry commander. Faced with the unusual circumstance of Soult's advance and apparently concerned about being subjected to more criticism by his superiors, General Long started to bombard Beresford with requests for orders:

14. Lapène, *Conquête*, p. 148.
15. The extent of the British intelligence network in the south of Spain in 1811 is discussed in Davies, 'Secret Intelligence', pp. 48–51.

Never in my life did I experience a greater anxiety of mind than during this period. My force was left in dispersed situations, whilst the enemy, whose advance and movements I was hourly reporting to head quarters, were concentrated in my front, and on my flanks. Not a single instruction had I received, nor could I obtain, though repeatedly applied for: my route or point of retreat were not even pointed out.[16]

Perhaps not surprisingly, this behaviour did not inspire confidence since Beresford considered that Long was 'making those applications [for instructions] far too frequently and most unnecessarily', and that he was displaying an indecisiveness and lack of initiative that ill-befitted a British officer.[17] Long also chose this moment to express discomfort with the ill-defined nature of his relationship with the different Spanish cavalry forces fighting alongside him, particularly that commanded by the Count of Penne-Villemur, who was senior in rank to Long. To be fair, that relationship was quite unusual and significantly informal:

[The Spanish cavalry] consists of two separate and distinct bodies. The one is under the command of Count Penne-Villemur, and belongs to the army of General Castaños, who allows this body to act for the present in connexion [sic] with our cavalry.

The other body of Spanish cavalry ... belongs to the army of General Blake, who has not placed it in connexion [sic] with us.

You will observe, therefore, that even the first-mentioned body is not placed in a formal manner under the orders of the senior general of the British cavalry, although there is no doubt that Count Penne-Villemur will act on all occasions of importance as if that were the case, and in that regard the [commander of the] cavalry of General Blake's army, as mutual communication and co-operation is (strictly speaking) all that can be required ... will no doubt see the propriety of carrying this understanding as far as possible.[18]

Nevertheless, Long's insistence on greater clarity caused an exasperated Beresford to realise he could no longer wait for the arrival of Erskine to make a change in the command of his mounted forces, and he had D'Urban inform Long that he was being superseded:

The Marshal further begs me to acquaint you that, to obviate the evils of undefined ranks and claims of command adverted to in your letter of last night, he has directed Major General Lumley to assume the command of the cavalry of this army.[19]

However, since Lumley was busy supervising siege operations on the right bank of the Guadiana, this change could not be effected immediately and so Long was told to continue in command until Lumley arrived.

16. Long to Brother, 30 May 1811 in Long, *Reply to Misrepresentations*, pp. 109–25 at 109.
17. Beresford, *Second Letter to Long*, p. 65.
18. This is the description of the relationship given to Sir Stapleton Cotton when he arrived in Extremadura some weeks later. Combermere, *Memoirs*, Vol. 1, pp. 200–1.
19. D'Urban to Long, 14 May 1811, in Long, *Reply to Misrepresentations*, pp. 79–81 at 80. The choice of Lumley was not completely random since he was a cavalry officer by training and had commanded the 22nd Light Dragoons earlier in his career.

While Soult was continuing to advance, Beresford and his men were going about the delicate task of undoing their siege works and moving the precious siege guns and equipment to safe locations: '. . . at one o'clock on the morning of the 13th, an order arrived to stop everything, and during that day and yesterday [the 14th] all our artillery and stores were removed back into Elvas.'[20] If that sounds simple, it was not, with the degree of difficulty increased by the watchfulness of the garrison and two straight days of rain. Noticing that the embrasures of the British batteries were now empty, the garrison sortied from the fortress around noon on the 15th and took possession of the works near the Picurina Fort, but were soon driven back by the elements of General Cole's 4th Division that had been left in place to deal with just such a development. At 3:00 p.m., some French cavalry made another sortie along the road to Talavera and surprised some Portuguese troops foraging in a bean field. The French 'wantonly sabred' the unarmed soldiers including 'a poor little drummer who had accompanied his father'.[21] More importantly, some of the men (including two officers) were captured. The officers then made the dreadful mistake of telling General Philippon about Soult's advance, so he now possessed the vital information that Soult had been unable to convey by cannon fire on the 12th.[22]

The last order of business for Beresford was to decide with Castaños and Blake how they would use the discretion given to them by Wellington for dealing with Soult's advance. Beresford moved his headquarters to Valverde on the 13th along with the 2nd Division and his Portuguese troops and was joined there in the evening by General Castaños and by General Blake early on 14 May.[23] The three leaders actually met five different times during the 14th and Castaños, who was suffering from a severe cold, seems to have left most of the discussion to Blake and Beresford.[24] From the start, Blake was strongly in favour of meeting Soult on the battlefield, while Beresford had numerous reservations about doing so. According to D'Urban's account of the conference, the key issue for Blake was the 'actual state and circumstances' of his own army, 'which could no longer retire by the way it had come'. The Spaniard stressed to Beresford that his men 'would, if . . . made to enter Portugal, desert and disperse to such a degree' that his army would no longer be fit for service and he even said he would prefer to fight the French alone with little prospect of success rather than lose his army in that way without striking a blow.[25] Beresford acknowledged the validity of these points and he was also painfully aware that a retreat across the Guadiana would have other disastrous consequences, including the end to any immediate 'prospect of taking Badajoz . . . for which so much had already been sacrificed, and which was so important to the common cause'.[26] Nevertheless, Beresford might still have opted for retreat but for one other factor – the possibility that even if he tried to retreat, he might not be able to do so because of bad weather and problems with crossing the Guadiana:

20. Jones to Father, 15 May 1811, in Jones, *Engineer Officer*, p. 103.
21. Peacocke, *Memoirs*.
22. Anonymous, 'Diario do Segundo Sitio', pp. 380–1.
23. Burriel, *Albuhera*, p. 7. This conference is often incorrectly said to have occurred on 13 May.
24. Castaños to España, 14 May 1811, in Prieto Llovera, *Castaños*, pp. 109–10 at 110.
25. D'Urban, *Report of Operations*, p. 21.
26. *Ibid.*

There was still another objection to a backward movement, perhaps the strongest of all; and this was the danger it posed to the army, for the weather was again threatening, the precarious passage of the Guadiana, and its capricious nature, had been fully proved, and it would perhaps have been necessary, as the enemy was rapidly advancing, either to abandon the siege supplies by passing the troops without delay to the right bank; or, by waiting to cover their removal, to have run the risk of his arrival while the army was in the act of crossing, a circumstance which could hardly have failed to be fatal.[27]

This consideration, plus the fact that he reckoned the allies had much to gain from a victory and had a reasonable prospect of battlefield success due to their superiority in numbers, finally caused Beresford to agree with Blake and to avail himself 'of the authority given him by Lord Wellington to fight a general action if he should think it expedient'.

The decision to fight energised the allies. Orders went flying in all directions from Valverde, calling on the allied contingents to make their way to the chosen battle-ground at Albuera, and morale soared as the allies prepared for their showdown with Soult. Castaños was moved to make another unselfish gesture and agreed that his few troops would be placed under the direct command of Blake to simplify matters in the coming battle.[28] Beresford himself, however, was far from happy with his decision and his remarkably candid communications with Wellington reveal he was a troubled man and very apprehensive about the events to come, albeit resigned to trying his best:

> We are now placed in that position that has always made me so uneasy, and from which I have not been able to extricate myself, as General Blake would not listen to crossing the Guadiana, and stated that, whether the situation was good or bad, you had pointed it out. I agreed with him that our numbers gave us every prospect of advantage, and that we had not much to fear. I yet could not agree with him on the propriety of undertaking anything so circumstanced. However the weather has decided the business, and we have only now to meet the enemy, if he desires it, to the best advantage we can.[29]

One unexpected positive result of the meeting at Valverde was that Beresford was able to take the measure of Blake and found him to be a worthy colleague. There was consequently some small bit of encouraging news for Wellington at the end of the marshal's letter:

> I acknowledge I have some confidence, as much as past experience and examples can possibly let me have, in the Spaniards; and this from Blake, who, whatever his politics towards us may be, seems an able and a determined man, and appears only a Spaniard in wanting to fight a battle, putting everything on the cast.[30]

Faint praise, perhaps, but praise nevertheless.

27. D'Urban, *Report of Operations*, p. 22.
28. Prieto Llovera, *Castaños*, pp. 111–12. This arrangement is also mentioned in Beresford, Official Report.
29. B. to W., 15 May 1811, *Supp. Despatches*, Vol. 7, p. 125.
30. *Ibid.*

Thanks to the decision taken at the conference at Valverde, all attention was now focused on the village chosen by Wellington as the best site for a battle with Soult. Albuera is found some sixteen miles south-southeast of the fortress of Badajoz on the Royal Road running between Badajoz and the city of Seville. At the start of 1811, it consisted of some 150 'very indifferent' houses and an ancient church with 'a good and respectable front'.[31] Its location, however, had the signal draw-back of making the village an obvious stopping point for the French when they advanced from Andalucia in February 1811 on their way to the first siege of Badajoz.[32] The drama of enemy occupation has been played out for innumerable villages, but the repetitive nature of the process has never made it any less tragic for those affected. We have no details of the occupation in this case because the voice of the villagers has been lost to history, but the broad outlines can be imagined. Most of the inhabitants probably fled before the French arrived for the first time. Those who did not, whether from ignorance or optimism, undoubtedly suffered personal outrages to varying degrees. All would have shared a catastrophic property loss as the French systematically consumed all foodstuffs, burnt all wooden furniture and fixtures for cooking and warmth and carried off any valuables found. By May the 'wretched' village was 'in ruins' and most of the houses had been unroofed.[33] Albuera had also been completely 'forsaken by its inhabitants' – or almost so, since one British soldier recorded that an old man and a cat were still living there at the time of the battle.[34]

The most obvious features of the countryside surrounding Albuera are the three watercourses that create the modest valley in which the village is situated. The Nogales Brook (sometimes called the Feria or Ferdia by British writers), which originates near the small village of Nogales, runs from south-east to north-west, while the Chicapierna Brook (called the Chicaspiernas on modern maps and sometimes labelled as the Albuera on older maps), which has its source in the hills near Almendral, runs from south-west to north-east. A French source says they were no more than one or two feet deep anywhere along their length.[35] When these two tributaries meet just south of the village of Albuera, they form a larger stream (generously called a river by almost all sources) that has the same name as the village and flows in a northerly direction until it feeds into the Guadiana River above Badajoz near Talavera la Real. The village is situated on a rise on the left, or west, bank of the Albuera River overlooking two bridges: 'one [the new bridge for the main road] about two hundred yards to the right [south] of the village, large, handsome and built of

31. Anonymous, 'Memoir on the Province of Andalusia', p. 10. The church, named for 'Nuestra Señora del Camino' (Our Lady of the Road), was built in the fifteenth century and then improved to a baroque style in the seventeenth century. The church is at the south end of the village.
32. The 14th French Dragoons were based at the village during the French siege, so Soult was certainly well-informed about the area when he returned in May. Menuau, *14e Dragons*, p. 248.
33. Sherer, *Recollections*, p. 153; [Dickens], Letter, 24 May 1811, p. 289.
34. [Dickens], Letter, 24 May 1811, p. 289; Emerson, 'Recollections', in Maxwell, *Peninsular Sketches*, Vol. 2, p. 236. This last memoir was first published in a periodical in 1830 under cover of a letter from J. Emerson that clarifies that Emerson was not the author, but the memoir has been associated with his name ever since. The memoir is actually the story of an un-named private of the 27th Foot and 'was written down by one of his friends from his own dictation'. 'A Private Soldier', 'Two Months Recollections of the Late War in Spain and Portugal', *United Service Magazine*, 1830, Part 1, pp. 287–94 and 415–22.
35. D'Héralde, *Mémoires*, p. 153.

hewn stone; the other [the old bridge], close to the left [north] of it, small, narrow and incommodious.'[36] There were also two fords across the Albuera, one just south of the new bridge and another just north of the junction of the Chicapierna and the Nogales.

North of the village, the banks of the Albuera are steep and uneven, making a passage of the river there an unattractive proposition for both cavalry and artillery. South of the village, however, none of the watercourses presents a formidable natural obstacle, since they are all relatively narrow and shallow, but the bridges and fords were certainly the favoured crossing points and General Long's notes state that the Chicapierna was 'an almost impassible ravine' that could only be crossed at established fords.[37] Along the watercourses were thin belts of cork trees and brush and there was some wooded high ground between the Nogales and the Chicapierna. The soil in the area is a distinctly reddish brown, accented in May by the bright green of new grasses and the scarlet blossoms of wild poppies.

Everywhere to the west of the line formed by the Albuera and the Chicapierna the land rises gently, but noticeably, for 600–1,000 yards to form the low north–south ridge on which the allies formed their line of battle. It was probably this feature of the position that caused Wellington to pick Albuera as the preferred site to confront a French relief force since it provided the allied army with a number of advantages. First, the upland was devoid of trees, brush or other significant vegetation, or even fences, to mark the open expanse of land, so the terrain provided a 'perfect glacis' for a force at the crest of the ridge defending against an attacker approaching from the east.[38] Second, the ridge was high enough to create the possibility of an initial reverse slope deployment of the type often used by Wellington in his own battles. Finally, there was a track running along the reverse slope that would facilitate troop movements. From the western side of this ridge, the ground slopes down gently to a narrow valley marked by the line of the Arroyo Valdesevilla watercourse, then rises again to another low ridge farther west. Accounts differ as to whether the Valdesevilla actually posed an obstacle to movements by horse or on foot, but when John Fortescue visited the battlefield in May 1903, he recorded that it was 'a watercourse fringed with thin low scrub, dry except in the very wettest weather, with no banks to speak of, not above four feet broad, and with a perfectly sound bottom'.[39] Nevertheless, the arroyo is marked prominently on contemporary maps and seems to have been treated as an obstacle by both the allied and French cavalry that skirmished over that area during the course of the day.

The ridge rises progressively higher the farther south from the village one moves, but, for purposes of discussion of the battle, its most important features are two high points on the ridge line, the first of which lies approximately one mile south-west of Albuera. The second is due south of the first and separated from it by a distance of perhaps 500 yards. These high points have been variously described, with some commentators characterising them as 'heights', but unless the ground has changed drastically since 1811, the conclusion of Beresford's quartermaster-general seems

---

36. Sherer, *Recollections*, p. 153.
37. A sketch map of the battlefield by Long that was enclosed in his 30 May letter to his brother is reproduced (albeit somewhat crudely) in the rear endpapers of McGuffie, *Peninsular Cavalry General*.
38. Scovell, Diary, Vol. 2, p. 52. Scovell noted that there was 'not a stick to be found' on the battlefield.
39. Fortescue, *History*, Vol. VIII, p. 184, n. 1.

closest to the mark: '. . . they are merely swells of an undulating country and are cavalry ground throughout'.[40] The summit of each of these high points is 928 feet above sea level and the ground between the two dips down to an elevation of 853 feet, but the vertical rise from the riverbank to either summit is less than a hundred feet.[41] The second high point is broader and longer than the first, but there is a spur of the ridge running east from the first high point down to a noticeable knoll near the banks of the Chicapierna. For ease of reference in further discussions of the Albuera terrain in this book, the high point closer to the village will be referred to as the northern knoll and the other high point will be called the southern knoll.

On the east, or French, side of the line formed by the Albuera and the Nogales, there is a small plain of level ground some 1,200 yards in breadth opposite the village itself.[42] South of the plain is a wooded area that afforded important concealment to the French: 'On the enemy's side the ground was low and a very large wood that came down to the rivulet masking all their movements was a great disadvantage to our troops.'[43] There was one road running due east from the bridge at Albuera towards Corte de Peleas. The only road running north from Albuera towards Talavera was on the allied side of the river.

The armies converging on Albuera on the 15th had many more similarities than they had dissimilarities, starting with their demographics. First, they were all organisations predominantly composed of young men. According to some relevant statistical samples, 61 per cent of the British private soldiers were 25 years old or younger as compared to 48 per cent of the French, with the oldest British soldiers being between 45 and 50 and the oldest Frenchman being only 42.[44] (The lower percentage of soldiers under 25 in the French forces undoubtedly reflects the fact that most units of the Army of the South had not received any replacements [that is new conscripts] for over a year.) Second, they were all small in stature by modern standards. Despite minimum height requirements, 82 per cent of the British were 5 feet 6 inches tall or shorter, while the equivalent percentage for the Frenchmen was 74 per cent, with the British having two 6-footers at the extreme, while the tallest Frenchman was only 5 feet 11 inches. By and large, the officers and men of the armies tended to come from opposite ends of the economic spectrum, with the officers being wealthy and aristocratic while the rank and file were men who had encountered sufficient economic difficulty in civilian life to choose a military career. This was less true for the French Army than the others, however, due to the levelling effects of the

40. D'Urban, Letter to Taylor, p. 23. Curiously, D'Urban did use the word 'heights' in his 1817 published work on the campaign: 'The ground . . . was a range of heights falling gradually into the Albuera in front and into the Arroyo de Valdesevilla in the rear. It was of gentle undulation and easy for cavalry throughout.' D'Urban, *Report of Operations*, p. 17.

41. The shallow space between the two summits is now marked by a short east–west secondary road running at right angles from the road from Albuera to Almendral to the far side of the ridge.

42. This dimension is provided by the notations on an 1812 manuscript map entitled 'Reconnaissance of the Country lying between the Guadajira [*sic*] and the Albuera Rivers' now lodged as item MR167(4) in the NA/PRO Map Room.

43. Scovell, Diary, Vol. 2, p. 54.

44. The age and height statistics for the British are taken from information about 757 men of the 57th Foot compiled on 9 May 1809. Woollright, *History of the Fifty-Seventh*, pp. 399–400. The French statistics come from the personal descriptions of 91 French soldiers taken prisoner at Albuera recorded by their British captors. See prisoner of war files for 1811, NA/PRO ADM 103. No equivalent information has been found for the Spanish and Portuguese Armies.

conscription system and the fact that so many officers had risen from the ranks. The men probably even smelled similar, since the pungent aroma of long-unwashed bodies in long-unwashed clothing could not have differed greatly among the different nationalities.

The armies were also similar in terms of military organisation because the rigid requirements of musket period warfare did not encourage or reward innovation. The men were dressed in similar types of uniforms, were burdened with similar heavy packs containing their worldly possessions, used similar means of transport, had similar arrangements for medical care, played music on similar instruments and suffered from similarly frequent supply and pay shortages. More importantly, since the key to success on the battlefield was the ability to deliver maximum firepower or shock effect in a consistent and effective manner, it is not surprising that all of the armies were similarly subdivided into regiments, battalions, companies, squadrons and batteries and that in battle they all marched in step and followed similar drill routines for loading and firing their weapons and forming into and deploying out of chosen battle formations. Even the formations themselves were similar, since the battalions and squadrons of each army were customarily arranged in column formations (that is, a formation that, when viewed from the front, is narrower than it is deep) for movement and in line formations (a formation that, when viewed from the front, is broader than it is deep) for combat. (Infantrymen had yet another formation in common in that they all were trained to form some type of square for protection if threatened by cavalry.) The last and most significant similarity is that they all used similar weapons – swords and bayonets (the proverbial 'cold steel') for close combat and smoothbore cannon, pistols and muskets for long-distance combat.

The primary weapon of all the armies was a smoothbore flintlock musket made of wood and steel that was easy to load and hard to damage. When the trigger was pulled, a piece of flint was struck against a metal plate, creating a spark that, if all went well, ignited a small amount of gunpowder in a pan attached to the barrel of the weapon. The flame from that small explosion would travel into the barrel via a small hole to ignite the main explosive charge and propel a lead ball out of the barrel towards the enemy with lethal force. These weapons were notoriously inaccurate for two reasons.[45] The first reason was that musket balls did not fit tightly into musket barrels. This so-called 'windage' was a good thing in terms of speed of loading, but it meant that the ball literally bounced around inside the barrel on its way to the muzzle when a musket was fired. The last contact of the ball with the barrel determined the direction of the shot, which could go straight, veer left, veer right, lift or sink. The other reason was the drag associated with the spherical shape of musket balls, which ordinarily caused a shot to lose most of its velocity within the first 200 yards of its flight. One British officer famously summarised the abysmal qualities of his own army's weaponry in the following terms:

> A soldier's musket, if not exceedingly ill-bored, *and very crooked, as many are*, will strike the figure of a man at 80 yards; it may even at a hundred, but a soldier *must be very unfortunate indeed* who shall be wounded by a *common musket* at 150 yards, PROVIDED HIS ANTAGONIST AIMS AT HIM; and as to firing at a

45. Kelly, *Gunpowder*, pp. 142–3.

man 200 yards [off] with a common musket, you may just as well fire at the moon and have the same hopes of hitting your object. I do maintain, and will prove, whenever called on, that NO MAN WAS EVER KILLED AT TWO HUNDRED YARDS by a common soldier's musket, BY THE PERSON WHO AIMED AT HIM.[46]

This inaccuracy was the reason that each army relied on massed volleys of musket fire rather than individual aiming to do its killing. A musketry trial conducted by Colonel Gerhard von Scharnhorst in 1813 provides some concrete data that backs up Colonel Hanger's conclusions. The test involved 10 infantrymen on level ground firing 20 rounds each at a wooden panel 6 feet tall and 100 feet wide that simulated an enemy company in line. The table below shows the results of the test for the British Short Land Pattern musket (or 'Brown Bess') and the French Charleville musket at different distances:

Weapons Effectiveness Tests 1813

Weapon	*100 paces/250 ft*	*200 paces/500 ft*	*300 paces/750 ft*	*400 paces/1,000 ft*
Brown Bess	94 hits/200 shots	116 hits/200 shots	75 hits/200 shots	55 hits/200 shots
	47.5 per cent	56 per cent	37.5 per cent	27.5 per cent
Charleville	151 hits/200 shots	99 hits/200 shots	53 hits/200 shots	55 hits/200 shots
	75.5 per cent	49.5 per cent	26.5 per cent	27.5 per cent

For shots at 100 paces, a French infantryman was instructed to aim at a point 3 feet above the ground while the aiming point for the British musket was 1 foot above it. The aiming point for longer distances for both weapons were 3 feet at 200 paces, 5 feet at 300 paces and 7 feet at 400 paces. Scharnhorst noted in passing that the time taken by the shooters to load and fire their 20 rounds was never less than 7 minutes, while the slowest shooters took up to 14 minutes.[47] Given this meagre level of speed and accuracy under ideal conditions, one can assume that the results in battle, affected by smoke, noise and enemy return fire, would be considerably worse.

There were, of course, some differences among the armies that did have significance for the battle ahead. In terms of weaponry, the British Army had two advantages: shrapnel and rifles. All armies had artillery shells, which were gunpowder-filled iron spheres with fuses set to explode when they arrived over or among the enemy. Only the British, however, had shrapnel, or 'spherical case shot', a form of artillery ammunition invented by a Lieutenant Henry Shrapnel in 1784, but not used in combat until the Peninsular War. Shrapnel rounds were exploding shells filled with musket balls, and this added ingredient made them able to inflict many more casualties than ordinary shells. The British Army was also the only one in Spain that included some soldiers armed with rifles instead of muskets. The favoured British weapon of this type, the so-called Baker rifle (created by Ezekiel Baker, an English gunsmith), was slow to load but was highly accurate in the hands of a skilled marksman. At Albuera, the rifles were carried not by men of the famous 95th Rifle Regiment, but instead primarily by men of the 5th Battalion of the 60th Foot, an

---

46. Hanger, *Letter to Castlereagh*, p. 78. This same quote, with slight variations in punctuation, is found in a number of publications written by Colonel Hanger.
47. Scharnhorst, *Results*, pp. 61–4.

unusual green-jacketed infantry unit whose companies were assigned individually to brigades and divisions to beef up their skirmishing capacity. There was also a company of rifle-armed sharp-shooters ('*Scharfschützen*') from the Brunswick-Oels Regiment under Captain Friedrich Ludwig von Wachholtz attached to the 4th Division,[48] and the light battalions of the KGL also had some designated riflemen. The French, Spanish and Portuguese troops all had designated skirmishers as well, but they were not armed with rifles.

The French had one weaponry advantage of their own in the form of the Lancers of the Vistula Legion, a veteran unit composed mainly of ethnic Poles. Although the Spanish Army did have some lancer units, none were present in Extremadura and none of the allied cavalry units on hand had ever encountered such a foe. In military circles of the day, there were many different viewpoints concerning the advantages or otherwise of the lance as the primary weapon of a cavalry unit. With its fluttering red and white pennon, the lance certainly was an impressive ornament on parade, but it is less clear how useful it was in action.[49] On the positive side, a trooper with an eight-foot spear could clearly outreach a sabre-wielding opponent and the pennon itself was said to spook enemy horses. If, however, that opponent avoided the lance point and slipped inside its arc, the lancer was at a decided disadvantage. The best the lancer could do at that point was to use the lance shaft defensively to unseat his enemy or ward off his blows. Against infantry, however, a lancer had the same advantage of reach without any disadvantage because his opponent (provided his weapon was unloaded) was using a shorter but equally unwieldy weapon in the form of his musket with bayonet attached. The length of the lance also meant that a lancer could spear a man lying prone on the ground who would be beyond the reach of a mounted man armed only with a sword. This capability deprived a foot soldier of his last resort of falling to the ground in case of a cavalry charge. One of the few points that all experts agreed on was that a lance was useless in the hands of an inadequately trained soldier. Another was that the Poles were the supreme practitioners of the lancer's art.[50]

Another area of significant difference between the armies is found in the details of how they created their lines and columns. The basic building blocks of these tactical formations in the British and Portuguese armies were units arrayed in two lines (ranks) of soldiers, one behind the other, while the building blocks for the French and Spanish

48. Wachholtz, 'Auf der Peninsula', pp. 270–4. This unit does not appear in Oman's order of battle for the British, but its presence was noted by Sir Julius Hartmann in his memoirs and is further evidenced by the fact that both Lieutenant Berner and Surgeon Beyer of the Brunswickers survived to receive the Military General Service medal with an Albuera clasp. Hartmann, 'Beitrage', p. 106.

49. According to Auguste Petiet, one of Soult's ADCs, Napoleon came close to replacing all the lances of the Legion cavalry with firearms when he inspected the regiment at Bayonne in 1808. In particular, Napoleon asked Colonel Konopka point blank if he believed that the lancers' 'red and white pennons could scare horses'. The colonel replied emphatically that they could and offered an impromptu demonstration to prove his point. When Napoleon accepted, Konopka ordered his men to lower their lances and make a mock charge on Napoleon and his retinue. The result was a rout in which Napoleon's horse 'turned tail rapidly and carried him off at the gallop'. After he recovered himself, Napoleon told Konopka, 'You can keep your lances and only the second rank will be given *carabines*.' Petiet, *Souvenirs Historiques*, p. 203.

50. The Poles have 'the lance as their national arm, have exercised, even from infancy, and exult and pride themselves upon their adroitness and dexterity in wielding the lance'. Raymond Hervey de Montmorency, *Proposed Rules and Regulations for the Exercise and Maneouvres of the Lance, Composed Entirely from the Polish System*, London, 1820.

armies were units with their soldiers arrayed in three ranks.[51] The consequence of that difference was an obvious one – a French battalion of 600 men formed in a three-rank line would have a frontage of only 200 men while a British battalion of equal strength in a similar formation would have a frontage of 300 men because of the two-rank line. This disparity in terms of frontage was matched by a similar disparity in firepower between the two units because the third rank in a French line did not participate in volley fire for fear of hitting the men in front. As a result, the British battalion could bring all 600 of its muskets to bear on the French battalion, but the latter could only reply with the 400 muskets in the front two ranks. Available firepower was also affected, albeit less directly, by the number and types of companies in each battalion (*see below*). When light infantry companies were detached for skirmishing duties, the effective manpower of a British battalion would be reduced by 10 per cent, while the reduction for a French battalion would be 16.67 per cent.

Battalion Organisation

Nationality	No. of Centre Coys/ Battalion	No. of Grenadier Coys/ Battalion	No. of Light Coys/ Battalion
British	8 (100 officers & men)	1 (100 officers & men)	1 (100 officers & men)
Portuguese	4 (152 officers & men)	1 (152 officers & men)	0
Spanish	4 (165 officers & men)	1 (120 officers & men)	1 (105 officers & men)
French	4 (140 officers & men)	1 (140 officers & men)	1 (140 officers & men)

The normal strength of each British company (approximately 100 men) was smaller than that for other nationalities (between 125 and 160 men), so battalion sizes were theoretically comparable despite the differing number of companies, but no army had units at regulation strength during the Albuera campaign. The French 12th Light came closest, with 700 men in each of its three battalions, but the average strength of the 19 battalions in V Corps was just 428 men. The 3rd Foot was the largest British battalion with 728 men but the overall average was much lower and the smallest unit, the 2nd/31st Foot, had only 398 soldiers present for duty. The Portuguese battalions all had a robust 500–600 men under arms, while the strength of the Spanish battalions ranged from 216 to 851 available rank and file.

The convergence of all these armies on Albuera began in earnest during the morning of 15 May as the British and Portuguese troops at Valverde moved towards the assigned rendezvous. By early afternoon, Stewart's 2nd Division, Hamilton's Portuguese division and the independent brigades of Alten and Collins had all arrived and were positioned in accordance with Beresford's expectation that the French would attack straight up the Royal Road. Stewart's three brigades were posted around a prominent knoll on the ridge about three-quarters of a mile distant from the river with their right resting on the road to Valverde, and Hamilton's men extended the line to the left across the road to Badajoz. Their arrival was timely because the allied cavalry, which had begun the day at Santa Marta, was being pushed back rapidly by the French. When General Long arrived at Albuera, he was greeted by Assistant Adjutant-General John Rooke and ordered to cross the river and take up a defensive

---

51. Even the French and Spanish, however, would use two-rank line formations if company strength dropped so low that the frontage of the company using three ranks would be unreasonably small.

position on the ridge occupying the position that the Spaniards would assume when they arrived. Unfortunately, that movement abandoned the whole of the right bank to the enemy cavalry who had skirmished with Long's men all the way from Santa Marta.[52] Long then conducted a reconnaissance of the proposed allied position and came to the conclusion that the southern knoll on the ridge beyond Stewart's right flank was the 'key to the position' and he was shocked that it was unoccupied.[53] He passed his views on to Rooke, but took no other action since he assumed that the heights would be occupied the next day.

As the cavalry regiments of General Briche set their pickets on the evening of the 15th, matched on the allied side by infantry and artillery as well, the Battle of Albuera was still not inevitable. Marshal Beresford was certainly committed to the position as a result of his instructions from Wellington, his conferences with the Spanish generals and the intelligence reports he had received indicating that the combined allied armies would certainly outnumber their French opponents, but Soult was not so tied down. When he received the first reports indicating that the allies were present at Albuera in strength, Soult rode from Santa Marta to examine the position for himself.[54] Soult undoubtedly noticed that the right of the allied position was not fully occupied and that there were hills in that direction that were higher than the ones closer in towards Albuera. He then needed to decide what his next move would be.

In very simple terms, Soult had four courses of action to consider – he could attack, he could withdraw, he could try to manoeuvre around the Albuera position or, as a last resort, he could do nothing and wait to see if Beresford would make a move first. Manoeuvring might have scared the allies back across the Guadiana and allowed the French to throw some supplies and reinforcements into the besieged fortress, but that course of action was dangerous and did not promise any real decisive result and would only have alleviated the danger to Badajoz temporarily.[55] If Soult's goal was merely to buy time for General Philippon to break up the siege works commenced by the allies, he did not have to do anything more since Beresford had already raised the siege in order to prepare to face Soult's relief force. In fact, however, the French commander seems to have had more ambitious thoughts on his mind, thoughts of how to eliminate the allied threat to the security of Badajoz and Andalucia for a long time to come. And to accomplish that goal, he would have to attack.

According to Soult's memoirs, he actually concluded on the evening of the 15th that he was facing nothing more than an allied rear-guard.[56] Whether that is true or not, we also know that he received reports around the same time that the Spanish force under Blake that was coming to cooperate with Beresford had been delayed and would not be able arrive on the scene until the 17th.[57] In addition, although his force

---

52. Long, Letter to Brother, 30 May 1811, in Long, *Reply*, p. 112. In the years following the battle, Beresford and D'Urban repeatedly stated that General Long alone was responsible for the mistake of abandoning the right bank, but that view is not supported by any facts.
53. Long, Letter to Le Marchant, 5 June 1811.
54. Lapène, *Conquête*, p. 150.
55. D'Urban asserts that he had 'every reason to believe that Soult originally intended to have made this movement to Talavera, and that in attacking where he did he was governed by the circumstances as they appeared on the 15th', but he does not give the specifics of those reasons. D'Urban, Letter to Taylor, p. 23.
56. Soult, *Mémoires*, p. 236.
57. Lapène, *Conquête*, p. 150.

was relatively small, Soult was justifiably confident about the fighting prowess of his men because all of his regiments had previously served in the Grande Armée at Austerlitz or elsewhere and had registered numerous victories over the Spaniards. Soult knew from his personal experiences at Corunna and Oporto that the British and Portuguese were formidable foes, but it was by no means far-fetched for him to believe that this force would be the one to avenge the French defeats of Talavera, Bussaco and Barrosa. In light of all these considerations (mistaken though some may have been), Soult decided that he wanted to attack the force in front of him. Consistent with his belief that Blake was on the march, he also decided that he should launch that attack as early as possible on the 16th so he could defeat the British before they joined forces with Blake. He consequently ordered the rest of his army to make haste to join him even if that meant they had to march through the night.

Beresford seemed to have many fewer worries than Soult. He already had a substantial force in position on his chosen field of battle and he had skillfully arranged for the concentration of the rest of his army to occur at precisely the right moment to give him numerical superiority over his possible French attackers. As the night wore on without the appearance of any of those other troops, however, the marshal must have begun to wonder if he had cut his timing too close. There were three components to his worries because he was looking for three different contingents – General Cole's 4th Division coming from Badajoz together with the small Spanish division of 5th Army under General Castaños, the Spanish 4th Army under General Blake coming from Almendral, and the Portuguese cavalry brigade of General Madden, who had been at Solano. Each of these forces had different experiences during the night.

Cole's 4th Division had been intentionally left behind at Badajoz to preserve the blockade of the town as long as possible on the remote chance that Soult might decide not to press his advance or approach from an unexpected direction. By noon on the 15th, those possibilities had become so remote that Beresford ordered Cole to hold himself in readiness to march on short notice and to unite his forces by collecting General Kemmis's brigade which, save for the light infantry companies of its three constituent regiments, was stationed on the right or Portuguese bank of the Guadiana River masking the Fort of San Cristoval.[58] Although Captain Alexander de Roverea, Cole's ADC, was able to get across a ford on horseback to deliver the order to depart, by early evening the river had risen abruptly and become so high that the infantrymen of Kemmis's brigade were unable to cross to the left bank using the ford and instead had to march via Elvas for the pontoon bridge at Juromenha.[59] This detour ensured that Kemmis's brigade would not be available for action on the 16th, since the distance it had to cover to reach Albuera by that route was nearly forty-five miles, as compared to the sixteen miles between Badajoz and Albuera along the Royal Road. Despite this loss of a significant part of the strength of the 4th Division, Beresford was unfazed by the development because he had already considered the possibility that Kemmis's men might not be available and had factored it into his decision to stand at Albuera.[60]

58. D'Urban, *Report of Operations*, p. 22.
59. A. de Roverea, Letter to Father, (?) October 1811, in F. de Roverea, *Mémoires,* Vol. 4, pp. 30–1. The peregrinations of Kemmis's brigade can be followed through Emerson, 'Recollections', in Maxwell, *Peninsular Sketches*, Vol. 2, p. 246.
60. 'I have some fear of not being able to get [Kemmis's brigade] over in time from the other side.' B. to W., 15 May 1811, in *Supp. Despatches*, Vol. 7, pp. 125–6 at 126.

Cole in the meanwhile rested his main force, consisting of Myers's fusilier brigade, Harvey's Portuguese brigade, Kemmis's three orphan light companies and the weak Spanish infantry division of Carlos de España. They finally departed for Albuera at 2:00 a.m. on the 16th (the time specified in Beresford's orders).[61] It is unclear why Beresford had them delay so long before setting out, but the late start left little margin for error in the timetable for their arrival on the battlefield. Given the normal problems of night marches, it is hardly surprising that a significant error did arise, as recounted by Surgeon Guthrie:

> The 4th Division raised the siege of Badajoz at one [sic] in the morning, with the intention of joining the Marshal at Albuhera, leaving the pickets in the trenches for the purpose of continuing the belief that the besieging force was present. Less than four hours of a night march, which is always very slow, should have brought them there at least by six in the morning. An accident prevented it. The road forked about half way; the left road leading to Albuhera, the right towards Jurumenha [sic] on the River Guadiana, and away from the field of battle, The assistant quarter-master general had placed two native guides at the fork to show the right road, instead of an English officer or non-commissioned officer, on whom confidence could be placed. The guides fell asleep, and gave no sign as the troops passed, who followed the wrong road for an hour before the mistake was discovered, when they had to countermarch for another, and thus arrived late on the field of battle.[62]

This delay was not overly concerning to Beresford, however, since he had envisaged a reserve role for Cole in the first place and since he was kept well-informed of Cole's progress and had absolute confidence that the 4th Division would be on hand well before it was needed.

The Spanish expeditionary force under General Blake also arrived later than expected. The 15th began with the components of that force spread out over a considerable portion of the Extremaduran countryside. Blake's headquarters was at Almendral, just under eight miles from Albuera, but his cavalry was near Santa Marta and his infantry divisions were at Salvaterra, Salvaleon and Barcarrota. Thus deployed, the Spanish troops were hanging on Soult's flank, but in fact the French in Santa Marta were closer to the Spanish headquarters, twelve miles, than Blake's own men in Salvaterra over twenty-one miles away. When the French pushed a reconnaissance force from Santa Marta towards Almendral, Blake matched it with his horse grenadiers and the 1o Voluntarios de Cataluña from the 5th Army and called in the rest of his forces to Almendral.[63] The French were driven off but, given the distances to be travelled, Blake's army was slow to concentrate at Almendral and even slower to move towards Albuera, despite being hurried along by periodic inquiries from Beresford. It was no wonder that Beresford was concerned – Blake had promised that his men would be at Albuera by noon on the 15th and Beresford's plan was predicated on the fact they would form the right wing of his army. In the event, the Spaniards did not make contact with their allies until the early hours of the 16th. Even

---

61. The timing of Beresford's order is given in D'Urban, *Journal*, p. 214.
62. Anonymous, 'Guthrie Biography', p. 731. Major Correia de Mello of the 11th Portuguese Line Regiment also mentions losing the road. Correia de Mello, Journal Excerpts.
63. Burriel, *Albuhera*, pp. 7–8.

worse, when they finally did arrive they botched the job of taking up the precise positions laid out for them by Beresford's staff officers: 'Blake and his division ... in spite of all instruction took up [the] wrong ground in the dark.'[64]

Command of the Spanish infantry was split among three respected officers. Mariscal de Campo José Lardizabal (b. 1777), the youngest of the three, came from a distinguished family but his rise in the Spanish Army was due as much to talent as it was to family connections. The military career of Teniente General Ballesteros (b. 1770) had nearly ended in 1804 when he was cashiered on charges of corruption, but the French invasion gave him a fresh opportunity to excel and he made the most of it. He was an impressive person, but some thought he had risen farther than his true talents merited:

> Ballasteros is excessively popular with the soldiers and with the peasantry, but though he has undoubted courage, loves his country, and never spares himself, yet from being entirely without an education, he is unfit for an independent command.[65]

During his many raiding expeditions from Cadiz, he made life miserable for the French, but never achieved a decisive success.

Mariscal de Campo José Pascual de Zayas y Chacón (b. 1772) was commissioned into a Spanish infantry regiment at the age of eleven and had fought both the French and the British by the time he participated in la Romana's expedition to North Germany in 1807. He returned to Spain on a special mission in time to join the insurrection against the French and distinguished himself in losing causes at the Battles of Medina de Río Seco, Medellin, Talavera and Ocaña. Zayas was an able trainer of troops and even wrote a manual for officers on campaign.[66]

While the Spaniards may have been slow to reach their rendezvous, General Madden and his brigade of Portuguese cavalry (consisting of the 3rd, 5th and 8th Portuguese Regiments) never showed up at all. Though Madden's force was a small one, Beresford had been anxious to make sure it was available for battle, given the size and quality of the cavalry contingent assembled by Soult. Madden was at Solana on the 14th and then was ordered to Talavera la Real to watch for troops advancing from the direction of Mérida.[67] When another set of orders was sent to him at Talavera, however, Madden was nowhere to be found: 'The Officer sent to Madden returned from Talavera without finding him – it appears that he ... retired from thence without orders, where no one knows.'[68] The definitive explanation for Madden's disappearance is none too flattering to that officer – he heard a rumour at Talavera that the entire allied army had withdrawn over the Guadiana and, without verifying the information, he retired to the Portuguese bank of the river.[69] Two squadrons of his

64. D'Urban, *Report of Operations*, p. 20; D'Urban, *Journal*, p. 214.
65. Bridgeman, *Letters*, p. 105.
66. The details of Zayas's life come from José Manuel Rodriguez Gómez and Arsenio Garcia Fuentes, 'José de Zayas', Article in the Research Section of the Napoleon Series <www.napoleon-series.org/research/biographies/c_zayas.html>.
67. D'Urban, *Journal*, p. 213.   68. *Ibid.*, p. 214.
69. Madden, Letter to D'Urban, 18 May 1811. There was also speculation at the time that Madden made himself scarce in order to avoid serving under General Long. The lengthy memoir about Madden's services in 1811 that appeared in the *Royal Military Calendar* in 1820 does not even mention, no less explain, his absence. *Royal Military Calendar*, Vol. IV, pp. 48–117, at 98.

command did turn up at Badajoz and accompanied the 4th Division to Albuera, but Madden and the rest of his men were not heard from until he wrote to D'Urban on the 18th from a bivouac near the river on the Portuguese side in a weak attempt to justify his conduct.[70] Madden was not censured at the time, but his absence was the subject of some harsh words in the pamphlet wars about Albuera that sprang up much later.[71]

Aside from concentrating his troops and arranging them across his position, Marshal Beresford had little else to do by way of planning for the morning. Having defined his immediate objective in terms only of preventing the French from reaching Badajoz, he had no plan to implement other than that of seeing what Marshal Soult would do when confronted by a well-positioned and prepared allied army. If he had any doubts about what the next day would bring, a deserter came in about 1:00 a.m. and said that the French planned to attack about 8:00 a.m.[72] On the French side of the river, Soult also had little to do once he made his decision to fight at Albuera, but he still had much to worry about. As 15 May drew to a close, he had only six light cavalry regiments facing almost the entire Anglo-Portuguese army and, without reinforcements, he would be at the mercy of the allies if Beresford chose to go on the offensive. Soult had ordered the rest of his army to march through the night so they would be at Albuera early on the 16th, but most of the units were starting from Santa Marta, over twelve miles away, while General Werlé's brigade was even farther back at Villalba. Given the normal French marching pace of between two and three miles per hour, the order was not unreasonable, but Soult was asking a lot of his men on top of the distance they had already travelled from Seville. If anything went wrong with those expected movements, the French would be in a very dangerous situation.

---

70. Madden to D'Urban, 18 May 1811.
71. Anonymous, *Further Strictures*, p. 121.
72. W. Napier, *Justification*, pp. 33–4.

Chapter 5

The French Feint

Sunrise (or as much of an appearance as the sun could muster given the overcast conditions) took place at Albuera at 4:20 a.m. on Thursday 16 May.[1] The night ended for the opposing forces well before then, however, because both armies followed the traditional precaution of standing to arms at first light to prevent a surprise attack: 'Reveille calls resounded through the French camp and we could hear at the same time the trumpets of the English army.'[2] The precaution was actually unnecessary, however, because the allies had no intention of taking the initiative and the main French forces were still arriving on the scene. The only excitement came from a brief appearance by Briche's cavalry recorded by Lieutenant Moyle Sherer of the 1st/34th:

> We stood by our arms an hour before break of day: it was a brilliant sight, at sunrise, to see the whole of the French cavalry moving on the plain: but in a short time they retired into the wood, leaving their pickets as before.[3]

Once it became clear that the French were not making any immediate offensive moves, the allies began to make adjustments in their overnight dispositions. Beresford first personally tackled the correct placement of the Spanish 4th Army on his right flank, a task that required much more effort than expected:

> At day-break the Spaniards commenced to get into their general alignment, which [because of] their total want of all system of movement, and consequent unwieldiness, took up such a length of time that they were not in [position] until 7 a.m.[4]

Notwithstanding the delays, Blake's infantry were eventually deployed in two lines on the western (or, in terms of orientation towards the French, reverse) slope of the ridge with their left flank resting on the Valverde road exactly as Beresford intended.

1. The website of the US Naval Observatory provides an application that can calculate the historical hours of sunrise and sunset for any particular location. See <http://mach.usno.navy.mil>. Daybreak is the only event of the day that can be timed with accuracy, since not all participants in the battle had timepieces and there was no universal time standard used by all the armies.
2. Gougeat, 'Mémoires', p. 335.
3. Sherer, *Recollections*, pp. 216–17.
4. D'Urban, *Journal*, p. 214. Beresford himself was in the saddle by 3:00 a.m. and was directly involved in placing the Spanish troops: 'I had been, all the early part of the morning, with Blake's division, with which I remained till I saw it fairly in the alignment.' Beresford, *Refutation*, pp. 157 and 163.

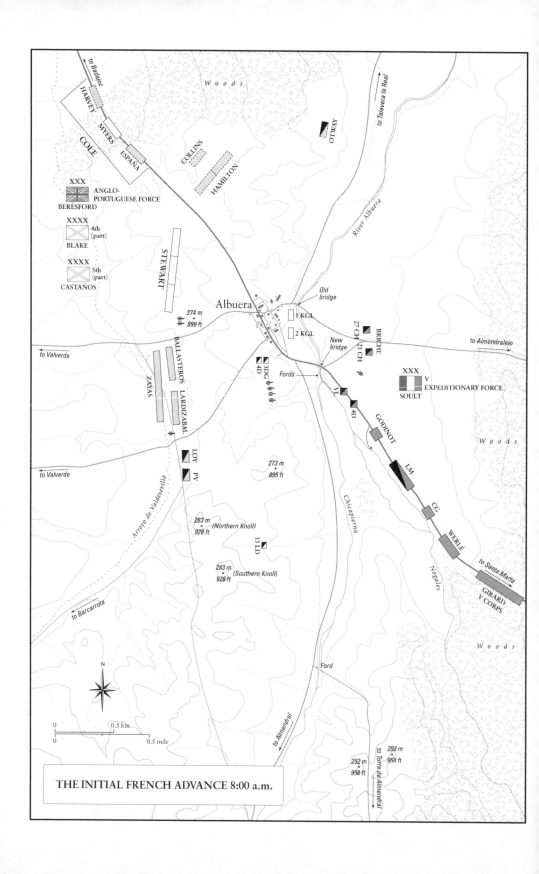

to Badajoz

HARVEY

MYERS

COLE

ESPAÑA

Woods

COLLINS

HAMILTON

OTWAY

to Talavera la Real

River Albuera

XXX

ANGLO-PORTUGUESE FORCE
BERESFORD

XXXX

4th (part)
BLAKE

XXXX

5th (part)
CASTAÑOS

STEWART

Albuera

274 m
899 ft

Old bridge

1 KGL

2 KGL

27 CH

21 CH

BRICHE

to Almendralejo

to Valverde

BALLASTEROS

ZAYAS

LARDIZABAL

New bridge

3 DG
4 D

Fords

V

4 D

XXX V

EXPEDITIONARY FORCE
SOULT

to Valverde

LOY

PV

273 m
895 ft

GODINOT

Woods

LM

Chicapierna

Arroyo de Valdesevilla

283 m (Northern Knoll)
928 ft

13 LD

CG

WERLÉ

Nogales

to Santa Marta

283 m (Southern Knoll)
928 ft

GIRARD
V CORPS

to Barcarrota

Woods

N

Ford

to Almendral

0   0.5 km

0   0.5 mile

292 m
958 ft

to Torre de Almendral

292 m
958 ft

THE INITIAL FRENCH ADVANCE 8:00 a.m.

The first line was composed of the divisions of Ballesteros and Lardizabal, with Ballasteros on the left. The regiments were in line formation (except for the last which was in column) in the following order from north to south: Infiesto, Cangas de Tineo, Castropol, Lena, Pravia, Barbastro, 1o Voluntarios de Cataluña, 2o León, Canarias, Murcia and Campo Mayor.[5] The last unit on the far right of the Spanish position was the combined light company battalion (Cazadores Reunidos) of Lardizabal's vanguard division, in column at the southern end of the infantry line.

The second Spanish infantry line was 200 yards to the west of (that is behind) the first and consisted of the division of General Zayas with the following units in line running south from the Valverde road: Reales Guardias Walonas (Royal Walloon Guards), Ciudad Rodrigo, Legion Extrangera (an unusual unit of foreign volunteers formed and commanded by Colonel Juan Omlin), Imperiales de Toledo, Voluntarios de la Patria, Irlanda, the 2nd and 4th Battalions of the Reales Guardias Españolas (Spanish Royal Guards) and then, last and least, a detachment of sappers.[6] The Spanish cavalry took position just to the south of the Spanish infantry and was also formed in two lines. First came the horsemen of the 5th Army under Count Penne-Villemur: the Lusitania, Borbon, Reina and Carabineros Reales Regiments supported by the Cazadores de Sevilla (formerly Tercio de Tejas), the Husares d'Extremadura and the Algarve Regiment. Next to them was the cavalry of the 4th Army: a first line consisting of three squadrons of mounted granaderos, the Instructional Squadron and one squadron of the provisional Regiment of Santiago, all under the command of General Casimiro Loy. Directly behind these troops was Lieutenant Colonel José Marron with four squadrons of the Husares de Castilla and a second squadron of the provisional Regiment of Santiago.

This set of dispositions gave the allies a solid defensive line along the ridge with the Portuguese on the left, the British in the centre and the Spanish on the right, but, given the number of troops available, it meant that the right flank of the Spaniards did not extend to either the northern knoll or, even more significantly, the southern knoll that had been identified the day before by General Long as 'the key of the position'. Captain de Roverea agreed with Long's concern about the terrain farther south on the ridge, but he seems to have focused initially on the importance of the northern knoll: '500 paces from the right wing of the Spanish line was a small hill that dominated our entire position. This hill was an essential point that should have been fortified in advance or at least strongly occupied.'[7]

The fact that the allies had done nothing to address this vulnerability left Long with a 'trembling heart', but he had more immediate problems to worry about. Long had placed his cavalry units at intervals along the allied front in order to be ready for any contingency and when he returned from visiting those on the far right, he was amazed to find Colonel D'Urban directing him to send all the British cavalry to the rear to rest and forage, after which the colonel 'marched off himself with the 4th Dragoons [that had been] posted for defence of the bridge and the ford near the

---

5. The sequence of Spanish units comes from the official Spanish reports in Burriel, *Albuhera*.
6. More details about the Legion Extrangera can be found in the biography of Prussian General Carl von Grolman, who served in the unit. Conrady, *Grolman*, Vol. 1, p. 231 *et seq*. This unit should not be confused with the Legion Extremeña, which was formed in 1810 by John Downie but which was not present at Albuera.
7. A. de Roverea, Letter to Father, (?) October 1811, in F. de Roverea, *Mémoires*, Vol. 4, p. 32.

village.'[8] There was some justification for this decision, since the cavalry had spent the night holding the ground eventually taken up by the Spaniards, but General Long felt strongly that it was imprudent to send off all the units at once. Rather than arguing with D'Urban, however, he simply disobeyed his orders and held back the 3rd Dragoon Guards and the 13th Light Dragoons as a practical matter:

> I ... assembled the rest of the cavalry in order to fulfill my instructions, but so convinced was I of the dangers attendant on the movement that I delayed their departure as long as I could.[9]

The lack of trust between Long and Beresford had become complete.

While the allied battle line was taking shape, the missing units from Badajoz finally made their appearance. The small Spanish 'division' under Brigadier de España arrived at 7:00 a.m. and since it had, by prior arrangement between Castaños and Blake, been put under Blake's orders, it was added to the second line of Spanish infantry already in position. The Voluntarios de Navarra fell in on the right of Zayas's division, while de España's other two units (the Rey and Zamora Regiments) extended Zayas's line farther to the left.[10] The leading elements of the 4th Division arrived somewhat later, probably around 8:00 a.m., but according to one source, 'The head of the 4th Division was [still] one mile distant from the nearest soldier under the orders of Marshal Beresford' when the first cannon shots were fired.[11] When the division did make its full appearance, Beresford placed it in a supporting position with its constituent regiments echelonned along the Royal Road just behind the centre of the British position.

It is impossible to calculate with certainty the exact strength of any army on any date because of the inherent inaccuracy of all military reporting systems. Nevertheless, as detailed in Appendix B, analysis of the most authoritative information available yields the following strength totals for the allied armies: 10,603 British and King's German Legion troops, 10,201 Portuguese and 14,552 Spaniards, for a grand total of just over 35,000 officers and men.[12] The allies had a disproportionately small amount of cavalry, but they did have 40 cannon of various calibres, as detailed below.[13] Overall, this force vastly outnumbered the approaching French army.

---

8. Long to Le Marchant, 5 June 1811. The circumstance is described by Major Leighton of the 4th Dragoons: '[W]e had, as usual, been under arms for an hour before day-break, and to the best of my recollection, between seven and eight o'clock, [we] received orders to proceed for forage.' Leighton to Gregory, quoted in W. Napier, *Justification*, p. 35. Beresford later disputed the existence of a general order to forage in reaction to criticism from Napier and Long's nephew, but D'Urban is clear on the point. D'Urban, *Journal*, p. 214.

9. Long to Brother, 30 May 1811, quoted in McGuffie, *Peninsular Cavalry General*, pp. 113–14.

10. Report of de España in Burriel, *Albuhera*, p. 41.

11. The time of arrival is given by D'Urban in his contemporaneous *Journal*, p. 214, and is corroborated by Capt. Thomas Peacocke of the 23rd Portuguese Regiment, who recorded that his unit arrived on the field between 8:00 and 9:00 a.m. Peacocke, *Memoirs*. (Inexplicably, D'Urban subsequently stated in his 1817 Report that the division arrived at 6:00 a.m.) The quote is from Anonymous, 'Guthrie Biography', p. 731.

12. See the figures in Oman, *History*, Vol. 4, pp. 631–3 (which do not include the Brunswick-Oels company) and Spain, *Estado*, pp. 117–19. For a discussion of alternate views, see Beresford, *Refutation*, pp. 113–33.

13. See table *above right* for details of the artillery types and calibres given in Dickson, Letter to Beresford, 25 July 1833, p. 1. This detail is more accurate than that given in either Beresford, *Refutation*, p. 112, or Duncan, *History of the Royal Artillery*, Vol. 2, p. 296 because it accounts for the presence of one howitzer with each British, KGL and Portuguese battery.

Allied Artillery

Nation	9-pounders	6-pounders	4-pounders	5½-in. howitzers	Total
British/KGL	5	13	0	4	22
Portuguese	5	5	0	2	12
Spanish	0	0	6	0	6
Total	10	18	6	6	40

On the French side of the river, Soult's first task of the day was to re-evaluate his projected attack in light of any new information revealed by early morning scouting reports. Amazingly, at this early point in the day the French either did not spot the new Spanish troops or mistook them for units of Castaños's force, so Soult remained convinced that Blake's army had still not united with that of Beresford.[14] Moreover, it also seems that Soult believed that Cole's division was still at Badajoz, because he is said to have personally questioned the first allied prisoners as to Cole's whereabouts. As a result of these mistaken beliefs, Soult never wavered from the decision to attack he had made the evening before. Now, however, he had to choose the specific form his attack would take. Since the main strength of the allies remained concentrated around the village and there was much open and unoccupied ground to the south of the main allied position around the southern knoll that obsessed General Long, it is perhaps not surprising that the French marshal opted for a classic envelopment that involved swinging the bulk of his forces around the allied right flank. By doing so, Soult knew he would be threatening to cut Beresford off from his preferred line of retreat through Olivenza to Juromenha and Elvas, as well as (so he thought) placing his troops between Beresford and Blake's approaching Spanish forces. If his plan succeeded to maximum effect, he might even trap the defeated allies against the Guadiana with no way to cross back to safety. To effectuate this plan, Soult made two significant tactical decisions. First, he continued to believe that he needed to attack as soon as all his men had assembled, despite the fact that the troops were 'exhausted by their long march and drained by the heat' when they finally reached Albuera.[15] Second, he chose to launch an initial attack directly at Albuera, precisely as expected by Beresford and the allies, in order to keep the allies guessing about his true intentions until the flank attack was ready. One decision was very successful; the other was not.

Since the French knew that a battle would be fought that day, the mood on their side of the river was decidedly sombre, with the preparations of officers and men alike affected by premonitions of mortality. One typical incident involved Captain Pierre-Andras de Marcy of the 20th Dragoons and his orderly, Louis-Antoine Gougeat:

> While I was bridling his horse, he [my captain] asked me for a bottle of *eau-de-vie* [strong liquor]. When I gave it to him, he took me by the hand saying: 'The fighting will be hot today; there are many who by this evening will no longer have need of physical possessions.' He took off his money belt and gave it to

---

14. Soult, *Mémoires*, p. 236; Soult, Unpublished Report. The late arrival of the Spaniards probably contributed to Soult's confusion because it meant that Blake's men were not in a position to be seen by early morning French observers.

15. Saint-Chamans, *Mémoires*, pp. 198–9.

me, adding: 'Ah! My poor Louis, this is perhaps the last time we will be together. If the English get me, this is for you. Adieu!' He then rode off at a gallop to take his place at the head of his company. I was more moved than I can say by his gesture.[16]

For the French infantry, there was less time for such scenes because the men had been on the march most of the morning from Santa Marta. Their priority on arrival at Albuera would have been to prepare a hasty meal or grab a few moments of repose before the fighting began. The most ambitious or conscientious soldiers, however, may have finished letters for loved ones and entrusted them to comrades for delivery in the case of death.

At approximately 8:00 a.m., Soult set his plan in motion by advancing 'a brigade of guns and a force of cavalry towards the [new] bridge' over the Albuera River near the village.[17] This force was General Briche's cavalry brigade (now reduced to just the 21st and 27th Regiments of Mounted Chasseurs (Chasseurs à Cheval) because the 2nd and 10th Hussars were held back by Latour-Maubourg), two detached cavalry regiments (the regiment of Lancers of the Vistula Legion and the 4th Dragoons), and a battery of horse artillery.[18] That battery, probably the 4th Company of the 6th Regiment of Horse Artillery under Lieutenant Bellencontre, seems to hold the dubious distinction of firing the first shots of the battle, since numerous accounts mention that the action opened with a cannonade and Lieutenant William Unger of the King's German Legion artillery recalled specifically that a 'Brigade of Horse Artillery . . . was drawn up about 600 yards in front of the bridge, and opened upon the troops defending the bridge and the village'.[19]

As the French approached the river, the horsemen split into two groups. General Briche's two regiments moved off to the north, driving in some allied skirmishers who had ventured to the French side of the river and taking up a position near the old bridge opposite the Portuguese forces on the far left of the allies. The Vistula Legion Lancers and the 4th French Dragoons meanwhile came straight on down the Royal Road, only to veer left before reaching the bridge and approach the river at a narrow ford just to the south.[20]

The approach of this cavalry and artillery alone would not necessarily have been taken as a serious threat by the allies, but Soult understood he had to make this attack convincing in order to achieve his overall objectives. He did so by adding two elements to the mix – a strong force of infantry and, even more spectacularly, the whole of the rest of his cavalry. The infantry troops were General Godinot's brigade, consisting of three battalions of the 16th Light and the single battalion present of the 51st Line, followed by General Werlé's brigade, consisting of the three battalions of the 12th Light and three (possibly four) of the 58th Line, but reinforced for the battle

16. Gougeat, 'Mémoires', p. 335.
17. Clarke Narrative in Groves, *The 66th Regiment*, p. 51. Lardizabal's Report says the attack began at 7:00 a.m., but that does not fit with other evidence. Burriel, *Albuhera*, p. 27.
18. Lapène says that Briche had the 10th and 21st Chasseurs, but that statement is surely wrong because the 10th Chasseurs were serving in the Army of Portugal. Lapène, *Conquête*, p. 155. Latour-Maubourg's Report gives the correct details as well as confirming the presence of the Lancers and 4th Dragoons.
19. Lapène, *Conquête*, p. 154; Unger, 'Description', p. 126.
20. Alten, Narrative, p. 1; Latour-Maubourg, Report, p. 1.

by three battalions of the 55th Line taken from Godinot.[21] The cavalry contingent consisted of every mounted unit in Soult's army except the four already headed toward the village – the 2nd and 10th Hussars, the 14th, 17th, 20th, 26th and 27th Dragoons and the 4th Regiment of Spanish Mounted Chasseurs in the service of King Joseph.[22]

The sight of these significant forces issuing forth from the woods on the French side of the river galvanised the allies into action. Dickson's Portuguese artillery and the four guns of Lefebure's under-strength mounted battery responded to the French artillery while the allied infantry and cavalry roused themselves to readiness. Although the French attack should not have come as a surprise to the allies, Lieutenant Sherer, at least, had presumed (incorrectly) that the French would not be coming at all since they had not attacked at dawn:

> The battalion having been dismissed, I breakfasted, and immediately afterwards set out to walk towards the Spanish troops, little dreaming, that day, of a general action. But the sound of a few shots caused me to return; and I found our line getting hastily under arms, and saw the enemy in motion.[23]

Rifleman Friedrich Lindau of the 2nd KGL Light Battalion was similarly caught unawares. He had miraculously discovered one live sheep in a stable as he was scavenging through the village for food. He quickly slaughtered his prize and wanted to share it with his brother, who was stationed in the steeple of the village church. Just then, however, the enemy were spotted and an officer ordered his company forward to skirmish. He barely had time to cut off a leg of mutton and stick the bloody haunch in his knapsack for later consumption.[24]

Lieutenant Charles Leslie of the 29th Regiment also recalled that the precise moment of the French advance had not been well anticipated:

> We had scarcely time to get a little tea and a morsel of biscuit, when the alarm was given – 'Stand to your arms! The French are advancing.' We accordingly instantly got under arms, leaving tents and baggage to be disposed of as the quartermaster and batmen best could.[25]

These last moments before fighting commenced were used in a variety of different ways by the men to settle themselves for the ordeal ahead:

> Each man then began to arrange himself for the combat in such manner as his fancy or the moment would admit of – some by lowering their cartridge boxes, others by turning theirs to the front in order that they might the more

---

21. Soult's Unpublished Report states Werlé's brigade, consisting of the 12th Light and 58th Line, was 'reinforced' with the 55th Line from Godinot's brigade at the start of the battle. It should be noted, however, that the regimental history of the 55th states unambiguously that the unit served with Godinot, not Werlé, while the history of the 12th Light is equally clear that the 58th was the only other regiment in Werlé's brigade, a view expressed as well by Lapène (who never mentions the 55th at all). Martin, *Le 55e Régiment*, pp. 70–1; Malaguti, *Historique du 87e Régiment (ex-12e Léger)*, pp. 367–8; Lapène, *Conquête*, p. 162.
22. Latour-Maubourg, Report, p. 1.
23. Sherer, *Recollections*, p. 217.
24. Lindau, *Erinnerungen*, pp. 35–6.
25. Leslie, *Military Journal*, p. 218.

conveniently make use of them; other unclasping their stocks or opening their shirt collars, and others oiling their bayonets; and more taking leave of their wives and children.[26]

The need to detach men to deal with an army's baggage is rarely mentioned in detail in military literature, but it certainly had a practical impact on the forces involved at Albuera beyond that suggested by Lieutenant Leslie. For instance, an entire company of the 34th Foot was ordered to the rear as part of the baggage guard of the 2nd Division, thus depriving the regiment of approximately a tenth of its fighting strength before the action began. Twenty-seven-year-old Captain George Gibbons, the commander of the chosen company, was so unhappy with that assignment that he volunteered to take command of the regiment's Light Company and, since he outranked the incumbent in that position, his request was granted.[27]

The 23rd Fusiliers likewise lost a company to baggage guard duty for the 4th Division, and its commander, Captain John Orr, was similarly unhappy with the prospect of missing the coming battle. When he heard cannon fire coming from the battlefield, both he and his second-in-command, 23-year-old Lieutenant John Harrison, sought permission to rejoin their regiment, but in the end only Harrison escaped his rear-echelon responsibilities:

> Here we joined the rest of the baggage of the army and I was not a little anxious to get rid of my troublesome office and join my regt. Orr at first objected to my going as I was second senior and he wished to go himself. However, I soon got over this obstacle and we both went forward to ask the [whereabouts of] the brigade which no one could give an account of. I discovered General Cole who we came up to and here I met with another obstacle for he would not hear at all of my leaving the baggage but after a few gentle remonstrances I soon overcame this . . .[28]

Lieutenant Colonel Henry Ellis of the 23rd was happy to have Harrison rejoin the regiment and even gave him command of the 7th battalion company in place of Captain John van Courtland, who was acting as a field officer. The colonel had an inkling that he would need every available man for the work ahead, however, so he first ordered Harrison to round up as many extra soldiers as possible:

> As soon as I saw Ellis he desired me to go back and bring the drums up and all the spare hands I could collect from the baggage. I got back to the rear with all haste and left my horse with my servant and a mule and moved forward with about forty men of the brigade.[29]

The French and Spaniards undoubtedly had to make similar arrangements for their baggage, so the available forces of those armies would likewise have been reduced to deal with this necessity.

General Cole discovered about this time that he had another, unexpected deduction from his strength because some of his men had been inadvertently left behind when

26. Grattan, *Adventures*, pp. 145–6.
27. J. L., 'Captain Gibbons', p. 431.
28. Harrison, Letter to Mother, 24 May 1811, in Glover, 'The Royal Welch Fusiliers', p. 150.
29. *Ibid.*

the 4th Division moved to Albuera. This oversight was the fault of the officer in charge of the thin cordon of sentries that had been left in place outside Badajoz early that morning to mask the British departure:

> This gentleman – a worthy old Scotchman [*sic*] ... as brave as his sword – having other duties to perform, soon forgot the pickets; and in his anxiety to be in for what was supposed to be an impending fight, followed the troops. When nearly on the field of Albuhera, he recollected he was to have brought off the pickets. The old gentleman – Randy Dandy, as he was affectionately called, for everybody liked him, who was rather bald, with reddish hair, a clear, florid complexion – turned rather pale, big drops of sweat broke out on his forehead, when the recollection of the deserted pickets suddenly flashed across his mind ... He rode up to Sir Lowry Cole, and manfully stated his forgetfulness. 'Go back, sir,' said the general, 'and do not let me see you again without the pickets.' Randy Dandy went off at a gallop, and slackened not his pace until he entered the trenches, where he found the pickets as quiet and as comfortable as possible. He withdrew them without molestation, although the distant firing could be distinctly heard.[30]

In its haste to prepare for action, the allied army made no effort to conceal itself from the attacking French troops. As recalled by Lieutenant Leslie, the allies took up their positions in the most conspicuous manner possible:

> We moved forward in line to crown the heights in front, which were intended for our position ... In occupying the position, the army was formed as follows:– The Portuguese, in blue, on the left; the English, in red, in the centre ... and the Spaniards, in yellow or other bright colours formed the right. The whole were drawn up as for a grand parade, in full view of the enemy, so that Soult could see almost every man, and he was enabled to choose his point of attack; which would not have been the case if we had been kept under cover a few yards further back, behind the crest of the heights, or had been made to lie down, as we used to do under the Duke of Wellington. That part of the 4th Division under Sir Lowry Cole, which had just arrived from Badajos [*sic*], were posted in the second line in our rear.[31]

Given this description, it is not surprising that Soult now came to realise that Blake's force had moved faster than he had expected:

> I had hoped to prevent the juncture of the Spanish troops from Cadiz under Blake with the English and Portuguese troops under General Beresford by attacking a day before they were due to arrive, but that in fact took place during the night before the battle and I consequently had to fight against a stronger enemy than I had supposed when I initiated the action.[32]

---

30. Anonymous, 'Guthrie Biography', p. 731.
31. Leslie, *Military Journal*, pp. 218–19.
32. Soult, Unpublished Report. The information about Blake was probably also conveyed to Soult via the report of a commissary officer named Hery who visited Almendral during the night looking for supplies and was told by the village priest there that Blake had marched for Albuera. D'Héralde, *Mémoires*, p. 151.

The French commander could easily have reacted to this development by postponing his attack or calling it off altogether, but he made no effort to do so. One can only speculate why Soult persisted with his chosen course of action in the face of this significant change of circumstances, but the Battle of the Gevora must have been prominent in his thinking. The beauty of his battle plan for Albuera was that, as a result of the Spanish being assigned to the allied right flank, it was calculated to bring about the same kind of confrontation between his proven veterans on the one hand and a motley assortment of Spaniards on the other as had taken place at the Gevora, and there was every reason for Soult to believe that the French would achieve an identical triumph.[33] So, despite what he later said for public consumption, far from concluding that the arrival of Blake made further offensive movement impossible, Soult seems to have embraced it as a potential advantage. But first he wanted to keep the attention of the allies focused away from his chosen point of attack as long as possible. He did so initially by having his cavalry make an unsupported attack on the allied right-centre.

This attack had two components. First, Latour-Maubourg sent some light cavalry across the river to test the allied response. The men chosen for this show of bravado were four platoons of Vistula Legion Lancers (approximately 100 riders) who waded through the narrow ford just south of the new bridge and took up a temporary position on the allied side of the river supported by the 4th French Dragoons. Two platoons of lancers (one commanded by Sous-Lieutenant Piotr Rogojski and one commanded by Sous-Lieutenant Kajetan Wojciechowski) then advanced in skirmish order towards the nearest British infantry, leaving behind the other two platoons in reserve at the edge of the river under the command of Captain Leszczynski.[34] General Long, gratified that his retention of two cavalry units near the village was being so clearly justified, immediately ordered Lieutenant Colonel Granby Calcroft of the 3rd Dragoon Guards to meet the attackers: 'Forward and charge, Sir Granby, if you please.'[35] The Lancers repulsed the first British squadron to attack, but the British horsemen then rallied and, reinforced by another squadron, forced the outnumbered Poles down the slope to the river. The fighting was sharp, but not continuous. At one point the two Polish officers rode up to each other and Rogojski offered Wojciechowski a drink from his flask. The two men were horrendously startled when a cannon ball passed between them just as Wojciechowski put the flask to his lips.[36]

The second component of the cavalry attack was an advance by all the rest of the French cavalry to the allied side of the river using a second ford located a further 'quarter league' to the south.[37] Once across, these units, joined by the 4th French Dragoons, halted between the two fords and formed regimental columns in echelon separated by 'full intervals'. The cavalry were accompanied by ten artillery pieces that were placed in line in front of the horsemen and began firing on the allied troops on the ridge. The return fire was so troublesome that non-combatants, such as Captain

33. Lapène says Soult's men were fully aware of the unfavourable odds they faced in terms of numbers, but that they were nevertheless full of confidence and eager to attack 'with their accustomed vigour'. Lapène, *Conquête*, p. 153.
34. Wojciechowski, *Pamietniki*, p. 70.
35. Quoted without attribution in Oatts, *I Serve*, p. 104.
36. Wojciechowski, *Pamietniki*, p. 70.
37. The details of the movements of the reserve cavalry come from Latour-Maubourg, Report.

de Marcy's orderly, who was leading the captain's spare horses, were ordered to retire in order to reduce the potential for casualties.[38] The French cavalry nevertheless maintained its position for 'more than two hours' in order 'to contain the enemy and allow time for [all] the infantry to arrive'.[39]

The arrival of Latour-Maubourg's force temporarily enabled the Poles to regain the advantage in their skirmish with the 3rd Dragoon Guards, but that advantage was not a lasting one. When the reserve cavalry (including the rest of the Lancer Regiment) departed for the extreme left flank of the French line, the Polish skirmishers on the allied side of the river were left in great danger. When the remaining squadron of the 3rd Dragoon Guards was committed to the fray, the Polish skirmishers were forced to retreat. Rogojski's platoon made it back to the French side of the river with the loss of only two or three wounded, but Wojciechowski's platoon was cut off at the ford despite covering pistol fire from Rogojski's men. Wojciechowski himself sabred his way through the surrounding English cavalrymen, but upwards of fourteen of his comrades were killed or wounded, most right at the ford.[40] In addition to these casualties, Captain Leszczynski had been shot dead early in the action. It was not an auspicious start to the day for the Lancers, who then moved off to join the rest of their regiment opposite the allied right flank.[41]

While the cavalry skirmished, Godinot's infantrymen finally reached the river and began their first attack on the village in accordance with Soult's plan. The two light battalions of the King's German Legion assigned to defend Albuera were well-positioned to receive them:

> The part of the village nearest to the large [new] stone bridge over the Albuera river was occupied by the 2nd Light Battalion, which with its skirmishers lined the mud walls enclosing the houses, and had advanced a party of their best marksmen to a well, surrounded by a stone wall and situated in front about half way between the village and the bridge. The churchyard in the centre of the village was occupied by two companies of the 1st Light Battalion; the skirts of the village on the left and some garden walls facing towards the Albuera river (where it is crossed by a minor bridge) were occupied by two more companies of the 1st Light Battalion. The rest of that Battalion, consisting of four companies remained in reserve on its ground in the rear of the village.[42]

Some of the KGL skirmishers closest to the bridge were concealed in a large patch of thistles that were eight or nine feet tall.[43] The French were veteran troops but, as a

---

38. Gougeat, 'Mémoires', p. 335.

39. The statement that the duration of the halt under artillery fire was two hours must be considered in light of the fact that Latour-Maubourg records the fight as starting at 7:00 a.m., an hour earlier than other sources. The exact location of the cavalry is also hard to discern because, even in the original French, Latour-Maubourg's description is peculiar: '*Elle [la cavalerie] était établi en face des hauteurs intermédiaires avec le village de la Albuhera et que l'ennemi commençait à faire occupait.*' Latour-Maubourg, Report.

40. The details of the skirmish come from Kujawski, *Z Bojow Polskich*, pp. 262–4, which in turn draws heavily on Wojciechowski, *Pamietniki*, pp. 69–70.

41. Curiously, Beresford claimed in 1833 that he had always thought that the Lancers had been driven off by infantry fire alone and that he had not previously been aware of the part played by the 3rd Dragoon Guards. Beresford, *First Letter*, p. 48.

42. Alten, Narrative, p. 2.   43. Lindau, *Erinnerungen*, p. 36.

tactical matter, they seem to have become fixated on capturing the new bridge rather than crossing the shallow river wherever they could (including over the old bridge) and pressing on to Albuera, so they made only modest progress towards the village:

> [A] close column [of French] ... advanced up to the bridge but owing to the well-directed fire of the 2nd Light Battalion and of its advanced marksmen, the latter repeatedly picking off the officers who led the enemy's column, the enemy failed several times in forcing this passage. After different fruitless attempts and a heavy loss, the column however succeeded in crossing the Albuera, partly by the bridge and partly by fording.[44]

Even that limited advance had the desired effect, however, as Beresford rose to the bait offered by Soult and ordered more troops towards his centre.[45]

The first thing Beresford did was to move Campbell's Portuguese brigade closer to the north side of the village. He then moved Colborne's brigade closer to the south side:

> The fire becoming extremely warm at the village and bridge, Sir William Beresford ordered forward our brigade to support the fatigued battalions of the German Legion, who were gallantly defending those posts.[46]

The marshal even brought forward two Spanish battalions from General Lardizabal's division, the Campo Mayor Regiment and the combined light companies (Cazadores Reunidos) of all the units in the division. These actions, of course, played right into the hands of the French:

> Soult must have been much delighted on observing this movement: it, no doubt, was precisely what he most wished; because the columns which appeared to threaten the village and our line were only a ruse to distract our attention and neutralise the English force which he most dreaded.[47]

The movement also put Colborne's men into range of the French artillery, which soon inflicted the first of the many casualties the brigade would suffer during the day:

> The 2/48th and its neighbours in Colborne's brigade suffered very considerably from the cannonade, losing several men killed and wounded by random cannon shot.[48]

The allies replied with fire from their own cannon posted on a rise 'about 750 or 800 yards from the bridge, and about 700 yards from the village'.[49] These were the twelve Portuguese guns under Dickson plus Hawker's 9-pounders and, at least initially, the guns of Lefebure's battery, though these last guns were withdrawn to

---

44. Alten, Narrative, p. 2. Curiously, Alten states that the whole French column turned left after crossing the river and 'continued its movement towards the right of the allied position'. This could not have been true for all of Godinot's force, but this evidence suggests that this initial attack may have involved parts of Werlé's brigade or the Combined Grenadiers.
45. Beauvais, *Victoires et Conquêtes*, pp. 238–9.
46. Brooke, 'Prisoner', p. 177.
47. Leslie, *Military Journal*, p. 219.
48. Brooke, 'Prisoner', p. 177.
49. Dickson to Napier, 7 September 1833, quoted in Dickson, *Manuscripts*, Vol. 3, p. 395.

support the allied cavalry on the right flank when the French cavalry moved off in that direction. But now, at approximately 9:00 a.m., just as the fighting intensified near the village, the French unveiled the second part of their attack.

The man chosen to lead the projected knock-out punch of the French was Division General Girard, the interim commander of V Corps. Soult had at first designated General Werlé to lead the attack, but Girard, a soldier eager to impress in his first opportunity to command a full army corps in a major battle, asked for the honour to be granted to him instead and, since he was a favourite of Soult, he persuaded the marshal to give pride of place to his own corps.[50] The choice was a logical one – Girard had proved himself many times over to be a fighting general who could relentlessly press an attack and, in fact, Napoleon himself later remarked that Girard was 'one of the most intrepid soldiers in the French Army' and one who eminently displayed the 'sacred fire' of a warrior.[51] Soult may even have judged that Girard's passion for battle would complement his own strengths as a commander since, by this stage of his career, Soult was thought by some to be more courageous on the eve of battle than he was on the day of action itself.[52]

The attack began shortly after Godinot's infantry became engaged at the bridge. The men of V Corps had just recently arrived from Santa Marta earlier in the morning, but they were nevertheless eager to come to grips with the enemy. After a quick breakfast, Girard and his whole staff led his men left off the Royal Road, then cross-country through the edge of the woods on the French side of the river, his own first division in front.[53] They crossed the Nogales unseen by the allies, then used the high ground and woods on the tongue of land between the Nogales and Chicapierna streams to conceal their approach as long as possible. Finally, Girard reached the point where he could see the first objective for the attack, the ford across the Chicapierna near where the track between Nogales and Albuera intersects with the road between Albuera and Almendral. Having thus far avoided premature exposure of the plans, the French were now ready to engage the enemy.

Boxes and arrows showing troop movements on maps drastically over-simplify the very real difficulties involved in moving bodies of men from one location to another on a battlefield and this is certainly a case in point. Girard's flank march looks easy on paper, but it was vastly complicated in practice and involved a delicate orchestration of cavalry, infantry and artillery units.

Throughout the initial French advance towards Albuera, there were some allied observers who remained unconvinced that this was the main French attack. Indeed, even one of the British medical officers thought it was clear that the French attack on the bridge was just a feint:

> 'These gentlemen below', [Mr Guthrie said] pointing to the French, 'do not mean to make their serious attack here; it will be over there [on the right] . . . where you now see nothing.'[54]

50. D'Héralde, *Mémoires*, p. 154. In recognition of the importance of the manoeuvre, Marshal Soult was equally insistent that he accompany the attack in person. Lapène, *Conquête*, p. 151.
51. Napoléon, *Correspondance*, Vol. 31, p. 173.
52. Lamarque, *Mémoires*, Vol. 2, p. 30.
53. D'Héralde, *Mémoires*, p. 154.
54. Anonymous, 'Guthrie Biography', p. 731.

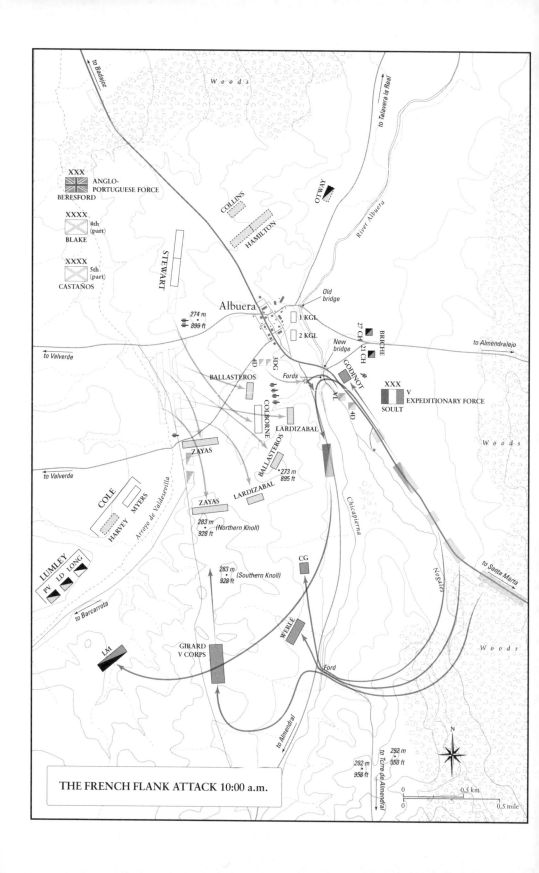

to Badajoz

Woods

to Talavera la Real

River Albuera

XXX
ANGLO-PORTUGUESE FORCE
BERESFORD

XXXX
4th
(part)
BLAKE

XXXX
5th
(part)
CASTAÑOS

COLLINS

HAMILTON

OTWAY

STEWART

Albuera

274 m
899 ft

1 KGL

2 KGL

Old bridge

27 CH
21 CH

BRICHE

to Valverde

to Almendralejo

4D

3DG

New bridge

GODINOT

BALLASTEROS

Fords

VL

XXX
V
EXPEDITIONARY FORCE
SOULT

COLBORNE

4D

LARDIZABAL

Woods

ZAYAS

BALLASTEROS

COLE

MYERS

273 m
895 ft

ZAYAS

LARDIZABAL

Chicapierna

HARVEY

to Valverde

Arroyo de Valdesevilla

283 m
928 ft

(Northern Knoll)

LUMLEY

283 m
928 ft

(Southern Knoll)

CG

to Santa Marta

Nogales

PV LD LONG

to Barcarrota

WERLE

LM

GIRARD
V CORPS

Ford

Woods

to Almendral

N

292 m
950 ft

292 m
958 ft

to Torre de Almendral

THE FRENCH FLANK ATTACK 10:00 a.m.

0   0.5 km

0   0.5 mile

The first person to catch actual sight of the second part of the French attack was, however, not the good doctor but a German serving on the staff of General Zayas who had arrived at Albuera by a very circuitous route. Lieutenant Colonel Andreas Daniel Berthold von Schepeler was a Westphalian who began his military service in the Austrian Army in 1797 at the age of seventeen.[55] That first experience and others (including being present on the losing side at Jena) instilled in him a fierce hatred of the French. In 1809, he fought along with the Duke of Brunswick in a vain attempt to free his homeland from the rule of Napoleon's brother Jérôme, then found his way to Spain in order to carry on in exile his personal fight against Napoleon. He had actually faced French troops commanded by Soult once before, in Switzerland in 1799, and had acquired some respect for the French marshal's military talents. That respect caused von Schepeler to believe that the attack on the village might be a diversion so, unlike almost everyone else in the allied high command, he kept his focus on the southern end of the allied position and the high ground that had so worried General Long:

> I was on General Zayas's staff and was eating breakfast when the French began to move and caused all telescopes to focus on the ground before the centre and left of our position ... I believed that he [Soult] would attack our right wing and so watched in that direction and I soon detected the gleam of the bayonets of the advancing enemy columns. When I blurted out 'That is where they are coming from and that is where they will deliver their attack!' all heads turned that way and General Blake came up and ordered me to ride toward the hill on the right.[56]

The soldiers von Schepeler spotted were, of course, the men of the vanguard of the French V Corps, who had become visible to the allies once they passed the crest of the high ground between the Nogales and the Chicapierna and began to descend towards their target ford.

The crossing of any watercourse, no matter how small, is a risky undertaking in the face of a prepared enemy and the precautions taken by Soult to mitigate those risks demonstrate the professionalism of the French command. As soon as the men of V Corps approached the stream, Latour-Maubourg sent the 2nd Hussars and the Vistula Legion Lancers (less the flankers already engaged with the British cavalry) rapidly south along the Almendral road to the ford to protect the advancing troops.[57] These horsemen were joined shortly thereafter by Battalion Chief Supersac of the 40th Line with the combined voltigeurs of the 34th and 40th Line Regiments (probably four companies, one from each battalion present), who crossed the ford in skirmish order to establish an infantry perimeter on the allied side of the stream.[58] The remaining mass of Latour-Maubourg's cavalry then also galloped south away from Albuera, turned west after passing the intended crossing point, climbed up and over the ridge

55. The biographical details concerning Colonel von Schepeler come from Juretschke, 'El Coronel von Schepeler', pp. 229–30.
56. Von Schepeler, *Histoire*, Vol. 3, p. 268. This quote has been changed to the first person voice for narrative effect even though von Schepeler refers to himself as 'the author' in his book. D'Urban, *Report*, p. 25.
57. Latour-Maubourg, Report.
58. The details of Girard's advance are provided by a surgeon attached to the 88th Line in Veilande's brigade. D'Héralde, *Mémoires*, p. 155.

and took up a position in the plain behind it, threatening the much smaller allied cavalry force. Only after all these preliminary moves had been completed did V Corps emerge from cover and head straight for the ford. General Brayer's brigade was in front followed in succession by the second brigade of the first division under General Michel Veilande and the two brigades of Gazan's old second division, now commanded by General Pépin.[59]

Surprise on a Napoleonic battlefield was a relative concept and, with all movement governed by human or equine capabilities, it was nearly impossible for an attacker to shift troops from one location to another in the presence of another army fast enough to prevent a response from the defending force. Thus it was in this case, and as soon as von Schepeler and other staff officers sent word confirming the French advance, Marshal Beresford began making changes in the alignment of his troops that were designed to thwart the new French attack. His most immediate response was to seek out General Blake for a personal conversation and ask him to take some of his Spanish troops and place them across the ridge at a right angle to their initial position so as to block any French attempt to roll up the allied right flank.[60] After Blake took leave of the marshal with the apparent intention of doing exactly what had been requested, Beresford also began to reposition the rest of the allied army. First, he recalled Colborne's brigade from near Albuera and put the whole of the 2nd Division in motion toward the allied right to reinforce the most directly threatened portion of the Spanish position. Next, he ordered General Hamilton's Portuguese division to occupy the ground being quitted by Stewart's men. After that, he re-deployed the 4th Division onto the open ground to the west of the ridge to protect the Valverde road and then sent all the Spanish horsemen, the 3rd Dragoon Guards, half (two squadrons) of the 4th Dragoons and Lefebure's under-strength horse battery even farther south and east to hold a line marked by the course of the Arroyo de Valdesevilla.[61]

It was around this time that General Lumley finally made his appearance on the expected field of battle, having made his way to Albuera via Elvas.[62] Beresford now had an opportunity to activate his plan to supersede General Long in command of the allied cavalry, but he was hesitant to do so with the action already under way. Nearly twenty-two years after the battle, D'Urban claimed some credit for stiffening the marshal's resolve:

> I recollect your reluctance, even then, to displace General Long, which occasioned me to express myself in these words, or words to the same effect[:] 'If you do not, sir, the cavalry will be worse than useless, and perhaps thrown away.'[63]

Whether D'Urban's recollection of how matters unfolded is accurate is questionable, but in any event Beresford finally authorised Lumley to take over and

---

59. D'Héralde, *Mémoires*, p. 154–5. D'Héralde differs from other sources in saying that the attack started at noon, but his recollection of the sequence of events seems accurate.
60. Beresford, *Refutation*, p. 150.
61. The details of Beresford's response are provided by D'Urban, *Report of Operations*, p. 29.
62. According to Long, Lumley did not arrive 'till an hour after the action of the 16th had commenced'. Long, Letter to Le Marchant, 5 June 1811.
63. D'Urban to Beresford, 26 January 1833, quoted in Beresford, *Second Letter*, p. 99.

he rode off to take command of the cavalry from Long. Long was extremely disappointed when Lumley superseded him even though he knew that this command change had been his idea: 'With regard to General Lumley's appointment it certainly arose out of an act [request] of my own.'[64] He seems to have been a genuinely loyal and helpful subordinate to Lumley for the remainder of the day, but Long thereafter never stopped complaining about the indignity of being relieved the midst of a battle:

> [Beresford] in my opinion, rather indelicately, permitted this command to be assumed after the action had commenced, and whilst I was manoeuvring [*sic*] the Troops. *This* I can never forgive.[65]

As a result of these prudent measures, the allies should have been in fine shape to face the French flank attack, but nothing can be taken for granted in combat. Beresford should therefore not have been completely surprised when, some time later, one of Blake's aides rode up and announced that his general had concluded that the principal attack of the French 'was still intended against the village and bridge' and that he had decided to 'suspend' the execution of Beresford's orders pending further clarification from the marshal.[66] British historians (including, in particular, Napier) have charged Blake with arrogance and insubordination in resisting Beresford's orders, particularly since Blake 'positively refused' to comply when the order was reiterated by Hardinge, who had been sent immediately by Beresford to assure the Spaniard that the village was well protected.[67] There is, however, a simpler explanation for Blake's actions – he was genuinely uncertain as to where the French were headed. The French cavalry were certainly committed on the allied right flank, but the French infantry had been disordered by the crossing of the Chicapierna and halted on the allied side of the stream to dress their formation and await the arrival of the last units in the column of march:

> The 1st Division [of V Corps] crossed the stream and formed up on the far bank; but then, to allow time for the 2nd Division to complete its crossing and Latour-Maubourg's cavalry to complete the grand turning movement it had been ordered to make against the enemy right flank, Girard waited close to an hour before giving the order to advance. It was consequently nearly 10 a.m. before the signal to attack was given.[68]

During this delay, the French were formed on a road running from Albuera to Almendral and were even better positioned for a sudden switch back towards Albuera than they were for further off-road movement around the allied right flank. In addition, the French cavalry had already demonstrated the feasibility of rapid movement across the front of the allied position. It was consequently not unreasonable in light of that circumstance for General Blake to believe it would be prudent to wait for the French to begin their next move before deciding the best way to commit his own troops.

64. Long to Brother, 26 June 1811, quoted in McGuffie, *Peninsular Cavalry General*, p. 118.
65. Long to Brother, 22 May 1811, quoted in McGuffie, *Peninsular Cavalry General*, p. 106 (emphasis in original).
66. Beresford, *Refutation*, p. 150.
67. Recollections of Hardinge quoted in W. Napier, *Justification*, p. 26.
68. Bouvier, *Historique de 96e Régiment (ex 21e Léger)*, p. 221.

Beresford reacted to the news relayed by Hardinge by moving immediately to the far right of the allied position to deal personally with Blake. He never did find his Spanish counterpart, but by the time he arrived, the situation had become clarified as the men of V Corps headed south away from Albuera for a short distance, then began to make their way cross-country to take a position on the summit of the ridge. Now that any doubt about the intentions of the French was dispelled, the marshal received immediate and complete cooperation from the three Spanish infantry generals on the spot – Lardizabal, Ballasteros and Zayas.

The execution of Marshal Beresford's plan for a new allied line facing south across the ridge involved more than just a change of direction for a few Spanish battalions. The left brigade of Ballasteros held its position, but his right brigade, the whole of Lardizabal's Division and the whole of Zayas's Division pivoted right on their right-hand units and then moved south *en masse* like a door closing across the ridge in the face of the French. When they were finished, they had created a new line of battle facing south, anchored on the northern knoll and running east from that summit down towards the Chicapierna. The 2nd Battalion of the Spanish Royal Guards under Brigadier Juan Urbina and the 4th Battalion under Colonel Diego Ulloa were placed in line across the summit of the northern knoll, with the 2nd Battalion on the right and the six cannon of José Miranda's artillery of the 5th Army in between. The 2nd Royal Guards was a pre-war unit with a traditional Spanish unit colour, while the 4th was a relatively new unit formed in 1808 that fought under a plain white banner bearing the inspirational words 'For King Ferdinand VII, Conquer or Die'.[69] The Irlanda Regiment (originally a mercenary unit composed exclusively of Irish expatriates fleeing British oppression, but by this time just a relatively ordinary line battalion) and a battalion of the Voluntarios de Navarra were in support on either wing in close column formation.

To the left of the 4th Battalion of Royal Guards was the small detachment of sappers from Zayas's division and then, in succession, the Murcia and Canarias Regiments of Lardizabal and the Barbastro and 1o de Voluntarios de Cataluña Regiments of Ballasteros. All of these were in line, but there were also two regiments (the 2o de León and Pravia) in column located behind Ballasteros's regiments and anchoring the end of the new position closest to the Chicapierna. The four battalions in Zayas's second brigade meanwhile deployed in line as a reserve some distance north of the new position. This new position still did not extend all the way to the southern knoll, but Zayas now made an effort to rectify that situation by sending the light companies of the two Guards battalions and of the Irlanda Regiment under Lieutenant Colonel Ramón Velasco to occupy the 'key' southern knoll before the French arrived.[70] In the end, the confusion relating to redeployment of the right wing probably cost the allies half an hour of preparation, but the new line was nevertheless ready for the French when at last they began to move forward along the ridge.[71]

Girard had in the meanwhile finally brought his leading units up onto the crest of the ridge well south of the new allied position. The formation used by the advancing

69. The exact words (in red) on the flag were 'POR EL REI FERNANDO VII./VENCIR O MORIR./SV QUARTO BATAon DE Rs GUAs España.' See description of Flag No. 21035 in Luis Sorando Muzás, *Banderas, Estandartes y Trofeos del Museo del Ejército 1700–1843 – Catálogo Razonado*, Madrid, 2000.
70. Reports of Zayas, Lardizabal and Ballasteros in Burriel, *Albuhera*, pp. 32–3.
71. D'Urban, *Report of Operations*, p. 30, first note.

French troops of V Corps has always been a subject of great interest to students of Napoleonic tactics in the context of the long-standing discussion of the respective combat merits of lines and columns of troops. The most relevant French sources are all consistent in stating that Girard sent his men forward in columns, although the precise description of the type of column used varies slightly from source to source. Lapène says Girard used *'colonnes serrées par bataillons'* – 'closed columns by battalion'.[72] Soult refers to Girard's *'colonnes d'attaque'* – 'attack columns'.[73] Surgeon d'Héralde of the 88th Line talks about *'colonnes par division'* – 'columns by division' and *'colonnes par peloton'* – 'columns by platoon'.[74] The definitive description, however, is that provided by Brigade General Jean Maransin, one of the commanders involved in the attack.:

> Having arrived at the point of attack [on the crest of the ridge], the V Corps changed direction by a movement of the head of the column to the right; Girard's division marched towards the enemy in attack columns, the second division was 150 paces behind in attack columns by battalion.[75]

Like most terminology relating to Napoleonic tactics, these words and phrases seem very confusing, but in fact they are easy to interpret. When Napoleon changed the basic composition of French battalions in 1808 from nine to six companies, he did not revise the French 1791 Drill Regulations, but he did provide guidance as to how those regulations should be interpreted in light of the new organisational structure:

> Article 7 – When all six companies of a battalion are present, they should march and manoeuvre by division. When the grenadiers and voltigeurs of a battalion are absent, the other companies should always march and manoeuvre by platoon [*peloton*]. Two companies will form a division; each company will form a platoon; [and] each half-company, a section.[76]

In light of Article 7, one can see from Maransin's description that every battalion in V Corps had adopted a column formation that was either two companies wide and three companies deep if all six of the companies were present, or one company wide and four or five companies deep if one or both of the elite companies were missing.[77] The term *serré* (serried) as applied to a column meant that the interval between each of the successive units in the column was minimised, and so from a distance the battalion would have appeared to be almost a solid square of soldiers. A *colonne serré* was consequently sometimes called a *colonne en masse*.

72. Lapène, *Conquête*, p. 156. The anonymous author of the Albuera section in Beauvais, *Victoires et Conquêtes*, uses similar terminology, but that is not surprising since the Appendix to that work acknowledges Lapène's assistance with the text. Beauvais, *Victoires et Conquêtes*, Vol. 20, pp. 239 and 241 and Vol. 25, p. 77.
73. Soult, Unpublished Report.
74. D'Héralde, *Mémoires*, pp. 154 and 155.
75. Maransin, Undated 'Observations' sent by Maransin to Lapène identifying errors made by Lapène in his book. Cambon, *Maransin*, p. 82. See p. 111 *below* for an illustration of this formation.
76. Decree of 18 February 1808 in Napoléon, *Correspondance*, Vol. 16, pp. 338–41 at 339.
77. The 18 February 1808 decree obviously fails to deal with the case where only one of the elite companies was absent. Since a number of basic manoeuvres would not operate correctly unless the battalion had an even number of sub-units, it seems likely a column by platoons was used in that circumstance as well.

Notwithstanding the clarity and consistency in French sources concerning the formation used by the French, an alternate view has held sway since 1909 when Professor Charles Oman disclosed in a lecture that he had discovered a report about Albuera in the French Army Archives that, in his opinion, settled the question once and for all.[78] Oman concluded that this report demonstrated that the French had employed a mixed tactical formation (*ordre mixte*) that combined some battalions in line with other battalions in column:

> At last I found the required information in the Paris archives [at the War Ministry, not the Archives Nationales], in the shape of an anonymous criticism of Soult's operations ... This document says that 'the line of attack was formed by a brigade in column of attack [that is a column formed of four battalions in column of double companies, one battalion behind the other]. To the right and the left the front line was in mixed formation, that is to say, on each side of the central column was a battalion deployed in line, and on each of the two outer sides of the deployed battalions was a battalion or regiment in column, so that at each end the line was composed of a column ready to form square.[79]

All subsequent British authors (including Fortescue and Brigadier B. P. Hughes in his book, *Firepower*) have relied on this information without further inquiry to advance their own treatments and analyses of the battle. Their reliance is certainly understandable given Professor Oman's well-deserved reputation as a careful historian but, in this one case at least, it is misplaced because the document simply does not contain the information described by Oman.[80] It is indeed a post-battle analysis of the action written by someone second-guessing the decisions made by Soult and his generals and it does describe the use of mixed column and line formation by the French. However, the author of the document was using that description to explain hypothetically what Marshal Soult *should have done* to ensure victory, not reporting factually what the French actually did. The text is unambiguous in this regard – the author states in a section entitled 'Projet de la Bataille' that the 'French army was formed in regimental masses [*masses par régiment*] **instead of** [emphasis added] being formed' in the manner described by Oman.[81] As a result of this mistake by Oman, Albuera has long been considered as an exception to the general rule that French armies in the Peninsula always fought in columns. In fact, the battle was not exceptional at all in this regard.

The information about Girard's formation that is available from the French sources is, however, incomplete in one important regard – it says nothing about the way in which the various French battalion columns were aligned in relation to each other.

78. Oman, 'Albuera', p. 58.
79. Oman, *History*, Vol. 4, p. 380.
80. Anonymous, 'Bataille d'Albuera'. Oman never provided a specific citation to this document, but I found it in the SHAT by means of his description of its contents. The only plausible explanation for Oman's misreading of the document is that he was working from an inaccurate translation or excerpt and never had a chance to examine the original.
81. James Arnold correctly concluded in an article that Oman was mistaken about the formation adopted by V Corps, but he did so for the wrong reason, expressing the opinion that the document in the French Army Archives was merely a 'pre-battle order explaining the intended French dispositions to be used'. Arnold, 'Reappraisal', p. 547.

The likeliest possibility is that all the battalions of a single regiment were arrayed one behind the other. It also seems likely that both regiments of a brigade would have been side-by-side with the lower numbered regiment on the right (as a matter of precedence) and with enough room (approximately the width of four companies) between the two regimental columns to allow the individual battalions to deploy into lines if circumstances required. If all that was true at Albuera, and if the generals of V Corps followed the 1808 decree, then Brayer's brigade would have been formed in two regimental columns, each one consisting of two battalions in column arranged one behind the other. Since the light companies of the regiments had been detached as skirmishers, each of these battalion columns would have been one company wide. (See below for a reconstruction of this formation.)

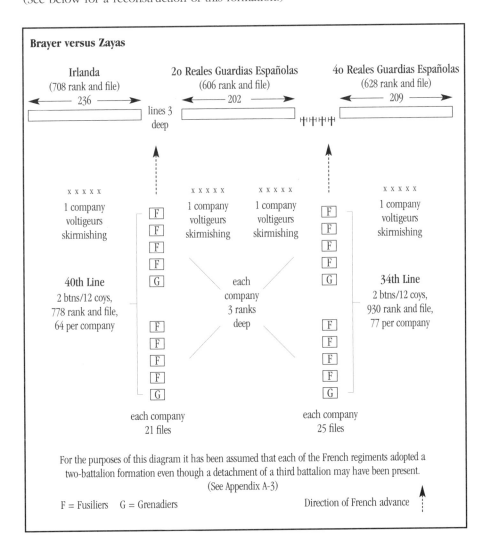

Brayer versus Zayas

Irlanda
(708 rank and file)
← 236 →

2o Reales Guardias Españolas
(606 rank and file)
← 202 →

4o Reales Guardias Españolas
(628 rank and file)
← 209 →

lines 3 deep

x x x x x
1 company voltigeurs skirmishing

x x x x x
1 company voltigeurs skirmishing

x x x x x
1 company voltigeurs skirmishing

x x x x x
1 company voltigeurs skirmishing

40th Line
2 btns/12 coys,
778 rank and file,
64 per company

each company
3 ranks
deep

34th Line
2 btns/12 coys,
930 rank and file,
77 per company

each company
21 files

each company
25 files

For the purposes of this diagram it has been assumed that each of the French regiments adopted a two-battalion formation even though a detachment of a third battalion may have been present.
(See Appendix A-3)

F = Fusiliers   G = Grenadiers

Direction of French advance

As Girard's men started to move north along the ridge they ran into another unanticipated delay – the troops of V Corps were literally stopped in their tracks by a dramatic squall blowing across the battlefield. General Maransin had never before seen such an unusual battlefield situation:

> During this strategic manoeuvre to flank the enemy, a powerful cloudburst with the rain driven by fierce winds forced us to turn our backs towards the enemy and left us unable to take a step for a quarter of an hour, a circumstance that was to have a great influence on the start of the battle.[82]

Surgeon d'Héralde experienced this weather first-hand:

> At this moment, a rain mixed with hail struck our faces and added to the difficulties of our infantrymen who, already wet to the knee from their stream crossings, struggled to reach the crest of the ridge.[83]

This squall is not mentioned specifically in any British memoir or history of the battle, but those sources do mention a 'chilling, and comfortless rain' that occasionally 'fell in torrents' and made the ground 'very heavy'.[84] When the rain finally stopped (probably a little before 11:00 a.m.), the sky was still dark but the prospects of the French were very bright indeed. They had accomplished exactly what Marshal Soult had planned and now had nineteen battalions of veteran infantry astride the allied right flank, well supported by strong forces of artillery and cavalry, and facing as their immediate opponents just a few battalions of the 4th and 5th Spanish Armies. Knowing how many times Spanish regular forces had already been defeated by the French in open combat since the start of the war, including most recently the rout at the Gevora, most of the soldiers present, no matter what their nationality, probably expected that the French would be able to sweep away the Spanish opposition and roll up the allied flank. On this day, however, those expectations were to be unfulfilled.

82. Cambon, *Maransin*, p. 82.
83. D'Héralde, *Mémoires*, p. 155.
84. 'chilling, and comfortless rain' – Sherer, *Recollections*, p. 158; '... torrents' – Close, *Diary*, p. 31; 'very heavy' – Clarke Narrative in Groves, *The 66th Regiment*, pp. 51–4, at 52.

Chapter 6

The Spaniards Hold Firm

The Spanish armies that fought at Albuera were in many ways legitimate objects of scorn and derision because of the pretensions of their generals, the incompetence of their field officers, the unpromising quality of their men and equipment and their miserable record of combat failure. General Long was probably not exaggerating when he commented on the appearance of the troops of the 5th Army:

> All the Spanish troops I see are of a most despicable description; neither clothed, paid, disciplined or even organised, and but precariously fed. They resemble more a motley banditti than Battalions of Infantry, and their great Generals have scarcely more than lieutenant colonel's commands. The Spanish Government appears to be doing nothing in a military point of view.[1]

Paradoxically, however, the Spanish soldiers were possessed of an abiding dignity and nobility derived from their astonishing perseverance in the face of so much adversity. Neither their allies nor their enemies had much love for the Spanish troops, but they had to acknowledge that the stubborn determination of the Spaniards to fight on, no matter how many times, and how badly, they were defeated, was nearly unprecedented in the annals of European warfare. The cause of that determination is not hard to find – the Spaniards had an unshakable faith in the righteousness of their cause of ridding Spain of the French invaders. It was their monarchy that had been overthrown, their country that had been occupied, their towns that were being pillaged and their people who were being killed.

At Albuera, that sort of determination changed the course of the battle and gave rise to an unusual (and, at least from a French perspective, unthinkable) result. Whether it was a matter of the units involved or of the officers who led them, or a combination of the two factors, on this day, instead of being thrown into confusion by French skirmishers, the Spanish were able to slow the French advance with effective skirmishing of their own. On this day, instead of running, the Spanish units positioned across the ridge held their ground with unparalleled tenacity. On this day, instead of wavering in the face of punishing musketry, the Spanish units involved met volley with volley in the first dramatic musketry duel of the day. It was a day of which the Spanish Army and nation could be justly proud.

The unexpected performance of the Spanish began, ironically, with the failure of

---

1. Long to Brother, 24 April 1811, McGuffie, *Peninsular General*, pp. 95–7, at 96.

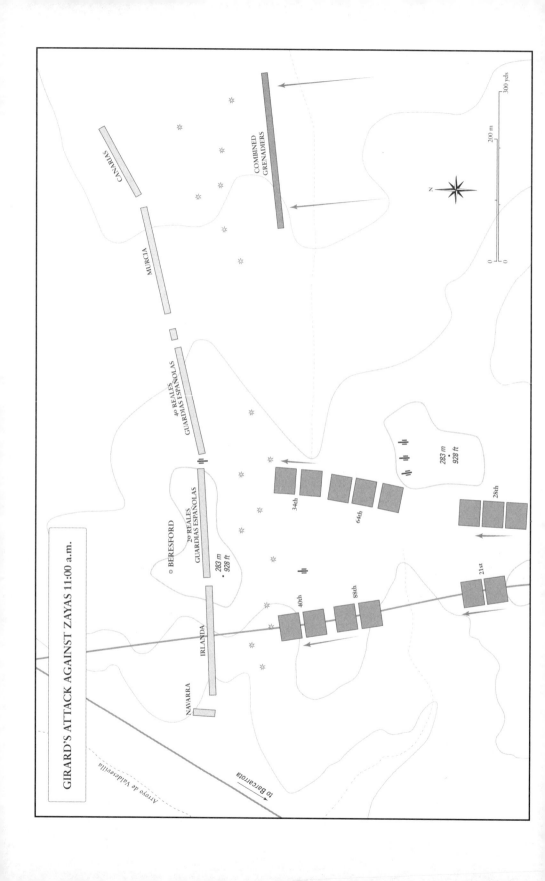

GIRARD'S ATTACK AGAINST ZAYAS 11:00 a.m.

the allies to defend the southern knoll with anything more than three companies of skirmishers. These troops drove off the French voltigeurs at bayonet point, but when the two regimental columns of General Brayer's brigade arrived on the scene, screaming their war cries of *'En Avant!'* – 'Forward!' and *'Vive l'Empereur!'* – 'Long Live the Emperor!', the Spaniards were quickly pushed back on their new line by sheer weight of numbers.[2] Girard, however, was puzzled by the ease with which he had conquered such a tactically significant position, and his puzzlement was increased by the amount of troop activity he could observe in the centre of the allied position. Like all French generals, he took pride in his *coup d'oeil*, his ability to assess a military situation at a single glance and decide the best course of action, but this time his ability failed him. He misinterpreted these facts as signs of an imminent allied retreat and decided that the best way to exploit that situation was to push his men forward as fast as possible:

> This mistaken conclusion, which was shared by the commander-in-chief, made Girard decide that he did not need to deploy his columns before chasing after an enemy who had abandoned their first position ... He therefore committed the fatal indiscretion of ordering the V Corps forward still formed in close columns [*'encore serré en masse'*] and assaulting the enemy in that formation.[3]

The words 'fatal indiscretion' were obviously written with the benefit of hindsight, but it is important to understand the practical implication of Girard's decision. Before he made that choice, there were three basic tactical options he could have used to defeat the Spaniards in front of him: superior firepower, superior force or a combination of the two. By opting to forego deployment into line, he eliminated the first and third possibilities and committed instead to having the outcome of his attack depend on his troops closing with their enemies so that the solidity of the column mass could make itself felt.

There was nothing inherently wrong with Girard's decision to use a column formation for his attack, but to use it correctly, a commander had to commit to advancing at full speed no matter what the cost because, once a column stopped in combat, its firepower deficiencies constituted a fatal weakness. That reality was the reason why the men in a French column would customarily advance with their muskets tucked under their right arms (*'l'arme au bras'*) so that they would not be tempted to stop and fire. When the first division descended into the narrow dip between the southern and northern summits, it needed to maintain its momentum until it made physical contact with the Spanish line. There was nothing about the terrain that could halt the French, so the only thing that stood in their way was the fire discipline and fire accuracy of their opponents. A first volley delivered at too great a distance would have little stopping power. A volley delivered at killing distance by soldiers who failed to load or aim properly would also fail to halt the attack. Everything, then, depended on how the Spaniards on the new front line performed in a critical five-minute span as Girard's veterans pounded up the slope towards the Spanish position. To the surprise of everyone (even, perhaps, including themselves), the Spaniards performed superbly, with particular assistance from the cannon in their

2. Report of Zayas in Burriel, *Albuhera*, p. 33.
3. Lapène, *Conquête*, p.160.

midst.[4] The heads of the French columns were hit by an intense fusillade at short range, not only from Zayas's men directly in front of them, but also from the troops of Ballesteros and Lardizabal shooting at the column's right flank. The Spanish artillery also provided critical close-range support despite a brief hiatus when an ammunition caisson was blown up by a French 'grenade'.[5]

This was a decisive moment of the battle. If the French could have covered the last yards to the Spanish line and engaged them at bayonet point, the charge might still have succeeded. Rather than continuing on, however, Girard stopped his men and ordered them to deploy. This might have been a good decision before the columns closed to killing range, but it was a disastrous one at this point. The columns lost their all-important momentum and yet were also unable to reply with their muskets as they sought to form line. Girard's fatal mistake was not that he attacked in column formation, but rather that he tried to change his form of attack at the last minute. Spanish volleys tore into the massed French formation and, within minutes, 400 men of Brayer's two regiments had been killed or wounded.[6] More importantly, French officers fell like ninepins:

> The Spanish artillery ... pounded the ranks of the 1st Division, which found itself in critical danger. General Brayer had his left leg broken by a gun shot. His aide-de-camp Carlier was killed. General Girard's horse was killed and he himself was wounded. His first aide-de-camp [Duroc-]Mesclops was mortally wounded, as was his engineer officer, Captain Andouan [Andoucaud]. Chief of staff Hudry had his horse killed. The two commandants [majors] of the 40th Line, Bonneau [Gaspard-Bonnot] and Supersaque [Supersac], Grenadier Captains Lamare [Delamarre] of the 40th Line, [and] Combarieux [Combarlieu] of the 34th ... were all already killed or mortally wounded.[7]

General Gazan rode to the scene hoping he might be able to bring some order out of the chaos, but he too was hit and forced to leave the field before he could make any impact.[8]

General Veilande, commanding Girard's second brigade, was known as a superb manoeuvrer, but he had limited scope here and apparently did nothing more than move his two regimental columns into the spaces alongside Brayer's beleaguered battalions. This gave the French a significant increase in the number of muskets able to fire, but this development could not overcome the inertia created by the appalling casualties the troops were suffering. Having lost their momentum, the French became unwilling participants in an unequal musketry duel. Veilande's 64th and the 88th Line Regiments were mowed down by the Spanish musketry just as Brayer's men had been before them – Battalion Chief Astruc of the 64th was killed while two other battalion chiefs of the 64th were wounded along with Colonel François-Joseph-Alexandre Letourneur and Battalion Chief Dubarry of the 88th.[9] Other officer casualties included:

4. Report of Burriel in Burriel, *Albuhera*, p. 17.
5. Report of Colonel Miranda, *Ibid.*, p. 49.
6. Dessirier, *Historique du 34e Régiment*, p. 111.
7. D'Héralde, *Mémoires*, p. 156. The names in brackets are the names of these officers as spelled in Martinien's list of French officer casualties.
8. Gazan, Letter to Berthier, 19 May 1811
9. Astruc had been a prisoner of war in England, but escaped in 1809 with the help of a young Englishwoman who accompanied him back to France and married him. Brooke, 'Prisoner', p. 193.

... [Captains] Dautrement and Leconte of the 88th Line, Sous-Lieutenant Hapecher [Hubscher] (the nephew of Marshal Lefebvre) of the 88th, brave Laurin [Captain Lorrain] of the 64th Line, officer of the Legion of Honour, and Grenadier Captain Chevaillon [Chevailleau] of the same regiment.[10]

Veilande's men also tried to deploy their now useless columns into lines so as to bring more muskets to bear on the enemy, but they had even less room for manoeuvre than the battalions of Brayer's brigade and had also suffered significant officer casualties. The men in the columns fought back as best they could against the enemy and a growing sense of disaster:

> Not a shot missed our column, still formed in serried masses, and we were only able to reply with the insufficient musketry of our first two ranks. Our soldiers were falling left and right without being able to defend themselves and the survivors fell prey to the darkest discouragement.[11]

Standing still, the French columns were no match for the Spanish line. Girard needed to regroup, and he needed to do it quickly. Unfortunately, before he could do anything, he and his men received another unpleasant surprise. Having outflanked the allied position, the French now found themselves assailed on their left flank by a newly-arrived brigade of British infantry.

General Stewart's part in the allied response to the French flank attack was to move his 2nd Division to a new position supporting the reconfigured right flank of the allied army. He was slow getting started because he wanted Colborne's brigade to lead the advance and he had to wait while that formation returned to the ridge from its earlier mission supporting the troops near the village. Once that was accomplished, he formed all three brigades into open company columns for the move to the right flank to support the Spaniards.[12] This formation was similar to the columns used by Girard's troops, but was only one company wide and had longer intervals between the companies in each battalion column. Once commenced, the movement was hampered by the same heavy rain that had hit the French and by the muddy state of the ground. Despite these hindrances, Lieutenant John Clarke of the 66th recalled that the whole division moved 'at the double'.[13]

The British troops travelled along the track on the reverse slope of the original allied position and came under fire much sooner than they expected. If any proof was needed of the importance of the southern knoll, it was provided by this circumstance because the occupation of that elevated ground gave the French artillery a clear view of the rear of the allied position and they opened fire as soon as the advancing infantry came into roundshot range. The accuracy of their gunnery can be judged by the remarks of Ensign Benjamin Hobhouse of the 57th Foot: 'During our advance in column the incessant and well-directed fire of the [F]rench artillery mowed down many of our poor fellows.'[14] Twenty-one-year-old Lieutenant Edward Close of the

---

10. D'Héralde, *Mémoires*, p. 156. The names in brackets are the names of these officers as spelled in Martinien's list of French officer casualties.
11. Lapène, *Conquête*, p.160.
12. Close, *Diary*, p. 31.
13. Clarke, Narrative in Groves, *The 66th Regiment*, p. 52.
14. Hobhouse, Letter to Father, 17 May 1811. This document was published in *The Times* in 1915 following its discovery in the Royal Archives by Sir John Fortescue, *(continued on p. 118)*

2nd/48th Foot agreed: 'A very heavy cannonading was scattering destruction amongst us at this time.'[15] Lieutenant Sherer of the 34th reported that the regiments of the third brigade suffered less than the others from this cause, but saw the results of the earlier passage of their comrades:

> I remember well, as we moved down in column, shot and shell flew over and through it in quick succession; we sustained little injury from either, but a captain of the Twenty-Ninth had been dreadfully lacerated by a ball, and lay directly in our path. We passed close to him, and he knew us all; and the heart-rending tone in which he called to us for water, or to kill him, I shall never forget. He lay alone, and we were in motion and could give him no succour.[16]

Stewart's lead brigade arrived on the extreme right flank of the allied position at approximately 11:00 a.m., 'just as the French were driving in the Spanish sharp shooters'.[17] Some sources say that Beresford had intended for Stewart to deploy all his brigades in a defensive posture behind the Spanish troops, but there is no evidence that he gave orders to that effect. Left to make his own choices, Stewart realised that the left flank of the French troops battling the Spaniards was completely exposed and that he had an unusual chance to wreak havoc on the enemy. He could not resist the opportunity. Napier says pejoratively that Stewart's 'boiling courage overlaid his judgment', but that view is far too harsh.[18] General Stewart was an experienced professional soldier who made a fast tactical decision based on reasonable risk and reward calculations. He consequently directed the regiments of Colborne's brigade to continue moving south in columns past the right flank of the improvised Spanish line of resistance while Hoghton's brigade took position directly behind the Spaniards and Abercromby's brigade came up on Hoghton's left.

As Colborne's men moved past the edge of the Spanish position, they immediately flanked the French troops engaged on the ridge, but they could not fire while on the march, so they needed to perform one additional manoeuvre before they could exploit their advantage. An attack in line would obviously bring maximum firepower to bear on the French flank, but the brigade itself was now the last unit on the allied right flank (barring a few British and Spanish cavalry regiments) and therefore now had an exposed flank of its own. Since the French had a significant force of cavalry in the vicinity, it would have been prudent for the British to have made some provision for protecting that flank before they advanced to the attack. One source suggests that Colborne proposed to take such action but that he was overruled by General Stewart:

(continued from p. 117) the Royal Librarian at Windsor Castle. Mr Fortescue (as he then was) was unaware that a large portion of the letter had previously been published anonymously in *The Times* on 24 June 1811, p. 3, col. B.

15. Close, *Diary*, p. 31.

16. Sherer, *Recollections*, p. 159. The wounded officer was John Humphrey, the only captain of the 29th killed at the battle. The regimental history of the 29th adds the detail that the cannon ball that struck Humphrey also carried away the limbs of two men behind him. The same source also states that, after he was wounded, Humphrey continued to encourage his company to perform its duty well '"for the honour of old Ireland", of which country he and many of his men were natives'. Everard, *History of the 29th*, p. 321.

17. Close, *Diary*, p. 31.

18. W. Napier, *History*, Vol. 3, pp. 542–3.

It has been understood that Colonel Colbourn [*sic*] wished to move to the attack with the two flank regiments in quarter distance columns, and the two centre ones in line; but Sir William Stewart, anxious to show a large front, was deploying the whole in line.[19]

Colborne himself never made a public statement about this issue, but one sentence in a private letter he wrote after the battle seems to support this interpretation of events: 'This has been a most unfortunate affair for me, although I had nothing to do with the arrangement, but merely obeyed the orders of General Stewart.'[20] A hitherto unknown description of the battle written by Sir James Wilson, the commander of the 1st/48th Foot (serving in Stewart's 2nd Brigade), sheds even more light on the case:

> The confusion and rout of the 1st Brigade appears to have originated in some little misunderstanding between Lt. Col. Colbourne [*sic*] of the 66th Regt. who commanded it and General Steuart [*sic*]. The latter being in charge of the Division would not have been supposed to interfere in the immediate formation of his brigade. He however directed it himself, . . . contrary to the wishes and suggestion of Col. Colbourne, who is a most excellent officer.[21]

Such interference is very understandable in context given that General Stewart himself had been the commander of the 1st Brigade until General Hill went on sick leave at the start of the year causing Stewart, as the senior brigadier, to move up to command of the whole division. Since Colborne had never commanded this or any brigade in combat, Stewart apparently felt the need to become personally involved in tactical arrangements that he might have been willing to leave to the discretion of a more experienced subordinate. Stewart likewise never provided an explicit explanation of how the 1st Brigade came to attack the French in line without some protection for its exposed right flank, but his after-action report to Beresford suggests that he was aware of the risks of the line formation but simply made a miscalculation concerning the amount of advance warning he would have of any threat to the brigade's flank:

> The form of the hill up which the brigade was led to the charge, and the obscurity occasioned by the smoke of musketry, and by a heavy fall of rain, prevented the enemy's cavalry from being seen, or their charge sufficiently early resisted.[22]

Lieutenant George Crompton of the 66th Foot was more blunt in his apportionment of blame in this regard: 'General Stewart . . . marched us wildly to this desperate attack without any support.'[23]

19. Leslie, *Military Journal*, p. 220. The author of *Further Strictures* also believes that this was the case: 'I apprehend that Col. Colborne requested Gen. Stewart to let him retain the right wing of his regiment in column.' Anonymous, *Further Strictures*, p. 159.
20. Colborne, Letter to Rev. Duke Yonge, 18 May 1811, in Smith, *Life of Seaton*, pp. 160–1.
21. Wilson, Journal. The author is grateful to Ms Page Life for sharing a typescript of the journal and to Ms Joy Austria of the Newberry Library in Chicago for verifying the text of the typescript against the original.
22. Stewart, *Cumloden Papers*, p. 88.
23. Crompton, Letter to Mother, 18 May 1811.

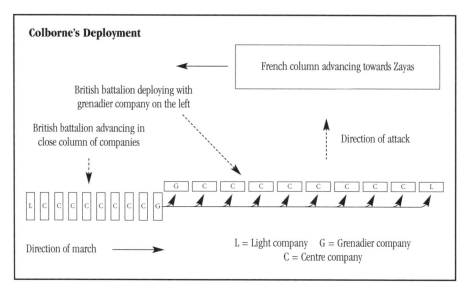

Colborne's Deployment

French column advancing towards Zayas

British battalion deploying with grenadier company on the left

British battalion advancing in close column of companies

Direction of attack

Direction of march

L = Light company   G = Grenadier company
C = Centre company

Once the decision to attack in line was made, the deployment of each battalion column of companies into a line facing toward the French should have been a relatively simple matter because, with one exception, the British units were advancing 'right in front', which means that each column was led by the relevant battalion's grenadier company (which normally occupied the right wing in any line of battle).[24] As a result, if the lead (grenadier) company in each battalion had continued to march south, after the intervals between companies had expanded to full company size, only a quarter wheel (90-degree turn) would have been needed to bring each company in each south-facing column neatly into a line of battle parallel to the old line of advance but now facing east towards the French (*see above*). However, the precise orders given by Stewart instead required the Buffs (3rd Foot) – and presumably the other battalions – to form the other companies in line to the right of its grenadier company, thus reversing the normal order of battle. This was a routine manoeuvre for the 95th Rifles that Stewart had once commanded, but it was a novel and confusing one for the line battalions from which it was now expected:

> ... what did my kind patron, Sir William Stewart, order them [the Buffs] to do? They were in open column of companies right in front, and it was found necessary at once to deploy into line, which Sir William with his light 95th had been accustomed to do on any company: he orders them, therefore, to deploy on the Grenadiers; by this the right would become the left, what in common parlance is termed 'clubbed'; and while he was doing this, he kept advancing the Grenadiers. It is impossible to imagine a battalion in a more helpless position.[25]

On top of this difficulty, the British encountered two immediate additional complications. First, the 3rd and 2nd/48th Regiments started to deploy before they had

24. Close, *Diary*, p. 31.
25. H. Smith, *The Autobiography of Lieutenant General Sir Harry Smith*, p. 278.

moved sufficiently far south to leave space for the full deployment of the two following battalions. What actually happened as a result is described in detail by Lieutenant Edward Close of the 2nd/48th:

> Our brigade began to form line, the Buffs on the right, 2nd Battalion 48th next, and the 66th Grenadiers being all that could be said to be formed – in line they were not, our left and rear companies being in the act of forming – and the 66th moving in echellon [sic] to form. Before the 31st Regiment, which was the last of our brigade, could open out, we were bayonet to bayonet with the enemy, and the hostile armies were met to decide the fate of many, if not of the day.[26]

Second, the 66th Foot was formed wrong-way round from a tactical point of view and had to conduct an unusual manoeuvre to put things right:

> When near the point on which we were to form, it was perceived that we were marching rear rank in front; we countermarched, on the march, under a tremendous cannonade, and I can safely say that the movement was never better performed by the 66th on its own parade ground.[27]

Despite these problems, the attack by Colborne's brigade was soon under way and it seems to have had three phases. First, the battalions exchanged a few volleys with the French. Next, they charged with the bayonet. Third, they regrouped and attacked again. The exact site of the attack is difficult to discern from individual accounts because of the many inconsistent descriptions of terrain and elevation they contain. However, if one assumes that the line held by Zayas was never pushed off its original position on the northern knoll, then the most logical follow-on conclusion is that Colborne hit the French while they were advancing along the ridge between the northern knoll and the southern knoll on which the French had deployed their artillery.

The British flank attack subjected Girard's already battered division to a demoralising crossfire. The French units targeted by Colborne's regiments cannot be identified with certainty, but they would have been the left-hand units of V Corps' columns (perhaps the battalions of the 40th and 88th and 100th Line Regiments based on the severity of their casualtiues).[28] There was nothing in the French drill regulations that would cover the situation in which these units now found themselves, but the British found that the French were somehow nimble enough to improvise a quick change of front so that they could defend themselves against the unexpected onslaught:

> On gaining the summit of the hill we discovered several very heavy columns of French troops ready to receive us. The British line deployed, halted, and fired two rounds; the heads of the French columns returned the fire three deep, the front rank kneeling.[29]

One British officer even thought that the French had the initial advantage in the ensuing fight:

26. Close, *Diary*, p. 31.
27. Clarke Narrative in Groves, *The 66th Regiment*, p. 52.
28. General Maransin specifically mentions the 40th Line being forced back by an attack at approximately this stage of the action. Cambon, *Maransin*, p. 82.
29. Brooke, 'Prisoner', p. 177.

We found the enemy, all Grenadiers, kneeling [in] several ranks, and pouring in a dreadful fire up [*sic*] the hill, for they had formed on the one side before we could effect a similar purpose on the other.[30]

This fire-fight was brief but intense. Lieutenant Robert Brown Dobbin of the Light Company of the 66th reported that he had never seen:

... the French fight so well as they did on this occasion. We were often firing at not more than ten yards distance before we came to the charge, and that for two or three minutes together.[31]

Captain Conway Benning's horse went down, but he extricated himself and immediately retook his place in the line. Benning himself was subsequently hit a total of three times, but he was able to remain on his feet and refused to leave the scene of the action.[32] Lieutenant Dobbin had the odd experience of noticing and surviving an aimed shot from an enemy musket:

A Frenchman made a snap at me when I was in Front, and not five yards distance, but his piece missed fire, and he was taken down in a moment by a man of ye [my] company named Boland.

Dobbin also recalled later that his own servant fell by his side while the lieutenant was 'clapping him on his shoulders for his gallant behaviour'.

Observing the fighting from afar, Lieutenant Charles Madden of the 4th Dragoons was struck by its intensity:

The French being strongly supported stood firm, and a more awful scene was never witnessed; it was a perfect carnage on both sides, bayonet against bayonet for nearly half an hour.[33]

The delivery of heavy and accurate musket fire against the enemy was undeniably the most salient characteristic of British tactics during the Peninsular War and it had certainly been achieved by the British flank attack. However, it was also well understood that firepower alone was usually insufficient to ensure a decisive victory. What was needed to achieve that result was a coupling of firepower with an actual advance by the British forces that could drive the enemy physically from their position on the field. In this case, according to Major William Brooke, the field commander of the 2nd/48th, it was General Stewart himself who organised the second step in the sequence:

Finding these [French] columns were not to be shaken by fire, the three leading battalions of the brigade prepared to charge with the bayonet, by order of Major General the Hon. William Stewart, who led them on in person to the attack in the most gallant manner.[34]

30. Close, *Diary*, p. 31.
31. Dobbin, Letter to Uncle, 23 May 1811.
32. The three superficial wounds Captain Benning received before his fatal one are mentioned in an undated note appended to Dobbin, Letter to Uncle.
33. Madden, 'Diary', p. 517.
34. Brooke, 'Prisoner', p. 177.

Further details of the charge are provided by Lieutenant Close, who relates that it even involved that rarest of all Napoleonic battlefield events, bayonet combat:

> Two or three shots were fired by our regiment [the 2nd/48th], when, irregularly formed as we were, we charged. The left column of the French became opposed to the left wing of the Buffs and our right. Their centre column faced our two left companies and the 66th Grenadiers. Their right column, which had escaped our notice, found its way to our rear. The French left column was broken, and was the only part of their troops which stood the charge. They remained as if powerless until they were bayoneted by our men. The rear companies fled. The centre column ... however, gave way as soon as we charged.[35]

This description is potentially confusing until one realises that Lieutenant Close is consistently describing the positions of each of the combatant units from its own perspective, so the French units on the 'left' were facing the 'right' flank of the British.

Major Brooke noted that the French officers did not give up as quickly as their men: 'We could see the officers trying to beat back the men with the flats of their swords.'[36]

The cost of the fire-fight and the charge was high. Captain Gordon of the 3rd Foot mentions that the ranks of his battalion, being on the right of the British advance, 'were thinned by cannon shot' coming from the French artillery posted to the south.[37] Lieutenant Close states that the 2nd/48th was 'literally cut to pieces' and that afterwards it 'stood on the hill like extended light infantry, [with] many of the intervals filled up by Spanish sharp shooters'.[38] The 66th suffered heavy casualties as well. Thrice-wounded Captain Benning led his battalion's charge, but he was soon hit again, this time by 'a Ball in his right side, which killed him on the spot'.[39] His men went on, however, despite fierce resistance from the French:

> ... when we did charge, the French never moved until we came Bayonet to Bayonet, and as soon as we dispersed one column another appeared which we served as the former.[40]

The British halted briefly at this juncture to consolidate their success and found themselves threatened on two fronts. First, the right-hand French column noticed by Lieutenant Close was working its way into the rear of the brigade in the interval between the 66th and the 31st. Second, the troops the British had routed in their first charge rallied and returned to the fight: 'Those of the French left and centre columns that had fled and laid down their arms, resumed the fight and commenced a murderous fire.'[41] Somehow or other, the conclusion was reached that the best course of action was another charge. This order left Lieutenant Crompton of the 66th with serious concerns about the propriety of that conclusion:

35. Close, *Diary*, pp. 31–2.
36. Brooke, 'Prisoner', pp. 177–8.
37. Gordon, 'Extract of a Letter.'
38. Close, *Diary*, p. 32.
39. Dobbin, Letter to Uncle.
40. Dobbin, Letter to Uncle.
41. Close, *Diary*, p. 32.

We fought them until we were hardly a Regiment. The Commanding Officer [Captain Benning] was shot dead, and the two officers carrying the Colours close by my side received their mortal wounds. In this shattered state our Brigade moved forward to the charge. Madness alone would dictate such a thing.[42]

It would be only a few minutes before Lieutenant Crompton received irrefutable proof that his concerns were well-founded.

42. Crompton, Letter to Mother, 18 May 1811.

Chapter 7

The Annihilation of Colborne's Brigade

The Battle of Albuera could well have ended at this point. The French tactical surprise of outflanking the allied right had been met by stubborn resistance on the part of the Spanish troops and now General Stewart had surprised the French in turn with his bold counter-attack that threatened to drive them from the field. Marshal Soult was already aware that Blake's force had arrived during the night and that his army was significantly outnumbered. The better part of valour could certainly have justified a withdrawal, or at least a regrouping, of his forces. Indeed, that might have been the logical next step for the French but for the occurrence of still one more surprise – a cavalry charge that obliterated Colborne's brigade and restored the initiative to the French.

The French Army of the Napoleonic era was blessed with many talented cavalry leaders. In addition to Joachim Murat, the charismatic inn-keeper's son turned marshal and king, and the less colourful, but more professional, Marshal Jean-Baptiste Bessières, the French cavalry boasted an astonishing array of gifted brigade and division generals such as Antoine Lasalle, Louis-Pierre Montbrun, the Colbert brothers (Auguste, Alphonse and Édouard), François-Étienne Kellerman, Édouard-Jean-Baptiste Milhaud, Étienne Nansouty, Jean-Joseph-Ange d'Hautpoul and Jean-Louis-Brigitte d'Espagne. In such company, there was at first little that a middle-aged ex-émigré cavalryman such as Latour-Maubourg could do to gain particular recognition in his chosen profession, despite the fact that he had already been an officer under the Bourbon regime. Nevertheless, by performing ably under the emperor's eye at Austerlitz, Jena and Friedland, he enjoyed a steady rise to the rank of division general and when he was assigned to the armies in Spain, he made the most of his chances in the early Peninsular campaigns. He had certainly achieved only mediocre results thus far in the spring of 1811, with the combats of Campo Mayor and Los Santos detracting from his prior record of success. After his short stint as interim commander of V Corps, he had reverted to the more familiar role of commander of the whole of the French cavalry for the campaign leading to Albuera.

For the first hours of the battle, Latour-Maubourg and his troopers had played a passive role, screening the gap in the French position between the troops attacking the village and those executing the manoeuvre around the allied right. As the French

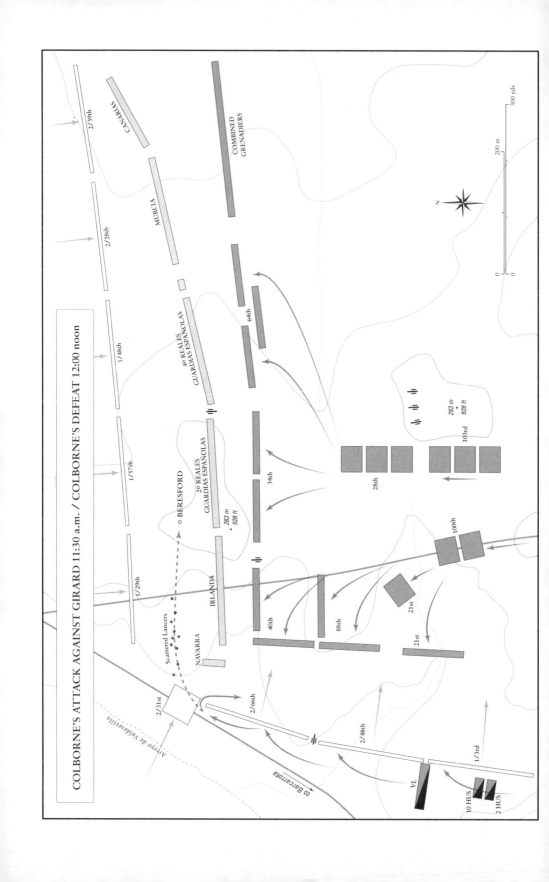

COLBORNE'S ATTACK AGAINST GIRARD 11:30 a.m. / COLBORNE'S DEFEAT 12:00 noon

flank attack began in earnest, Latour-Maubourg shifted most of his horsemen to the extreme left of the new French position so they could protect his infantry from attacks by the massed English and Spanish cavalry under Lumley. But this post had offensive as well as defensive possibilities, as the allies were soon to discover. As Stewart pushed Colborne's brigade up the ridge, Latour-Maubourg must have been amazed at what he saw – enemy infantry in line formation presenting their flank and rear to a force of French cavalry in the middle of a major battle. Recognition of the opportunity and the decision to seize it must have been nearly simultaneous events. A few hurried commands sent Captain Jakub Kierzkowski, a staff officer with V Corps, galloping off with orders for an immediate attack.[1]

The first recipient of Latour-Maubourg's orders was Colonel Jan Konopka, the commander of the Lancers of the Vistula Legion. Like so many Polish officers in Napoleon's forces, Konopka had fought in the hopeless campaign preceding Poland's final partition in 1795. In 1796, he joined the French Army as a volunteer and passed very quickly through the lower ranks until he was appointed as a captain in the first Polish Legion formed by the French in 1797. He was promoted to command of the Vistula Lancers in 1807, so by 1811 he and the 576 officers and men waiting behind him knew each other very well. They also knew that this was a perfect situation for use of the special weapon that was carried by half of the men in the regiment.

The situation called for a larger force than the Poles alone could muster, so Latour-Maubourg's commands also went out to other cavalry regiments. There is still some uncertainty as to exactly which regiments these may have been. Based on Latour-Maubourg's own account, one of them was undoubtedly the 305-strong 2nd (or Chamborant) Hussars commanded by Colonel Gilbert-Julien Vinot (b. 1772). Vinot was another true son of the Revolution, having volunteered for service in 1792 when he was twenty years of age, but his early Republican sentiments apparently did not preclude him from becoming an enthusiastic supporter of Napoleon. His service in Italy, Egypt, Germany, Poland and Spain had been rewarded both with the colonelcy of the 2nd, one of the premier regiments of light cavalry in the Grand Army, and the title of 'baron of the empire' borne by so many members of Napoleon's military aristocracy. Latour-Maubourg's action report also confirms the involvement of the 10th Hussars under Colonel François-Marie Laval, another veteran who had worked his way up from the ranks during the Wars of the Revolution. However, given that the 10th suffered comparatively few casualties in the course of the entire action, it may be that it served only as a reserve for the other units. Other sources variously state that the 4th, 20th and 26th Dragoons were also participants in the charge, but none of those regiments is specifically mentioned by Latour-Maubourg. One reason for confusion about the exact number and identity of the units involved in the attack may be the fact that Latour-Maubourg's personal escort, composed of dragoons from the 1st, 2nd, 4th, 9th, 14th and 26th Regiments, is known to have joined in the action.[2]

As in all cavalry charges of this period, the horsemen would have started off at a brisk walk and then progressed to a faster, but still relatively unthreatening trot. The

---

1. This identity of the officer who carried the orders for the charge comes from Kierzkowski's 1836 *Pamietniki* [Memoirs], discussed in Kujawski, *Z Bojow Polskich*, p. 291.
2. The escort was commanded by Lieutenant Gaudelet of the 2nd Dragoons, an 'outstanding officer', who was killed in the charge. Latour-Maubourg, Report.

Lancers of the Vistula were the lead unit, with the 1st Squadron of the Lancers under Squadron Chief Kostanecki in front.[3] Since French cavalry commanders understood that the essential element of a truly successful cavalry charge was control of the fury being unleashed, one or both of the hussar regiments would have followed in reserve, available to exploit new situations as they arose or to respond to any setback to the primary effort. Given the favourable nature of the ground for cavalry action, the last stages of the charge would probably have been conducted precisely in accordance with the prescriptions of the French cavalry regulations. At approximately 150 yards from the enemy formation, Colonel Konopka would have given the order for the Lancers to accelerate to a gallop for maximum shock effect and perhaps 50 yards after that (and only seconds from impact) the trumpeters would have begun to sound the charge and the lancers would have lowered their weapons to killing position.

Amazingly, the British almost averted disaster at the last second because of the vigilance of two alert staff officers on the extreme right flank of the British advance, Captain Robert Waller of the 103rd Foot, the assistant quartermaster-general of the 2nd Division, and Lieutenant Charles Bayley of the 31st Foot, the division's deputy assistant adjutant-general. Despite the poor visibility on the battlefield, they spotted the French threat while it was still some distance off: 'The fact is that though the atmosphere was dark, these lancers were observed in time to have been opposed.'[4] Bayley unfortunately concluded that the threat could be ignored because the lancers would be intercepted by the allied cavalry: 'We saw them coming on, but expected our cavalry would have assisted us and continued our charge.'[5] Waller, however, recognised the danger and initiated a counter-measure that consisted of having the Buffs throw back their right wing 'to cover the rear of the Brigade'.[6] This was a 'dangerous manoeuvre when near the enemy', but it is just possible that the well-drilled British infantry could have pulled it off. This formation would not have been as effective as a proper defensive square, but any solid front presented by unbroken infantry to attacking horsemen was likely to increase the brigade's prospects for survival because horses have as much of a sense of self-preservation as men and will tend to shy off from an encounter with a wall of humanity, especially when it bristles with bayonets. Unfortunately, these prospects were never realised due to a combination of bad judgment and bad luck

The bad judgment was provided by a senior field officer of the Buffs who chose the wrong moment to raise a pedantic point about the proper chain of command for such an order:

> The Buffs being then in line were requested by Capt. Waller of the Quarter Master General's Department to refuse their right and receive the charge of cavalry. This was communicated to Major [Henry] King, who not being in command of the Regt. very injudiciously and imprudently hesitated in instantly making this movement with the right wing, replying that Col. [William] Stewart [no relation to the general] commanded the Regt.[7]

3. Kujawski, *Z Bojow Polskich*, p. 270.
4. Anonymous, *Further Strictures*, p. 162.
5. Bayley, Letter to Miss Sally Smith.
6. Clarke's Narrative, in Groves, *The 66th Regiment*, p. 52.
7. Wilson, Journal.

Even this hesitation might not have been fatal, however, but for some final confusion about the identity of the attacking force. As the right wing of the regiment prepared to meet the approaching cavalry onslaught with a volley, 'a cry was raised that they [the lancers] were Spaniards', and the British soldiers held their fire.[8] This was not an irrational mistake since the British troops had never encountered French lancers before and the horsemen were coming from the same general area as was occupied by the allied cavalry, but on top of all the other factors at work it was disastrous. Untouched by musketry and unopposed by a solid formation, the French crashed into, over and through the Buffs and burst into the unprotected flank and rear areas of Colborne's brigade.

There is no record of the thoughts which went through the minds of the first British soldiers to recognise their mistake about the identity of the lancers or of the curses which must have come to their lips, but as professional soldiers, and as human beings, they would have known the worst kind of battlefield disaster was striking them. They had already endured artillery fire, infantry charges and hand-to-hand infantry combat, and now enemy cavalry had caught them unawares. If discipline is the glue which makes a mob into an efficient fighting force, fear is the solvent which can reverse the transformation. The men of Colborne's brigade seem to have had three primary responses to their predicament. Many, perhaps most, fled for their lives, with or without their weapons. Others banded together in clusters with bayonets facing outward, hoping to achieve a semblance of the solidity of the prescribed square formation by a sheer mass of bodies. A last group simply surrendered, attempting to avoid their extraordinary peril by formally declaring themselves vanquished. The stories of all these groups expand our knowledge of the human reality represented by the dry recitation of action in a Napoleonic battle.

The Buffs took the brunt of the charge and were, for all immediate practical purposes, annihilated as a fighting force: 'The soldiers lost all presence of mind, broke, and fled in every direction, the French cutting them down and showing no quarter at the moment.'[9] On the morning of the 16th, the Buffs had a strength of approximately 27 officers and 728 other ranks. By the end of the day the battalion mustered only some 85 unwounded men (including 7 officers), with most of the others having disappeared in the few harrowing minutes of the French charge. The term 'shock tactics' merely hints at the stupendous physical and psychological mayhem wreaked by a galloping half ton of horseflesh bearing a hostile, heavily armed rider into a mass of men on foot. The experience of one anonymous private of the Buffs is probably representative of what happened to many of his comrades:

> I was knocked down by a horseman with his lance, which luckily did me no serious injury. In getting up I received a lance in my hip, and shortly after another in my knee, which slightly grazed me. I then rose, when a [French] soldier hurried me to the rear a few yards, striking me on the side of my head with his lance. He left, and soon another came up, who would have killed me had not a French officer came [*sic*] up, and giving the fellow a blow told the

8. Beresford, Official Report; Anonymous, *Further Strictures*, p. 162. According to a 'British private soldier', the Poles encouraged this crucial mistake of identity by 'shouting in Spanish, "Vivan los Ingleses!" [and] "Vivan los amigos de España!"' Fraser, *The Soldiers Whom Wellington Led*, p. 151.

9. Wilson, Journal.

fellow to spare the English [prisoners], and to go on and do his duty against
... [the rest] of my unfortunate comrades. This officer conducted me to the rear
of the French lines and here, the sight that met the eye was dreadful! Men dead,
where the column had stood, heaped on each other; the wounded crying out
for assistance and human blood flowing down the hill! I came to where the
baggage was where I found a vast number of my own regiment, with a good
proportion of officers prisoners, like myself; numbers of them desparately [sic]
wounded even after they were prisoners! Here then I offered up my most fervent
thanks to Heaven for having escaped so [relatively] safe.[10]

Captain William Stephens had been shot in the arm during the attack on the French
infantry and so, when the Poles arrived, his company was actually commanded by
Ensign Edward Price Thomas, a boy not yet sixteen years old, because there were no
other officers present. Thomas was an orphan who had been raised by his aunt and
her husband, who happened to be a surgeon attached to the Buffs, so he was basically
a child of the regiment.[11] Despite his youth, he displayed remarkable composure in
the face of disaster. The last moments of Thomas's brief military career were
recounted by Captain Stephens in a letter written to the lad's uncle four days after the
battle:

I cannot refrain from tears while I relate the determined bravery of your gallant
little subaltern, who fell on the 16th instant, covered with glory; and it must in
some measure alleviate the grief I know you will feel at his loss, to know that
he fell like a hero. He rallied my company after I was wounded and taken
prisoner, crying out 'Rally on me, men, I will be your pivot.' Such glorious
conduct must surely meet its reward in that world where all troubles cease, and
all grief is at an end.[12]

Any rally inspired by the ensign was short-lived, however, as the French cavalry
overwhelmed the remains of Stephens's company. Ensign Thomas miraculously
survived the dispersal of his men, but his luck gave out when he ran to help an officer
defending the regimental colour: 'The colours he died in protecting, it appears he took
possession of at the moment the officer who held them was killed.'[13] Captain Vincent
Konopka, the brother of the Legion's colonel, was apparently the individual who rode
off in triumph with the colours.[14]

The standards or colours of a Napoleonic military unit were the physical symbols
of that unit's traditions and honour, so fights over flags were extraordinarily intense.
In the British Army, each regiment carried two colours into combat. Each one of these
was a large (6 feet 6 inches wide by 6 feet tall) near-square of painted silk attached
by nails to a 9-foot 10-inch staff topped with a spearhead finial. (They were so

10. Anonymous, 'Letter from a Private in the 3rd Regiment of Foot', p. 240.
11. The family history of Ensign Thomas is provided by his aunt in Matthews, Letter to Londonderry,
    which was published in an Appendix to the third edition of the second volume of Londonderry's
    Narrative, but was omitted from later editions.
12. Letter of Captain Stephens to Dr Matthews, Olivenza, 20 May 1811, quoted in Matthews, Letter to
    Londonderry, *Narrative*, Vol. 2, p. 318.
13. Matthews, Letter to Londonderry, in Londonderry, *Narrative*, Vol. 2, p. 318. Based on circumstantial
    evidence, the officer Thomas replaced was probably Ensign William Chadwick.
14. Kujawski, *Z Bojów Polskich*, pp. 270–1.

unwieldy to manage that they were usually kept partially furled in all but the calmest wind conditions.) One was the king's colour (the familiar Union flag with a regimental crest in the centre) and one was the regimental colour (a flag the colour of the regimental facings with the Union flag in the upper canton nearest the staff and, once again, the regimental crest in the centre). Each colour was carried by an officer (usually an ensign) accompanied by NCOs serving as the colour guard. Since the capture of an enemy's flag was almost certain to lead to rewards and advancement for the captor, while the loss of one's own standard was a crushing blow to unit pride and morale, it is not surprising to find that the other colour of the Buffs also became a focal point for the attacking cavalry and gave rise to a spectacular example of what one senior British officer quite accurately called the 'incomprehensible valour' of the men fighting at Albuera.[15]

The first bearer of the king's colour was Ensign Charles Adam Walsh, who was also only fifteen years old (although he had already been with the unit for over a year).[16] As Walsh and the colour party struggled with the attacking lancers, Lieutenant Matthew Latham went to the ensign's aid. Most traditional accounts of Latham's actions depict him successfully taking possession of the colours and their staff from Walsh and then gallantly resisting his attackers, albeit with drastic personal consequences:

> He was attacked by several French Hussars, one of whom seizing the flag-staff, and rising in his stirrup, aimed a stroke at the head of the gallant Latham, which failed in cutting him down, but which sadly mutilated him, severing one side of the face and nose; he still however struggled with the dragoon [*sic*], and exclaimed, 'I will surrender it only with my life.' A second sabre struck severing his left arm and hand, in which he held the staff, from his body. The brave fellow, however, then seized the staff with his right hand, throwing away his sword, and continued to struggle with his opponents, now increased in number, when ultimately thrown down, trampled upon and pierced by the spears of the Polish lancers, his last effort was to tear the flag from the staff as he thus lay prostrate, and to thrust it partly into the breast of his jacket.[17]

A second version of these events, recorded only four years after the battle by Joseph Carpue, the doctor who treated Latham's disfigurement in 1815, is more prosaic (and therefore perhaps more accurate), but no less astonishing:

> ... in attempting to seize the colour [from Ensign Walsh], he [Latham] lost an arm by a sabre-cut. Still persevering, he tore the colour from the staff, but not before

---

15. Sir Charles Stewart, Letter, 22 May 1811. See Appendix E for more details about the British colours captured during the battle.
16. Manuscript account of Walsh's life, Archive Item No. 2001-11-56:3, NAM.
17. This account of Latham's ordeal comes from a little-known 12 April 1840 letter published in the *United Service Gazette*, No. 382, p. 3, col. 1. The author, John Morrison, was a doctor who joined the 3rd Foot after Albuera and who cared for Latham after his restorative operations, and he wrote to correct inaccuracies in the account of Albuera contained in the first history of the regiment, Richard Cannon's *Historical Record of the Third Regiment of Foot*, London, 1839. Cannon responded by writing a supplement to his history that incorporates much of Morrison's letter, but still has some mistakes. Cannon, 'Memorandum Relating to ... Albuera'. This memorandum is the source of most modern versions of the Latham story.

he received five wounds, one of which took off part of his cheek and nose. One of the lancers charged through the others, and, with his lance, hit him with such force in the groin, as to throw him to the distance of some yards, almost in a state of insensibility, but still with the colour in his possession.[18]

Whichever version of the ordeal is correct, the key point is that Latham at the end managed to preserve much of the colour from the enemy. Ensign Walsh was wounded and taken prisoner while Latham was fighting for his life and when he returned to the regiment he corroborated the main points of Latham's story. This corroboration must have included the otherwise implausible utterance attributed to Latham ('I will surrender it only with my life!'), since those words were eventually immortalised on a special medal Latham received from the regiment to commemorate his heroism.[19]

The case of Lieutenant Latham is extraordinary, but few of the Buffs' officers fared well that day. Captain Arthur Gordon catalogued their tribulations in a letter he wrote after the battle:

> I shall endeavour, however, to give you some facts respecting the First Battalion of the Buffs: Captain [Richard] Burke is killed, Captain [Charles] Cameron is shot in the neck, wounded in the breast with a pike, and a prisoner; Captain [Henry] Marley was wounded twice in the body with a pike, badly; Captain [William] Stevens [*sic*] was shot in the arm, was a prisoner, and made his escape; Lieutenant [Richard] Woods had his leg shot off by a cannon ball; Lieutenant Latham's hand is shot off, also part of his nose and cheek; Lieutenant [William] Juxon is wounded in the thigh with a pike; Lieutenant [Richard] Hooper shot through the shoulder; Lieutenant [Richard] Houghton has received a severe sabre cut on the hand, and through the skull; Lieutenant [Arthur] Herbert is dead; Ensigns [William] Chadwick and [Edward] Thomas are also dead; Lieutenants [Preise] O'Donnell and [William] Tetlow, with Ensign [Charles] Walsh, were wounded and made prisoners, they have since escaped and joined ... I was stabbed at the time with a pike in the breast, in the back, and elsewhere, and the enemy's cavalry galloped over me.[20]

Ironically, Major King, one of the most significant contributors to the disaster, escaped unscathed, as did Lieutenant Colonel Stewart who, according to Major Wilson, 'in the confusion took himself to the rear and left his Regt. to its fate'.[21]

The next unit to be overrun was the 2nd Battalion of the 48th (or Northamptonshire) Regiment of Foot. The 48th theoretically had more time to react to the attack but, once again, the British were unable to muster any organised resistance.

---

18. Carpue, *Account*, pp. 91–2.
19. When Parliament gave thanks for Beresford's victory early in June, Latham's heroism had yet to be recognised and these words were incorrectly attributed to Ensign Thomas by the Chancellor of the Exchequer. Hansard, *Parliamentary Debates*, Vol. XX, col. 524; see also *The Times*, 8 June 1811, p. 3, col. B.
20. Gordon, "Extract of a letter, 20 May 1811'. The identification of Captain Gordon as the author of this letter is the work of C. R. B. Knight: 'It is almost beyond doubt that the writer of this letter was Captain Arthur Gordon who was wounded during the course of the day.' Knight, *The Buffs*, p. 343, n. 1. Knight, however, never explained why he was so certain of his attribution.
21. Wilson, *Journal*.

Twenty-one-year-old Lieutenant Edward Close of the Light Company of the 2nd/48th later wrote in his diary:

> ... their cavalry ... rode through us in every direction, cutting down the few that remained on their legs. There was nothing left for it but to run. In my flight I was knocked down by some fugitive like myself, who, I suppose, was struck by a shot.[22]

In fairness to Lieutenant Close, it should be noted that he may not have had a weapon during this crucial period.

> At Albuera my sword, or rather sabre – for it was a Spanish weapon – was broken in two, in what way I never could tell – whether it was done by a shot or from the tread of the Cavalry I never could decide.[23]

The destruction of the battalion was almost complete: 'Our muster on coming out of the field [at the end of the action] was, including non-commissioned officers and drummers, just twenty-five [men] and six officers.'[24] Many scattered survivors quickly returned to the ranks and improved these figures, but the number of casualties was nevertheless appalling. One officer of the 48th wrote afterwards: 'I have been in several general actions, but never witnessed such a dreadful slaughter.'[25] The extreme casualties inflicted by the French may have been caused in part by the difficulty they had in distinguishing between those soldiers who were still resisting or fleeing capture and those who had already given up the fight and were trying to surrender. It also seems, however, that the proverbial 'heat of battle' led to some despicable behaviour such as that experienced by Major Brooke of the 2nd/48th Foot. In rare contrast to the many boy officers in the British ranks, Brooke was 'a grey haired old man of 66 years of age' (who had begun his military career in 1778) when the French horsemen rode down his unit:

> Part of the victorious French cavalry were Polish Lancers[;] from the conduct of this regiment on the field of action I believe many of them to have been intoxicated, as they rode over the wounded, barbarously darting their lances into them. Several unfortunate prisoners were killed in this manner, while being led from the field to the rear of the enemy's lines. I was an instance of their inhumanity: after having been most severely wounded in the head, and plundered of everything that I had about me, I was being led as a prisoner between two French infantry soldiers, when one of these Lancers rode up, and deliberately cut me down. Then, taking the skirts of my regimental coat, he endeavoured to pull it over my head. Not satisfied with this brutality, the wretch tried by every means in his power to make his horse trample on me, by dragging me along the ground and wheeling his horse over my body. But the beast, more merciful than the rider, absolutely refused to comply with his master's wishes, and carefully avoided putting his foot on me![26]

22. Close, *Diary*, p. 31.   23. *Ibid.*, p. 36.   24. *Ibid.*, p. 33.

25. Anonymous, Letter 'From an Officer', 19 May 1811. Internal evidence indicates that the writer was an officer of the 48th.

26. Brooke, 'Prisoner', p. 178–9. Brooke's description and age can be found in Woods, 'Second Prisoner', p. 7.

Major Brooke was injured and upset from the loss of his sword and a family heirloom watch, but he soon discovered that the French were capable of kindness as well as cruelty:

> From this miserable situation I was rescued by two French infantry soldiers, who with a dragoon guarded me to the rear. This last man had the kindness to carry me over the river Albuera, which from my exhausted state I could not have forded on foot.[27]

Lieutenant William Woods had succeeded to command of his company only a short time before the charge when his commander, Captain H. F. Wood, was shot through the thigh. The young lieutenant found his unit dispersed before he could take any action to organise resistance:

> At this time more than half the brigade were either killed or wounded, and I found myself left with only four men of the company, surrounded on all sides. In a minute after I was struck smartly on the right leg by a ball which had rebounded from the ground, and the next minute a number of hussars came upon us and rode me and the four men all down together. Before I could get up, a French Officer came [and], I called out in French 'I am an English Officer.' The scoundrel made no reply, but spurred his horse violently to get him over me. He was followed by several Dragoons, and I was trampled upon and bruised in several places, but not half so severely as I expected. I got up as soon as I could, and was cut at by two Dragoons in all directions. I evaded many cuts and expected to have got away, as some of our Dragoons were coming up the hill, when someone gave me a blow on the back of the neck that brought me down again.[28]

Woods was immediately set upon and robbed by the two dragoons, but his life was spared by the intercession of another, more sympathetic French officer who arranged for the captive to be escorted to the French lines.

There are no surviving accounts that describe in detail the fate of the colours of the 2nd/48th, but the total loss of twenty-three officers killed, captured or wounded (including four ensigns) suggest that they must have been defended as obstinately as those of the other regiments of Colborne's brigade.[29] In all the battles for British colours, there is a certain irony derived from the fact that the sergeants of the colour guards were all armed with long, spear-tipped pikes similar to the lances of the attacking French cavalry, but that similarity in weaponry could not offset the advantage of the attacking horsemen. In the end, both colours of the 2nd/48th were captured, with the king's colour being carried off by Maréchal des Logis (Sergeant) Michel-François-Dion d'Aumont of the 10th Hussars.[30]

The wave of French cavalry next engulfed the 2nd/66th (or Berkshire) Regiment of Foot, with much the same result. The battalion had been seriously weakened by its fire-fight with the French infantry and the death of Captain Benning had left it

---

27. Brooke, 'Prisoner', p. 178–9.
28. Woods, 'Second Prisoner', p. 6.
29. Gurney, *History of the Northamptonshire Regiment*, p. 364.
30. Close, *Diary*, p. 32; Lamathière, *Pantheon de la Légion d'Honneur*, Vol. 1, pp. 425–6. This feat won a cross of the Legion of Honour for d'Aumont.

leaderless. When the 'Polanders' appeared, 'armed with lances which they handled with great dexterity', the unit's cohesion disintegrated.[31] Of this moment, Lieutenant George Crompton wrote, 'It was then that our men began to waver, and for the first time (and God knows I hope the last) I saw the backs of English soldiers turned upon the French.'[32]

Some of the British soldiers nonetheless continued to resist. Nineteen-year-old Lieutenant John Clarke later remembered:

> ... at this moment a crowd of Polish Lancers and Chasseurs-à-Cheval swept along the rear of the Brigade; our men now ran into groups of six or eight, to do as best as they could; the officers snatched up muskets and joined them, determined to sell their lives dearly. Quarter was not asked, and rarely given. Poor Colonel [*sic*] Waller, of the Quarter-Master-General's staff, was cut down close to me; he put up his hands asking for quarter, but the ruffian cut his fingers off. My Ensign, [James] Hay, was run through the lungs by a lance which came out of his back; he fell, but got up again. The Lancer delivered another thrust, the lance striking Hay's breast-bone; down he went, and the Pole rolled over in the mud beside him ... The Lancers had been promised a doubloon each, if they could break the British line. In the melee, when mixed up with the Lancers, Chasseurs-à-Cheval and French infantry, I came into collision with a Lancer, and being knocked over was taken prisoner; an officer ordered me to be conducted to the rear.[33]

Lieutenant Stepney St George of the 2nd/66th Foot also had a brush with capture, but escaped due to some very peculiar circumstances. St George was severely wounded early in the action and rendered unconscious. A Polish lancer, 'probably attracted by his bright scarlet coat and gold epaulettes (for he [St George], having plenty of private means, was always well-dressed)', tried to drag him off by his collar into captivity. The lancer was shot dead, and his blood trickling down revived St George, who crawled back to the British lines.[34]

Given the breakdown of discipline, it is not surprising that the French captured both colours of the battalion from the soldiers who carried them after the original bearers were killed in the musketry duel. A stunned Lieutenant Crompton wrote to his mother about this development:

> The worst of the story I have not related. Our Colours were taken. I told you before [that] two Ensigns were shot under them; two Sergeants shared the same fate. A Lieutenant seized a musket to defend them and he was shot to the heart; what could be done against cavalry? General Stewart ... praised rather than censured our conduct, but I should think the malicious World will take hold of it with scandal in their mouths.[35]

31. Dobbin, Letter to Uncle, 23 May 1811.
32. Crompton, Letter to Mother, 18 May 1811. Crompton was so upset by the disaster that he described himself in the letter as 'A miserable Lieutenant of the unfortunate 66th Regt.'
33. Clarke Narrative in Groves, *The 66th Regiment*, pp. 53–4.
34. L'Estrange, *Recollections*, p. 194. The author of these recollections was the nephew of Guy Carleton L'Estrange, the commander of the 31st at Albuera.
35. Crompton, Letter to Mother, 18 May 1811.

Lieutenant Robert Brown Dobbin thought the casualties amongst the colour guards were even higher than those reported by Lieutenant Crompton: 'I am sorry to say that the French got our colours, but not until we had two officers killed, two wounded, and nine sergeants killed and wounded, defending them.'[36]

General Stewart, Colonel Colborne and the divisional and brigade staffs were somewhere near the 2nd/66th Foot when the cavalry charge occurred, which makes sense both because that unit was in the middle of the brigade formation and because it was Colborne's regiment. These officers were mounted, but that did not prevent them from sharing the tribulations of their men. According to Lieutenant Dixon of the 48th, acting as orderly adjutant to General Stewart, the general responded to the disaster by ordering his staff to scatter: 'And at this moment, the General said, "It is of no use gentlemen, we must make the best of our way."' Dixon galloped away and managed to outrun some pursuing French cavalrymen:

> Mr. Dixon was then closely pursued by two of the enemy's dragoons to the left of the Fusilier brigade (of Cole's Division); his poor animal, though having received his death wound, leaped a drain at the left of the fusiliers and by that means escaped, and the two dragoons fell into the hands of the fusiliers.[37]

Lieutenant Bayley, serving on Stewart's staff, related that the general and his entourage were surrounded by the enemy cavalry and that:

> General Stewart, myself & . . . Captain Waller, our Qr. Master Gen'l (who was cut down) actually cut our way through them . . . My poor General Stewart was wounded twice, in the foot & breast.[38]

Bayley himself had some close calls, but emerged unscathed. As he reported emotionally to his fiancée,

> Thank God, my ever dearest Sally, once more your Charles has been spared . . . [although] [m]y horse was shot in the head & a ball lodged in the hind part of the saddle & one passed through my coat.

Colborne's only remark about his own adventures was the terse statement that 'I did not receive any injury personally, although in the hands of the Poles for some minutes.'[39]

Captain Andrew Cleeves and four of the six guns of his company of King's German Legion artillery were also near the 66th, probably in the interval between that battalion and the 31st. In any event, as the Berkshires scattered before the French cavalry, they ran through the battery and prevented Cleeves from immediately moving his weapons. As the Lancers arrived on the scene, however, the sheer mass of the company's guns and horse teams, plus the stubborn resistance of men such as Gunner Friedrich Grass, who battled the enemy cavalrymen with a hand-spike, bought time for Sergeants Wilhelm Hebecker and Friedrich Bussman to limber up the two cannon farthest from the onslaught.[40] Their efforts would have been for naught, however,

36. Dobbin, Letter to Uncle, 23 May 1811.
37. Manuscript records of the 48th quoted in Gurney, *History of the Northamptonshire Regiment*, p. 149.
38. Bayley, Letter to Miss Sally Smith.
39. Colborne, Letter to Yonge, 18 May 1811, in Smith, *Life of Lord Seaton*, p. 161.
40. Beamish, *History of the KGL*, Vol. 1, p. 338–9; Vigors, *Hanoverian Guelphic Medal*, Entry 617.

without the ingenuity of yet another courageous and quick-thinking non-commissioned officer whose actions were described later by Captain Cleeves himself:

> [The French] turned us, and cut and piked the gunners of the right division down. The left division limbered up, and both guns would have been saved; but the shaft horses of the right gun were wounded, and came down, and the leading driver of the left gun got shot from his horse. Corporal Henry [Heinrich] Fincke had presence of mind enough to quit his horse, to replace the driver, and then galloped boldly through the enemy's cavalry; his own horse, which ran alongside of him, secured him from the enemy's cuts and saved the gun, which I immediately made join the fight again. At this moment I was made prisoner, but had the good luck to escape unhurt. Two guns were nearly immediately retaken; but the howitzer was carried off. Lieutenant Blumenbach was taken and wounded with the left division; Lieutenant Thiele and myself were taken with the right; the former badly wounded by the Polish lancers.[41]

The howitzer was taken by the 2nd French Hussars.[42] The French were unable to carry off the other two guns because equipment train personnel and camp followers who swarmed onto the field in the wake of the charge cut the harnesses of the surviving draught horses and quickly led them to the rear as valuable prizes.[43]

The phenomenal success of the French charge posed a serious dilemma for General Lumley, the commander of the allied cavalry on the right flank. He was certainly aware that the most important strategic task for his mixed Anglo-Spanish force was to observe and contain Latour-Maubourg's cavalry: 'Had their cavalry, which was three to one of ours, charged round our right flank, which they might have done, and so came in our rere [sic], the day was lost.'[44] On the other hand, despite the clouds and smoke of battle, he could see from his position the plight of Colborne's brigade and knew that he ought to take some positive steps to stop the charge in progress. The compromise action chosen by Lumley was to send a small force of only four squadrons to Colborne's rescue. Two of these were Spanish, led by Lieutenant William Light, the British liaison officer to the Spanish cavalry, while the other two were the squadrons forming the right division of the 4th Dragoons under Major Burgh Leighton. The results of the intervention were decidedly mixed.

First, in the words of Lieutenant Light, the Spaniards 'did not execute the order exactly as could be wished':

> After our brigade of infantry, first engaged, were repulsed, I was desired by General [sic] D'Urban to tell the Count de Penne-Villemur to charge the lancers, and we all started, as I thought, to do things well; but when within a few paces of the enemy the whole pulled up, and there was no getting them further; and in a few moments after I was left alone to run the gauntlet as well as I could.[45]

41. Beamish, *History of the KGL*, Vol. 1, pp. 385–6.
42. Latour-Maubourg, Report, p. 5. This howitzer was recaptured by the British at Seville in 1812. An Eyewitness, 'The Attack Upon Soult's Rear-Guard', p. 91.
43. Lapène, *Conquête*, pp. 167–8.
44. Madden, 'Diary', p. 517.
45. The first quote comes from Light's diary reproduced in Dutton, *Founder of a City*, p. 54; the second comes from a letter written by Light that is reproduced in W. Napier, *History*, Vol. 3, p. 640.

Second, although the 4th Dragoons certainly charged home, the cost for them was high as they faced lancers in combat for the first time. In particular, it seems that the pennons of the Lancers were indeed effective in distracting the British riders and their mounts:

> The charge of our right wing was made against a brigade of Polish cavalry, very large men, well-mounted; the front rank [was] armed with long spears, with flags on them, which they flourish about, so as to frighten our horses, and thence either pulled our men off their horses or ran them through. They were perfect barbarians, and gave no quarter when they could possibly avoid [it]. We had ... two captains [Carlisle Spedding and John Phillips, the two squadron commanders] and one lieutenant taken and one captain and one lieutenant severely wounded, with a great proportion of men and horses killed and wounded.[46]

According to Captain Jean-Étienne Pernet of the French 5th Horse Artillery Regiment, the allied horsemen did temporarily manage to drive back one of the French hussar regiments, but were taken in the flank by some French dragoons and driven off in turn.[47] Captain Poitiers, the commander of the elite company of the 2nd Hussars, claimed to have killed three British dragoons himself, but received in return a sabre cut to his jaw.[48]

The counter-charge initiated by Lumley was effective in one sense, however, since it created a diversion sufficient to allow many British soldiers, Colonel Colborne among them, to free themselves from captivity. Lieutenant Clarke of the 66th was one such lucky escapee:

> Presently a charge was made by our Dragoon Guards [sic] in which I liberated myself, and ran to join the Fusilier Brigade at the foot of the hill. When I got close to the 7th regiment, they knelt down to receive cavalry, and I threw myself down to avoid their fire[.] I got up, and passing through the regiment met Lieutenant [James] Anderson carrying a colour. He said, 'I thought, my dear fellow, you must have been riddled, it was only [your] presence of mind [that] saved you.' I went a few paces to the rear, and fell exhausted.[49]

Lieutenant Close of the 2nd/48th was another man saved by the advance of friendly horsemen:

> Whilst on the ground I was ridden over by a number of Lancers, one of whom passing close to me was about to save me the trouble of recording this event, when a Spanish Dragoon rode up to him and struck him with his sabre, which brought him over his horses [sic] head. I then got up and ran again.[50]

46. Madden, 'Diary', p. 519. This quotation provides further proof that the pennons of the lancers contributed noticeably to their battlefield success against other cavalry.
47. Pernet, 'Journal', in Remy & Rey, *Général Bourgeat*, p. 100.
48. D'Espinchal, *Souvenirs Militaires*, Vol. 2, p. 29. Poitiers was reputed to be one of the best light cavalry officers in the French Army, but his advancement had been limited by 'an unfortunate passion for drink'.
49. Clarke Narrative in Groves, *The 66th Regiment*, pp. 53–4.
50. Close, *Diary*, p. 31.

By this point, the French cavalry regiments were undoubtedly in some disarray, with units intermingled and horses and men starting to show the effects of exertion, but they had still not met sufficient resistance to halt the momentum of their charge. That circumstance was to change as they bore down on the 2nd/31st Foot. As mentioned earlier, the 31st had not been able to deploy because it was the last unit in the line formed by Stewart and it had instead advanced in some type of column formation. When the enemy cavalry arrived, Major L'Estrange was able to form the unit into a square by means of an 'impromptu manoeuvre' of his own devising, which may have simply involved closing the intervals between sections of the column and having the side files face outward. Although its details have not been recorded for posterity, his formation was enshrined in regimental tradition as the 'Albuera Square' and practised regularly until 1856.[51] An anecdote concerning Maurice Quill, one of the assistant surgeons of the regiment and an Irishman with an army-wide reputation for self-deprecating humour, suggests that the mood in the square was not entirely sombre despite the danger posed by the attacking horsemen:

> A mass of the enemy's cavalry, including a regiment of Polish lancers, prepared to charge the 31st. Colonel [L'Estrange] ordered the regiment to form square, in the centre of which he discovered Maurice, shaking from head to foot with well-dissembled terror. 'This is no place for you, Mr. Maurice,' said [L'Estrange] ... 'By Jove, I was just thinking so, colonel,' replied the droll ... Finding it impossible to break the square, the enemy's cavalry retired with great loss, when, ordering the regiment to deploy, 'Fall in,' said the colonel; 'Fall out,' said Maurice, and scampered off; but hearing that a captain of the regiment was severely wounded, he returned into the fire, and dressed him. He had just finished this operation when a twelve-pound shot struck the ground near Maurice and his patient, and covered them with earth. 'By Jove, there is more where that came from,' said Quill, and again took to his heels.[52]

General Stewart's official report states flatly that the 2nd/31st was not actually attacked by the French cavalry, which is certainly wrong, but it is easy to imagine that the French horsemen may have moved on quickly to seek easier targets when they found the 2nd/31st prepared for resistance. Stewart goes on, however, to praise the battalion's overall conduct:

> The 31st Regiment, the left of the brigade, not having been attacked by the cavalry, retained, by its steadiness and spirit, the summit of the hill which had been gained by the rest of the brigade. The conduct of this small corps (it had only 320 firelocks in action) under the command of Major L'Estrange was so particularly remarked by me during the whole of the action that I feel it to be my duty to state the same in the warmest terms.[53]

The full impetus of the charge had dissipated by this time, but some thirty or forty of the lancers who were 'drunk with victory' (and encouraged by the possibility that

51. Pearse, *History of the 31st Foot*, Vol. II, p. 122.
52. G. R. Cutter, *Biographical Sketches of Eccentric Characters*, Boston, nd, p. 132. The anecdote inexplicably names Duckworth as the colonel of the 31st, although that is clearly wrong.
53. Stewart, *Cumloden Papers*, p. 89.

they had only Spanish troops left to contend with) continued on and penetrated into the heart of the allied army rather than rallying on their reserves.[54] This small and reckless group of individuals should not have posed a significant threat to anyone but, amazingly, by riding into the space between the Spaniards on the northern summit and the British troops who had advanced to support them, they came very close to inflicting two significant blows to the allied army. First, they exposed Zayas's division to a critical peril by causing the British to open fire on the rear of their Spanish allies and, second, they engaged Marshal Beresford and some other senior Spanish and Portuguese officers in hand-to-hand combat that could have inflicted serious casualties on the allied high command.

While Colborne's brigade was being destroyed, the two other brigades of the 2nd Division had halted a short distance behind the Spanish troops resisting Girard's attack and immediately formed into a line composed of (from British right to left): the 29th, 1st/57th, 1st/48th, 2nd/28th, 2nd/39th and 2nd/34th. They were still under fire from the French artillery that had harassed them during their march to the right of the allied position, but this did not prevent them from carrying out the necessary deployment. One eyewitness account concerning Lieutenant Colonel Inglis of the 57th brings home forcefully the point that the commander of each unit had very real practical tasks to perform in order to ensure that his men were formed in proper battle order:

> Sir William, close to and immediately in front of the colours, was dressing the line on the centre; he had finished with the right wing, and having turned to the left, was cooly scanning the men as they formed, when a shot brought his charger to the ground, leaving his master erect on his feet. At that critical moment, I observed his unchanged countenance, and that while he extricated his feet from the stirrup, he never once turned his eye from the line he was continuing to perfect, and not until that was completed did he cast a glance on the remains of his noble steed.[55]

Incidents such as these played an important role in steadying and inspiring the troops as their time of combat trial drew near – if their officers disdained danger, then so could they. Officers of all nations understood this psychological reality and even sought out opportunities to demonstrate their disdain for danger by acting calmly under fire. Then as now, it was desirable to be 'cool' under fire in the sense conveyed by the following incident involving the commander of the 2nd Brigade that was witnessed by Lieutenant Leslie:

> When in our first position Major General [Daniel] Houghton [sic] was on horseback in front of the line, in a green frock coat, which he had put on in the hurry of turning out; some time afterwards his servant rode up to him with his red uniform-coat, [and] he immediately, without dismounting, stripped off the green and put on the red one; and it may be said that this public display of our national colours and of British coolness, actually was done under a salute of French artillery, as they were cannonading us at the time.[56]

54. The estimate of the number of French cavalrymen involved in this phase of the attack comes from Burriel, *Albuhera*, p. 19. The characterisation of their behaviour is from von Schepeler, *Histoire*, Vol. 3, p. 273.

55. A Die Hard, 'Letter', p. 107.   56. Leslie, *Military Journal*, p. 224,

Front-line leadership of this sort was also important because even with close supervision from the senior officers, tactical evolutions could and did go wrong. For instance, Colonel Inglis (referring to himself in the third person) recalled many years later that his efforts to form the 57th in line of battle were initially unsuccessful:

> Colonel Inglis ... was ... at that moment wholly employed in the act of correcting an error that had occurred in the formation of the centre of his regiment; in which, owing to the rain that fell, and the thickness of the atmosphere which it occasioned, joined to their having met with a piece of hollow ground, the fifth company had lost its perpendicularity, and doubled behind the fourth, whereby the centre of the regiment became crowded.[57]

The 'friendly fire' incident came about as the lancers galloped past the flank of the Spanish line, then turned and crossed into the rear of that formation. This action brought the Poles in front of the two deployed brigades of Stewart's division so that they were actually between two lines of allied troops (mixed in, according to Lieutenant Leslie of the 29th,[58] with some Spaniards in front of his regiment who had begun to give way, but rallied and held their ground under the guidance of the 29th's adjutant, Lieutenant Benjamin Wilde):

> At this period, the Spaniards were warmly engaged with the enemy, and were behaving most gallantly. [The second brigade of] Gen. Stewart's division was brought up to support them ... After the 29th and the right wing of the 57th had formed, a body of the French [*sic*] lancers got between the two lines. The right platoon of the 29th was ordered to disperse them: the fire from this body flew rapidly to the left, and in consequence was taken up by the 57th.[59]

Leslie acknowledged in his memoirs that the British were aware that they were firing on friend and foe alike, but justified that operational necessity by reasoning that they 'had no alternative left but to stand firm, and in self defence fire on both' because they were exposed 'in line on the slope of a bare green hill'.[60] To add to the confusion, some of the men in the rear rank of the Spanish formation faced about and fired on the French cavalry themselves, thus creating the spectre of a fire-fight between the two groups of allied soldiers.[61] The situation was perilous, but the allied commanders on the scene reacted immediately and stopped the firing before serious harm was done. Marshal Beresford sent Lieutenant Colonel Arbuthnot and General Cole's ADC, Captain de Roverea, galloping towards the brigade with an order to cease firing, but even before he arrived General Hoghton brought the 29th under control while Inglis ran to the front of his right wing 'and gave the command to order arms, which was instantly obeyed'.[62] Marshal Beresford himself then rode up to the 57th Foot 'and rebuked them for their inadvertence', an action that seems uncalled for and that suggests that the marshal was already feeling the pressures of combat.[63]

57. Inglis, Letter, pp. 241–2.
58. Leslie, *Military Journal*, p. 221–2.
59. Inglis, Letter, pp. 241–2, at 241.
60. Leslie, *Military Journal*, p. 221.
61. Burriel, *Albuhera*, p. 19.
62. The role of Arbuthnot is described in Anonymous, *Further Strictures*, p. 164; the quote concerning the 57th comes from the Inglis Letter, p. 241.
63. Anonymous, *Further Strictures*, p. 165. The timing and details of this incident were significantly misunderstood by Napier and his description of this event is consequently replete with errors.

The marshal, the Spanish commanders and their respective staffs had avoided the dangers of the exchange of volleys between the two allied forces, but they now became themselves the targets of the rogue French cavalrymen. General Zayas's ADC von Schepeler first became aware of the threat when he received a lance thrust in the back that, fortunately, was too weak to do him any serious harm.[64] His staff colleague, Lieutenant Colonel Oppen (another German who had come to fight in Spain), unhorsed a lancer and when Brigadier de España prepared to strike the dismounted man, Oppen chivalrously prevented the general from doing so.[65] It was probably also at this time that Grenadier Juan Pastor of the 2nd Battalion of Royal Spanish Guards earned a mention in General Zayas's report by unhorsing a lancer who attacked him.[66] Another Pole made straight for Marshal Beresford. The allied leader could have been killed or disabled, but the Pole had not reckoned on the physical prowess of his adversary: 'One of them grabbed the marshal by the collar, but Beresford lifted him from his horse and threw him to the ground where he was killed.'[67] The *coup de grâce* was delivered by one of the men of the marshal's personal escort, which consisted of an officer and six troopers of the 9th Regiment of Portuguese Line Cavalry.[68] Another Pole who attacked the rest of Beresford's staff about the same time proved even harder to overcome:

> A lt [lieutenant] of these Polish heroes upset & discomfitted the whole of the Portuguese staff. He charg'd one, knock'd another with the butt of his pike overset a 3rd & in short the DQM [deputy quartermaster?] who had neither the nerve nor the force of the Marshal had great difficulty in dispatching him. They swear he bit the ground & was a very devil.[69]

The few remaining lancers scattered after this last effort and one of the most successful cavalry charges of the entire Napoleonic era finally came to an end.[70] From start to finish, it had probably lasted no more than twenty minutes. General Latour-Maubourg and Marshal Soult both had reason to be well pleased with the results. Marshal Beresford did not.

---

64. Von Schepeler, *Histoire,* Vol. 3, p. 268 n. 1, at 269.
65. *Ibid.,* p. 276.
66. Burriel, *Albuhera,* p. 38.
67. A. de Roverea, Letter to Father, (?) October 1811, in F. de Roverea, *Mémoires,* Vol. 4, p. 35. Another eyewitness gives a slightly different version of the incident: 'Lord Mulgrave told me he had had a letter from Major L'Estrange, who saw the attack of the Polish Lancers upon the rear of the British in the battle of Albuera; when Marshal Beresford, riding with his sword undrawn, was suddenly made at by a Polish officer, who was endeavouring to cut him down, Beresford put his spurs to his horse, rode at the Polish officer, seized him by the throat, threw him off his horse upon the ground, where the infantry dispatched him.' Entry for 4 June 1811 in Abbot, Charles, *The Diary and Correspondence of Charles Abbot, Lord Colchester, Speaker of the House of Commons 1802–1817,* 3 vols., London, 1861, Vol. 2, p. 334.
68. Chaby, *Excerptos Historicos,* p. 403, n. 1.
69. Stewart, Letter to Unidentified Colonel, 22 May 1811. This individual may have been Sous-Lieutenant Rodbicki, the only known officer fatality of the Vistula Legion at the battle.
70. General Lardizabal reported that the Murcia Regiment captured one of the standards of the Vistula Legion lancers during the battle, but that claim can be dismissed on the basis of the careful analysis presented by Luis Sorando Muzás in his article, 'The Standards of the Vistula Lancers', posted on www.napoleon-series.org.

Chapter 8
Stalemate

The end of the French cavalry charge seems to have given rise to a spontaneous pause in the fighting. There was, of course, still plenty of activity going on, but the fierce musketry battle between Girard's first division and Zayas's men had ceased. Both sides needed this respite, but Beresford particularly wanted to relieve the Spanish troops who had borne the brunt of the assault by V Corps. There were numerous Spanish units as yet unengaged, but there seems to have been no thought given by Beresford or the other allied commanders to using them for this purpose. Instead, Beresford once again chose to rely on his British regulars and made plans to substitute the remaining brigades of the 2nd Division for Zayas's men. According to Lieutenant Leslie of the 29th, General Stewart, apparently none the worse for wear following the harrowing experience of the French cavalry charge, was directly involved in overseeing the advance of his troops to replace the Spaniards:

> The formation of our [Hoghton's] brigade now being completed, and Lumley's [Abercromby's] brigade having taken post on the left, and all being now ready for the attack, Sir William Stewart rode up to our brigade, and with a few energetic words, said, 'Now is the time – let us give three cheers!' This was instantly done with heart and soul, every cap waving in the air.[1]

De Roverea thought that the ensuing 'Hourra[s]' from the British troops were more 'military and impressive' than the accompanying battle cry of 'Viva, Viva' from the nearby Spanish troops.[2] These shouts were the signal to start a 'passage of lines' manoeuvre in which the Spanish soldiers filed off to the rear using the intervals between the British battalions, which then moved up to face the enemy in place of the troops who had retired. One Spanish officer felt the need to inform any British officer who would listen that he was only retreating because he had been ordered to do so: '. . . a very noble-looking young Spanish officer rode up to me, and begged me, with a sort of brave and proud anxiety, to explain to the English, that his countrymen were ordered to retire, but were not flying.'[3] The men of the 4th Battalion of the Spanish Royal Guards were so intent on keeping up the fight that they had to be literally elbowed out of the way by their British allies.[4] This successful passage of lines

---

1. Leslie, *Military Journal*, p. 221.
2. A. de Roverea, Letter to Father, (?) October 1811, in F. de Roverea, *Mémoires*, Vol. 4, p. 36.
3. Sherer, *Recollections*, 218. 4. Von Schepeler, *Histoire*, Vol. 3, p. 274.

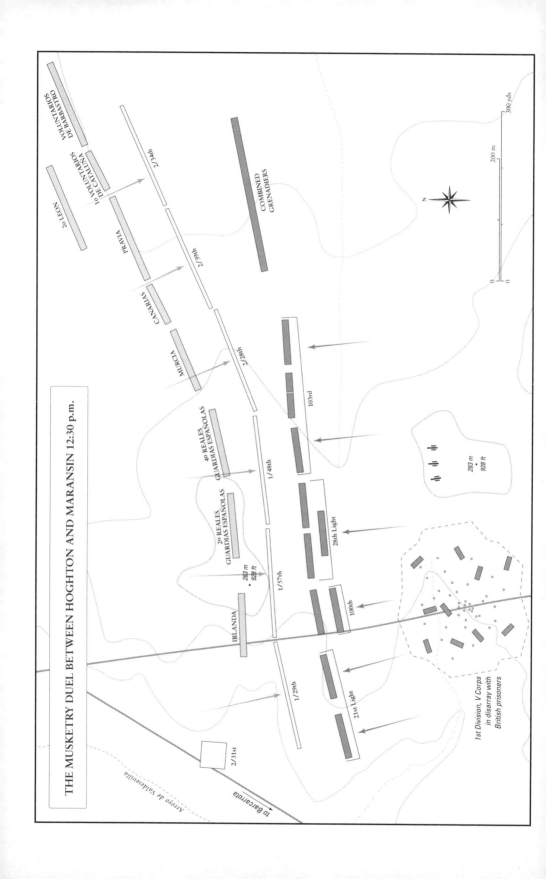

THE MUSKETRY DUEL BETWEEN HOGHTON AND MARANSIN 12:30 p.m.

VOLUNTARIOS DE BARBASTRO

2o LEON

1o VOLUNTARIOS DE CATALUÑA

PRAVIA

CANARIAS

MURCIA

4o REALES GUARDIAS ESPAÑOLAS

2o REALES GUARDIAS ESPAÑOLAS

IRLANDA

2/34th

2/39th

2/28th

1/48th

1/57th

1/29th

COMBINED GRENADIERS

103rd

28th Light

100th

21st Light

2/31st

283 m
928 ft

283 m
928 ft

283 m
928 ft

1st Division, V Corps
in disarray with
British prisoners

N

300 yds

200 m

Arroyo de Valdesevilla

to Barcarrota

was a remarkable feat since it involved units of mixed quality who were in the immediate presence of the enemy at the time the manoeuvre took place.

No matter how well the manoeuvre was performed, however, it exposed the allies to extreme danger because the northern knoll occupied by the Spaniards had to be briefly abandoned as they moved off before the British could move up. The French immediately pushed some skirmishers forward to where the Spaniards had been and they opened up on the approaching British line: 'We ... advanced up the hill under a sharp fire from the enemy's light troops, which we did not condescend to return, and they retreated as we moved on.'[5] The French had not otherwise occupied the vacated ground and their failure to do so is one of the key mistakes they made during the battle. Their failure is, however, quite understandable as a practical matter because, in a fluke coincidence, the French were carrying out their own passage of lines at precisely the same time as the allies. The first division of the French V Corps had been so roughly handled by both the attack of Colborne's brigade and the stubborn resistance of Zayas's troops, and then so further disorganised by the task of taking prisoner the British soldiers fleeing the French cavalry attack, that it was in complete disarray and had begun to fall back on its support. If the allies had attacked at that moment instead of pulling back themselves, a rout might have ensued. Instead, the Spanish withdrawal gave the French an opportunity to regroup, and that opportunity was seized by Brigade General Jean-Pierre Maransin, who had succeeded to command of the second division when his superior, Brigade General Pépin, was wounded and carried from the field.

Maransin, like Girard, had volunteered to serve his country early in the French Revolution. His progress through the ranks was steady but not spectacular, in part because he had never served in any of Napoleon's personal campaigns. He finally made brigade general in 1808 and seemed to thrive in his new rank. He certainly made the most of the opportunities for independent command given to him by Soult and now the greatest challenge of his military career presented itself. The units of his division had been formed in columns of attack by battalion, trailing those of the first division by an interval of some 150 paces. Seeing that V Corps' first division was in no condition to carry on the fight, General Maransin took charge of both brigades of his division and led them forward through the disorder of Girard's men:

> Maransin had already had two horses killed beneath him but, happily for the honour of the French Army, he had not yet received the wound that would later disable him. Placing himself in the centre of the line, he delivered a short address to the carabiniers of the 28th Light who were near him and ordered them to fix bayonets; they greeted his words with cheers that seemed to presage victory. Girard's division had just recoiled through the intervals in the second division and already the enemy was pressing forward. Maransin ordered a charge which he led at the head of the carabiniers of the 28th Light.[6]

Since Maransin does not specifically describe the formation used by his troops for this advance, it seems likely that they were still formed in the attack columns they had used for the earlier stages of the flank attack.

5. Leslie, *Military Journal*, p. 221–2.
6. Cambon, *Maransin*, pp. 82–3. Although they are written in the third person, the words quoted are those of General Maransin himself.

The scene was thus set for another spectacular collision – both the French in columns and the British in lines were pushing forward at the same time to occupy the ground previously defended by the Spaniards. According to Lieutenant Leslie of the 29th Foot, the British reached the position first:

> On arriving at the crest of the height, we discovered the enemy a little in the rear of it, apparently formed in masses, or columns of grand divisions, with light troops and artillery in the intervals between them … This was the moment at which the murderous and desperate battle really began.[7]

The clash of Hoghton's brigade and the second division of the French V Corps at Albuera provides yet another textbook example of a confrontation between troops in column and troops in line. In many ways it differed little from the confrontation between the first division and Zayas's Spanish troops, but the superior training and discipline of the British troops and their use of a two-rank line made them the ultimate test for a general seeking to use shock tactics to achieve victory. When Maransin led forward his gallant troops, he was gambling that their speed could bring them successfully through the volleys that the opposing British battalions could produce. Like General Girard earlier in the battle, Maransin lost his gamble. Once the French columns were stopped, they were devastated by the superior firepower of the British lines. The French then struggled to deploy into lines of their own, but that effort, too, failed. As Wellington said of a French attack at Sabugal a month earlier: 'But really these attacks in columns against our lines are very contemptible.'[8]

This clash, however, had a unique twist to it. Careful scholarship and analysis of British tactics over recent decades has established that the British battlefield triumphs in the Peninsula were not simply the result of more muskets firing more shots more accurately at the enemy.[9] It is now clear that their successes were generally the product of a combination of factors including, in addition, the use of reverse-slope positions, aggressive support from skirmishers and artillery, and well-timed counter-charges. The combination of a few well-executed volleys followed by a charge had already played an important role in Colborne's successful attack against the flank of Girard's division. In the case of the attack of Hoghton's brigade on Maransin's division, however, something went drastically wrong with the formula – whether because of the death of Hoghton, the impediment presented by the number of casualties already strewn across the battlefield or some other reason, no offensive movement by the British ever took place. Unable to exploit their firepower advantage over the opposing columns with cold steel, Hoghton's battalions took extraordinary casualties themselves. The result was a prolonged and bloody stalemate.

The British were able to open fire first under the calm gaze of their brigade commander:

> Gen. Houghton [sic] directed Colonel Inglis not to engage till he should receive his orders to do so, and said that he himself was going to the right of his brigade, and would take off his hat to the Colonel as a signal to him when he wished him to commence. When the signal was given (the Spanish having retired), it

---

7. Leslie, *Military Journal*, p. 221–2.
8. W. to B., 4 April 1811, *Dispatches,* Vol. 7, pp. 426–9, at 427.
9. See, e.g., the chapter on 'Infantry Combat', in Muir, *Tactics*.

was returned by the Colonel, who then ordered arms to be shouldered, and his regiment then threw in a very heavy and well-directed fire by files from the right of companies.[10]

The proverbial 'hail of lead' unleashed by the British staggered Maransin's troops, but the French were able to respond with '[a] most overwhelming fire of artillery and small arms' of their own.[11] This return fire felled both General Hoghton and his horse at the moment he was 'waving his hat and cheering his brigade on to the charge'.[12] The general's ADC, Captain George Ramsden, ran to assist his commander, only to find that Hoghton had been hit numerous times and was too severely wounded to retain command.[13] Ramsden helped him from the field, realised that the general was dying and then rode to inform Inglis that he had inherited command of the brigade.

The musketry duel around the crest of the northern knoll did not have a uniform progression. Ensign Hobhouse noted that the passage of lines split Hoghton's brigade into unsupported segments that quickly lost touch with one another: 'In passing the Spaniards, the different regiments of our brigade were separated, and fought alone for the remainder of the action.'[14] The death of Hoghton certainly contributed to the continuation of this isolation, since it would have been difficult for Inglis to establish control over the brigade and correct the problem. As a result, each of Hoghton's battalions fought its own battle isolated from the other units of the brigade.

The 29th Foot was led into action by Lieutenant Colonel Daniel White, who had held this rank in his regiment for over three years. The 29th had distinguished itself at Roliça, Vimeiro and Talavera, but had not been in action since the last of these battles (although it had been present at Bussaco). By 1811, the appearance of the men was not impressive, although they carried themselves in a manner befitting veterans:

> Nothing could possibly be worse than their clothing; it had become necessary to patch it; and as red cloth could not be procured, grey, white, and even brown had been used, yet, even under this striking disadvantage, they could not be viewed by a soldier without admiration. The perfect order and cleanliness of their Arms and appointments, their steadiness on parade, their erect carriage, and their firm and free marching, exceeded anything of the kind I had ever seen. No corps of any Army or Nation, which I have since had the opportunity of seeing, has come nearer to my idea of what a regiment of infantry should be, than the old Twenty-Ninth.[15]

The regiment was accompanied into battle by a corps of musicians that included four black drummers.[16]

10. Inglis, 'Letter to the Editor', pp. 241–2.
11. Leslie, *Military Journal*, p. 221–2.
12. W. to Marquess Wellesley, 22 May 1811, in *Supp. Despatches*, Vol. 7, p. 134. Wellington went on to praise Hoghton's 'cool and collected' behaviour before his death.
13. Hoghton's coat was afterwards found to have more than a dozen bullet holes. Ramsden's account is summarised in a history of the British Cemetery at Elvas, Portugal, found at <http://planeta.clix.pt/british.cemetery/descren.htm> on 14 June 2001.
14. Hobhouse, Letter to Father, 17 May 1811.
15. Sherer, *Recollections*, p. 61.
16. Ellis, 'The Black Soldiers of the 29th', pp. 186–201. The names of the drummers present at Albuera were George Wise, John Freeman, Peter Askins and Thomas Bohannon.

As the right-hand unit of Hoghton's brigade, the 29th found itself in a very isolated position, too far from both the 4th Division and the 31st Foot on its right and the 57th Foot on its left to benefit from supporting fire. The regiment was also in an odd spot from a topographical point of view. The ground occupied by the 29th was near the highest point on the northern knoll, so the men of the regiment were initially looking down on the masses of French troops directly in front of them. This had the unfortunate result of exposing the British to more enemy fire than would otherwise have been the case:

> ... the three or four front ranks [of the French] in some cases could fire [at us] over the heads of one another, and some guns were posted on a bank and fired [at us] over one of these columns.[17]

Lieutenant Leslie states that there was at first no allied artillery on the spot to return fire, but that some guns came up later in the action:

> This dreadful contest had continued for some time, when an officer of artillery – I believe a German – came up and said that he had brought two or three guns, but that he could find no one to give him orders, our superior officers all being killed or wounded. It was suggested that he could do no wrong in opening directly on the enemy, which was accordingly done.[18]

This officer might have been Lieutenant William Unger of the KGL artillery, who later drew up a plan of the battle that detailed the positions of all the allied batteries. Unger reported that Hoghton's brigade was supported by two guns of unspecified calibre while Abercromby's men were accompanied by four 9-pounders.[19]

The 29th stood its ground in the face of the French fire, but the casualties were heavy:

> ... our ranks were at some places swept away by sections ... Our line at length became so reduced that it resembled a chain of skirmishers in extended order; while, from the necessity of closing in towards the colours, and our numbers fast diminishing, our right flank became still further exposed. The enemy, however, did not avail himself of the advantage which this circumstance might have afforded him.[20]

The officer corps was particularly hard hit. Lieutenant Colonel White was mortally wounded early on and his second-in-command, Major Gregory Way, fared little better. Mounted on Black Jack, a celebrated brown horse 'nearly 17 hands high ... with a famous long tail', Way was an easy target; he was shot through the body and then hit again by a musket ball that fractured his left arm at the shoulder joint.[21] As usual, the

17. Leslie, *Military Journal*, p. 221.
18. Leslie, *Military Journal*, p. 222.
19. Unger, 'The battle of Albuera', p. 127.
20. Leslie, *Military Journal*, p. 222.
21. Landmann, *Recollections*, Vol. 2, p. 137. Black Jack originally belonged to Colonel George Lake of the 29th, but was captured by the French when his master was killed at the Battle of Roliça. The horse was recovered by the 29th when the French evacuated Portugal after the Convention of Cintra. Everard, *History of the 29th*, p. 289. The details of Way's injuries are given in his obituary in *The Annual Register*, London, 1845, pp. 212–13.

losses among the officers holding the colours were appalling since the large silk squares made an obvious target for the French. Seventeen-year-old Ensign Edward Furnace carried the king's colour. He was a slim individual who was 'an agile and successful rider at the races, and from that circumstance, and his general amiable deportment was the pet and almost spoiled child of General Hill's division.'[22] Furnace was hit and nearly fell with the flag, but was propped up by a sergeant. By the time he was hit again and killed, there was no one left to attend to the colours, which fell to the ground, still in the young ensign's grasp.[23] The regimental colours were carried at first by Ensign John Lovelock, but he was hit in the forehead by a shot that ricocheted off the staff of the colour and then wounded through both thighs.[24] Ensign Richard Vance next took charge of the colour and guarded it while all around him were slain. When he himself was mortally wounded he evidently feared that the French were on the verge of winning the battle, for with his last bit of strength he tore the colour from its staff and stuffed it in his jacket. Amazingly, while this act of desperation was taking place, the 29th was still in the fight:

> We continued to maintain this unprecedented conflict with unabated energy. The enemy, notwithstanding his superiority of numbers, had not obtained one inch of ground, but, on the contrary, we [the 29th] were gaining on him.[25]

Until Albuera, the 57th Foot was an undistinguished regiment that had never earned a single battle honour, but this one day changed all that. By displaying an extraordinary tenacity of purpose in its struggle with the French, the 57th gave posterity a new exemplar of behaviour for British soldiers facing adversity and earned the immortal nickname of the 'Die Hards'.[26] The experience of the 57th is captured in a letter written the day after the battle by Ensign Benjamin Hobhouse to his father, Lord Broughton. He noted that his unit received a 'most raking and continuous cross-fire of musketry' from the French right from the start of the action, and that due to the relative position of the opposing forces the heads of the French soldiers 'were scarcely exposed above the brow of a hill'.[27] The result was a protracted musketry duel that nearly wrecked the regiment:

> At this time, our poor fellows dropped around us in every direction. In the activity of the officers to keep the men firm, and to supply them with the Ammunition of the fallen men, you could scarce avoid treading on the dying and the dead. But all was still firm … Tho' alone, our fire never slackened, nor were the men the least disheartened. Tho' by closing to the right we appeared to be no more than a company, we still advanced and fired; and the Spaniards moved upon the left with the greatest bravery.[28]

22. Norton, *Captain Norton's Projectiles*, p. 101.
23. The stories of Ensigns Furnace and Vance were handed down as part of regimental tradition and in 1931 they were incorporated into a narrative of the battle written for the regiment. Anonymous, 'The 29th at Albuhera'. There is no known first-hand source for these stories.
24. In 1937, the regimental museum acquired a portion of that very colour staff adorned with the inscription describing Lovelock's wounds. Anonymous, 'The Regimental Museum', p. 307.
25. Leslie, *Military Journal*, p. 222.
26. See Appendix D for a complete discussion of the origins of the regimental nickname. There is no direct evidence that the Colonel Inglis actually uttered those famous words attributed to him.
27. Hobhouse, Letter to Father, 17 May 1811.   28. *Ibid.*

To complete the horror of these scenes, squalls of rain continued to rake the battlefield: 'During the principal part of the action it rained most violently, which prevented us from seeing the enemy through the thickest part of the fire.'[29]

Some glimpse of the men of the 57th who endured this prolonged musketry duel can be gleaned from the regimental records. They were two-thirds English and one-third Irish, with a handful of Scots and foreigners mixed in, and the great majority had seen more than six years of military service. Although the largest number of privates (as noted in the casualty records for the battle itself) listed themselves simply as 'labourers', the civilian occupations represented in the ranks of the regiment ranged from smiths, weavers, tailors and shoemakers to watchmakers, silversmiths, masons and hair dressers, with at least one lawyer thrown in for good measure.[30] From Wellington's perspective, the soldiers of his army may have been the 'scum of the earth', but there is little to support that view in the demographics of the 57th. However, during the early years of the Peninsular War, the regiment earned the nickname of the 'Steelbacks' because of the frequent use of flogging to enforce discipline.

One officer set the standard of individual conduct for the unit by selflessly refusing medical attention after he was wounded:

> In the late battle, a Captain of the 57th Regiment was so severely wounded, that he ought to have quitted the field; but instead of allowing himself to be removed, he directed his men to lay him on the ground at the head of his company, where he continued to give his orders, and was observed to urge, that in firing at the enemy, the musquets [sic] might be levelled low.[31]

The first regimental history of the 57th states that this officer who urged his men to 'fire low' was Captain Ralph Fawcett, a 23-year-old who was killed during the battle.[32] The author of that book, Lieutenant General H. J. Warre, is a respectable authority for this identification because he actually commanded the 57th later in the nineteenth century, but since Fawcett was the junior captain of the regiment and did not command a company, it seems possible that this courageous individual might actually have been one of the four company commanders who were severely wounded in the action: Thomas Shadforth, Walter M'Gibbon, John Jermyn or John Stainforth. The attrition among senior officers was so drastic that Ensign Hobhouse at one point found himself briefly in command of the regiment's Light Company (which apparently formed part of the line of battle as opposed to being detached for skirmish duties):

> ... many companies were without officers, and as the light company was next to me, I could not do otherwise than take command of it which I did, until it was my turn to take up the shattered colours.[33]

As had happened with Colborne's brigade, some of the highest drama took place around the colours of the regiment. Ensign Robert Torrens, carrying the king's colour,

29. Hobhouse, Letter to Father, 17 May 1811.
30. Casualty Returns of the 1st Battalion, 57th Regiment, May–July 1811, NA/PRO WO 25/1893.
31. *The Times*, 6 June 1811, p. 3, col. A. See Appendix D for a discussion of the possible confusion between this behaviour and that attributed to Lieutenant Colonel Inglis.
32. Warre, *Historical Records of the Fifty-Seventh*, p. 53.
33. Hobhouse, Letter to Father, 17 May 1811.

was severely wounded and the flag dropped to the ground, a development that called forth a fast reaction from the bearer of the regimental standard:

> Ensign [James] Jackson immediately directed one of the non-commissioned officers to pick it [the king's colour] up, and taking it from him, gave the regimental colour to the sergeant, which he retained until an officer was brought to take charge of it. The king's colour, which Ensign Jackson carried, received thirty balls through it, and two others that broke the pole and carried away the top. Nine balls passed through his clothes, of which four wounded – one through the body.[34]

The fourth time Ensign Jackson was hit, he was compelled to withdraw to the rear to have his injury attended to and he passed the king's colour to Lieutenant James Veitch. When Jackson gallantly returned to the field of battle after being bandaged, he found that Veitch had also been wounded, but Jackson was unable to persuade his superior officer to give the flag back. In spite of his wound, Lieutenant Veitch kept hold of the colour to the end of the action.[35] The officer who took up the regimental colour after Jackson was the ubiquitous Ensign Hobhouse. He counted seventeen bullet holes in that colour after the battle.[36]

By Hobhouse's calculation, his regiment was 'actually engaged' with the enemy for 'at least 4 hours'. This is almost certainly an exaggeration, but demonstrates as well as any other piece of evidence the deep impression left by the fire-fight on the survivors. The regiment had almost literally been shot to pieces, since it suffered over 425 killed and wounded including Lieutenant Colonel Inglis, who was hit late in the fighting. The surgeon who treated Inglis left a detailed record of the wound he suffered:

> The ball . . . struck the lower part of his stock & made a deep incision in his neck a little above his collar bone, luckily escaping the artery. I thought it had passed, but on stripping and examining him I found that it had lodged in the back upon the surface of the blade bone – it was immediately extracted and proved to be grape.[37]

Beresford also singled out the regiment for particular praise in his official dispatch about the battle:

> It is impossible by any description to do justice to the distinguished gallantry of the troops; but every individual most nobly did his duty, which will be proved by the great loss we have suffered, though repulsing the enemy; and it was observed that our dead, particularly [those of] the 57th regiment, were lying as they had fought in ranks, and every wound was in front.[38]

---

34. Carter, *War Medals*, p. 130.
35. Fraser, *The Soldiers Whom Wellington Led*, pp. 166–7. Veitch is identified as an ensign in this source, but the *Army List* for 1811 shows he had been a lieutenant since 1809.
36. Hobhouse, Letter to Father, 17 May 1811. Both colours were presented to Inglis when they were retired.
37. Letter from Inglis's surgeon, Olivenza, 21 May 1811, in Lady Inglis, Manuscript History. The lead ball removed from Inglis is now held by the NAM.
38. Beresford, Official Report to W., 18 May 1811.

Later in the same report, the marshal added: 'Nothing could exceed the conduct and gallantry of Colonel Inglis at the head of his Regiment.'

The last unit in the brigade was the 1st Battalion of the 48th Regiment. It was unusual to have two battalions from the same regiment serving in the same action, but this had previously happened to the 48th at Talavera. Now it was happening again, and the 2nd Battalion had already been annihilated in the French cavalry charge against Colborne's brigade. If the men of the 1st Battalion knew of the fate of their regimental comrades, it did not affect their professional calm as they advanced to replace the Spaniards in front of them. The passage of lines does not, however, seem to have been as smoothly executed here as it was elsewhere because the Spaniards in front of the 48th 'were in some confusion' and 'The intervals through which the Regt. had to pass were scarcely sufficient for a company.'[39] The battalion nevertheless completed the manoeuvre, re-formed its line and opened fire on the enemy.

One characteristic of the musketry duel on the northern knoll was the heavy loss suffered by the officers of each battalion. They were normally stationed, for obvious reasons, on the flanks and in the rear of the firing line, but this does not seem to have kept anyone from harm. The commander of the 1st/48th was one of the first to fall in the hail of musket and cannon balls, but he was followed by many others:

> Lieut.-Col. Duckworth was first severely wounded in the left breast by a musket-ball, while gallantly leading his regiment to the charge; but . . . he could not be induced to quit the field. Shortly after another shot struck him in the throat and he expired without a groan.[40]

In all, sixteen officers were killed or wounded.

One of those killed at Albuera came to his fate in a particularly unusual way. On 25 January 1811, Lieutenant John Ansaldo was found guilty of charges brought against him by Duckworth and he was suspended from rank and pay for a period of three calendar months.[41] The charges arose because Ansaldo felt that Duckworth had impugned his honour, and Ansaldo chose to insist that Duckworth should order an investigation that would vindicate him. Since Duckworth took the position that he had never said anything untoward in the first place, he denied Ansaldo's request. Ansaldo's sense of honour was so over-wrought that he could not accept his commander's response. In his frustration, Ansaldo persisted in his demand and wrote Duckworth several letters that were 'most disrespectful and offensive'. It was these communications that led to his court martial and conviction. Sadly for Lieutenant Ansaldo, his sentence was up at the end of April and he consequently returned to active duty just in time to meet his death at Albuera, along with his accuser and Captain Conway Benning of the 66th, the acting deputy judge-advocate in the case.

Duckworth was succeeded by Major James Wilson, a veteran of Egypt and Corunna. He was able to move the unit slowly forward, but not in any decisive way

39. Wilson, Journal.
40. Letter from 'an Officer high in rank in Gen. Beresford's army' quoted in an obituary for Duckworth that appeared in *Gentleman's Magazine*, June 1811, p. 679. Surgeon Guthrie examined Duckworth's body post-battle and found the cause of death to be 'a ball . . . which divided the carotid artery, and killed him almost instantly'. Guthrie, *On Gunshot Wounds*, p. 26.
41. The judgment against Ansaldo is contained in, Vol. 3 (1811) of the *General Orders [for the Army in] Spain and Portugal*, pp. 15–17.

that could break up the same sort of destructive fire-fight that had been encountered by the 29th and the 57th:

> Our brigade stood their ground most gallantly and behaved in the most glorious manner, keeping up a most destructive fire on the enemy's columns which were endeavouring to gain the ground which we had driven them from and maintained. Every field and mounted officer of the brigade was either killed or wounded ... The glorious conduct of the soldiers was most conspicuous.[42]

Wilson himself went down late in the battle: 'I received a musket ball through my leg and another near my ankle. My horse likewise had one through his hind quarter.'

At the same time that Hoghton's brigade advanced, the last brigade of the 2nd Division also went into action. Lieutenant Colonel Alexander Abercromby of the 28th Foot, the acting brigade commander in place of Lumley, was the son of Sir Ralph Abercromby, who had commanded the British army in Egypt in 1800. He, too, led the regiments of his brigade through the Spanish position and engaged in a musketry duel with French troops in their front, although one that seems to have been less fierce than the clash taking place to their right. The battalions of Abercromby's brigade were arrayed in a customary battle order from west to east with the 2nd Battalion of the 28th on the right of the brigade (as it faced the French), the 2nd/39th Foot in the middle and the 2nd/34th on the left. In accordance with Wellington's General Order of 4 May 1809 the light companies of these regiments were grouped together with the rifle company attached to the brigade to form a detached force under the command of Captain Charles Carthew of the 34th.[43] The description of their opponents given by Lieutenant Sherer of the 34th Foot suggests that they may have been facing the Combined Grenadiers that formed part of Soult's reserve:

> Just as our line had entirely cleared the Spaniards, the smoky shroud of battle was, by the slackening of the fire, for one minute blown aside, and gave to our view the French grenadier caps, their arms, and the whole aspect of their frowning masses. It was a momentary, but a grand sight; a heavy atmosphere of smoke again enveloped us, and few objects could be discerned at all, none distinctly. The coolest and bravest soldier, if he be in the heat of it, can make no calculation of time during an engagement ... This murderous contest of musketry lasted long. We were the whole time progressively advancing upon and shaking the enemy.[44]

There is no other source that provides a location for the Combined Grenadiers during the battle, but it does seem logical that they would be stationed to cover the large gap in the French line between Girard and Godinot

The experience of the men engaged in this close musketry duel is hard to imagine. The most prominent sights, noises and smells of the battlefield all came from one very pedestrian source – the gunpowder used by every musket and cannon. This granulated compound, composed of approximately 75 per cent saltpetre, 15 per cent charcoal and 10 per cent sulphur, was very simple, but the chemical reaction set off

42. Wilson, Journal.
43. Wellington, *General Orders (Alphabetical)*, p. 205; *Royal Military Calendar*, London, 1820, Vol. V, p. 364.
44. Sherer, *Recollections*, pp. 159–60.

by the spark from a gun flint was very complicated.[45] In a few thousandths of a second, the deflagration of the powder at its burning temperature of over 2,000 degrees Centigrade produced a huge volume of gas that propelled a musket ball toward the enemy, but it also produced a loud sharp bang as well as gritty deposits on the inside of the gun barrel and vast clouds of dense, dirty grey smoke reeking of sulphur. The billowing smoke produced by artillery fire was even more impressive and the noise of the cannon would have been truly deafening to those nearby, who would also have felt the concussion from each shot. In the humid conditions prevailing at Albuera, the smoke hung low over the battlefield and significantly hampered visibility. The smoke was so thick in fact that it was seen from the ramparts of Elvas by Robert Bakewell, an officer in the 27th Foot:

> Albuera is, I should suppose, about 16 or 17 miles, over a flat and even country from Elvas, in consequence of which the field might be plainly seen from it. I went to the top of one of the convents ... [W]e had a quantity of telescopes with us, [and] as the day was very fine and clear, we could clearly ascertain the success each belligerent power obtain'd, but the smoke that arose from their musketry was our truest director.[46]

Susan Dalbiac, the wife of the commander of the 4th Dragoons who was nursing her sick husband at Elvas, was also a spectator: 'Saw most distinctly the smoke etc of the engagement at La Albueira [sic] so spent the day in much anxiety. D much distressed at his illness and being away etc.'[47]

The soldiers of both armies engaged in this fight had been drilled over and over to create a maximum volume of fire in a minimum amount of time, and that is what they began to do as soon as their officers gave the command to open fire. The only skill that mattered was the ability to load and fire as fast as possible, to compress the intricate steps of prescribed musketry loading drill into a blur of movement punctuated by searing blasts of noise, fire and smoke. Shoulders were bruised, faces blackened and fingers burned in the process, but the volleys kept coming. Lieutenant Sherer of the 34th Foot later mused that one of the better soldiers in this desperate situation was a private named Kit Wallace, a simpleton who was 'one of his Majesty's hard bargains'. He was neither crazy nor an idiot, so he could not be discharged. Instead, he was the despair of every drill sergeant: 'He had a slouch; and he was a sloven. He never stood in the proper position of a soldier; nor did he ever put on his clothes or equipment like one.' His simple-mindedness gave him one inestimable advantage, however:

> ... he had apparently no fear of death. He stood in his place – had a pouch full of ball cartridges and fired them away during the battle; whether guilty or innocent of blood, he could not on that occasion know, and little heeded.[48]

One of the great mysteries of Albuera is how a fire-fight of the intensity reported by the survivors was able to last such a long time. A well-supplied soldier in any of

45. Kelly, *Gunpowder*, pp. 115–16.
46. Bakewell, Diaries, p. 120.
47. Entry for 16 May 1811, Diary of Susan Dalbiac, Archive Item TD2004/7/1602, Archives of the Innes-Ker Family, Dukes of Roxburgh, NRAS 1100, Scotland.
48. Sherer, 'Kit Wallace', p. 8.

the armies at Albuera would have carried approximately sixty cartridges about his person and he could, in theory, fire three or four shots a minute. These statistics suggest that any action longer than thirty minutes in duration would have been unusual, but in this case the musketry duel apparently lasted at least a full hour. This duration indicates that the efficiency of the shooters must have declined precipitously after they were in action only a short time. There would have been a number of reasons for this drop-off. Although no participant in the battle makes express reference to this specific issue, the periodic rain must surely have had an adverse effect on the fire efficiency of the troops since it was almost impossible to load and successfully discharge a flintlock musket in a downpour. Even in the temporary absence of actual precipitation, water from damp clothing and equipment could easily have been communicated to carelessly handled powder, causing similar problematic results. There were also likely to be problems with flints in such conditions that would also lead to misfires. One particularly grumpy British officer noted that even in good weather the poor quality of the regulation flints distributed by the army often detracted from battlefield performance: 'It was well known that sometimes after a volley nearly a fourth of the muskets were still loaded, owing to the inferiority of the flints then supplied.'[49] Fouling of gun barrels was another problem that would have been encountered by every soldier. Ironically, the number of casualties may have contributed to the length of the action because there would have been numerous abandoned muskets and cartridge boxes available for appropriation by anyone whose musket or ammunition failed.

Death and injury were everywhere. There are no first-hand accounts of Albuera that describe actual combat deaths, but the few that do exist relating to other actions help to illuminate what the men at Albuera would have experienced. William Tone (the son of Irish patriot Wolfe Tone) who joined the French Army as a cavalry officer, observed that:

> ... soldiers in general suffer and expire with great calmness, and complain very little on the field of battle. It should seem that, in the ranks, the inevitable fate which comes equally to all, and the idea of being at their post, and in their duty, represses such feelings [of anguish]; at least there I have seen but small difference between the countenance and demeanour of one man and another.[50]

The possibility that battlefield death could be painless has probably given comfort to many a fighting man, but painless death was certainly not the only way for a soldier to meet his fate. As Lieutenant Frederick Pattison of the 33rd Foot noted in the aftermath of the fighting at Waterloo:

> [I]n pursuing my examination of the dead ... I was struck by the diversity of expression still lingering on the countenances of those around me. From the distortion of their faces ... many of them must have had a terrible struggle 'with the king of terrors'; others, from the placidity of their expression, seemed as if they had sunk into refreshing slumber. The separation between soul and body must have been instantaneous.[51]

49. Moorsom, *History of the Fifty-Second Regiment*, p. 137.
50. Tone, 'Narrative of My Services', in *Life of Theobald Wolfe Tone*, Vol. 2, p. 629.
51. Pattison, *Personal Recollections*, p. 35.

An extraordinary case of an apparently painful death is recorded in the following vignette from the memoirs of Captain William Cooke, a British infantry officer who had an especially clinical (or, one might say, morbid) interest in the more grisly aspects of Napoleonic warfare:

> It was here that I saw the remarkable death of one of the rifle corps, who ... received a ball through his body, which caused him such excruciating agony, that his face was all at once distorted, his eyes rolled, and his lips, blackened with the biting of cartridges, convulsively opened. His teeth were tightly clenched; his arms and legs were thrown into an extended position, and he held out his rifle, grasped at arm's length, and remained stationary in this extraordinary attitude for a few moments, until he dropped down dead, as suddenly as if struck by a flash of lightning.[52]

This description highlights the extensive physical damage that could be done to the human body by the weapons of the time. The average lead musket ball could, and sometimes did, pass cleanly through flesh, but it had such a low velocity that it could also carom about with horrendous results if it hit bone. In many cases, the ball, or pieces of it, remained lodged in the unfortunate victim. Cold steel could also cause tremendous physical trauma, particularly in the area of the head and upper body. Finally, and most obviously, cannon shots could tear off whole limbs, and often struck down an entire file of men in sequence. Artillery could even turn the human body into an indirect weapon, as was discovered by Jean-Baptiste Barrès, a French officer who had a wound inflicted by 'the head of a sub-lieutenant, which had been hurled into' his face.[53] On the other hand, there are many cases in which men were struck by spent musket balls and pieces of shells without suffering great harm. Captain George Dean, General Long's ADC, was one such lucky soldier:

> Captain Dean had a hard knock on the shoulder blade, which however being a grazing shot only incommoded him for the moment. He was riding by my side when it took place. I heard it strike him, and after a short exclamation he begged me to look and see if the shot had gone through him. At the first view of his coat, I really thought it had, but told him not, and sent him to the rear to have his wound dressed. In ten minutes, to my utter surprise, he returned to me all alive and well, and only a little sickened by the blow.[54]

The sources on Albuera are full of statements by individuals who were wounded, but there are no accounts that describe the precise moment when musket ball or cannon shot met flesh, or steel blade cut into bone. Once again, the few Napoleonic letters and memoirs that do contain such information provide perspective on the type of trauma and suffering that was the lot of so many at this stage of the battle. One detailed description of a wounding by Thomas Brotherton, a British cavalry officer, is a classic of understatement:

> I was run through the body from the right side to the navel, about six inches. When the point of the sword came out, and as I staggered and fell, my

52. Cooke, *Memoirs*, p. 27.
53. Barrès, *Memoirs*, p. 161.
54. Long to Brother, 22 May 1811, quoted in McGuffie, *Peninsular Cavalry General*, p. 107.

antagonist, instead of withdrawing his sword from my body altogether, drew it up a little and then made another thrust, which went into the cavity of my chest. I was then led off the field faint and sick . . .[55]

'Faint and sick' hardly seem the correct words to cover this case, but this was certainly an age which valued stoicism as a virtue. Coincidentally, those same words appear in another narrative of a wounding left by Private John Green of the 68th Foot that gives more information about the feelings and state of mind of the typical sufferer:

> . . . a ball struck me, entering my left side a little below the heart. At first I felt nothing; in about ten seconds, however, I fell to the ground, turned sick and faint, and expected to expire, having an intolerable pain in my left side. I thought it was all over with me, being confident that I had received a mortal wound. . . . They [some of his comrades] attempted to lift me up; but I begged them to let me alone, saying 'For God's sake, let me die in peace!'[56]

The most comprehensive first-person description of a serious combat injury during the Napoleonic Wars is contained in the diaries of Thomas Austin, an English infantry officer:

> The instant after . . . another cannon-ball swept off my left leg below the knee-joint; and although felled to the earth by the irresistible force of the blow, I experienced no sensation of faintness; but felt excessively hot, thirsty and savage. As the balls had by this time broken down some of the palisades, and made gaps sufficiently wide for the men to pass through, I said to them with, I imagine, less of that Christian feeling which all ought to possess, 'Go on, and give it them!'
> The moment after being struck down, I had sufficiently recovered from the shock, or more correctly had not been prostrated by it, as to be able to sit up and examine my wound. I found the bones were laid bare for some distance up the limb, and appeared as white as the finest ivory, the tendons dangling and quivering like so many pieces of thread; while the haemorrhage was much less than might have been expected . . . Soon after receiving my wound, however, there came on a burning sensation in the injured part which gradually spread over my whole frame, and I felt a parching thirst which seemed to have converted my tongue into a fire-brand; but there was no water at hand to allay the heat which seemed as though it would consume me . . . The battle-field was, to me, now divested of all the excitement and dignity of glorious war. It was present to my sight in its most appalling form, in all its hideous aspects. Its pomp had been transformed into the horrid reality of a charnel house. The dead were lying in every conceivable position – poor mangled creatures who in the morning had laughed and joked with comrades now writhing with pain; and with imploring accents besought those comrades to save them from a painful protracted death by depriving them of the few brief moments that yet remained for them to live.[57]

55. Brotherton, *A Hawk at War*, pp. 53–4.
56. Green, *Vicissitudes*, pp. 188–9.
57. Austin, *'Old Stick-Leg'*, pp. 140–5.

This type of horrific experience was commonplace on the slopes of the northern knoll. The problems faced by wounded men were compounded under these combat conditions because there were no unwounded men who could be spared to give aid to the those who had been hit: '. . . such of the wounded as could not walk lay unattended where they fell:– all was hurry and struggle; every arm was wanted in the field.'[58] The only exception to this rule was the exception that was always made for wounded officers – they, by and large, had friends, subordinates or servants who would help them in distress.

As mentioned above, the French attack on Hoghton's brigade was led by the three battalions of the 28th Light from Maransin's brigade and they were followed immediately by the three battalions of the 103rd Line Regiment. The 28th Light was commanded by Colonel Jean-André Praefke (b. 1758), one of the oldest officers in Soult's army. Praefke, who had joined the 28th Light when it was formed in 1797 and had been its commander since 1804, had a strong bond with the men of his regiment and believed they would follow him anywhere. His leadership, however, was not enough to prevent the regiment from being brought to a halt by musket fire 'from hell':

> Its brave commander, Colonel Praefke . . . was mortally wounded and fell at the head of his regiment; he raised himself to a sitting position and ordered his men not to budge. His three battalion chiefs and three most senior captains were killed outright and Aide-Major [Surgeon] Latouche was shot through the chest when he went to minister to one of them. The men of the regiment, faithful to the command of their dying colonel, kept firing and held their ground. Command of the regiment fell to Captain Jacques Jean, the eighth commander of the day.[59]

The extraordinary number of officer casualties suffered by the French provides evidence that the rifle companies of the 5th Battalion, 60th Foot, plus that of the Brunswick-Oels, were operating at peak efficiency during the battle. Soult was aware of the unique danger posed by these riflemen and in 1813 even asked the Minister of War to form a similar force in the French Army:

> The English army has a special battalion of the 60th Regiment . . . It is armed with rifles and the men are chosen among the best marksmen in the army . . . and their assigned task in battle is to shoot down our officers, particularly the commanders and generals. As a result, whenever one of our senior officers comes close to the action . . . he is ordinarily killed or wounded . . . This style of making war puts us at a severe disadvantage.[60]

Although the French did not have riflemen at Albuera, their specialised skirmishers, called voltigeurs, were probably targeting British officers in return. One anonymous British participant in the battle noticed French sharpshooters lying on the ground and using their shakos as rests to steady their muskets for more accurate fire.[61]

58. Sherer, *Recollections*, p. 159.
59. D'Héralde, *Mémoires*, pp. 157–8. The courageous behaviour of Colonel Praefke suggests that his regiment could claim to be the 'Die Hards' of the French Army.
60. Soult to the Duke of Feltre, 1 September 1813, quoted in Hennet de Goutel, *Le Général Cassan et la Défense de Pampelune* (Paris, 1920), p. 145, n. 1.
61. Quoted without attribution in Fraser, *Soldiers Whom Wellington Led*, pp. 165–6.

The pounding being administered to the French was immensely demoralising because the men in the columns felt that they had no way to strike back at the enemy and were in equally desperate circumstances. Ironically, William Napier, the British Peninsular veteran and historian who wrote so passionately (and inaccurately) about Albuera, may have best captured the essence of this feeling in another passage:

> The close column ... [is] unequal to sustain the fire and charge of a good line, aided by artillery. The natural repugnance of men to trample on their own dead and wounded, the cries and groans of the latter, and the whistling of the cannon-shots as they tear open the ranks, produce the greatest disorder, especially in the centre of attacking columns, which, blinded by smoke, unsteadfast of footing, and bewildered by words of command coming from a multitude of officers crowded together, can neither see what is taking place, nor make any effort to advance or retreat without increasing the confusion; hence no example of courage can be useful, no moral effect can be produced by the spirit of individuals, except upon the head, which is often firm and even victorious at the moment when the rear is flying in terror.[62]

The other brigade of the second division of V Corps, consisting of the 21st Light and 100th Line Regiments and probably commanded by Colonel Quiot of the 100th Line in place of Pépin, moved up alongside Maransin's men. According to Sous-Lieutenant Perrin-Solliers of the 21st Light, these regiments were also formed in closed battalion columns and also advanced at the *pas de charge*, counting on their audacity and impetus to strike home. They did not fare any better than the first brigade:

> They soon found themselves in the hottest possible fire. All the generals and superior officers who were mounted were put out of action in minutes, as were a large number of other officers. This development left the soldiers to their own devices and led to wavering and hesitation. The head of each column, crushed by musket fire of ever-increasing violence, was stopped at pistol-shot distance from the enemy line. The battalions deployed without orders and this infantry, deprived of its officers, still had enough tenacity to fire almost all their cartridges. They held their position until they were outflanked by a converging movement by several enemy units.[63]

The 21st was the only regiment in the whole of V Corps that had room to deploy fully. Perrin-Solliers estimated that more than 21 officers and 500 men of his regiment were killed or wounded in less than 20 minutes (although actual casualties were in fact lower). The fighting was at such close quarters that Colonel Quiot was stabbed in the left thigh by a British bayonet.[64]

The combatants of both armies fighting between the knolls were now hanging on through sheer determination only and were in equally desperate circumstances. The French were on the verge of headlong flight, but at the same time a British officer thought that any further French advance would inevitably break through the British position.[65] The French hopes for success now suffered another severe blow when

62. W. Napier, *History*, Vol. 1, p. 266. 63. Perrin-Solliers, [Review], p. 365.
64. Girard, Report to Marshal Soult, 16 May 1811.
65. A. de Roverea, Letter to Father, (?) October 1811, in F. de Roverea, *Mémoires*, Vol. 4, p. 39.

General Maransin was struck down by a musket ball that went straight through his stomach. The wound appeared to be a mortal one and he was immediately carried to the rear. As he neared the Chicapierna stream, Maransin was approached by Squadron Chief Tholosé, one of Soult's ADCs, who asked for a report. Maransin told him what had happened, then added a flourish that reflected both his outlook for survival and his dedication to army life: 'Tell the marshal that I die happy to have been able to give my life in a way that has been so beneficial to the glory of our armies.'[66] Maransin, perhaps understandably due to his condition, was overly optimistic about what his men had achieved. The grim reality was that the outcome of the battle would most likely be decided in favour of the next army able to mount an offensive effort.

66. Cambon, *Maransin*, p. 85.

Soult, engraving by Tardieu after
Lambert, from Portrait Volume relating to
G. T. Beauvais de Préau (ed.), *Victoires,
Conquêtes, Désastres, Revers et Guerres
Civiles des Français de 1792 à 1815*
(Paris, 1818). Many of the stock
illustrations of Marshal Soult found in
Napoleonic history books depict him as
an older man. This portrait shows him
in the prime of life and shows how he
would have looked at Albuera.
(Anne Brown Military Collection)

Marshal Beresford, engraving by R. Young
after portrait by W. Beechy, from J. Wilson,
*A Memoir of Field Marshal the Duke of
Wellington* (2 vols., London, 1853–4).
This portrait depicts Marshal Beresford
just after the close of the Peninsular War.
(Author's Collection)

'La Bataille d'Albuera', engraving by Couché (?) after Pierre Martinet, from Abel Hugo, *La France Militaire* (4 vols., Paris, 1838). This seems to illustrate the defeat of Colborne's brigade, but pride of place has been given to the hussars rather than the Lancers of the Vistula, who can be seen charging in the background. *(Author's Collection)*

'Trooper, Elite Company, 17th Dragoons', from the print series *Troupes Françaises* published by Aaron Martinet (Paris, 1811). The composition of this particular print of a French dragoon waving a captured British regimental colour was undoubtedly inspired by the events of Albuera. *(Author's Collection)*

'Chasseur of Light Infantry', from the
Troupes Françaises series of prints
published by Aaron Martinet
(Paris, 1808). *(Author's Collection)*

'Voltigeur of Line Infantry', from the
Troupes Françaises series of prints
published by Aaron Martinet
(Paris, 1811). *(Author's Collection)*

'Carabinier of Light Infantry', from the
Troupes Françaises series of prints
published by Aaron Martinet
(Paris, 1808). *(Author's Collection)*

General Girard, contemporary
print after portrait.
(Courtesy of Tony Broughton)

General Werlé, contemporary
print after portrait.
(Author's Collection)

General Maransin, contemporary
print after portrait.
(Courtesy of Tony Broughton)

General Godinot, contemporary print after portrait.
(Courtesy of Tony Broughton)

General Ruty, contemporary print after portrait.
(Courtesy of Tony Broughton)

General Latour-Maubourg, contemporary print after portrait.
(Author's Collection)

General Brayer, engraving by Tardieu after portrait by
Forestier, from Portait Volume relating to G. T. Beauvais
de Préau (ed.), *Victoires, Conquêtes, Désastres, Revers
et Guerres Civiles des Français de 1792 à 1815*
(Paris, 1818). *(Anne Brown Military Collection)*

'Lancer of the Vistula Legion', print by Carle Vernet. *(Anne Brown Military Collection)*

'General Konopka', engraving by Hulk after Pierre Martinet, from F. Ternisien d'Haudricourt, *Fastes de la Nation Française* (Paris, 1821). *(Anne Brown Military Collection)*

Above: An anonymous contemporary panorama of Badajoz: the Fort of San Cristoval, the bridge over the Guadiana River and a view of the fortress from the west. *(Anne Brown Military Collection)*

Right: Anonymous contemporary panorama of Badajoz: a view of the fortress from the south-east. *(Anne Brown Military Collection).*

'Badajoz 1811', map by Lamare, a French engineer officer. *(Author's Collection)*

Breach D the Small Stream running into the Guadiana au encircling this part of the works.
N. O. other big Batteries. ⊞ Fort La Picolina Ⓞ La Pardalera R. ridge of high gro
are and deep in all colours the point belt is worn round the body. — if part the
was raised —

An anonymous contemporary panorama of Albuera. This panorama exaggerates the size of the mountains in the background, but accurately depicts the village and nearby countryside as viewed from the north-east. *(Anne Brown Military Collection)*

'The Battle of Albuera, May 16th, 1811', engraving by W. Heath, coloured by Sutherland, from Jenkins, *The Martial Achievements of Great Britain and Her Allies* (London, 1814). This does not provide an accurate depiction of any particular phase of the battle, but it does convey some sense of the formations used and the effect of gunpowder smoke on battlefield visibility. *(Anne Brown Military Collection)*

'The Buffs at the Battle of Albuera', engraving by Dubourg after Manskirch, from Edward Orme, *Historic, Military and Naval Anecdotes* (London, 1819). This curiously unemotional print depicts an unwounded Latham tucking one of the colours of the Buffs into his jacket. The soldiers are shown wearing the so-called Waterloo shako rather the plainer 'stovepipe' shako actually worn by British troops in the Peninsula. *(Anne Brown Military Collection)*

'Captain Latham Rescuing the Colours of the Buffs at Albuera', engraving by R. Ackermann after J. Atkinson from *Ackermann's Incidents of British Bravery during the Late Campaigns on the Continent* (London, 1817). The silver regimental centrepiece depicting Latham's bravery is modeled from this print. *(Courtesy of Donald Graves)*

'Marshal Beresford Engaged with the Polish Lancer, at the Battle of Albuera', engraving by Dubourg after Manskirch, from Edward Orme, *Historic Military and Naval Anecdotes* (London, 1819). *(Author's Collection)*

Above: General Cole, engraving by
R. Young after portrait by T. Lawrence,
from J. Wilson, *A Memoir of Field
Marshal the Duke of Wellington*
(2 vols., London, 1853–4).
This portrait depicts General Cole just
after the close of the Peninsular War.
(Author's Collection)

Left: 'Lieut. Col. Sir Wm. Myers,
7th Fusiliers', print from *Royal
Military Chronicle* (1811).
(Author's Collection)

'Sergeant of the 31st Foot', facsimile of
a drawing in the Frankfurt Collection,
a set of watercolour paintings made by
a soldier serving in the Peninsula.
(Author's Collection)

General Robert Long, print after
portrait. This print depicts Long early
in his career. *(Author's Collection)*

'Marshal Beresford with the Allied Forces under his command gained a Glorious victory . . . near Albuera', woodcut published by G. Thompson (London, 4 July 1811). This is the earliest depiction of the battle. *(Author's Collection)*

'British Artillery in Action', print by George Jones. *(Author's Collection)*

'Drummers, 57th Foot', print after watercolour. The shakos and overalls of these drummers are probably more accurate than the bearskins and gaiters depicted in Lady Butler's famous painting of the 57th at Albuera. *(Author's Collection)*

'13th Light Dragoons at Campo Mayor', print after painting by Stanley Wood. *(Author's Collection)*

'Officer of 13th Light Dragoons', print from Goddard and Booth, *The Military Costume of Europe*. *(Author's Collection)*

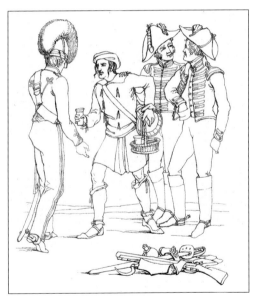

'British Cavalry 1811', from John Luard, *History of the Dress of the British Soldier* (London, 1852). Luard was an officer in the 4th Dragoons, so this is an eyewitness depiction of men of the 13th Light Dragoons, the 3rd Dragoon Guards and the 4th Dragoons purchasing lemonade from 'a Valentian seller of that refreshing beverage'. *(Author's Collection)*

'British Officers 1811', from John Luard, *History of the Dress of the British Soldier* (London, 1852). Shown are (*from right to left*) a staff officer, an infantry officer, and officer of the 4th Dragoons and one of the assistant surgeons of the 4th Dragoons – either Thomas Hickson or Gavin Hilson, 'a despiser of dress' but a clever businessman who lent money to officers in his regiment. *(Author's Collection)*

'Spanish Royal Guard 1811', after Pacheco. *(Author's Collection)*

'Officer of Canarias Regiment 1811', after Pacheco. This regiment, like many others in the Spanish Army, had a dress uniform and a campaign uniform. *(Author's Collection)*

'Patria Regiment 1811', after Pacheco. *(Author's Collection)*

General Castaños, contemporary print after portrait. *(Courtesy of Luis Sorando Musa)*

General Ballasteros, contemporary print. *(Courtesy of Luis Sorando Musa)*

General Blake, contemporary print. *(Courtesy of Luis Sorando Musa)*

'Portuguese Infantry Repulsing French Cavalry', contemporary print. *(Author's Collection)*

General Zayas, print after portrait. *(Author's Collection)*

'The Die Hards', print by Marshman. This illustration is one of the few depictions of the battle that attempts to show the prevailing bad weather. *(Author's Collection)*

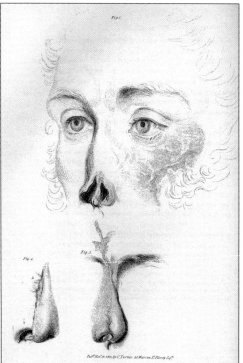

Lieutenant Matthew Latham, engraving from J. Carpue, *An Account of Two Successful Operations* (London, 1816). This is the only known portrait of the much wounded Lieutenant Latham, who seems to have been a handsome man before his injuries. *(Author's Collection)*

Chapter 9

The Charge of the Fusiliers

The men of Hoghton's brigade might have felt themselves isolated from the rest of the army during their trials, but that feeling would have been unjustified because the army's commander was right there with them. Command and control on a Napoleonic battlefield was a very limited geographic concept and, to his credit, Marshal Beresford stationed himself exactly where he was needed the most, at the point of resistance to the French flank attack. He was thus in a perfect position to identify and assess developments and devise an appropriate response to them. At the start of the musketry duel between Hoghton's brigade and the French, Beresford had reason to consider himself a lucky man. The initial French flank attack had been thwarted, his army had survived the destruction of Colborne's brigade, he himself had survived hand-to-hand combat with a Polish lancer and Hoghton's brigade had successfully changed places with Zayas's Spaniards. He was, nevertheless, also a man who still had a significant problem – Hoghton's brigade was outnumbered and was wasting away before his eyes despite its superior firepower. The marshal consequently needed to find a way to break the tactical stalemate that had arisen and restore the initiative to the allied army.

Beresford's first plan for achieving that objective was to bring forward some of the nearby Spanish forces that had not yet been engaged with the French:

> After having placed the 57th in the front line, and remained with them a short time ... I afterwards went to the right. There it was that I endeavoured ... to induce the Spaniards to turn the right of Houghton's [sic] brigade, and attack the left and flank of the French columns.[1]

The easiest way to accomplish this goal would have been to coordinate the move with General Blake, but that possibility never seems to have been considered by Beresford. In fact, it seems that the allies had failed to make any arrangements for keeping in touch once the action was joined, and the astonishing result was that Beresford and Blake never encountered each other again on the battlefield after the French flank attack began: 'I neither saw, nor heard any thing more of General Blake till after the conclusion of the battle.'[2] This was a spectacular breakdown in coordination on the part of the allies and one that must be attributed to Beresford

---

1. Beresford, *Refutation*, p. 193.
2. Beresford, *Refutation*, p. 150. Beresford also went the whole day without seeing Castaños, although that was not significant because Castaños had ceded command to Blake.

since he was the agreed-upon leader of the combined force. As a practical matter, this situation prompted Beresford to use an unorthodox approach when he tried to persuade some nearby Spanish units to move forward in support of Hoghton:

> [F]inding several Spanish battalions in column to the rear, he [Beresford] exerted every mode of authority and persuasion to induce them to descend the hill, and to make the desired charge. His orders and expostulations were equally disregarded. In his eagerness to forward the measure, he laid hold of a colonel commanding one corps, and taking him forcibly to the front, desired him to order his men to follow, the Marshal declaring that he himself would lead them on. All was in vain.[3]

There is an obvious British bias to this version of the events. Judged more objectively, Beresford's actions can be recognised as highly peculiar. First, Beresford made no effort to request the required troop movement via the Spanish chain of command – he went straight to the unit commander instead of seeking out a senior officer like de España, Zayas or Ballasteros. Second, that course of action was probably a very rash one, since there is no evidence that the marshal was known by sight to the Spanish troops or fluent enough in Spanish to make his intentions fully known to the troops he was wildly ordering about. Finally, Beresford's bizarre behaviour in physically assaulting a senior Spanish officer almost ensured that the Spanish battalions would balk at following his commands. Indeed, the outcome was no different than that which would have resulted if a Spanish general had tried to give orders to a British unit in a similar fashion. This incident also provides more evidence that the stresses of the day had begun to affect Beresford's ability to make sound tactical and strategic decisions, although British contempt for the fighting qualities of their allies probably obscured its significance to Beresford's staff at the moment.

The allies were still in the middle of a desperate fight, however, and the failure of Beresford's attempt to bring forward fresh Spanish troops meant that his original tactical problem remained unsolved and, indeed, had become worse as the musketry duel wore on. The nearest other allied troops who could have had an immediate impact on the situation on the ridge were the eight battalions of the 4th Division but the marshal was clear in his own mind that those troops were best left where he had put them originally because they were performing the vital twin services of deterring the superior French cavalry from overwhelming his own mounted troops and protecting his own line of retreat towards Valverde. Abercromby's brigade of the 2nd Division was also at hand, but there is no evidence that Beresford ever gave it a thought in this context and there is no obvious explanation for that omission.

Yet another possible asset Beresford might have used was his cavalry, but that force was, according to General Long, well and truly occupied with its primary task of containing the opposing French mounted forces:

> Their Cavalry was so much superior to ours both in quality & numbers, that our services during the day of action were limited to keeping them in check, & counteracting their attempt to gain our flanks, & deprive the Infantry of our

3. Anonymous, *Strictures*, p. 249.

Support – We only came in contact with them, partially, twice, but our Artillery made considerable havoc among them.[4]

Beresford agreed that it was crucial for his cavalry to avoid full engagement with the enemy and later praised Lumley for the circumspect way he handled his command. The confrontation between the allied and French cavalry was consequently like a boxing match in which each fighter circles the other looking for an opening but does not throw any serious punches unless that opening can be found. Latour-Maubourg has been criticised for not attacking more aggressively, but in fact his available force did not outnumber that of the allies at the critical point on the right flank (after deducting on both sides the units that were still recouping from the charge on Colborne's brigade and the allied counter-attack).[5] The cavalry combat was still eventful, however. For instance, Lieutenant Edward Whinyates of Lefebure's Royal Horse Artillery battery wrote to his family that although he himself 'did not get a scratch', one of his guns 'was for a moment in the hands of the enemy' and he also 'lost some horses and men'.[6]

By a process of elimination, then, Beresford arrived at the conclusion that his best alternative would be to break the stalemate on the ridge with some of the Portuguese troops from his left flank. The fighting in that sector had, after Godinot's first rush at the bridge, settled down to a relatively desultory skirmish and artillery fight, but it certainly did not seem any less dangerous to the participants. José Jorgé Loureiro, a Portuguese officer stationed near the village, felt that the French were aiming at him in particular:

My regiment advanced in support of the [KGL] riflemen and suffered terribly heavy cannon fire and so many bombs and bullets flew right by me that I consider myself very fortunate to have escaped with my life; for a while I felt I was the target.[7]

On the French side, the men of General Briche's two regiments of chasseurs à cheval had to endure the extended misery of waiting patiently in formation while they were targeted periodically by Portuguese artillery posted on high ground near Albuera. Sous-Lieutenant Théophile de Bremond d'Ars of the 21st Chasseurs was luckily hit only in the arm, but at the same time he was wounded, his orderly, 'the unlucky Poijeux', was killed at his side by a cannonball.[8]

Assuming that the French efforts against the village were unlikely to intensify in the short run, Beresford dispatched Lieutenant Colonel Arbuthnot to Major General Hamilton 'with orders to send along the back and under the shelter of the ridge, one brigade to attack the enemy's left'.[9] Unfortunately for Beresford, however, Hamilton

4. Long to Brother, 22 May 1811, quoted in A. Uffindell, *The National Army Museum Book of Wellington's Armies*, p. 104. This passage differs by a few words from the same passage as quoted in McGuffie, *Peninsular Cavalry General*, pp 105–6.
5. The total strength of all the French dragoon regiments was just under 2,000 officers and men, while combined strength of the available Spanish cavalry plus the squadrons of British cavalry assigned to the allied right flank was over 2,400 men.
6. Whinyates, Letter to his Uncle, 20 and 22 May 1811.
7. Loureiro, Letter to Father, 20 May 1811.
8. Bremond d'Ars, *Historique du 21e Chasseurs*, pp. 250 and 252.
9. Anonymous, *Strictures*, 249–50.

had moved his division from its original position to a location by the village of Albuera and Arbuthnot was unable to find the Portuguese commander quickly and efficiently. As time passed without either word from Arbuthnot or the arrival of the expected reinforcements, the marshal became exceedingly anxious because of the deteriorating situation on the northern knoll and his anxiety caused him to make another bad decision – he decided to go and find Hamilton himself:

> Lord Beresford having waited some time for the approach of the Portuguese brigade from Hamilton, and finding that it did not arrive, supposed some mistake must have occurred, and proceeded to the rear to discover the cause of the delay.[10]

Leaving aside the question of how an entire Portuguese division came to be misplaced on a field with almost no trees and vegetation to obscure sight lines, this was an extraordinary development. Beresford was abandoning his rightful post at the scene of the action and, because he rode off without first having a word with General Stewart or with any of his Spanish counterparts, he effectively left the allied army leaderless at a crucial moment in the battle. There is no possible justification for Beresford's action, but there is an explanation – Beresford was so concerned about the possibility that the French would prevail in their flank attack that he personally wanted to make arrangements to ensure the safe withdrawal of his army in case of that eventuality. Hence, while he was looking for the 'lost' Portuguese, Beresford also gave orders to Major Dickson and General Alten to pull the KGL light battalions and their supporting artillery back from the village. Dickson, for one, was certain that these orders reflected an acknowledgment of defeat on the part of Beresford:

> The Marshal himself, for a moment, thought he was defeated, as I received an order to retreat, with my artillery, towards Valverde, and Baron Alten absolutely, by order, quitted the village for a moment.[11]

When, on the strength of this order, Napier and others later accused the marshal of having panicked in the field, Beresford indignantly argued that his critics had missed the key point of his actions. In a nutshell, Beresford claimed that he had simply and calmly taken reasonable precautions against the possibility of defeat, not conceded the outcome of the day:

> I must maintain that it is the commander's duty to provide against the occurrence of either probable or possible danger. Such, at that moment, was my case ... [M]y order to [Dickson and to] Alten's brigade was to provide against the forced retreat, or the defeat, of our line engaged, and not to order the retreat of the army, as Colonel Napier would infer.[12]

In other words, he ordered a tactical withdrawal to make the KGL battalions available to respond to adverse developments on the right of his line of battle, not to cover a

---

10. Anonymous, *Strictures*, 250.
11. Dickson, Letter to McLeod, 22 May 1811, quoted in Duncan, *Royal Regiment of Artillery*, p. 296. (This letter is mentioned in Dickson, *Manuscripts*, Vol. 3, pp. 394–5, but went missing some time after it was used by Colonel Duncan for his book but before the Dickson manuscripts were published in 1908. Its current whereabouts are unknown.)
12. Beresford, *Refutation*, p. 229.

retreat from the battlefield. General Alten's recollection of what happened supports Beresford's view of the matter:

> Meanwhile the engagement on our right had become very serious and doubtful for the allies, and it was at this time of day that I received Marshal Beresford's order to get loose of the village with my brigade, with the ultimate view of taking up a position in the rear of it, covering the Valverde road.[13]

The marshal's version is also supported by the fact that he simultaneously directed Campbell's Portuguese brigade to move up on either side of the village, an order that would make no sense if he was really contemplating a retreat but that would mitigate any problems arising from the redeployment of Alten's men. With two battalions of the 10th Portuguese Regiment just north of the village and two battalions of the 4th Portuguese Regiment just to the south, there was little danger that the withdrawal of the KGL troops could have led to an enemy breakthrough along the Royal Road.[14]

Beresford's concern for his line of retreat was certainly reasonable, but he was definitely guilty of a lapse of judgment in the way he addressed it. Fortunately for the allies, however, when Beresford set off on his own, he happened to leave behind on the ridge one of his most trusted staff officers and this oversight proved to be one of his most decisive actions of the day. Twenty-five-year-old Lieutenant Colonel Henry Hardinge was thought by his contemporaries to be destined for great things. He was one of the first graduates of the Royal Military College and had received a staff appointment to the expeditionary force sent to the Peninsula in 1808, but he soon proved that he was no mere staff officer. At the Battle of Vimeiro he so distinguished himself that Benjamin D'Urban, a friend and colleague then and at Albuera, could scarcely find enough praise for his conduct:

> I grieve to tell you that our inestimable friend, Captain Hardinge, was wounded at the hottest point of attack. It is his custom to be foremost in every attack, where an unaffected gallantry of spirit irresistibly carries him. Here he was conspicuous where all were brave ... He is now an example of fortitude and tranquility; and highly as I thought of him before, it remained for me to see him in his present state to be aware of all the excellences of his nature.[15]

Hardinge served on the staff of Sir John Moore in the campaign at the end of 1808 and used his own sash to staunch the mortal wound of his general at the Battle of Corunna. It was during that campaign that Hardinge came to the attention of Beresford who remembered the young officer when he was assembling the staff of the new Portuguese Army in 1809. He accordingly offered Hardinge a post in his military 'family' as the Deputy Quartermaster-General of the Portuguese Army (with the local rank of lieutenant colonel). Nothing had occurred in Hardinge's next two years of service to change the marshal's favourable impression of his subordinate.

At Albuera, Hardinge apparently spent most of the morning with his commander-in-chief at or near the site of the French flank attack, but they became separated when Beresford went to find Hamilton's division. Beresford states explicitly that the reason

13. Alten, Narrative, p. 2.
14. Statement by Sir Archibald Campbell (1833?) in Beresford, *Refutation*, pp. 234–6.
15. Letter from D'Urban dated 22 June 1808 quoted in Hardinge, *Rulers of India*, p. 14.

for this was that he had sent Hardinge to Lumley with orders shortly before his own departure: 'It was also at this period that I despatched Sir Henry Hardinge, with instructions to Sir William Lumley, commanding the cavalry.'[16] Hardinge for his part is equally clear that nothing of the sort occurred:

> I carried no order to Sir William Lumley at this period of the battle … In Sir William's published letter, he states that he was in communication with General d'Urban about this time, which may have led to the error, but he does not allude to any order conveyed to him by me, nor is it stated what that order was.[17]

Of these two recollections, Hardinge's seems to be the more accurate because there is no doubt that he found himself at that moment a close observer of the fighting on the ridge. What he saw horrified him:

> The 29th, 57th and 48th Regiments, in a military sense, were almost exterminated. My former regiment, the 57th, had scarcely any officers left. Every Commanding Officer was at this time either killed or wounded; Sir Wm. Stewart, the General of the division, twice wounded – [sic], the General of the brigade, killed; and it was evident that the whole brigade was in such a crippled and exhausted state, that it could not be expected to hold the position much longer.[18]

Hardinge concluded 'that nothing but an offensive flank movement could retrieve [the situation]'.[19]

What Hardinge did next was controversial at the time and has remained so ever since. Although he was aware that Beresford was already taking steps to bring about such a flank attack in his own way, Hardinge nonetheless decided that the situation was so pressing that some more immediate response was urgently required and, furthermore, that there was no time to consult with his commander before taking action: 'In this emergency, I could not refer to Marshal Beresford, who had proceeded to the left to hasten the arrival of the Portuguese brigade.'[20] Since the 4th Division was the only unengaged force in the near vicinity, Hardinge made straight for its commander:

> In this desperate state of things, not admitting of delay, but requiring an instant remedy, I rode to Sir Lowry Cole to propose to him to attack the enemy's column with his division.

Hardinge's arrival at the 4th Division was certainly dramatic, since he galloped up to General Cole brandishing his sabre, which he had drawn along the way when he briefly stopped to direct an effort to drive back some French skirmishers 'who had collected within twenty paces of our right flank'. Without further formality or ceremony, Hardinge described the state of affairs on the ridge and then boldly and

---

16. Beresford, *Refutation*, 194.
17. Cole, *Correspondence*, p. 9.
18. Hardinge, Letter to the Editor of the *United Service Magazine*, 9 September 1840, reprinted in Cole, *Correspondence*, p. 9.
19. Hardinge, *Rulers of India*, p. 22.
20. This and the next two quotes are from Hardinge, Letter to the Editor of the *United Service Magazine*, 9 September 1840, reprinted in Cole, *Correspondence*, p. 9.

passionately urged Cole to launch an immediate attack on the French to relieve the pressure on the surviving brigades of the 2nd Division. This extraordinary behaviour on the part of Hardinge violated all standards of military decorum and protocol. It also helped save the day for the allied army because, as it turned out, Hardinge's plea fell on receptive ears despite the fact that Cole had been explicitly ordered not to leave his position without special instructions from Beresford.[21]

Although Sir Lowry took that order very seriously, he had himself been keeping track of the action on the ridge with an increasing sense of dread, even though he could not see exactly what was happening because of the thick smoke caused by the incessant artillery and musket firing taking place there. Despite the fact that Hardinge did not carry any instructions from Beresford, his first-hand report on the desperate situation of Hoghton's brigade caused Cole to wonder if his original orders, given many hours earlier in much different circumstances, were still valid. As the general pondered what he should do, Lieutenant Colonel John Rooke, the assistant adjutant-general, rode up and joined the group. When Cole announced to him that 'Hardinge is pressing me to attack the enemy's column,' Rooke immediately replied that he agreed with Hardinge and added his voice to those in favour of an attack.[22] Lieutenant Colonel Sir William Myers, the senior officer of the 7th Fusiliers and the temporary commander of the whole fusilier brigade, also expressed a similar opinion.[23]

General Cole's choices were clear – he could either hold his position in accordance with his original orders or he could violate those orders and move his division to support the troops on the ridge. He had sent his ADC, de Roverea, to Marshal Beresford early in the day to await further instructions, but none had come from that source or from Hardinge, so he could not claim to have been released from his original restrictions.[24] He was also aware of the negative way in which Beresford (and Wellington, for that matter) had reacted to the supposed failure of the British cavalry to obey orders at Campo Mayor. Cole therefore knew that if he did what Hardinge was suggesting, anything less than complete success on his part would almost certainly mean a court martial and potential disgrace and dishonour. It is a measure of the man that he nevertheless concluded that he would rather take the risk of action than the risk of inaction and so he decided to bring his division forward. The opinions so vehemently expressed by other experienced officers in favour of just such a movement may have been a factor in General Cole's decision, but the responsibility for making that decision was his alone. The moral courage required to do so was no

21. Cole, Letter to the Editor of the *United Service Magazine*, 6 January 1841, in Cole, *Correspondence*, p. 19. D'Urban at one point argued that Hardinge was merely 'anticipating' an order that had already been sent by Beresford to Cole. D'Urban, *Report of Operations*, p. 29. This is certainly wrong. De Roverea, who was with Beresford at the relevant time, reports that he did not receive a single order from Beresford until *after* the Marshal became aware that the 4th Division was attacking. A. de Roverea, Letter to Father, (?) October 1811, in F. de Roverea, *Mémoires*, Vol. 4, pp. 27–45.

22. Hardinge, Letter to the Editor of the *United Service Magazine*, 9 September 1840, reprinted in Cole, *Correspondence*, pp. 10–12.

23. Anonymous, 'Life of Sir William Myers', p. 473.

24. Some sources state that Cole sent de Roverea to Beresford to request permission to move shortly before the arrival of Hardinge, thus suggesting that Cole was the first person to have this idea. However, there is no doubt that Cole sent de Roverea to the Marshal 'at the first sound of gunfire'. A. de Roverea, Letter to Father, (?) October 1811, in F. de Roverea, *Mémoires*, Vol. 4, p. 35.

less than the physical courage soon displayed by the men of the 4th Division, particularly since Cole was acutely aware of the large mass of French cavalrymen in the near vicinity and of the fact that four of his five Portuguese battalions had never before been in combat.

Cole realised, however, that he needed to temper the boldness of his decision with care in its execution so that the risk he was running by disobeying Beresford's order would be minimised. He consequently crafted a unique formation for his advance that was intended to achieve his tactical offensive objective while continuing to protect the exposed right flank of the allied army. The heart of the formation was seven battalions of infantry in line – the three battalions of the fusilier brigade on the left and four battalions of his Portuguese brigade (two battalions each of the 11th and 23rd Portuguese Regiments) on the right. (According to Blakeney, 'the 1st battalion of the Royal [7th] Fusiliers [was on the left] . . . , my battalion, the 2nd [Battalion of the Royal] Fusiliers, next; and the 23rd Welch Fusiliers on the right.'[25] There is no information available about the exact sequence of the four Portuguese battalions.) Cole was also aware, however, that in light of the fate suffered by Colborne's brigade, he had to make some provision for securing his own flanks:

> Thinking it desirable (with all due confidence in the Portuguese Brigade), to have some British troops on the extreme right of the division, I directed the light companies of the Fusilier Brigade to form in column on the right of the Portuguese, where I also placed the brigade of guns [Sympher], and sent the Lusitanian Legion to the left of the Fusiliers.[26]

As a result of these arrangements, Captain John Hill, the commander of the Light Company of the 23rd Fusiliers, found himself 'on the right of the Portuguese in a hollow square . . . (which outflanked their infantry, but in return was outflanked by the enemy's cavalry).'[27]

The use of the light companies of the three battalions of the fusilier brigade as an independent unit (known as the 'light battalion' of the brigade) had been standard practice since the formation of the brigade in 1810 and the regular commander of the combined companies was Major Thomas Pearson of the 23rd Regiment.[28] The quotation from Cole implies that these three light companies were the only ones on the right of the formation, but this seems odd given that three companies alone would have made for a very small flank guard. De Roverea states that there were **four** 'elite' [light?] companies in square on the right of the Portuguese while Charles Broke Vere, the assistant quartermaster-general for the division, adds to the confusion with the statement in his memoir that the extreme right of the division was protected by all 'the flank companies **of the division** [emphasis added] in column of quarter distance'.[29]

25. Note from Sir Edward Blakeney, 7th Fusiliers, quoted in Wade, Letter to Editor of the *United Service Magazine*, 19 March 1841, reprinted in Cole, *Correspondence*, p. 17.
26. Cole, Letter to the Editor of the *United Service Magazine*, 6 January 1841, reprinted in Cole, *Correspondence*, p. 19.
27. Hill, Letter to Mother, 22 May 1811, quoted in Hall, 'Albuera and Vittoria', p. 194.
28. Pearson's role as commander of the light battalion at Albuera is discussed in Graves, *Fix Bayonets!*, pp. 1–3 and 231–2.
29. A. de Roverea, Letter to Father, (?) October 1811, in F. de Roverea, *Mémoires*, Vol. 4, p. 37; Vere, *Marches, Movements, and Operations*, p. 13.

Since the Portuguese line battalions did not have light companies and since the Lusitanian Legion was itself a light infantry unit, he must be referring to the three light companies (those of the 2nd/27th, 40th and 97th Regiments) from Kemmis's brigade present at the battle and perhaps also to the one company of Brunswick-Oels attached to the 4th Division.[30] Sergeant Cooper of the 7th Fusiliers reports on the other hand that the Portuguese brigade was 'supported by three light companies' and that the fusilier brigade itself was accompanied by 'some small detachments [the light companies?] of the brigade left at Badajoz'.[31] Given these contradictory recollections, it seems unlikely that the true facts will ever be known.

The other key element of Cole's plan of attack was a refusal of his right flank. This was achieved by having the battalions of the division advance in echelon with the fusilier brigade leading and the Portuguese brigade trailing so that the British battalions would come into action sequentially before the Portuguese battalions. Cole thus hoped to prolong the period of time during which the Portuguese would be able 'to show front to the enemy's cavalry, and at the same time . . . cover the right flank of, the Fusilier Brigade'.[32] Given this concern, it would certainly have made sense for Cole to have coordinated his proposed attack with General Lumley, the commander of the allied cavalry, posted to Cole's right and many historians (including both Fortescue and Oman) state explicitly that Cole rode over to consult his colleague before putting his division into motion. Amazingly, however, Lumley himself stated many years after the battle that nothing of the sort occurred and, to the contrary, he was taken by surprise by the 4th Division's attack:

> Frequently, as time and circumstances would permit, I scanned with no small anxiety the whole line of infantry on those hotly and effectively contested, and most important heights, the key to our position; but, to the best of my recollection, I was not aware of the advance of the two brigades (the Fusiliers and Harvey's) until they passed my left flank. They then came under my eye; and . . . the rain and smoke having at that time cleared away, I saw them, as one body, moving to engage.[33]

All sources nevertheless agree that the allied cavalry did move in support of Cole's attack, even if it did not do so by prearranged design.

Cole's decision to advance was greeted enthusiastically by his men. Colonel Myers appeared in front of his regiment and exclaimed to the men, 'It will be a glorious day for the fuzileers [*sic*]!'[34] Like most warriors, his men preferred the stimulus of action to the boredom of waiting: 'The words, "Fall in Fusiliers," roused us; and we formed line.'[35] A Royal Welch Fusilier officer recalled later that the Fusiliers first advanced in 'contiguous columns of battalions at quarter distance' and did not deploy into line 'till

30. The only light company associated with the division that was definitely not at Albuera was Captain Prevost's company of the 5th Battalion, 60th Rifles, attached to Kemmis's brigade, which spent the day of battle on the wrong side of the Guadiana. Butler, *King's Royal Rifle Corps*, Vol. 2, p. 138.

31. Cooper, *Rough Notes*, p. 60.

32. Cole, Letter to the Editor of the *United Service Magazine*, 6 January 1841, reprinted in Cole, *Correspondence*, p. 19.

33. Beresford, *Refutation*, p. 225.

34. Anonymous, 'Life of Sir William Myers', p. 473.

35. Cooper, *Rough Notes*, p. 60.

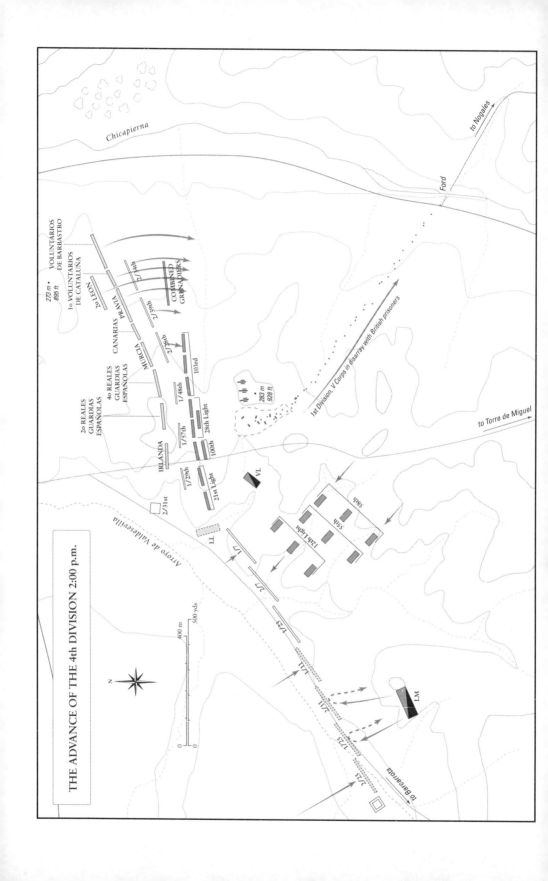

THE ADVANCE OF THE 4th DIVISION 2:00 p.m.

N

0 — 400 m
0 — 500 yds

Arroyo de Valdesevilla

2/31st

IRLANDA

2o REALES
GUARDIAS
ESPAÑOLAS

4o REALES
GUARDIAS ESPAÑOLAS

MURCIA

CANARIAS

PRAVIA

2o LEÓN

1o VOLUNTARIOS
DE CATALUÑA

VOLUNTARIOS
DE BARBASTRO

273 m •
895 ft

1/34th

COMBINED
GRENADIERS

2/39th

2/28th

1/48th

103rd

1/57th

28th Light

100th

1/29th

21st Light

VL

283 m •
928 ft

to Torre de Miguel

1st Division, V Corps in disarray with British prisoners

Chicapierna

Ford

to Nogales

58th

55th

12th Light

TT

1/7

2/7

1/23

1/7

1/7C

1/23

2/23

LM

to Barrancila

within a musket shot of the French', but he may have been describing an earlier point in the battle or a different approach taken by the Royal Welch Fusiliers alone.[36] In any event, the task ahead of the fusilier brigade seemed a daunting one:

> When we reached the part of the position allotted to us, the action in our front had been going on very severely. A fog and rain prevented our seeing what had occurred; but when it cleared up, which was in about ten minutes, we saw the French columns placed in echellon [*sic*] on our side of the hill, with the artillery, twenty-three pieces, above, and an echellon of cavalry on their left flank, covering the whole plain with their swords.[37]

Despite the formidable appearance of the French array, the advance of Cole's division posed an extremely serious threat to Soult's army because the French marshal was running out of fighting men. The V Corps had been so severely punished in its successive fights on the ridge with the Spaniards, Colborne's brigade and with Hoghton's brigade that it was almost entirely spent as a fighting force. Despite heroic personal efforts on the part of General Girard, his troops now 'formed nothing more than a confused mass of men beginning to fall back in disorder'.[38] Colonel Konopka, mounted on a magnificent British charger, tried to rally the infantry by sending forward the standards seized earlier by his lancers and reminding them of what had already been accomplished that day: 'My friends! Hold firm and victory will be ours! Here are the flags that my regiment alone just captured from the enemy!'[39] His exhortations, however, were in vain. Soult even threw himself and his staff into the middle of this mass to encourage his men, but he also realised more concrete help was needed to stabilise the situation.[40] He consequently ordered forward General Werlé's reserve brigade and then called upon Latour-Maubourg to repeat his earlier success.

The cavalry struck first but, unfortunately for the French, the allied troops were ready for them this time:

> The French Cavalry, under General Latour Maubourg, was in front of the advancing line in the plain, and charged twice on the line of the Portuguese Infantry during its movement. [Footnote omitted.] The French Cavalry was received with, and repulsed by a well directed fire from the line, and the Artillery on its flank, in both charges. The line shewed great steadiness; and conduct, that would have done honour to the best and most experienced troops.[41]

The Portuguese troops who so impressed all observers with their calm demeanour were the 9th Portuguese Brigade, consisting of the 11th and 23rd Infantry Regiments under the command of Brigadier General William Harvey (late of the 79th Foot). Harvey had led the brigade since January 1810, so he knew his men well and they

36. Harrison, Letter to Mother, 24 May 1811, quoted in Glover, 'The Royal Welch Fusiliers', p. 150.
37. Note from Sir Edward Blakeney, 7th Fusiliers, quoted in Wade, Letter to Editor of the *United Service Magazine*, 19 March 1841, reprinted in Cole, *Correspondence*, pp. 16–17.
38. Lapène, *Conquête*, p. 161–2.
39. Entry concerning Colonel Konopka in Société d'Hommes, *Les Fastes de la Gloire*, Vol. 4, p. 185.
40. Lapène, *Conquête*, p. 162.
41. Vere, *Marches, Movements, and Operations*, p. 14.

had been trained to a high standard even if they had never before been in a major battle.[42] He was ably supported by two of his regimental commanders. Lieutenant Colonel Donald MacDonell of the 11th Portuguese Regiment was a British officer in the 91st Foot when he transferred to the Portuguese Army in 1809.[43] Lieutenant Colonel Thomas William Stubbs (b. 1776) of the 23rd Portuguese Regiment was an Englishman by birth, but he had converted to Catholicism, married a Portuguese woman and joined the Portuguese Army before the war began.[44] Their performances at Albuera provide further evidence of the benefits obtained by mixing British officers with Portuguese rank and file when the Portuguese national army was reformed under Beresford's aegis after the French invasion of 1808.

The French troops involved in this attack were probably the 4th and 20th Dragoons and they may have been over-confident because they could see that they were approaching blue-coated Portuguese. There is considerable confusion as to exactly how many times these cavalrymen charged Harvey's brigade during its advance, but there is considerable clarity as to how little they achieved. Latour-Maubourg noted in his after-action report on the battle that the two dragoon regiments started to charge enemy infantry from the 'plateau', but were unable to press home their attack because of the 'difficulties of the terrain and the depth of the enemy column [sic]'.[45] According to the report, the lead elements of the two regiments cut down or captured some allied soldiers at significant cost to themselves, but the French cavalrymen could not deter the allied advance.

Freed from concerns about the enemy cavalry, the fusilier brigade pressed its attack enthusiastically. Lieutenant Harrison of the 23rd Foot thought that the French had the early advantage:

> Their infantry formation was covered by their field pieces which kept up a heavy fire with grape shot and round shot on our line at very short distance … The French infantry were formed on an eminence and we had every disadvantage of the ground. They soon opened their fire.[46]

Sergeant Cooper of the Royal Fusiliers had a very similar and equally vivid recollection of the course of events:

> Having arrived at the foot of the hill, we began to climb its slope with panting breath, while the roll and thunder of furious battle increased. Under the tremendous fire of the enemy our thin line staggers, men are knocked about like skittles; but not a backward step is taken. Here our Colonel and all the field officers of the brigade fell killed or wounded, but no confusion ensued. The orders were, 'Close up'; 'Close in'; 'Fire away'; 'Forward'. This was done.[47]

---

42. The details of Harvey's tenure with the battalion come from Ward, 'Portuguese Infantry Brigades', pp. 107–8.
43. The surname of this officer is spelled in different ways by different sources, but this is the spelling he used in one of his own letters. See MacDonell, Letter to Cousin, 23 May 1811.
44. D'Urban, *Report of Operations*, p. 48. According to Halliday, *Observations*, p. 32: 'The Twenty-third is commanded by Lieutenant Colonel Stubbs, who has the Portuguese rank of Colonel, and who has great merit in bringing his corps to such perfection.'
45. Latour-Maubourg, Report, p. 3.
46. Harrison, Letter to Mother, 24 May 1811, quoted in Glover, 'The Royal Welch Fusiliers', p. 151.
47. Cooper, *Rough Notes*, pp. 60–1.

Eighteen-year-old Second Lieutenant Revis Hall of the 23rd Fusiliers, one of the shortest officers in his regiment, was standing in this hail of shot in front of one of the tallest officers, Second Lieutenant Isaac Harris. Hall playfully called out 'Harris, the ball that goes over my head will kill you,' then ironically was felled by a shot to the forehead minutes later.[48]

The exact details of how Colonel Myers was wounded are given in a short biography written in 1812:

> The order and exact line preserved by Sir William's exertions in ascending the hill, of which the enemy had possession, was remarked by every officer present. Here his horse was wounded under him; he proceeded on foot, giving his people an example of that unconquerable spirit they till the last displayed. Another charger was brought, which he had hardly mounted when the fatal shot struck him, passing from under the hip upward in an oblique direction through the intestines. He did not fall, but continued, with his wonted firmness, to address his soldiers. It [soon] became necessary, however, to take him from his horse, when he was carried off the field by his trusty comrades, expressing more pride at their conduct than sense at his own suffering, and only regretting his separation from his gallant fusileers.[49]

General Cole was also wounded, but he was able to remain in command because his injury was 'merely a flesh wound through the thigh.'[50]

The French troops who were pounding the fusiliers were the men of General Werlé's reserve brigade, supported by the French artillery firing from the rise to the south of the main battle ground. Werlé's lead unit was the 12th Light, an exceptionally strong three-battalion regiment commanded by 31-year-old Louis-Étienne Dulong de Rosnay, one of the finest fighting officers in the French Army. Dulong's heroism during Soult's retreat from Portugal in 1809 had been instrumental in saving the French from defeat, but it had earned him a disfiguring wound to the face, one of eleven he suffered during his military career.[51] The other regiments of Werlé's brigade were the 55th Line and 58th Line. The 58th was a four-battalion unit under Colonel Jean-Baptiste-Henri Legrand. Legrand was a 54-year-old greybeard who had enlisted as a private in 1774, but his age had not prevented him from actively leading his regiment against the British in two prior battles, Vimeiro and Talavera (where he was wounded in the head). The 55th was a three-battalion unit that had been commanded since 1807 by Colonel Henry-César-Auguste Schwitter, a life-long soldier who had been enrolled as a child in the Swiss Guard of Louis XVI and nearly killed when that unit was massacred at the Tuileries early in the Revolution.

General Werlé himself was one of Soult's most trusted subordinates, having served with the marshal since 1799. The two men had a very strong friendship, so the

48. This incident was related to the family and recorded in the memoirs of Hall's younger brother. Hall, *Retrospect of a Long Life*, pp. 588–9.

49. Anonymous, 'Life of Sir William Myers', p. 473.

50. Cole to Lord Eniskellen, 21 May 1811, quoted in Cole, *Memoirs*, at pp. 75–6. Cole's wound was attended in the first instance by his long-time orderly, Johann Kramer of the 1st Hussars of the KGL. Vigors, *The Hanoverian Guelphic Medal*.

51. Titeux, 'Le Général Dulong de Rosnay.' Dulong's exploits in 1809 have a prominent place in Bernard Cornwell's *Sharpe's Escape*, London, 2003.

marshal was confident that Werlé would do his best to turn the tide of battle back in favour of the French. Werlé had also risen from the ranks and was 'personally a very brave and very honest man', but some said that, like many former rankers, he was more comfortable following orders rather than giving them.[52] That concern was moot in this circumstance, because the task at hand did not call for much creativity or initiative. He simply had to take his troops straight at the allied attack and buy enough time for the V Corps' survivors to avoid encirclement. Unfortunately, before he could do so, he had to avoid two obstacles that complicated his mission. First, his men were disrupted by the flood of British prisoners being transported back to the French lines because many individual soldiers broke ranks in order to plunder the captives: 'Each man wanted his own prisoner.'[53] Second, Werlé's formations were also disrupted by the disarray of the very troops they were assigned to cover:

> General Werlé advanced with confidence at the head of the 12th Light and the 58th Line Regiments [and the 55th Line]. Nevertheless, as soon as these units reached the scene of combat and were getting ready to deploy they found themselves under pressure from the troops of General Girard, who, having been repulsed, fell back abruptly on their reinforcements. This mingling of fresh and used troops threw the men of the reserve into confusion.[54]

Because of this confusion, Werlé's men remained in column formation as they pushed through the debris of V Corps and they were still in column when they encountered the fusilier brigade. The scene at this juncture was later described by Lieutenant Colonel Blakeney of the 2nd/7th Fusiliers:

> We moved steadily toward the enemy, and very soon commenced firing. The men behaved most gloriously, never losing their ranks, and closing to the centre as casualties occurred. From the quantity of smoke, I could perceive little but what was immediately in my front. The first battalion [of the 7th] closed with the right column of the French, and I moved on and closed with the second column, and the 23rd with the third column.[55]

Thus, for the third time in the battle, there was a stark confrontation between allied troops in line and French troops in column. Blakeney is clear that he saw three columns, which Oman concludes were the three regiments of Werlé's brigade in separate regimental columns. That is not the only possibility, since the French might have been advancing in three successive lines of regimental columns, each composed of three battalions in columns abreast of one another, but it is impossible to confirm the exact order of battle of the French. However the three columns were formed, this formation meant that the French once again had the superior force at the point of contact in terms of sheer numbers, but were once again outflanked and outgunned. The three fusilier battalions deployed in lines of two ranks each could bring to bear the fire of 1,900 muskets, while the French brigade, notionally over 3,600 men strong,

52. Bouillé, *Souvenirs et Fragments*, Vol. 3, p. 389.
53. D'Héralde, *Mémoires*, p. 156.
54. Lapène, *Conquête*, p. 162. Lapène actually makes no mention of the 55th, but he may never have been aware that the 55th was transferred from Godinot to Werlé at the start of the battle.
55. Note from Sir Edward Blakeney, 7th Fusiliers, quoted in Wade, Letter to Editor of the *United Service Magazine*, 19 March 1841, reprinted in Cole, *Correspondence*, p. 17.

could respond with only 600 muskets in the first two ranks of its columns. Once again, it is likely that, if the French columns had pushed ahead aggressively, they would have broken through the thin British line and caused another change in the course of the battle. Once again, however, the French faltered and Werlé instead committed the same error as Girard and Maransin before him and ordered his columns to deploy in order to bring more muskets into action. Unfortunately, when the columns halted to do so, they first lost momentum and the opportunity to charge and then lost cohesion when they found that they were unable to execute the necessary manoeuvre under the fierce British fire. Blakeney had a clear view of what happened:

> I saw the French officers endeavouring to deploy their columns, but all to no purpose; for as soon as the third of a company got out [of the column] they immediately ran back, to be covered by the front of the column.[56]

Despite the obvious distress of the French force, the British still faced the risk of becoming involved in another devastating fire-fight like the one on the ridge. This time, however, they avoided the trap by making use of the shock tactics that the French had failed to utilise: 'We returned it [the French fire] handsomely, came down to the charge and cheered.'[57] The account of an officer of the 23rd emphasises that the tactical offensive they adopted was particularly effective because of the close range at which the preceding British volley was delivered: '. . . we advanced to within about twenty paces of them without firing a shot. When our men gave three cheers and fired, the enemy broke in great confusion.'[58] In some instances, however, the French were apparently able to rally and put up a fight, albeit one that they could not ultimately sustain:

> They [the French] faced about after a few paces and, others coming to their assistance, the contest soon became general and a most determined fire kept up on both sides, so near as to be almost muzzle to muzzle. They again drew us on by showing us their backs and we twice repeated our former treatment.[59]

The 55th Line was one of the French regiments exposed to this assault. Colonel Schwitter was wounded in the leg and had two horses killed beneath him, but he calmly mounted a third and held his men together by force of his example. Captain Martin Lacroix, a twenty-year veteran who held the Legion of Honour because he had won a sabre of honour at the Battle of the Trebbia in 1799, was hit in the head by a spent musket ball and knocked to the ground.[60] He immediately jumped back up, but only had time to shout *'En Avant!'* once to his men before he lost consciousness. Lieutenant Auzerac, the bearer of the regiment's eagle standard, was shot down and a sudden rush of British soldiers allowed them to take momentary possession of the eagle. Lieutenant l'Heureux witnessed this development and realised he had to act quickly if the regiment was going to avoid disgrace. Rallying a small party of

56. Note from Sir Edward Blakeney, 7th Fusiliers, quoted in Wade, Letter to Editor of the *United Service Magazine*, 19 March 1841, reprinted in Cole, *Correspondence*, p. 17.
57. Harrison, Letter to Mother, 24 May 1811, in Glover, 'The Royal Welch Fusiliers', p. 151.
58. Philipps, Letter to Father, 19 May 1811, in Goodridge, 'Letters Home', p. 24.
59. Harrison, Letter to Mother, 24 May 1811, in Glover, 'The Royal Welch Fusiliers', p. 151.
60. Lacroix's biography can be found in Lievyns, *Fastes de la Légion d'Honneur*, Vol. 2, p. 47.

veterans, l'Heureux led his men forward in a counter-rush and rescued the eagle from enemy hands.[61]

In these desperate circumstances, Soult dramatically called on Colonel Konopka and his lancers for one last effort: 'Colonel! In the name of God, save the honour of the French!'[62] The Poles responded bravely and even achieved a brief success:

> The Fusilier Brigade was now hotly engaged, and the Portuguese line was closing up to it and covering well its right, and in echellon [sic] to it; when the right of the Fusilier Brigade was charged and partially broken by the same Polish Cavalry which had attacked the right of the 2nd Division.[63]

This report of a cavalry attack against the Fusiliers is corroborated by Lieutenant Hill of the 23rd Fusiliers, who adds some interesting details of the cat and mouse game played by horsemen and infantrymen in combat:

> The Fusilier Brigade, [having] arrived on the heights, were attacked in front by cavalry who, receiving the fire of all our companies, put themselves in order and prepared to charge, thinking the whole [of the regiment was now] unloaded. The spurs were in the horses' sides, [and] they were coming on, [when] the Grenadiers then fired on them at about 15 paces distant and file fire recommenced from those who had first fired ... [and] they went to the right about and galloped off. During this [attack] some small parties of cavalry had got in our rear and took prisoners the wounded who were getting away from the fire.[64]

This incident explains how a noticeable number of Royal Fusilier officers, including Major John Nooth (commander of the 1st Battalion of the 7th), Captain Andrew Fernie and Captain William Despard, came to be captured during their successful advance.[65] Whatever the true circumstances of this last charge of the Vistula Legion Lancers might be, it was too little and too late to save the day for the French. Order was soon restored by Harvey's Portuguese regiments, who continued to behave coolly under pressure: 'The Portuguese received the Lancers with a steady fire. The Poles were repulsed, and the Fusiliers resumed their formation.'[66] De Roverea provides some additional details of the final triumph of the Portuguese over the Poles: 'The brigade awaited this cavalry with the first rank kneeling and then delivered a *coup de grâce* volley at pistol-shot range.'[67] The battle had now been effectively won by the allies. It remained to be seen whether the French defeat would become a rout.

The allied conduct of the battle had been halting and indecisive until the moment of Cole's advance, but now, with the French giving way on all fronts, there was still a chance to convert a bloody repulse of the enemy into a decisive victory. The first favourable development was the appearance of the Portuguese of the Loyal Lusitanian Legion, which came up on the right flank of Werlé's men and ended their stubborn resistance:

61. Martin, *Le 55e Régiment*, pp. 70–1
62. Wojciechowski, *Pamietniki*, p. 72.
63. Vere, *Marches, Movements, and Operations*, p. 15.
64. Hill, Letter to Mother, 22 May 1811 in Hall, 'Albuera and Vittoria', pp. 194–5.
65. *The Times*, 18 June 1811, p. 3, col. C. All these officers quickly escaped after the battle.
66. Vere, *Marches, Movements, and Operations*, p. 15.
67. A. de Roverea, Letter to Father, (?) October 1811, in F. de Roverea, *Mémoires,* Vol. 4, p. 37.

> The enemy ... artillery ... kept up a tremendous fire on us, and as we advanced, did considerable execution; but at length, on our coming within a few yards of the columns they gave way with the greatest precipitation, notwithstanding the exertions of their officers to prevent it.[68]

The flight of Werlé's troops ended the fight between Maransin's division and what was left of Hoghton's brigade:

> ... the gallant Fusilier brigade ... moved up from the plain, bringing their right shoulders forward. They thus took the enemy obliquely in the flank, who, although already much shattered, still continued to make a brave resistance.[69]

As the last units of V Corps finally gave way, 'a cry of "They run, they run!"' passed down the line. Astonishingly, the survivors of the 57th had to be restrained from joining the ensuing general advance:

> Just as we mounted the heights from which they [the French] had fought we saw them running over the plain in the greatest disorder. Marshal Beresford passed us at the time, and ordered us to halt; upon which we drew up, and a shell that was thrown from a great distance blew up the horse of our last field officer [Major Spring?], and wounded him slightly. The french [sic] Artillery, which was covering their retreat, annoyed us most dreadfully on the height; and we went under the brow to count our numbers.[70]

An officer of the regiment recalled many years later the exact words used by Marshal Beresford when he exempted the 57th from pursuit of the French: 'Stop, stop the 57th; it would be a sin to let them go on!'[71]

Hardinge, meanwhile, fresh from his contribution to the attack of the fusilier brigade, had ridden around Hoghton's brigade to reach Abercromby and to urge him to bring his men to the charge. This reprise of his mission to the 4th Division was less controversial but also no less successful since Abercromby readily agreed to the suggested move. The 34th Foot seems to have played a leading role in the advance, which brushed aside the French Combined Grenadiers and threatened the right flank of all the French troops still in the dip between the two knolls:

> We kept up a lively fire as we advanced against them, they briskly returned it until we came within twenty or thirty yards. We then gave three cheers, and prepared for the charge. This had an instantaneous effect. They went right about in the utmost confusion and disorder, and we were after them. For a short time our firing ceased, as they were ingenious enough to pass themselves for Spaniards. We soon discovered our error and pursued them from hill to hill until they reached their reserve, which consisted of cavalry and a train of artillery, which was extremely well served. If we had had cavalry and artillery to have supported us and to have kept up with us, their loss would have been infinitely

68. Mayne, *Narrative*, p. 111.
69. Leslie, *Military Journal*, p. 222.
70. Hobhouse, Letter to Father, 17 May 1811. The *Royal Military Calendar* for 1820 states that Major Spring commanded the regiment after Inglis was wounded.
71. A Die Hard, 'Letter from "A Die Hard"', pp. 106–7.

greater, and their artillery would have been taken, as their infantry had abandoned it. We should have advanced and taken it, had we not observed a column of their cavalry ready to attack us, and our line, as you may conceive, was rather in confusion, from the pursuit and number of casualties.[72]

The threatening cavalry were probably the 2nd and 10th Hussars, both of which units had been moved by a direct order of Soult to cover the gap in the centre of the French position between his two main infantry forces.

The Spanish troops, too, joined in the advance, led by Ballesteros. According to Ensign Hobhouse, the Spanish general demonstrated some quick thinking when his men found a bloody French general's coat on the battlefield:

> Ballesteros seized it and cried out, though I believe he knew to the contrary, 'Soult is dead, my lads, look at his coat,' as he rode in front of the lines, and he held up the embroidered coat. He said this in my hearing, and it produced an admirable effect; for both Spaniards and British advanced to the attack with redoubled vigour.[73]

Another Spanish leader who distinguished himself was Teniente General Mendizabal, the commander defeated at the Gevora, who was serving as a mere volunteer. According to Blake, Mendizabal encouraged the troops 'by his exhortations and the example set by his bravery ... wherever the struggle appeared most dangerous or uncertain'.[74] This stage of the battle also gave Spain a new hero when Emetrio Velarde, an officer of the Spanish General Staff, was mortally wounded. Velarde is now remembered for having proclaimed after being struck down: 'What does it matter that I am dying when we have won the battle'.[75]

Beresford himself shook off his fears of defeat and sent Captain de Roverea to bring forward some reinforcements for General Cole:

> When the marshal saw that the 4th Division was moving forward and realised that there was still some hope of success, I received the first and only order that he gave me: I was sent to find a Spanish brigade that had not yet been engaged and to bring it forward to support the 4th Division's attack. I obeyed and found the Walloon Guards. After I gave the marshal's orders to the commanding officer of the Guards, I returned to the fusilier brigade where I found that my general [Cole] and all his staff had been wounded.[76]

The battlefield was still a very dangerous place. As de Roverea marvelled at how the strange caprices of fate had brought together Frenchmen, Englishmen, Poles, Germans, Portuguese, Spaniards and at least one Swiss to try to kill each other over a small village in Spain, he was hit on the head by a piece of artillery shell and

72. [Dickens], Letter, 24 May 1811, p. 290. The writer of this letter is not actually named in the text, but he can be identified because he states, 'I am now in command of a company, vacant by the death of Captain Gibbons.' *Ibid.*, p. 292. The officer who received that promotion was Lieutenant S. R. Dickens.
73. Hobhouse, Letter to Father, 17 May 1811. Hobhouse must have understood Spanish to be able to report this event.
74. Letter of Blake in Burriel, *Albuhera*, p. 3.
75. Report of Ballasteros in Burriel, *Albuhera*, p. 32.
76. A. de Roverea, Letter to Father, (?) October 1811, in F. de Roverea, *Mémoires*, Vol. 4, p. 38.

knocked unconscious from his horse. When he came to, he tried to get back on his horse and ride to safety, but that simple plan proved difficult to execute:

> I fell several times while trying to remount my horse, and when I finally got into the saddle, instead of heading to the rear as I intended, I ended up galloping left and right over the battlefield, bleeding profusely, until someone took pity on me and led me to a surgeon.[77]

The French army's ability and will to resist were now fading fast. All available troops had been committed and defeated and the remnants of the vanquished V Corps and Werlé's brigade were retiring quickly down the slopes of the ridge in a state of confusion that threatened to turn into headlong flight. Marshal Soult himself rode into the flood of humanity and tried to stop it by shaming his disordered troops: 'Where are you going? If you face the enemy, no one will pursue you!'[78] His efforts and those of the few surviving officers were unavailing, however, and he was forced to recognise that his men had nothing left to give. In a final effort to stem the rout, Soult halted one drummer, then a few more and ordered them to sound retreat. The familiar if discouraging notes of the drums sanctioned the withdrawal and restored some semblance of order to the French movement. Ultimately, however, the French army was saved from destruction not by Marshal Soult but by General Bourgeat and the artillery of V Corps.

Because of the presence of General Ruty with the expedition, General Bourgeat did not have at Albuera an independent artillery command appropriate for his rank, but, 'As always, he could be found anywhere where his services were needed or there were dangers to be faced.'[79] As Bourgeat watched the jumble of defeated French infantry making for the fords across the Chicapierna stream and blocking any retreat for the artillery, he realised that he would be unable to get his guns safely back to the French side of the river until the rest of the army had passed. To buy time for that to happen, Bourgeat ordered his chief of staff, Colonel Bouchu, to take command of the twelve cannon constituting the reserve artillery and deploy them in line facing the approaching enemy troops. Bourgeat then formed the seventeen guns of the divisional artillery of V Corps into a second battery and deployed it alongside that formed by Colonel Bouchu.[80] The only infantry support available was the 1st Battalion of the 12th Light, which maintained its cohesion under Battalion Chief Louis, as well as some of the voltigeurs who had been operating in the intervals of the French formations throughout the day, but this would-be last stand was also protected in part by Latour-Maubourg's cavalry, which was still manoeuvring on the extreme left flank.[81]

It nevertheless seemed doubtful that the guns could turn the tide, but, as the French infantry filed to the rear, the French artillery was left with a clear field of fire towards the approaching masses of allied troops. When this wall of metal opened fire with canister rounds at relatively short rage, the allies were stopped in their tracks: 'Each

77. A. de Roverea, Letter to Father, (?) October 1811, in F. de Roverea, *Mémoires*, Vol. 4, p. 41.
78. Soult's efforts to rally his troops are recounted in d'Héralde, *Mémoires*, p. 158.
79. Lapène, *Conquête*, p.257.
80. Part of this battery may have been under the direct command of Colonel François Berge of the 5th Horse Artillery Regiment, who was serving as Ruty's chief of staff.
81. Malaguti, *Historique du 87e Régiment (ex-12e Léger)*, p. 368.

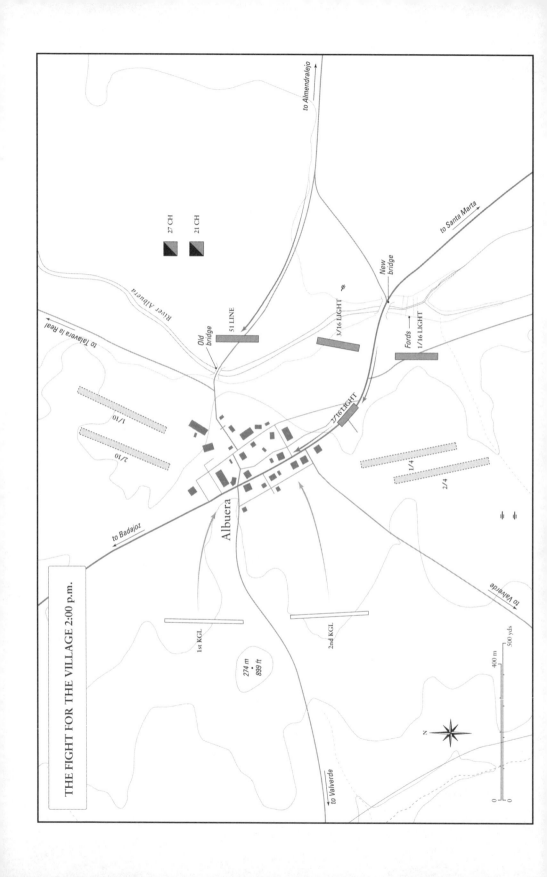

THE FIGHT FOR THE VILLAGE 2:00 p.m.

to Badajoz

Albuera

to Talavera la Real

River Albuera

Old bridge

51 LINE

3/16 LIGHT

New bridge

Fords

1/16 LIGHT

2/16 LIGHT

27 CH

21 CH

1/10

2/10

1/4

2/4

to Almendralejo

to Santa Marta

to Valverde

to Valverde

1st KGL

2nd KGL

274 m
899 ft

N

0   400 m   500 yds

time the enemy advanced in pursuit, we crushed them with our artillery fire.'[82] (Unfortunately, the French were also unavoidably firing at the same time on their own wounded, who had been left behind during their retreat on the slope running down to the stream.) The officers and artillerymen serving the guns realised that the safety of the army depended on their ability to hold their ground and they never faltered in their duty. Lieutenant Kernier of the 3rd Horse Artillery (who was 'carrying a telescope and wearing a bearskin cap') was, for instance, wounded twice but refused medical treatment in order to stay and encourage his men.[83]

The unexpected success of this dramatic stand of an unsupported artillery force against an entire army had its intended effect – the French troops were comforted by the roar of the guns and began to recover some composure. Another rallying point was provided by the regimental eagles of V Corps. The eagle-bearers stopped before crossing the stream and formed up behind the artillery, where they were joined by assorted stubborn veterans unwilling to concede that they were being driven from the field. Typical of these was a simple voltigeur of the 88th Line, who ended up with the eagle of the 103rd Line when the Lieutenant d'Egremont, the eagle-bearer of the 103rd, had his leg broken by the explosion of a howitzer shell.[84] When the last stragglers came in, the French infantry were able to finish crossing the stream in an orderly fashion and re-formed on the other side, but now one last crisis loomed – the guns themselves had to be saved. With ammunition running low and allied skirmishers swarming closer and closer, Bourgeat improvised a simple but effective plan. The two groups of guns were withdrawn in alternate stages, with one battery providing covering fire while the other battery retired and then provided covering fire in turn for the first battery.[85] This rear-guard action, culminating in the escape of the French artillery without the loss of a single gun or caisson, was a remarkable achievement and was even recognised as such by Marshal Beresford: 'His [Soult's] overbearing cavalry ... and ... his artillery saved his Infantry after its rout.'[86] This outcome also reveals indirectly how battered the allied army was (physically and psychologically) at this late state of the action and therefore how incapable it was of any additional offensive effort. Von Schepeler was particularly bitter that Lumley did so little to challenge the French at the last stages of the battle. He likened Lumley's behaviour to that of Lord George Sackville, who, after the Battle of Minden, 'built a bridge of gold' for the enemy by not harassing their retreat.[87]

82. The details of Bourgeat's actions come from a memoir written by his ADC, Captain Jean-Étienne Pernet of the 5th Foot Artillery Regiment of the Line, that is quoted in Rey & Remy, *Bourgeat*, pp. 99–101 at 100. In his *Mémoires*, p. 238, Soult gives General Ruty the credit for this use of the artillery to cover the retreat of the infantry, but Soult only mentioned Bourgeat, and not Ruty, in his Unpublished Report.

83. Unfortunately, Kernier ultimately succumbed to a third wound. D'Héralde, *Mémoires*, p. 159. D'Héralde does not actually name the 'light artillery' lieutenant who turned down his assistance, but Kernier is identified by Lapène and, in fact, was the only horse artillery officer killed at the battle. Lapène, *Conquête*, p.257.

84. D'Héralde, *Mémoires*, p. 159. The name of the eagle-bearer of the 103rd Line comes from Martinien's *Tableaux*. D'Egremont later died of his wounds.

85. Rey & Remy, *Bourgeat*, p. 100. D'Héralde says that the last artillery pieces did not cross back to the French side of the Chicapierna stream until the evening but, even if that is true, they must have been very close to the banks of the stream in the interim. D'Héralde, *Mémoires*, p. 159

86. Beresford, Report to Wellington, 18 May 1811.

87. Von Schepeler, *Histoire*, Vol. 3, p. 176.

The fighting was still not done, however. Back at the village, the withdrawal of the KGL had been so quietly executed that the French did not recognise the opportunity presented to them until it was too late. They did manage to advance some men of the 16th Light into the village, but they had barely begun to settle themselves when Alten received a countermand of the withdrawal order. He immediately launched a successful counter-attack that swept away the new defenders:

> Several companies of the 2nd Light Battalion, which were the nearest at hand instantly faced about and retook the village cheering and advancing in double quicktime, without meeting with any serious opposition. The enemy was found to have thrown only a very few straggling tirailleurs into the place, and even these were not met with, till the churchyard, situated in the centre of the village, had been passed. The 1st Light Battalion in the mean time rapidly advanced on the right of the village, its left wing closely skirting the same, and then throwing a strong line of skirmishers forward. These became briskly engaged with the enemy who kept possession of the bridge and the broken ground on the margin of the Albuera river.[88]

Rifleman Lindau was a participant in the counter-attack:

> We stuck our sword bayonets on our rifles and with a 'Hurrah!' went into the village, which was already occupied by the French. In the beginning they shot at us, but they yielded and retreated, indeed in such a hurry that I alone chased ten Frenchmen out of the ruins of a house and only managed to get my bayonet into the last of them, running him through as he jumped over the wall.[89]

Given the outcome on the other flank, Soult could not afford to lose any more men, so he ordered the 16th Light to withdraw completely to the French side of the river. The officer commanding that unit was a stubborn man, however, and he was unwilling to give up possession of the bridge since it represented the only tangible accomplishment of the day for his regiment.[90] He consequently ignored the first summons from Godinot and then another before he finally concluded there was nothing more that he and his men could accomplish and led them back to the French side of the river.[91] Unfortunately, this withdrawal led to the temporary recapture of the bridge by the British:

> The bridge ... was for some time retaken by part of our skirmishers making a dash at it, but these being unnecessarily exposed in so advanced a situation, they were recalled, however, without the enemy's retaking possession.[92]

After all the firing had ceased, the commander of the 16th Light indulged himself with a last act of stubborn defiance. He 'placed a small advanced Picket on the bridge', thus having the figurative last word in the battle on that part of the field. It was approximately 4:00 p.m.

88. Alten, Narrative.
89. Lindau, *Erinnerungen*, p. 37.
90. It is likely that the 16th was commanded at Albuera by Battalion Chief Ghenezer, the senior battalion commander, rather than its colonel, Morio de l'Isle.
91. Beauvais, *Victoires et Conquêtes*, Vol. 20, p. 245.
92. This and the following quote are from Alten, Narrative.

Chapter 10

The Aftermath of Battle

When the fighting finally stopped and it became certain that there would be no last push made that day by either side, the commanders of the opposing forces still had a lot to do. The three highest priority concerns were the same for all the armies: regrouping the surviving troops for a possible renewal of battle; taking care of the wounded; and securing the prisoners. Although no army was especially successful in dealing with these issues, they all managed to address them well enough to stave off serious problems.

The post-battle steps taken by Marshal Soult are detailed by Captain Lapène, but similar ones were probably also taken by Marshal Beresford:

> The commanding general [Soult], after having made arrangements to secure his camp from surprise attack and visited his advanced posts, went to the aid station where he personally made sure that the wounded were receiving the best treatment possible under difficult circumstances. Returning to his bivouac, he sent orders to all his division commanders and other senior officers to report on the state of their troops.[1]

One thing Soult must certainly have learned from those reports was that V Corps was no longer an effective fighting force – both divisions had been smashed beyond recognition. Werlé's brigade and the Combined Grenadier force could probably be rallied during the night, but the only unbroken force of infantry Soult could count on was Godinot's brigade, bruised but not broken during its fight for the village. In addition, he still had a powerful force of cavalry and artillery, but the ammunition stores for the latter were severely depleted.

The allied army was certainly in rather better shape than that of the French, but it was also unprepared for immediate action. Marshal Beresford had nearly 15,000 Spanish and Portuguese troops who had hardly fired a shot, but the 2nd and 4th Divisions had suffered truly horrendous casualties, so the only 'British' troops he had to deploy until the arrival of General Kemmis's brigade were the light battalions of the KGL.

Soult and Beresford could take steps to stabilise the military situation on both sides of the river, but there was little or nothing they could do to alleviate the shock that seemed to affect most survivors of the battle, no matter what their nationalities,

---

1. Lapène, *Conquête*, p. 169.

due to the extraordinary number of casualties suffered by the combatants.[2] A military unit is normally considered useless as a fighting force when it has taken over 30 per cent casualties. After Albuera, many units needed to cope with far worse outcomes. For instance, according to a surviving officer of the Buffs, only 5 officers and 94 men (less than 15 per cent) of the regiment remained to draw rations the day after the battle (although these numbers improved so rapidly thereafter due to the return of escaped prisoners that the Buffs became known as the 'Resurrection Men').[3] The 2nd/48th lost 23 of 29 officers and 320 of 423 men (76 per cent) killed, wounded or captured, while the 1st Battalion of the same regiment lost 57 per cent of its 497 soldiers. The 57th left 428 (66 per cent) of its 647 officers and men on the field of battle and the survivors were commanded by Lieutenant-Adjutant William Mann, who had been the fourteenth officer in seniority at the start of the action.[4] According to Lieutenant Crompton, the 66th Foot lost 320 of 400 soldiers, an astonishing 80 per cent of its fighting strength (although, once again, the final casualty figures tallied a few days later were somewhat lower).[5] Strangely enough, command of the whole of Colborne's brigade had devolved by way of seniority onto a Frenchman, Captain Gilbert Cimitière of the 48th, who had emigrated from France during the Revolution and joined the British Army in 1794.[6]

There were so many officer casualties that anyone who survived unharmed was worried about being taken for a shirker. Ensign Hobhouse was one of the officers in this situation despite the many dangers he had encountered during the day:

> Among all the officers in the regiment, another and myself were the only ones who had not some scratch or shot through their cloathes [*sic*]. We were in vain looking for some hole to show our brother officers; our anxiety to find one, and our want of success created a laugh against us.[7]

The Portuguese forces had been only slightly engaged, so their losses were relatively light. Casualties for the Spanish armies were unequally distributed, but almost every unit had some men killed and wounded. Zayas's division suffered the worst. The two battalions of the Spanish Royal Guards that defeated Girard lost, respectively, 167 and 169 officers and men, while the Irlanda Regiment suffered 272 casualties.

The French casualties were even worse in both absolute and relative terms, although their exact total loss will never be known with certainty. Soult ultimately filed an incomplete return of losses in July that accounted for a total of at least 5,936 officers and men killed, wounded or missing, but the real number was certainly higher than that. According to Beresford, the French 'left 2,000 dead upon the field' as well as 'about 1,000 prisoners, almost all [with] desperate wounds'.[8] Soult meanwhile

2. Appendix B contains the best information available from primary sources concerning the strengths and casualties of the units that fought at Albuera. All these numbers must be treated with caution because that they may reflect both innocent error and intentional under-reporting.
3. Gordon, 'Extract of a Letter'.
4. The casualty figures come from Hobhouse's letter; the detail about Lieutenant Mann comes from a letter written by Colonel Inglis printed in the *United Service Journal*, 1829, Part I, p. 350.
5. Crompton, Letter to Mother, 18 May 1811.
6. Gurney, *History of the Northamptonshire Regiment*, p. 151.
7. Hobhouse, Letter to Father, 17 May 1811.
8. B. to W., 20 May 1811, *Supp. Despatches*, Vol. 7, pp. 133–4 at 133.

admitted on 4 June that he had at least 5,600 more casualties: 'Of the wounded, 4,500 have arrived at Seville; 600 remain with their regiments; 500, who could not be moved, are under treatment in the commune of Extremadura; the rest remain in the field; the enemy, I think, have made 200 prisoners.'[9] These figures from Beresford and Soult suggest a total French loss of approximately 8,600 and this 44 per cent larger loss is consistent with the fact that the total number of officer casualties (362) listed in Martinien's *Tableaux* and supplement is 38 per cent larger than the total (262) reported by Soult in his official return. Even using just Soult's official casualty figures, unit losses were severe. The 12th Light, the largest regiment in the field, lost 769 men (36 per cent of its strength). The 64th Line had 651 killed, wounded or captured, equal to 41 per cent of its pre-battle complement. The highest percentage loss was suffered by the 34th Line, one of the lead regiments in Girard's flank attack. That unit lost 44 per cent of its original 953 officers and men. Surprisingly, despite the fact that they were engaged in combat on multiple occasion during the day, the Lancers of the Vistula Legion lost only 130 officers and men from their original strength of 591, a relatively small number of casualties given the spectacular results they achieved. As with the allies, the staggering losses suffered by the French officer corps made it especially hard to ready the remaining troops for any additional combat activity.

The most urgent post-battle activity for all the forces was caring for their wounded. In all the armies engaged at Albuera, there was at least one surgeon attached to each regiment and, in the French and British Armies, there were also medical personnel attached at the division and corps levels.[10] None of the armies, however, had a systematic plan for treating casualties on the scale encountered in an action as bloody as Albuera, so wounded men generally had to fend for themselves both during and immediately after the battle. The result was a hotchpotch of experiences for the wounded of Albuera, with a noticeable line of demarcation between the experiences of wounded soldiers who could move to safety and assistance under their own power and those who could not.

A wounded man who was very fortunate might actually have received relatively prompt treatment from medical personnel serving near the front line or working out of a first aid station established close to the fighting. The only one of these at Albuera that can be identified with certainty is that organised by Surgeon George Guthrie for the 4th Division. It was close enough to the action that even the medical officers were in danger:

> Mr. Guthrie placed himself on the plain a little in the rear of the two British divisions of infantry with the cavalry on the right. It was impossible to keep out of the way of either shot or shell. Assistant-staff-surgeon Bolman was struck by one in the chest, which went right through him. Rain came down in torrents; the lightning was more terrific than the flashes of the guns, the thunder louder . . .[11]

9. Soult, Letter to Berthier, 4 June 1811. Soult's estimated number of wounded in Extremadura may be low, since British reports indicate they encountered as many as 720 such cases. See text accompanying Notes 27 and 28 *below, p. 217*. There does not appear to be a copy of this letter in the files of the SHAT.

10. For information about the French and British medical services, see Brice and Bottet, *Le Corps de Santé Militaire*, and Cantlie, *The Army Medical Department*. No similar works are available for the Spanish and Portuguese Armies.

11. Anonymous, 'Guthrie Biography', p. 731.

Surgeon d'Héralde of the 88th Line actually accompanied his regiment into battle and experienced first-hand the fighting on the ridge. Because V Corps was constantly on the move, he was ordered to leave his medical supplies packed up and told that the first casualties would be sent back to a field hospital (*ambulance*) set up on the French side of the river. D'Héralde asserts that a total of fifteen French surgeons were wounded during the battle and that three subsequently died.[12]

Once the battle ended, the doctors available were overwhelmed by the vast numbers of wounded needing care. The best that could be achieved was a rigorous triage to maximise the efficient use of the time and skills of the few surgeons on the scene. The following recollection by Rifleman William Green (who was not at Albuera but whose experience is representative) indicates that subtlety was not the order of the day in terms of treatment in such situations. Green was hit by a musket ball which went through the thick part of his thigh and then lodged in his left wrist. He was fortunate enough to be carried to a nearby aid station on a stretcher made of 'two slant poles with a piece of sacking nailed to them':

> ... at the distance of about a mile we reached the tents, where ... there was a doctor standing by the tent-pole, with his coat off, a pair of blue sleeves on, and a blue apron; a large wax taper was burning, and there was a box of instruments laying by his side. The tent was full of wounded, all laying with their feet towards the pole; it was an awful sight to see, and to hear their groans was truly heart-rending. I stepped up to the doctor, he saw the blood trickling down my leg, and tore off a piece of my trousers to get at the wound, which left my leg and part of my thigh bare. He then made his finger and thumb meet in the hole the ball had made, and said 'The ball is out my lad!' He put in some lint and covered the wound with some strapping, and bid me lay down and make myself as comfortable as I could, saying 'There are others who need dressing worse than you!' I said 'I have another wound in my wrist,' so he cut the back part of my wrist, about an inch and half, put in an instrument and pulled out a piece of the thumb bone, about half an inch long, which had been broken off by the ball, and driven into the back of the wrist. The ball could not be extracted. He then dressed the wound, and bid me lay down outside the tent as there was no room inside.[13]

The experience of Major Brooke of the 2nd/48th Foot demonstrates that the situation in the French aid stations at Albuera was much the same. He was astonished to find that he received excellent, if brusque, treatment from a French doctor even though he was an enemy prisoner:

> When I arrived at the French hospital, one of their own surgeons, seeing me so badly wounded, left his own people and examined my head. He cut off much of my hair, and, having put some lint on my two wounds, tied up my head so tightly, to keep the skull together, that I could not open my mouth for three days, except to take a little to drink. He told me that at the expiration of that time I might venture to loosen the bandage a little ... Of my final recovery he gave

12. D'Héralde, *Mémoires*, pp. 155 and 162. Martinien lists only three medical officer casualties for Albuera, but the records for these non-combatants may not have been kept meticulously.
13. Green, *Where Duty Calls Me*, pp. 36–7.

me little hope, as my skull had received fractures of whose consequences he was fearful.[14]

One certain point about all the aid stations was that a wounded man could not expect any treatment normally covered by the concept of nursing. A drink might be proffered, but there was no cleaning of wounds, nor was there any attempt to make the patients comfortable in either the physical or mental sense of that term. Major Brooke reports, for instance, that it was not until three days after the battle that he was able to wash his head wounds and the clotted blood on his face and clothing.

The end of the fighting gave hope to the non-ambulatory wounded strewn over the battlefield. They could not find medical attention on their own, but now others could come to their aid and indeed many survivors returned to the scene of the action urgently seeking missing comrades or relations. Sometimes the result was a happy one, as was the case for Lieutenant Clarke of the 66th:

> In the evening I went to seek my friend [Ensign James Hay], and found him sitting up to his hips in mud and water. He was quite cool and collected, and said there were many worse than him.[15]

Other searches had more sombre results. Lieutenant George Browne of the 23rd Fusiliers took a corporal's guard out specifically to search for Second Lieutenant Hall, the 'pet of the regiment'. When they eventually found him, Hall was still alive but unconscious from the gunshot he had suffered to his head and he had been stripped of his clothes by scavengers. Browne told Hall's brother years later: 'I carried him in my arms to the hospital, and in my arms the next day he died.'[16]

Colonel von Schepeler, the Spanish staff officer, was willing to provide succour to wounded of all nationalities. He first came upon a soldier of the Buffs lying face down in the mud and he was surprised to find that the wounded man's first words after being saved by von Schepeler were: 'Who won the battle?' 'We did,' responded von Schepeler, but the wounded man was perhaps understandably confused over the identity of a man in a blue uniform speaking English with a German accent. 'Who is "we"?' he managed to inquire. When von Schepeler confirmed that the allies had been the victors, the soldier muttered 'Ah, well, well', and breathed his last. Von Schepeler next met a handsome French officer with a broken leg who seemed more upset at having been defeated than at having been wounded. When von Schepeler arranged for some Portuguese soldiers to pick him up, the Frenchman 'said seriously "I thank you very much, Monsieur," but no other sound or complaint crossed his lips.'[17]

Such individual efforts to help the wounded left on the battlefield were, overall, insufficient given the sheer magnitude of the task. There were just too many wounded and too few survivors to make a difference. As a result of these circumstances, most non-walking wounded at Albuera (but especially those abandoned on the field by the defeated army) were forced to spend at least one night where they fell without any attention whatsoever. General Long noted that the weather made this reality particularly unpleasant after Albuera:

14. Brooke, 'Prisoner', p. 179.
15. Clarke Narrative in Groves, *The 66th Regiment*, p. 53.
16. Hall, *Retrospect of a Long Life*, p. 589.
17. Von Schepeler, *Histoire*, Vol. 3, p. 272 n. 1.

A violent rain fell during the action & a still heavier one during the evening & the following day. This made the situation of the wounded most pitiable. Not a house presented itself for [shelter], not a carriage or beast of burden was to be found to transport them to the rear. On the ground therefore they remained, some for 24 many for 48 hours, with bleeding wounds where they fell, exposed to cold & a drenching rain & many of them stripped to the skin.[18]

Sergeant Cooper of the 7th Fusiliers attributed the neglect of the British wounded to the coincidence of a number of unfortunate circumstances:

What was now to be done with the wounded that were so thickly strewed on every side? The town of Albuera had been totally unroofed and unfloored for firewood by the enemy [in a prior visit], and there was no other town within several miles; besides, the rain was pouring down, and the poor sufferers were as numerous as the unhurt. To be short, the wounded that could not walk were carried in blankets to the bottom of the bloody hill and laid among the wet grass. Whether they had any orderlies to wait on them, or how many lived or died, I can't tell.[19]

Cooper condemns the Spaniards for failing to assist with the wounded, but he also mentions a specific incident involving himself that suggests that the unwounded survivors were so stunned by the trauma of battle that they had temporarily lost the ability to feel pity for their less fortunate comrades:

Once [during the night] I looked out of my wet blanket and saw a poor wounded man stark naked, crawling about I suppose for shelter. Who had stript [sic] him or whether he lived till morning I know not.[20]

Friedrich Lindau also had a bizarre encounter with a wounded man. After finding it impossible to sleep because of the cold and wet, he went scavenging into the village and found one of his officers, Captain Georg Arnold Heise, lying wounded in an abandoned house. Heise had been shot in the head and was in such pain that he begged Lindau to finish him off. Lindau declined and offered what comfort he could before returning to his bivouac. After some fitful sleep, he roused himself at daybreak to find that he had been sleeping next to a corpse. He then spent much of the morning carrying canteens of water to the wounded men still in the field.[21]

Wounded Frenchmen who were unlucky enough to be left on the field of battle were exposed to an even greater danger than mere neglect. Because of the unrelentingly homicidal nature of the warfare between French and Spaniards in the Peninsula, they knew they could expect little mercy or pity if they fell into Spanish hands. One British officer noticed that such fears led the French wounded to seek assistance from him:

Who are these, that catch every moment at our coats, and cling to our feet, in such a humble attitude? The wounded soldiers of the enemy, who are imploring

18. Long to Brother, 30 May 1811, p. 712.
19. Cooper, *Rough Notes*, p. 62.
20. *Ibid.*
21. Lindau, *Erinnerungen*, p. 38. Heise was evacuated to Elvas and died there on 10 June.

British protection from the exasperated and revengeful Spaniards. What a proud compliment to our country![22]

This anxiety of the French was well-founded. An anonymous British officer recorded some years later the experience of meeting a Spanish peasant who announced that his object in life 'was to kill as many Frenchman as he could' and that he had been particularly successful in pursuing that object in the immediate aftermath of Albuera:

> [H]e pulled a tremendous knife from his side-pocket, with which he assured us, he sent eleven Frenchmen to sleep with their fathers on the morning subsequent to the Battle of Albuera. On upbraiding him for his cruelty, and inquiring how he could perpetrate such cold-blooded atrocities, he very coolly replied that it was the duty of every loyal Spaniard like himself, to send as many Frenchmen into another world as they could, wherever they might find them, whether in the field of battle, or in a private retreat – whether armed or unarmed – or whether they might be in the enjoyment of health, or writhing under the effects of severe wounds.[23]

Many of the British were appalled at such treatment of wounded men, but von Schepeler noted that it was easy to have such a smug attitude if one's homeland had never been invaded by a cruel and heartless foe. However, von Schepeler himself took steps to safeguard some German-speaking wounded men (Alsatians?) of the French army from precisely that kind of fate. He wondered at the time how surprised they must have been to find a German-speaking 'Spaniard' answering their pleas for protection.[24]

By way of contrast, those wounded men who were able to get away from the battlefield usually obtained better treatment in the short run, with officers generally having more success in this regard than others. Lieutenant Harrison of the 23rd Regiment was hit in the leg but, with the assistance of his sword, 'hobbled about a half mile to the rear'.[25] There he met an NCO with a horse who conveyed him another half mile to the place where the regimental baggage had been left. He lay there in the rain for four hours, then decided to ride to Valverde on a mule with another wounded officer: 'The road presented a shocking scene, numbers exerting themselves to avoid the inclemency of the night.'[26] He arrived there soon after 10 p.m. and ended up sharing accommodation with some soldiers of the Buffs. Harrison looked for a doctor on the field and at Valverde, but never found one and ended up giving first aid to himself:

> Still, no 'Pill' [doctor] was to be procured, being few in number and having many subjects … I refreshed myself with a little tea and bread which was all the sustenance I had that day, but notwithstanding slept pretty well on a little straw 'till morning when I proceed to operations myself and cut open my overalls. As

22. Sherer, *Recollections*, pp. 161–3.
23. Anonymous, The Military Memoirs of an Infantry Officer, pp. 138–9.
24. Von Schepeler, *Histoire*, Vol. 3, p. 277
25. Harrison, Letter to Mother, 24 May 1811, quoted in Glover, 'The Royal Welch Fusiliers', p. 151.
26. *Ibid.*

no mark was through I was afraid the ball had lodged in [my leg]. It entered about three inches above the knee and luckily had passed through on the under side and lodged in the overalls under the knee where I found the gentleman myself and mean to keep [it] for a memento of the day.[27]

Sir William Myers of the 7th Fusiliers, who was wounded in the abdomen, wanted his servants to build him a shelter so that he could stay near his regiment, but 'fondly hoping his recovery possible, [they] persisted in removing him to where they could procure a bed. On the road he appeared free from pain, and not altogether aware of the extremity of his situation.'[28]

The French wounded who had retired to their side of the river were not noticeably better off, even though they found some shelter in the woods in that vicinity and were spared the additional horror of mingling with the corpses left on the battlefield:

> Our wounded, lying here and there under the trees, begged insistently for prompt medical attention, but it could not be provided because their numbers swamped the available medical resources. The sky, already dark during the battle, clouded up even more towards evening and the abundant rain that followed destroyed in part the benefit obtained by those who had received medical treatment. These miserable conditions led to the unfortunate deaths of some men who might otherwise have survived their wounds.[29]

The only shelter from the rain available to General Maransin, who had been severely wounded by a musket ball that passed through his stomach, was a blanket held over him throughout the night by some faithful grenadiers.[30] A French engineer, Captain Armand Andoucaud, who had been wounded in the arm by a musket ball, only found shelter by striking out on his own:

> He believed it would be healthier to avoid exposure to night air, so he left the army bivouac and made his way to a little hamlet near the French lines where he could find some shelter. He went to sleep there, believing himself safe, because he did not imagine that the French might abandon the field of such a bloody and indecisive battle without having gained their objective of relieving Badajoz. Twenty-four hours after the French army had departed for Seville, the owner of the house in which he was staying gave him the shocking news that a Spanish patrol had just arrived at the village. Despite suffering from a fever, Andoucaud roused himself immediately and was able to make his escape and rejoin the French army by forced marches.[31]

Unfortunately, Andoucaud's wound became infected and he died of tetanus at Seville, 'speaking sadly in his last moments of the wife and [five] children he would never see again'.[32]

---

27. Harrison, Letter to Mother, 24 May 1811, quoted in Glover, 'The Royal Welch Fusiliers', p. 151.
28. Anonymous, 'Sir William Myers', p. 473.
29. Lapène, *Conquête*, p. 168.
30. *Ibid.*, pp. 168–9.
31. Petiet, *Mémoires*, p. 350.
32. *Ibid.*, p. 335. Out of the officers present at the death of Andoucaud, one, his good friend Colonel Delapointe, later married Andoucaud's widow, and another, Captain Auguste Petiet, married one of his daughters.

Having been driven back across the river, the French were deprived of the opportunity to search actively for wounded comrades. They could only wait on their side of the river and hope that missing soldiers would be able to make their way back to safety on their own. Orderly Dragoon Louis Gougeat spent the whole afternoon anticipating the return of his captain:

Towards 4 or 5 o'clock, having heard no news about my regiment, I went looking for him. The cannon and gunfire had quieted down by then and the battle seemed to be coming to an end. Moving through the locations where the dragoons had been during the day, my heart was broken by the sight of the numbers of dead and dying that littered the ground. When I arrived at the position that had been occupied by the dragoons earlier in the day, gunfire had completely ceased. I found my comrades in a pitiable state: they were defeated and exhausted; their faces blackened by the smoke from gunpowder were unrecognisable. I soon, however, had the satisfaction to learn that my captain was safe and sound – someone pointed out to me that he was lying on his cloak a short distance away . . . he was sad and preoccupied; of the food I offered him, he accepted only a small piece of bread which he ate slowly and silently. When he was finished, he lay down again.[33]

Searching for missing men was not the only motivation that brought soldiers out to survey the field of battle. Some returned to the site of the most intense fighting simply to fix the scene in their memories or to try to make sense of the horrendous experience they had just endured. Many could barely cope with the reality that so many comrades who had been hale and hearty in the morning had been killed, wounded or captured. Lieutenant Sherer recorded the vivid and appalling scenes he encountered when he walked the battlefield late in the day on the 16th:

Look around – behold thousands of slain, thousands of wounded, writhing in anguish, and groaning with agony and despair. Move a little this way, here lie four officers of the French hundredth [100th Line], all corpses. Why, that boy cannot have numbered eighteen years? How beautiful, how serene a countenance! Perhaps, on the banks of the Loire, some mother thinks anxiously of this her darling child. Here fought the third brigade; here the fusileers: how thick these heroes lie! Most of the bodies are already stripped; rank is no longer distinguished. Yes: this must have been an officer; look at the delicate whiteness of his hands, and observe on his finger the mark of his ring. What manly beauty; what a smile still plays upon his lip! He fell, perhaps, beneath his colours; died easily; he is to be envied. Here charged the Polish lancers; not long ago, the trampling of the horses, the shout, the cry, the prayer, the death stroke, all mingled their wild sounds on this spot; it is now, but for a few fitful and stifled groans, as silent as the grave. What is this? A battered trumpet; the breath which filled, this morning, its haughty tone, has fled, perhaps, for ever. And here again, a broken lance. Is this the muscular arm that wielded it? 'Twas vigorous, and slew, perhaps a victim on this field; it is now unnerved by death. Look at the contraction of this body, and the anguish of these features; eight times has some

33. Gougeat, 'Mémoires', p. 337.

lance pierced this frame. Here again lie headless trunks, and bodies torn and struck down by cannon shot; such death is sudden, horrid, but 'tis merciful.

Lieutenant Sherer concluded that 'it would be well for kings, politicians, and generals' to experience such scenes for themselves lest they be inclined to 'talk of victories with exultation, and of defeats with philosophical indifference'.[34]

One unusual consequence of exploration of the battlefield was the recovery of three more British colours (one intact and two damaged) in addition to the regimental colour of the Buffs that had been found during the advance of the fusiliers. The intact colour was the king's colour of the 29th which had been carried by Ensign Furnace. The first damaged colour was the regimental colour of the 29th which had been torn from its staff and hidden by Ensign Vance. The other damaged colour was the king's colour of the Buffs. The portion that Lieutenant Latham had torn from the staff was discovered hidden under his mutilated and apparently lifeless body. The exact circumstances of this discovery were never recorded, but the fact that the finder of the colour failed to notice that Latham was actually still alive condemned the officer to spend more time on the battlefield with his wounds untended:

> After lying some time on the ground in a state of insensibility, Lieut. Latham revived, and crawled towards the river, where he was found endeavouring to quench his thirst. He was removed to the convent, his wounds dressed, the stump of his arm amputated, and he ultimately recovered.[35]

The great mass of survivors did not even have the strength or inclination to visit the scene of the action. They were more concerned with the need for rest, food and shelter, but those items were in very short supply:

> Having returned to the top of the ridge we piled arms and looked about. What a scene! The dead and wounded lying all around. In some places the dead were in heaps. One of these was nearly three feet high, but I did not count the number in it ... But if [the wounded] were ill off our case was not enviable. We were wet, weary and dirty; without food or shelter.[36]

Officers were no better off. Captain Thomas Gell, who led the 'poor remains' of the 29th Foot off the field due to the death or disability of all the more senior officers, was exhausted and hungry, but found that Spaniards had plundered his baggage.[37] When Lieutenant Rice Jones of the Royal Engineers reached Albuera after the fighting had ended, he discovered that not even the commander-in-chief was guaranteed a hot dinner and a place to sleep:

> Joined Marshal Beresford and remained with the staff [for the rest of the day]. Towards evening the Marshal and suite went into the village of Albuera, intending to dine there on what could be procured, but obliged to evacuate; though the Germans under General Alten did not give up possession of it. The

34. Sherer, *Recollections*, pp. 161–3.
35. Cannon, 'Memorandum Relating to ... Albuera'. See Appendix F, pp. 307–9, for more information about Latham's life after the battle.
36. Cooper, *Rough Notes*, pp. 61–2.
37. Gell, Letter to his Father, 17 May 1811.

enemy having the bridge could force them out when they liked. Lay on the field near the 34th Regiment. Major [Henry Charles] Dickens affording us all the aid he could; rainy and uncomfortable all night; the ground being so very wet and no shelter to be found.[38]

Lieutenant James Lindam of the 2nd Light Battalion of the KGL recalled that they had better luck with rations than the marshal because his men were able to improvise a meal from the flesh of the numerous horses killed in action by cooking it using debris from the battlefield:

But we young fellows soon found out we were ravenously hungry; and so, while some gathered splinters of gun-carriages and the like, others made rough gridirons out of broken iron ramrods which were lying all about the place, and others cut steaks out of the bodies of the horses that had been killed, and grilled them over the fire; and I don't think I ever had a better dinner in my life.[39]

The appearance of the battlefield took on an even more sinister cast with the fall of night.[40] In particular, darkness brought out hordes of scavengers who, motivated by a thirst for plunder, had no compunction about finishing off a wounded man to facilitate stripping him of both property and clothing. Daniel Long of the 48th Foot was only saved from such a fate by the exertions of Mary Anne Hewitt, the wife of Sergeant Thomas Hewitt of the 48th, who was on the battlefield looking for her missing husband:

As Mary Anne was moving along, here and there lifting a head to see if life could be perceived . . . she came upon two or three trampers stripping a body, and a painful groan was uttered by the very man whom they were robbing. It was well she heard it. In another moment she would have heard no more, for already a Portuguese hag raised a hammer to strike the blow upon his forehead, when her arm was arrested by the powerful grasp of the soldier's wife. There are times when a woman feels the strength and daring of a man, and such was the moment with our heroine. She forced back the miscreant's arm with such violence that it was dislocated at the shoulder in an instant – the hammer fell from her grasp and she herself fled cursing from the field. Our heroine called to her companions of the 48th, two or three of whom immediately came up, and they helped to lift the wounded man; when, what was at once her horror and delight, to discover, that the soldier who was stripped, was her old friend, Dan Long![41]

Mrs Hewitt was eventually reunited with her husband, who was unwounded himself but had been occupied assisting casualties of his regiment. Other men were not so fortunate as Dan Long.

38. Jones, *An Engineer Officer*, pp. 99–109, at p. 105.
39. Obituary of Colonel James Ohle Lindam, *The Times*, 11 January 1882, p. 6, col. E. Seventy-four allied horses and four allied mules were killed in the fighting, while one source states that the French lost a remarkable 502 horses killed (plus 302 wounded). Berthier, Report of Losses.
40. Sunset at Albuera on 16 May was at 6:38 p.m., local time, according to the US Naval Observatory website.
41. Cobbold, *Mary Anne Wellington*, Vol. 2, pp. 129–30.

It was certainly the case that civilian camp followers were not the only persons seeking plunder on the battlefield during the hours of darkness. As exemplified by the behaviour of the British forces after the storming of Badajoz and San Sebastian, the personal conduct of soldiers during the Napoleonic Wars was not always on the highest moral plane. The men were under-paid and under-appreciated, so it is not surprising that they might take a cavalier attitude towards property.[42] As one Peninsula veteran confessed in his memoirs:

> It is one of the worst results of a life of violence, that it renders such as follow it selfish and mercenary: at least, it would be ridiculous to conceal that, when the bloody work of the day is over, the survivor's first wish is to secure, in the shape of plunder, some recompense for the risks which he has run and the exertions which he has made. Neither does it enter the mind of the plunderer to consider whether it is the dead body of a friend or of a foe from which he is seeking his booty.[43]

The night of 16/17 May was consequently a long one for all the survivors of Albuera, French or allied, wounded or unwounded. Exhaustion probably overcame wet and cold for most, so that the soldiers had some sleep, but prudence dictated that both armies were once again roused before dawn to guard against the risk of an early renewal of the fighting:

> Before daylight [on the 17th] we were under arms shivering with cold, and our teeth very unsteady; but the sun rose and began to warm us. Half a mile distant were the French, but neither they nor we showed any desire of renewing hostilities. A little rum was now served out, and our blood began to circulate a little quicker. We then rubbed up our arms and prepared for another brush; but nothing serious took place except cavalry skirmishes on the plain before us.[44]

Amazingly, many of the French thought that Soult would actually be the one to renew the conflict:

> The outcome of the fighting on that day [the 16th] was so extraordinary and the unfortunate events that had led to retreat in spite of the excellent conduct and intrepidity of our soldiers were so unexpected that a reasonable number of soldiers believed that Marshal Soult would have the intention of launching another attack the next day that would be more successful because he would have learned from his mistakes.[45]

Soult, however, was more realistic about his situation and there is no indication that he ever contemplated taking any such action.

---

42. Stanhope, *Notes of Conversations*, p. 14. See also, Cross, 'The British Soldier in the Peninsular War'.
43. Farmer, *The Light Dragoon*, p. 160.
44. Cooper, *Rough Notes*, p. 63.
45. Lapène, *Conquête*, pp. 169–70

Chapter 11

The Second British
Siege of Badajoz

Daylight on 17 May brought reinforcements for the allies in the form of Kemmis's brigade, and, from that moment on, the allies were indisputably in a position to dictate what the next military events of the campaign would be. The only initiative left to the French was the decision of when and how their retreat would be effected. However, none of this was immediately clear to most of the shocked survivors. It was not even clear to Kemmis's men, who were exhausted from marching through the night to reach Albuera and stunned by the sights that greeted them:

About six o'clock, a.m., we came in sight of our troops on the field of battle at Albuera: the French were discerned near a wood, about a mile and a half in their front ... With awful astonishment, we gazed on the terrific scene before us; a total suspension took place of the noisy gaiety so characteristic of Irish soldiers; the most obdurate or risible countenances sunk at once into a pensive sadness, and for some time speech was supplanted by an exchange of sorrowful looks, and significant nods.

Before us lay the appalling sight of upwards of 6,000 men, dead, and mostly stark-naked, having, as we were informed, been stripped by the Spaniards, during the night; their bodies disfigured with dirt and clotted blood, and torn with the deadly gashes inflicted by the bullet, bayonet, sword, or lance, that had terminated their mortal existence. Those who had been killed outright, appeared merely in the pallid sleep of death, while others, whose wounds had been less suddenly fatal, from the agonies of their last struggle, exhibited a fearful distortion of features. Near our arms was a small stream almost choked with bodies of the dead, and from the deep traces of blood on its miry margin, it was evident that many of them had crawled thither to allay their last thirst. The waters of this oozing stream were so deeply tinged, that it seemed actually to run blood. A few perches distant was a draw-well, about which were collected several hundreds of those severely wounded, who had crept or been carried thither. They were sitting, or lying, in the puddle, and each time the bucket reached the surface with its scanty supply, there was a clamorous and heart-rending confusion; the cries for water resounding in at least ten languages, while a kindness of feeling was visible in the manner the beverage was passed to each other.[1]

As the day progressed, it became obvious that neither side intended to renew the battle. The focus of attention thereupon once again shifted to dealing with the vast numbers of wounded men, both in terms of collecting those who had still not been gathered from the battlefield and in terms of evacuating all the most serious cases to more appropriate hospital facilities away from Albuera. This was a more pressing problem for the French because they were facing the possibility of retreat by their whole army, but they were fortunately better equipped than the British in this regard since they had a number of purpose-built ambulances for their soldiers, and many more wagons overall:

> The French are generally well-supplied with conveyances for this purpose [the evacuation of wounded]; on this occasion they had not less than eighty or a hundred large covered wagons for the use of the worst cases, exclusive of many horses, mules and asses.[2]

As a result, the French were able to send off a large convoy of wounded on the 17th under the command of Colonel Pierre-Louis Varé using 'supply wagons, ambulances and empty artillery caissons'.[3] Even so, the resources available were insufficient for the task and the French also had to resort to the extreme expedient of forcing British prisoners to carry their wounded captors:

> ... on this occasion, from the enormous number of wounded that they had to remove, they found it necessary to force the British soldiers, who had fallen into their hands as prisoners, to carry some of their generals and other officers of note on litters. Being disgusted with this burden, through fatigue and the heat of the sun, one of the prisoners exclaimed to his comrades: 'D—n this rascal, let us throw him down and break his neck.' To the surprise of the soldiers, the wounded general lifted his head and replied in English: 'No, I hope not.' Those of the prisoners who did not escape were handsomely paid for their trouble.[4]

There is also one report that the French 'made their cavalry dismount to carry away their slight wounded'.[5] By way of contrast, on the allied side at the end of the fighting, 'Mr. Guthrie found three thousand wounded men at his feet, with four wagons only for their removal ... the nearest village of Valverde being seven miles off.'[6] To make up for this deficiency, the British assigned the whole of Kemmis's brigade to moving wounded men to Valverde on the 19th.[7]

1. Emerson, 'Recollections', in Maxwell, *Peninsular Sketches*, Vol. 2, pp. 233–4.
2. Brooke, 'Prisoner', p. 180.
3. Lapène, *Conquête*, p. 171.
4. Brooke, 'Prisoner', p. 180; see also Lapène, *Conquête*, p. 171–2, specifically mentioning the use of prisoners to assist with the evacuation of wounded senior officers. This English-speaking French general cannot be identified with certainty, but he must have been Gazan, Maransin or Brayer.
5. Letter to Archibald Shettleton [his father-in-law] dated Almondrelego [sic], 28 May 1811, in Drummond, Documents. Surprisingly, Drummond makes no specific mention of his experiences or those of his regiment other than the comment that '[I]t was a Very bloody day.'
6. Anonymous, 'Guthrie Biography', p. 731.
7. Boutflower, *Journal*, p. 93.

Initially, no systematic attempt was made to bury the dead, allied or French, although there were some instances of individual interments. Lieutenant Dobbin of the 66th, for one, was driven by respect and friendship to recover the body of his beloved Captain Benning and to make certain it was given a proper burial:

> I was for two hours after the Battle, searching for him among the dead, and when I found him Surgeon S. [Assistant Surgeon Robert Shekleton] and I paid the last sad offices to the best and bravest of men, seeing him covered in the spot on which he fell.[8]

Young Ensign Thomas of the Buffs 'was buried with all care possible, by a sergeant and a private, the only two survivors out of my [Captain Stephens's] company, which consisted of sixty-three when taken into action.'[9] General Pépin, attended by his staff officers, expired from his wounds before he could be evacuated. Some grenadiers from his division dug him a shallow grave and marked it with a tree limb.[10]

An officer of the 57th recorded that the few men left in his regiment did specifically go out looking for both dead and wounded:

> Though wet to the skin we slept soundly during the night, expecting another attack this morning. The enemy, however, has not yet thought proper to attempt it. They are still in the wood just in our front. We have been occupied the whole day in collecting our wounded and burying our dead who were this morning lying on the field of battle in two distinct lines where we stood the fire. We found the bodies of our major [John McKenzie Scott] and a captain, who was my particular friend and messmate.[11]

Most of the dead, however, were simply left where they fell, forming heaps that enabled survivors to identify immediately where the fighting had been most fierce. Lieutenant Sherer walked about the battlefield on the 20th and recorded the following scene:

> This same day I went down to that part of the field, which was covered with the slain; they lay ghastly and unburied: here and there, indeed, you might remark a loose-made grave, where some officers or soldiers had been to perform a private act of friendship. I was much struck with one affecting, though simple proof of the attachment of our peninsular allies: the hands of vast numbers of the British corpses had been clasped together in the attitude of prayer, and placed by the Spaniards in the manner they superstitiously imagine it is important to lay out their dead.[12]

The stripping of bodies was a point noted by several eyewitnesses as contributing disproportionately to the shocking spectacle of the field on the day after the battle:

8. Dobbin, Letter to Uncle, 23 May 1811.
9. Letter of Captain Stephens quoted in Matthews, Letter to Londonderry, in Londonderry, *Narrative,* Vol. 2, p. 318.
10. Lapène, *Conquête,* p. 168.
11. Hobhouse, Letter to Father, 17 May 1811.
12. Sherer, *Recollections,* p. 226

The dead, actually amounting to thousands, were in heaps, and the scene was rendered more horrible by the Spaniards plundering and stripping the bodies and thus exposing the wounds in all their horror.[13]

Eventually, concerns about both the morale of the surviving troops and the noxious effects of decomposition of the dead forced the allies, as the proud possessors of the battlefield, to take some action. They started with 'burials' that consisted of dumping bodies with little ceremony into common graves, including one that was 'a trench ... 5 or 6 hundred yards long and 4 or 5 wide'.[14] The burial task was, however, an overwhelming one: 'Our people ... buried 'til they could work no longer, and there still lay immense numbers that could be interred.'[15] As a result, many of the dead were deprived of even the minimal courtesy of interment and their corpses were burned instead.

Although the threat of French attack had faded, the situation of the remaining allied troops on the night of the 17th was little improved from that on the night of the battle itself. The simple problem was that the weather remained bad and supplies remained scarce:

On this night our situation was, if possible, more gloomy and uncomfortable than any we had yet experienced, war on every hand presenting one of his most horrid and terrific forms, while at the same time we laboured under the greatest privation. Neither provisions nor liquors could be had at any price, as to bid defiance to all attempts to better our state, even by marauding. The only place of rest, if such it could be called, was sitting on our knapsacks in the mud, into which many occasionally dropped, overcome with sleep and fatigue, and remained for a time as insensible as the gory corpse[s] on the field.[16]

The only fuel available for fires was debris found on the battlefield, a circumstance that made even keeping warm an adventure:

From the heavy rain that had fallen the preceding day, and the trampling of men and horses, the field of battle was at this time a perfect puddle, without one dry or green spot on which we could repose or be seated. Wearied and chilled after our forced march, and wading through the sloughs, we kindled fires, and as fuel could not be had, the muskets lying about were thrown on promiscuously for that purpose. These arms made truly a crack fire, for several being charged immediately exploded, the balls whistling through the mud and casting it in our faces. Alarmed at those salutes, we for some time examined if the guns were discharged, but tired of those researches, several again exploded, happily without doing any mischief.[17]

One soldier vividly described how the sounds of the battlefield at night were in some ways as shocking as those heard during the hours of combat:

13. Whinyates, Letter to Sisters, 30 May 1811, pp. 233–4.
14. Account of Lieutenant P. Gordon of the 27th Foot recorded in Bakewell, Diaries, Vol. 1, pp. 122–3.
15. This observation resulted from a battlefield visit on 21 May. Scovell, Diary, Vol. 2, p. 56.
16. Emerson, 'Recollections', in Maxwell, *Peninsular Sketches*, Vol. 2, pp. 240–1.
17. *Ibid.*, p. 240.

During those heavy and lengthened hours, when about to fall into the mire, I several times started up and gazed on this strange and appalling scene. The ghastly lines of the dead were faintly visible through the gloom, while the deep snoring of those lying about, or who still maintained their balance on their seats, nearly drowned the calls of the sentinels and the low moanings of the mutilated soldiers who still continued to feel. The dull monotony of those sounds was at times broken by others in strict unison with such a time and place. From about midnight, the howling of wolves was heard in the direction of the river; they had probably left their dens in the adjacent woods to feast on this field of carnage. Their howls seemed at times as if answered by the calls and croakings of the birds of prey which kept hovering about.[18]

The prisoners of both armies were, understandably, even worse off than their captors because they faced the same dreadful circumstances with even fewer resources to sustain them. All the prisoners had been stripped of personal property, so they lacked even knapsacks and blankets, and they received no rations. Since the armies were still within sight of one another, there was a strong incentive to escape, but, as noted by Major Brooke, the captors made a corresponding effort to be vigilant:

Weak as I was, I reconnoitred the French guard over the prisoners in the evening: it had been reinforced, and their sentries being posted three deep, I found it impossible to get past them, although on the other side of the river I could see my friends resting on their arms after their victory. The night was extremely cold and damp: we had but few clothes left, and no blankets. We made a fire by gathering boughs from the trees near us, but could get no sleep from the pain of our wounds, the loss of blood, and our distressing condition.[19]

One contemporary letter suggests that the French may have tricked some of the English out of trying to escape by promising that a prisoner exchange would be organised in short order:

In the general confusion of the engagement, our Officers and men who were taken prisoner were making their escape very fast, when Soult addressed Captain Cameron [of the Buffs], and told him it would be useless to run such risks, as in the morning they would all be exchanged. This had the effect of inducing them to remain, or it is said they would all have got off; the French General, however, did not stay to perform his promise.[20]

Although all prisoners were under guard, a certain amount of fraternisation nevertheless took place. Despite having been captured, one French officer could not allow himself to concede that the enemies he had faced at Albuera were the most stubborn he had ever encountered:

On the morning after the battle of Albuera, a number of French officers who were taken prisoners, being in friendly conversation with some British officers,

---

18. Emerson, 'Recollections', in Maxwell, *Peninsular Sketches*, Vol. 2, p. 241.
19. Brooke, 'Prisoner', pp. 179–80.
20. Anonymous, 'Extract from a letter dated Lisbon, 24 May 1811'.

one of the latter, among many questions, said, addressing himself to a bronzed Frenchman 'I suppose, in all the service that you have seen, you never witnessed so hard fought a battle as that of yesterday.' The French officer replied, 'It was a most sanguinary fight, but if you were campaigning against the Russians, you would see many such.'[21]

By the end of 17 May, Soult had resolved that the only prudent course of action left to him was to retreat, but he did not do so hastily. During the night he sent off the remaining wounded who could be moved and the rest of his baggage and equipment trains, but he kept his fighting men in position until he was certain that Beresford would not take the offensive early on the 18th. Once that fact had been ascertained, the units began to move off one by one on the road to Santa Marta until only Soult's cavalry and the 12th and 16th Light were left to form a rear-guard under the intrepid Colonel Dulong of the 12th.[22] There was certainly some skirmishing during the retreat, in which Captain François Bourbon-Busset of the 27th Mounted Chasseurs was captured when his horse was shot, but in general the allies made no serious attempt to interfere with the departure of the French.[23] The lack of a pursuit was particularly fortunate since the French were running short of all types of supplies. The chief administrative officer, or intendant-general, of the French army was named Mathieu-Favier, but his nickname was 'Mathieu-Famine' because of his notorious failures to keep the army supplied with food. There were no distributions of supplies during the retreat, but, for the most part, the French were able to live off the land, albeit not luxuriously:

> Our soldiers would have died of hunger if not for the fact that, happily, they found extensive bean fields along the road. Our horses were able to eat grass and grain we cut for them . . . The rapacious administrators had failed to prepare for any of our needs. We lacked every medical supply – bandages, wine, medicine . . . everything . . . There was not even a bit of opium to give to the wounded men suffering from tetanus.[24]

The escape of the French from the numerically superior allied army was so well-conducted that it might even have been termed a great success except for one unfortunate fact – they had to abandon some of their most severely wounded men. This expedient was understandable, but certainly one that confirmed that the French had been soundly beaten by the allies. Lieutenant Sherer was a witness to how these doubly unfortunate wounded and abandoned men fared:

> Our wounded were removed, with as much expedition as possible, to Valverde; but the field hospitals, for two or three days after the engagement, presented scenes, at the recollection of which humanity quite shudders. I can never forget seeing, on the 20th, the small chapel at Albuera filled with French wounded, very great numbers of whom had suffered amputation, and who lay on the hard stones, without even straw, in a dirty, comfortless state; all which was

21. Norton, *A List of Captain Norton's Projectiles*, p. 139.
22. Lapène, *Conquête*, pp. 172–3.
23. Eeckhoudt, *Les Chevau-Légers Belges*, p. 139.
24. D'Héralde, *Mémoires*, pp. 145 and 163.

unavoidably the case, for we had nothing to give them on the spot, and, owing to the want of conveyances, they were forced to wait till our own people had been carried to the rear.[25]

The British tried to deliver some of these wounded Frenchmen to their compatriots at Badajoz, but General Philippon rebuffed the attempt:

> The Marshal sent a Flag of Truce to Badajoz [on 21 May], demanding Medical Assistance, clothing, &c. for the French Wounded. We have none for them. We have fed and dressed and attended them, but we can't cover, or remove them. He [Philippon] answered 'We can't,' and thus they must perish.[26]

As a continuing reminder of their failure, the French were forced to resort to this expedient of abandoning wounded men again at Almendralejo and at various other points along the high road to Seville: 'The French have left four hundred wounded in this Town, and our cavalry are taking them every hour.'[27] Colonel D'Urban recorded in his journal on 21 May: '320 wounded French found here [at Zafra]. Most of them never dressed.'[28] The treatment of these men seems to have been very generous:

> The Hon. William Stewart, our division general, paid great attention to such of the enemy as were left in Almendralejo; he almost daily visited their hospitals, and satisfied himself, by personal inquiries, whether they were properly taken care of. I have more than once been present at these visits and the gratitude of these poor fellows was strongly pictured on their countenances, and in every thing they said. In speaking of their own commander, they called Soult blood-thirsty, and avaricious, saying that he cared not how he sacrificed his men, and that he was wholly bent on the pursuit of dignities and wealth.[29]

The military aftermath of Albuera began as soon as Marshal Soult retreated from the battlefield on 18 May. From a British perspective, the only reason Albuera had been fought was to give the allies another opportunity to capture Badajoz, so the best way to justify the extraordinary loss of life in the battle was to finish the job Soult had interrupted. As a result, rather than pursuing Soult with some of the many allied units that had survived the battle intact, Beresford's first priority was to put Badajoz under siege again. So, as Soult headed south, Hamilton's Portuguese division hastened north and re-established a blockade of Badajoz. After Wellington arrived, he too focused on Badajoz, although he assigned Beresford and a small force to follow Soult at a distance and at a leisurely pace.

Although Wellington demonstrated his support for Beresford time and time again in the weeks and months following the battle, he was astute enough to understand that popular opinion concerning the battle made it imperative for him to replace Beresford, at least temporarily. Fortunately for all concerned, it was just at this time

25. Sherer, *Recollections*, p. 165.
26. D'Urban, *Peninsular Journal*, p. 217.
27. Dobbin, Letter to Uncle, 23 May 1811. Beresford officially reported the number of abandoned French wounded as 350 (Beresford, *Refutation*, p. 145), while Whinyates counted only 300 (Whinyates, *The Whinyates Family*, p. 232).
28. D'Urban, *Peninsular Journal*, p. 217.
29. Sherer, *Recollections*, p. 166.

that General Rowland Hill was returning from sick leave. Hill was well-respected and well-liked and many regretted that his illness had opened the way for Beresford to take charge of the forces in the south in the first place, so it was only natural that he should resume his command, a prospect that was eagerly anticipated: 'I am exceptionally glad to hear by your letter of the 7th May that Genl Hill is now on his way to this country, where his arrival will be hailed with the most sincere joy.'[30]

At the same time, reports from Lisbon about administrative difficulties with the Portuguese Army provided another natural and ostensible reason for a change to be made other than Beresford's performance at Albuera. Wellington made his decision quickly; on 23 May he informed Lord Liverpool:

> When Hill comes he must return to his command; and I will confine Beresford to the management of the detail of the Portuguese army, which has suffered much from his employment in this campaign.[31]

Wellington's brother thought that this plan provided a most elegant solution to the Beresford problem:

> Of course I have been cautious in saying a word, but ... the truth is that Beresford has entirely lost all hope of being considered by us lookers on as a general and I think it most fortunate that you did not leave him longer to himself. And also that you propose to give his command to Hill or rather let Hill take what is naturally his and leave Beresford to arrange the Portuguese.[32]

Beresford handed over command of the southern corps to Hill on 27 May 1811, and immediately left for Lisbon.[33] Edward Pakenham, who had once commanded the fusilier brigade and who was appalled by the losses that unit had suffered, may have expressed in writing what others also felt about this development:

> He is gone, Thank heaven, to Lisbon, – to stir up the Portuguese Government, whom he is better calculated to bully than to contend with Soult. I personally wish him no ill, but most sincerely do I pray he may never command another British Soldier.[34]

The French read something more significant into the fact of Beresford being replaced by Hill. There is a document in the French archives that asserts optimistically that Beresford had been recalled to England to stand trial for having sacrificed the lives of so many of his soldiers.[35]

Because of Beresford's departure, the second siege of Badajoz was entirely a Wellington affair. This time, he intended that the British force would have sufficient resources, so he drew 46 cannon from Elvas, 12 more than Beresford had for the first siege. Wellington also made sure he had more men to work on the siege by bringing along the 3rd and 7th Divisions of his northern army. Despite all his good intentions, however, the second siege did not get off to a strong start. Dickson was once again

30. Somerset, Letter to the Duke of Beaufort, 23 May 1811.
31. W. to Liverpool, 23 May 1811, *Dispatches,* Vol. 7, p. 598–9, at 598.
32. Wellesley-Pole, Letter to W., 16 June 1811.
33. D'Urban, *Journal,* p. 218.
34. EP to Lord Longford, 3 July 1811 in Pakenham, *Letters,* pp.105–7, at 106.
35. Report of 21 July 1811, AF IV 1630 Plaq 1(iv), AN.

in charge of transporting the siege guns and equipment from Elvas and, once again, the process was painfully slow. The convoy did not reach its destination until 30 May. In the meanwhile, Wellington set his plan of attack, which was based on the assumption that Soult would renew his offensive as soon as he could find reinforcements. He therefore concluded that the British should continue to focus first on taking the Fort of San Cristoval, although this time he ordered a simultaneous bombardment of the castle in the north-east corner of the fortress so it would already be weakened when San Cristoval fell.

The plan, as before, was not a bad one, but it was undermined from the start by the insufficient quantity and poor quality of the siege material:

> The guns, it has been stated, were of brass, false in their bore, and already worn by previous service; and the shot was of all shapes and diameters ... The howitzers used as mortars were defective equally with the guns; their chambers were all of unequal size, the shells did not fit the bore, and their beds were unsteady, so that the practice was necessarily vague and uncertain, and they proved of little service.[36]

The responsibility for this state of affairs rests squarely with Wellington. The defects of the guns were clearly known before the siege began and were even the subject of gallows humour by General Thomas Picton, who quipped that 'Lord Wellington sued Badajoz *in forma pauperis* [as a pauper]' and that 'instead of breaching, the operations appeared more like beseeching Badajoz.'[37] Wellington nevertheless went ahead on a gambler's hunch that his artillery would last long enough to get the job done:

> I undertook the siege of Badajos, entertaining a belief that the means of which I had the command would reduce the place before the end of the second week in June, at which time I expected that the reinforcement for the enemy's southern army ... would join Marshal Soult. I was unfortunately mistaken in my estimate of the quality of these means.[38]

Of course, it also mattered that the allies were opposed by a particularly determined and resourceful foe in the person of General Philippon, who had used the respite provided by Soult's advance to destroy the works constructed for the first siege. Philippon reduced his men to half rations, but he nevertheless inspired them to put up a fierce resistance. The French artillery in the fortress was well-supplied with ammunition and wreaked havoc with allied efforts to progress the siege:

> The boarded platforms of the batteries, damp with the blood of our artillery-men, or the headless trunks of our devoted engineers, bore testimony to the murderous fire opposed to us.[39]

The besiegers and the besieged were so close to each other that their struggle had a distinctly personal aspect, as evidenced by an incident observed by a British officer on duty in the trenches:

36. Jones, *Journals*, Vol. 1, p. 71.
37. H. B. Robinson, *Memoirs of Lieutenant General Sir Thomas Picton*, 2 vols., London, 1835, Vol. 2, p. 26.
38. W. to Liverpool, 13 June 1811, *Dispatches*, Vol. 8, pp. 12–17, at 13.
39. Grattan, *Adventures*, p. 92.

When at last he [Colonel Richard Fletcher, Wellington's chief engineer] had satisfied himself, he quietly put up his glass, and turning to a man of my party who was sitting on the outside of an embrasure . . . said, 'My fine fellow, you are too much exposed; get inside the embrasure, and you will do your work nearly as well.' 'I'm almost finished, Colonel,' replied the soldier, 'and it isn't worth while to move now; those fellows can't hit me, for they've been trying it these fifteen minutes.' They were the last words he ever spoke! He had scarcely uttered the last syllable when a round shot cut him in two, and knocked half his body across the breech of the gun. The name of the soldier was Edward Mann . . . When he fell, the French cannoniers [sic], as was usual with them, set up a shout, denoting how well satisfied they were with their practice.[40]

Wellington did, however, have a back-up plan – he tried to use the valour of his soldiers to take the fortifications that his guns could not completely breach. Twice, on 6 June and again on 9 June, he sent storming parties against the Fort of San Cristoval. Each assault was led by a so-called 'Forlorn Hope', a squad of volunteers intended to navigate the breach or die trying, and each Forlorn Hope was commanded by the same officer, Ensign Joseph Dyas of the 51st Foot. On each occasion, 'Dyas and his companions did as much as men could do, but in vain.'[41] Unfortunately for the British, valour was found on both sides of the walls of San Cristoval and the attacks were repulsed with heavy casualties.

The failure of the second assault marked the effective end of the second siege of Badajoz:

Both attempts failed . . . upon which we were decidedly of the opinion that we had it not in our power to take the place, and therefore we raised the siege on the 10th, although we continued the blockade until the 17th.[42]

This decision was hastened by the fact that on 10 June Wellington had sight of a captured dispatch revealing that Marmont had agreed to come south to support Soult.[43] This was stunning news – the idea that two French marshals could collaborate successfully in a military operation was very ominous for the allies. Marmont noted in his memoirs that Soult was stunned as well: 'Soult was so little accustomed to cooperation, which unfortunately was very rarely offered in Spain, that he was overjoyed.'[44] Considering that the cooperation might not come to pass in reality, Wellington assembled his available forces at Albuera on 13 June with the intention of offering battle to Soult if he was in fact advancing alone, but on 14 June he received a first-hand report from one of his scouting officers, Lieutenant John Ayling of the 40th Foot, confirming that Marmont was less than two days' march away.[45] In addition, on 15 June, General Drouet d'Erlon finally rendezvoused with V Corps and turned over the missing battalions of its regiments, thus bringing that

40. Grattan, *Adventures*, p. 93.
41. Grattan, *Adventures*, p. 98–102. Dyas was promoted to lieutenant after the siege, but it was another ten years before he was promoted to captain.
42. Memo of Operations in 1811, 28 December 1811, *Dispatches*, Vol. 8, pp. 494–520, at 510.
43. W. to Liverpool, 13 June 1811, *Dispatches*, Vol. 8, pp. 12–17, at 14.
44. Marmont, *Mémoires*, Vol. 4, p. 45.
45. W. to Liverpool, 20 June 1811, *Dispatches*, Vol. 8, pp. 37–9, at 37.

corps back to a respectable strength. As the forces of Marmont and Soult made contact with each other at Mérida on 18 June, the allies were completing their withdrawal across the Guadiana. With the allies gone, the French relief forces moved forward to Badajoz and entered the fortress on 20 June. It was the very day on which the rations for Governor Philippon's garrison ran out.

Chapter 12

The Wounded of Albuera

There were three groups of individuals who felt the effects of Albuera in a particularly personal and permanent way – men who were wounded, men who were taken prisoner and the family members and friends of the many men who were killed. For soldiers in the first of these groups, surviving long enough to receive medical treatment was just the start of a long and painful set of experiences that had to be endured before their situation resolved in death, recovery or permanent disability. Treatment would generally take one of three forms: external procedures (including the splinting of broken bones and the sewing of gaping wounds); internal procedures (including probing and the extraction of musket balls and foreign matter); and amputation. This last treatment was not used as extensively as is ordinarily believed, since doctors did try to save wounded extremities when possible.[1] Nevertheless, tales of amputations predominate in the literature of Napoleonic warfare, probably because this particular operation left a tremendously powerful physical and mental impression on wounded and unwounded alike:

> A little farther on, in an inner court were the surgeons. They were stripped to their shirts and bloody. Curiosity led me forward; a number of doors, placed on barrels, served as temporary tables, and on these lay the different subjects upon whom the surgeons were operating; to the right and left were arms and legs, flung here and there, without distinction, and the ground was dyed with blood. Dr. Bell was going to take off the thigh of a soldier . . . and he requested I would hold down the man for him. He was the best-hearted man I ever met with, but, such is the force of habit, he seemed insensible to the scene that was passing around him, and with much composure was eating almonds out of his waistcoat-pockets, which he offered to share with me, but, if I got the universe for it, I could not have swallowed a morsel of anything. The operation upon the man . . . was the most shocking sight I ever witnessed; it lasted nearly half an hour, but his life was saved.[2]

The following account by William Tone, an Irishman serving in the French Army, indicates that conditions were exactly the same for the French:

1. Surgeon Guthrie reported that after the Battle of Toulouse in 1814, less than 10 per cent (98 of 1,407) of the British wounded underwent amputations, with the vast majority (76 of 98) of those operations involving the leg and thigh. Guthrie, *On Gunshot Wounds*, pp. 43–4.
2. Grattan, *Adventures*, pp. 76–7.

I entered a large tavern-looking house, and ascended to an upper hall, where an appalling spectacle lay before me. A long table occupied one side of it, the rest was strewed with straw, and crowded with maimed and bleeding wretches. A dozen of young surgeons, naked and bloody from the middle upwards, eating and drinking and passing jokes in the intervals of their occupation, were cutting off limbs with all expedition, as the wounded were successively laid on the table, and casting the amputated legs, arms, hands, and feet, into a corner, where they formed a hideous pile; the floor streamed with blood; the straw was soaked with it, and it ran down the stairs. I threw myself on the ground, waiting for my turn. The sight was better calculated to cure a passion for war than that of the field of battle; it had all its horrors, and none of its brilliant accompaniments.[3]

The medical procedure for amputation during the Napoleonic era was quite straightforward. First a tight bandage was applied to the affected limb above the point of amputation, or the relevant arteries were compressed by hand. Then an incision was made down to the bone, the flesh was retracted to reveal the bone, and the bone sawn through: 'The saw should be used, not with short strokes backwards and forwards, but with a long steady motion nearly its whole length, placing the heel first on the bone and drawing it towards you.'[4] Finally, the arteries found in the stump of the wound were drawn out of the flesh with forceps and either sutured or cauterised with a hot iron. There was apparently a gruesome on-going debate about which stage in this process was the worst for the patient:

Near the gate an assistant-surgeon was taking the leg off an old German sergeant of the 60th. The doctor was evidently a young practitioner, and Bell, our staff-surgeon, took much trouble in instructing him. It is tolerably general received opinion, that when the saw passes through the marrow the patient suffers the most pain; but such is not the case. The first cut and taking up the arteries is the worst. While the old German was undergoing the operation, he seemed insensible of pain when the saw was at work; now and then he would exclaim in broken English, as if wearied, 'Oh! Mine Got [*sic*], is she off still?' but he, as well as all those I noticed, felt much when the knife was first introduced, and all thought red-hot iron was applied to them when the arteries were taken up.[5]

By way of contrast, another amputee recalled that the pain of taking up the arteries was, as a relative matter, not terribly daunting. As the operation on his leg proceeded, Captain Charles Boothby spoke to his surgeon:

'Is it off?' said I, as I felt it separate.
'Yes,' said Fitzpatrick. 'Your sufferings are over.'
'Ah, no! You have yet to take up the arteries!'
'It will give you no pain,' he said, kindly; and that was true – at least, after what I had undergone, the pain seemed nothing.[6]

3. Tone, 'Narrative of My Services', in *Life of Theobald Wolfe Tone*, p. 629.
4. Guthrie, *On Gunshot Wounds*, p. 89.
5. Grattan, *Adventures*, p. 77.
6. Boothby, *A Prisoner of France*, pp. 19–20.

It is almost impossible from this distance of time to understand how, in an era before anaesthetics, men were so often able to bear with equanimity the immense pain of the primitive medical treatment meted out to them. The effects of shock and adrenaline surges may provide part of the answer, but another part was certainly the near-universal recognition that wounds could be badges of honour, especially if they were borne in a manner which displayed mastery over pain. The French attitude in this regard is best expressed by Napoleon himself: 'I will admit no one into my Guard who does not have four quarterings of nobility – that is to say, four wounds received on the field of battle.'[7] The British attitude is reflected in the experiences of the Napier brothers, Charles, George and William (the author referred to elsewhere in this book), all of whom were wounded in the Peninsular War. George at one point had the unusual experience of being present at a field medical procedure involving his brother Charles:

> The ball had entered on the side of his nose and, passing through, had lodged in the jawbone of the opposite side, from which it was extracted with much difficulty, [a] great part of the jaw coming away with it, as well as several teeth. During this long and painful operation he never uttered a word or winced under the hands of the surgeon who performed the operation, and who told me he never saw a man who bore pain so patiently and manfully.

Given such an example, it is perhaps understandable that George found reason to reproach his own behaviour when he later found himself undergoing similarly drastic medical treatment:

> I must confess that I did not bear the amputation of my arm as well as I ought to have done, for I made noise enough when the knife cut through my skin and flesh.

The operation was performed by Staff Surgeon Guthrie himself, so he had an excellent professional for the job, but:

> ... for want of light, and from the number of amputations he had already performed, and other circumstances, his instruments were blunted, so it was a long time before the thing was finished, at least twenty minutes, and the pain was great. I then thanked him for his kindness, having sworn at him like a trooper while he was about it, to his great amusement ...

Napier's musings on this topic conclude with a touching, and revealing, note to his children:

> ... I hope, boys, you will do the same [as your Uncle Charles] when your time comes to be wounded ... It is no joke, I assure you, but still it is a shame to say a word, and is of no use.[8]

Sang-froid was, however, by no means a universal trait. One French officer observed that wounded men could present very different demeanours:

> Some old soldiers displayed the most intrepid coolness, smoking whilst the surgeons amputated them, and crying '*Vive l'Empereur*', when the operation was

---

7. N. to Fouché, 11 September 1809, *Correspondance*, No. 15787, Vol. XIX, p. 575.
8. G. Napier, *General George Napier*, pp. 135–6.

over. But most appeared to lose all command over their nerves, and shrieked in a hideous manner, when laid on the table.[9]

In one very real sense, soldiers whose wounds were treated by amputation in the field were lucky. By the third year of the Peninsular War, most surgeons were sufficiently experienced to be able to perform that operation relatively efficiently. Once the limb was off, the healing process could begin cleanly and chances of survival were good. In cases where the wound was more complicated, and particularly if it involved penetration of the trunk of the body affecting the lungs or intestines, the doctors could do relatively little, and the wounded man usually faced a protracted period of suffering before the situation resolved itself by death or recovery. For example, Private James Dilley of the 1st Battalion, 40th Foot, was wounded during the first siege of Badajoz by a shot that 'went in at my belly and was cut out of my side' and he languished in hospital for four months before he could return to duty. He was inspired by that experience to include a suggestion for his brother in his next letter home: 'I hope to God that my brother will never think of going for a soldier for I cannot express the Sufferings in the compass of a letter that we undergo in this distressed country.'[10]

The variety of the experiences undergone by wounded combatants from Albuera has been captured in case notes published afterwards by Surgeon Guthrie:

1. Private J. Barnes of the 29th Regiment was shot in the right thigh, behind and above the knee. After the wound 'was dressed in the usual slight manner', he was left at the aid station for two days. Infection ensued and on 3 June his foot was amputated. He survived as an invalid.

2. Thomas Canyon of the 3rd Regiment was wounded on the inside of the calf of the right leg. The wound began bleeding again on 15 June, and his leg was amputated on 7 July. He died a few days later from arterial damage.

3. Sergeant Jean-Baptiste Pontheit of the 64th Line received a wound on his upper thigh which injured the femoral artery. Bleeding began again on 26 May, which led to the death of the patient despite an operation by Guthrie to repair the artery.

4. An unidentified soldier 'was wounded in the right side of the chest by a sword, which had passed slantingly under the shoulder-blade'. (This soldier may have belonged to Colborne's Brigade, because his injury is consistent with an attack by a mounted cavalryman on a fleeing infantryman.) His chest and neck swelled to a point where it was impossible for him to breathe, so Guthrie re-opened the wound until he 'could distinctly hear the air rush out', thus relieving the problem. At the end of three weeks, the soldier was determined to be 'in a favourable state for recovery'.

5. An unidentified soldier of the 3rd Regiment was wounded by a lance on the left side between the fifth and sixth ribs. On 26 May he appeared to be dying because swelling had made it difficult for him to breathe. Guthrie opened his chest and he recovered completely.

9. Tone, 'Narrative of My Services', in *Life of Theobald Wolfe Tone*, p. 629.
10. Dilley, Letter to Parents, 5 November 1811.

6. Captain Henry Tarleton of the 7th Fusiliers was struck in the groin by a large, flat piece of shell. He initially suffered a severe bruise, and as time went on a hernia developed in the exact spot he was hit, but his life was never in danger.

7. A soldier of the 48th had a musket ball pass straight through his body just above the liver. The case was considered hopeless because of the large quantity of blood and bile being discharged from both the ingress and exit wounds. Under Guthrie's care the patient was bled several times, his wounds were dressed simply and he was kept 'perfectly quiet'. The soldier's strength failed under the treatment and he 'became thin and looked ill', but he nevertheless gradually improved and his wounds finally healed.[11]

8. Captain de Roverea received a blow to the head that left a noticeable dent in his skull 'as if it had been a tin vase struck against a hard surface'. His friend, Surgeon Guthrie, initially wanted to remove part of de Roverea's skull to relieve the pressure on his brain, but ultimately decided not to risk the dangerous trepanning operation. De Roverea ended up with no recollection of the ten days following the battle, but otherwise recovered fully.[12]

There are no comprehensive statistics available to inform us about the percentage of wounded men who did or did not recover from their wounds, but the muster rolls of the 57th Foot reveal that 15 per cent (3 sergeants and 45 other ranks) of the men of that battalion who were wounded in the battle died of their wounds in the next two months.[13] Similarly, 22 per cent of the wounded men of the 29th Foot (53 out of 245) did not survive their injuries.[14]

Many times there was simply nothing that Surgeon Guthrie or any other doctor could do for a patient. The case of Captain Felix Cappanegra, another officer of the French 12th Light Infantry, was particularly gruesome in this regard:

> Le capitaine Negre [Cappanegra] ... was struck on the left side of the hip ... by a musket-ball, which went through the upper part of the ... colon, and came out behind ... As urine came through this opening, the ureter or lower part of the kidney must have been wounded; and, as he had lost the use of one leg and much of that of the other, the spinal cord must also have been injured. He was left on the field of battle, supposed to be about to die, and was brought to me ... at Valverde three days afterward, in a most distressing state. The ... pain he suffered on any attempt to move him was extreme ... and he at last implored me to allow the box of opium pills, of which one was given at night to each man who was most in need of them, to be left within his reach, if I would not kindly do the act of a friend and give them to him myself.

Guthrie could not, on moral grounds, bring himself to assist in the officer's suicide, but this gave little solace to the Frenchman. 'He died at the end of ten days, after

11. Guthrie, *Commentaries*, pp. 191, 193, 195, 438, 510, 528 & 532.
12. A. de Roverea, Letter to Father, (?) October 1811, in F. de Roverea, *Mémoires*, Vol. 4, pp. 42–3.
13. Manuscript Casualty Report for the 1st/57th Foot dated 4 July 1811, Archive Item No. 6504-52-15, NAM.
14. Everard, *History of the 29th*, p. 333.

great suffering, constantly regretting that our feelings as Christians caused ... [its] prolongation.'[15]

For many wounded men, the realisation that recovery was not going to occur was less dramatic. Sir William Myers was a remarkable example of the best side of the purchase system, since he came to command his battalion at the extraordinarily young age of eighteen, but was widely recognised as a skilled and diligent soldier: '[A]t an early Age he had attained very high rank ... his superior Abilities excessive zeal and entire devotion to the Service however proved he was admirably qualified for the situation he filled.'[16] After he was wounded in the field, his servants banded together to find a way to move him to Valverde so he would at least have a bed to rest in. Unfortunately, the musket ball that had broken his thigh remained lodged in his body and gave rise to gangrene of the intestines.[17] The end for Sir William was relatively swift and painless:

> He expressed much emotion at the tears and distress of those around him; but until about 40 minutes before his dissolution he was not sensible that it was so near. His servant then conceived it was his duty to acquaint him [that] his death approached, and asked him his last commands: he received the communication with the same intrepidity which characterized him through life. He desired a ring, which he wore, to be taken to his sister, with an assurance that he died as a soldier. The names of a beloved mother and sister lingered on his lips, and, without a struggle, his gallant spirit ascended to its creator.[18]

Captain Colin MacDonald of the 23rd was also taken relatively unawares by a deterioration in his condition. He had 'received a shot which enter'd through his shoulder blade pass'd through his lungs, and fractur'd his collar bone' and his wound had remained untreated until the 18th because he was a prisoner of the French for two days. He was evacuated to Valverde and, although 'he seemed to have suffered much from the ill-treatment he received', his wound nevertheless did not seem to be life-threatening. That appearance was deceiving, however, because on 23 May he was informed his death was imminent:

> [A]bout 24 hours before his death, he was told his wound was mortal and that he had but a short time to live ... he received the intimation with great fortitude, call'd the Surgeon and the soldier who attended him and in their presence dictated how he wish'd to bequeath his property. This the Surgeon instantly took down in writing.

MacDonald 'expired on the 24th retaining the perfect use of his faculties to the last'.[19]

In a few cases, the lag between being wounded and succumbing to the wound was astonishingly protracted. Twenty-year-old Lieutenant Henry Jones of the 7th Fusiliers, 'a young man of very promising talents', lingered on until the end of the year before

15. Guthrie, *Commentaries*, p. 563–4. Since there is no officer named 'Negre' listed in Martinien's compilation, I have assumed that the wounded man must be Captain Cappanegra, who is shown by Martinien as having been killed in the battle.
16. Boutflower, *Journal*, p. 95.
17. Guthrie, *Commentaries*, p. 25.
18. Anonymous, 'Life of Sir William Myers', pp. 473–4.
19. Obituary in the 1 February 1812 issue of *The Monthly Magazine or British Register*, p. 74.

dying from his wounds.[20] The case of Sous-Lieutenant Pierre Fornerol of the 12th Light is even more tragic. On 22 March 1812, he gained the unenviable distinction of being the last direct casualty of the battle when he died in the hospital at Olivenza 'of wounds received 16 May 1811'.[21]

The psychological attitude of the wounded man could also have a significant influence on his recovery or demise. Lieutenant Harrison of the 23rd noted this phenomenon in the case of his fellow officer, Lieutenant Robert Castle:

> We have lost Castle since my last [letter]. Though his wound was not of a very serious nature, it took such an effect on his spirits that the poor fellow died almost in a fit of despondency. We came together from the field to Elvas and I never could stimulate him to smile the whole way.

Harrison himself was wounded in the leg during the battle, but his more positive attitude helped him achieve a full recovery:

> My journey down here [to Lisbon] has thrown me back a few days but I shall soon recover this. I am quite an adept with a pair of crutches, yet do not mean to place myself on the Chelsea list this bout. My wound is healed up, tho' my leg is very weak from long confinement in bed (near a month), and want of exercise, which I shall treat it with gradually every day, and I expect another week or two will reinstate me in all my strength and vigour. From the ball passing so near the tendon it feels a little contracted at present, but a short time will conquer this. The eighth of an inch more and I must have lost my leg, so I consider myself a lucky fellow.[22]

Lieutenant Gordon Booker of the same regiment lost the forefinger and thumb of his right hand to a sabre cut, but nevertheless continued to be 'in great spirits and christened himself, "Obi [sic] or Three-fingered Jack".'[23]

The ordeal of a seriously wounded soldier did not end once he received initial medical care for his wounds. The next stage of treatment was usually evacuation to a distant city or hospital for further care and convalescence, but being moved even by one's own army could add significantly to a man's sufferings given the primitive level of transport available. The ubiquitous wooden bullock carts of the local farmers provided a slow and painfully bumpy ride that was accompanied by the annoying squeals of the ungreased axles and the fixed wheels. John Murray, an assistant surgeon with the 66th, described one such convoy to Lisbon in the aftermath of Albuera:

> The most disagreeable and unpleasant duty I ever had in my life has again brought me to this capital. I came down from Elvas with 170 badly wounded men in bullock carts, which is a distance of 100 miles and took 9 days ... As almost all the cases were broken limbs and amputations the poor creatures were quite helpless and suffered dreadfully from the jolting.[24]

20. MacDonnell, Letter to his cousin, 23 May 1811.
21. Malaguti, *Historique du 87e Régiment*, p. 471.
22. Harrison, Letter to Father, 22 June 1811.
23. A pair of portrait miniatures depicting a very young and blond Lieutenant Booker and his wife, Loveday Sarah Booker, was sold at Sotheby's in London on 1 December 1980.
24. Murray, Letter to Father, 29 June 1811.

A British cavalryman travelling in the opposite direction from Lisbon shortly after Albuera encountered a similar convoy of wounded men from the battle and was appalled by the suffering he saw:

> . . . at the village where we halted there arrived on cars, about 700 wounded men from Albuera, whose plight was as pitiable – I might have used a stronger expression, and said horrible – as it is easy for the human imagination to conceive. No doubt they had received, when first taken in hand by the surgeons, all the care which the nature of their condition would allow, But they had performed since that period a long journey, through a barren country, and under a broiling sun – and their wounds remaining undressed all this while, were now in such a state as to defy description.[25]

The new British troops did their best to help the wounded men despite the 'fearful' smell from their 'hurts'. They could not, however, ease all the pains of the Albuera men:

> One pair of wretches I particularly remember, an Irishman and a Frenchman, who travelled in the same car, both of whom had lost their legs – not partially, but entirely – and who yet ceased not to abuse and revile one another from morning to night. It was melancholy to hear them railing, in their respective tongues, and threatening one another.[26]

The Good Samaritan cavalryman was much affected by his brief experience:

> We did our duty faithfully by our mutilated countrymen; so faithfully, indeed, that weeks passed away ere I was able entirely to overcome the effect which the distressing occupation had produced upon me. I could neither eat nor sleep, for everything seemed to be tainted with the effluvia from those cankered wounds, and my dreams were all such as to make sleep a burden. Fortunately for us, however, we were not long condemned to the torture; for war must be fed for ever with new victims, and we turned our back upon those already smitten on the morning after we had met them.[27]

Amputees obviously suffered permanently from the effects of their wounds but so did many others who became invalids or were otherwise unfit for further service. In fact 31 officers received government pensions for loss of a limb or other wounds from Albuera. Even those who were able to return to active duty sometimes had lingering problems that lasted for months and even years after the battle. Captain Thomas Wade, an ADC to General Cole, was wounded in the left side by a musket ball which passed through his pelvis and remained in his abdomen. He never fully recovered his health:

> [A] small fungous protrusion and discharge continued from the wound for several years, with a certain degree of pain, and occasional lameness in the leg and thigh. The wound closed sometimes for a few months, and [then] reopened with an attack of pain, with great lameness and swelling of the hip, and a discharge of matter from the original site.[28]

25. Farmer, *The Light Dragoon*, p. 33.
26. *Ibid.*
27. *Ibid.*, p. 34.
28. Guthrie, *Commentaries*, p. 567. See Appendix F, p. 313, for further information about Wade.

Lieutenant Samuel Crammer of the 28th was still on active service in 1832 suffering 'more pain than at first' from his Albuera wound.[29] The official casualty returns from Albuera state that Captain James Morisset of the 48th Regiment was 'slightly' wounded, but that is true only in that his wound was not life-threatening. In fact, he was hideously and permanently disfigured by a shell burst that left him with 'a strange face, one side considerably longer than the other, with a stationary eye as if sealed on his forehead; his mouth was large, running diagonal to his eye.' Overall, the side of his face resembled 'a large yellow over-ripe melon'.[30]

Popular opinion tended to find fault with the medical services, in part because most wounded men who survived had stronger memories of suffering and hardship than they had of the benefits of medical science. The skill of the doctors caring for the wounded could vary significantly from individual to individual, and it was certainly true that lower-level functionaries such as surgeon's mates often had only minimal training:

> In this army there are men in charge of sick who till they came here never prescribed in their lives, and there are others who have had no practice beyond answering a prescription in an apothecary shop in England. Such are the men entrusted with the lives of soldiers, but it must always be the case in a great degree while the pay remains so small as to induce those only to enter the service who would starve at home. I have myself heard a surgeon say that he had no doubt that two-thirds of the deaths in the army were due to the inattention and ignorance of the medical officers.[31]

The senior men on the British side were, however, unquestionably dedicated and skilled medical practitioners, as the many references to Surgeon George Guthrie in this chapter attest. Indeed, one of the few undeniably positive results of the Battle of Albuera was a medical advance attributable to Guthrie. In treating the many wounded, Guthrie was able to perfect a new technique for dealing with arterial wounds which contradicted prior teaching but eventually became the standard procedure:

> The first effort made for the improvement of surgery made in the Peninsular War was the publication, in 1811, of a paper on wounded arteries, which I sent to London after the Battle of Albuhera.[32]

George Napier undoubtedly had men such as Guthrie in mind when he expressed the following view:

> ... it is a very general but very erroneous and unjust idea in the army to think slightly of the medical men and to consider their profession as inferior to others ... yet (and I speak from thirty years' experience) I never met anything but kindness, generosity, and manly honourable conduct, combined with skill and judgment, in those medical gentleman with whom I have served.[33]

---

29. Cadell, *Campaigns of the 28th Regiment*, p. 110.
30. Fyans, *Memoirs*, p. 92. A miniature portrait of the Captain reproduced in Champion, 'James T. Morisset', p. 210, reveals that he was a reasonably handsome man before Albuera.
31. Aitchison, *Ensign*, p. 95.
32. Guthrie, *Commentaries*, p. 7. See also Cantlie, *Army Medical Department*, Vol. I, p. 331.
33. G. Napier, *General George Napier*, p.134.

The quality of French military doctors was similarly mixed and, once again, the best men were clearly very skilled professionals. The pinnacle of professional achievement was recognition by the emperor, who made barons of his top doctors such as Dominique-Jean Larrey and Pierre-François Percy. Other honours were available at other levels. Indeed, no fewer than three French surgeons – Cassé of the 88th Line, Fillod of the 100th Line and Buthiau of the 28th Light – received the Cross of the Legion of Honour for their conduct at Albuera.[34]

Much less is known about the medical services of the Portuguese and Spanish Armies, but the former had been reorganised by British doctors at the same time that the army as a whole was being upgraded by Marshal Beresford.[35] Since, however, almost all aspects of Spanish military administration were inferior to those of other military forces of the period, it is likely that the quality of their medical services left something to be desired. On the other hand, the following comment by British Lieutenant George Gleig seems unduly harsh:

> Of all the classes of men with whom I ever had intercourse, the Spanish surgeons are, I think, the most ignorant and the most prejudiced. Among the many amputations which, during the war, they were called upon to perform, about one-half, or more than half, proved fatal. Their mode of dressing other wounds was, moreover, at once clumsy and inefficient; and hence the mangled wretches who passed us this morning were not only suffering acutely from the natural effect of their hurts, but were put to more than ordinary torture on account of the clumsy and rude manner in which their hurts had been looked to.[36]

34. Lacepéde, *État Général*, Vol. 2, p. 448.
35. Cantlie, *Army Medical Department*, Vol. I, pp. 320–1.
36. Gleig, *The Subaltern*, p. 52.

Chapter 13

The Prisoners of Albuera

Albuera is a rather unusual battle in that the rapid shifts of fortune during the course of the day left both armies with significant numbers of prisoners taken from the other side. For the French, the main haul came from the cavalry charge that overran Colborne's brigade. According to official British casualty returns, just 530 British officers and men were missing after the battle, but a tally of prisoners prepared for Soult on 17 May records that the French at that point had captured a total of 816 British soldiers.[1] The British did not make a contemporaneous count of their French prisoners and accurate assessment of the numbers involved is further complicated by the fact that some French soldiers who became prisoners merely because they were wounded and abandoned were recovered by their own army when the French advanced again in June. All in all, however, the number given by Oman of just under 900 French officers and men captured and retained as prisoners seems reasonable.

The act of surrender – the transformation of a combatant into a non-combatant who acknowledges that he is no longer willing or able to offer resistance – has been called one of the most complex transactions that can take place on a battlefield. In the heat of battle, it is very hard for a soldier to switch from attacking to protecting his enemies and that is one of the reasons why there were so many reports after Albuera that the Polish lancers continued to kill and wound British soldiers even after the men had attempted to surrender. At the time of Albuera, there were no international conventions in place governing how a prisoner should be treated once surrender was acknowledged, but there were certainly accepted practices and norms which all sides followed. One point was absolutely clear – the act of surrender was bound to subject the surrendering soldier to a thorough plundering. Soldiers of all armies tended to carry all their portable personal wealth with them into battle and they all understood that the involuntary transfer of that wealth on the battlefield was a potential result of combat. Indeed, the possibility of being a recipient of such a transfer was a significant incentive for soldiers to do their utmost to capture their enemies.

The experience of being plundered is well described by a British light dragoon who was taken prisoner near Badajoz a month after Albuera:

> The fighting was over now, and there began a scene, of which I cannot think
> without blushing for the chivalry of our adversaries. Not content with taking our

---

1. This tally is quoted in Soult, Letter to Berthier, 4 June 1811.

horses and arms, or even the purses and watches of such as possessed them, they proceeded to strip us of our jackets, boots and even our overalls; apparently bent, as it seemed to me, on leaving us nothing whereby we might be distinguished as British soldiers. I do not know how far this system might have been carried, had not our captain, who spoke French fluently, remonstrated with the officer in command; upon which an order was given to put a stop to the plunder; and to most of us our jackets, at least, were restored. But of watches, money and boots, no account was taken; and we marched off, some of us in a very sorry plight, to the rear.[2]

This pattern of behaviour was repeated time and time again at Albuera. In one odd case, a French soldier 'forced [Captain] MacDonald's ring off his finger with his teeth'.[3] In another lurid (but unverified) case reported in a letter written by an anonymous officer of the King's German Legion, the plundering was punctuated by the infliction of bodily harm on the captive:

> In one instance an officer of the 4th dragoons who had fallen into ... [the] hands [of the Poles], was, as usual, stripped of his watch and money, of which I suppose he had rather a small stock, as there had been no pay issued for some time. On being asked if that was all, and replying in the affirmative, they deliberately cut off one or both of his ears, I believe both.[4]

Once they were formally taken into the custody of the capturing army, prisoners usually fared badly in terms of medical treatment and food simply because these things were in short supply for their captors. A complaint by one British prisoner about having to eat beans to survive is, ironically, exactly the same one made by the French against their own supply services:

> I remained a prisoner for seven days, and the whole I received from our enemy (marching six leagues a day on the road to Madrid) was three ounces of rice, nine ounces of bread and a pound of meat. However when on the line of march they indulged us by entering bean-fields, using the same language as the Spaniards use to the Swine, 'Hurrah! Hurrah!' Conceive my feelings, for believe me I cannot describe them.[5]

Another British prisoner acknowledged explicitly that he and his countrymen were not singled out for special mistreatment in terms of provisions:

> I believe, however, in point of feeding we were not by many degrees worse treated than the French themselves, who could derive no supplies at all from the surrounding country.[6]

Immediately after the battle, the British and French prisoners faced very different futures. A British captive being escorted back to the French base at Seville was travelling through regions populated with civilians actively hostile to his captors and,

2. Farmer, *Light Dragoon*, p. 42.
3. Harrison, Letter to Mother, 23 May 1811.
4. Anonymous, Letter from KGL Officer, 27 May 1811.
5. Anonymous, 'Extract from a letter from a private of the Buffs'.
6. Farmer, *The Light Dragoon*, p. 45.

for the most part, actively friendly to the prisoner. Under these circumstances, it is not surprising that a large number of British prisoners were able to make their respective escapes. In each case, the success of the escapee depended on a combination of his own resourcefulness and assistance from helpful Spaniards, as is demonstrated by an escape narrative written by a Corporal Dutton of the Buffs, who had been wounded during the battle:

A great grenadier, with his sword under his arm, took me in charge until we arrived at Serena [Llerena?] . . . finding himself hungry [he] stepped into a house to demand some bread, thinking I should not have the presumption to move from the door; but he was mistaken; for as soon as I got him housed, I forgot my sore feet, and ran down the street, entering the first house that was open; and upon explaining what I was, they received me with open arms, and taking part of the cockloft down, handed me up, and closing it after me, supplied me with plenty to eat and drink, and bedding, and kept me close prisoner two days and nights, until all the French had marched away; when collecting some twenty more who like myself had been concealed by the friars and others in the town; supplied us with plenty of victuals; and started us upon our road. Here again I was unfortunate, for exclusive of sore feet, I was seized with a severe fit of an ague; and the rest for their own safety were obliged to leave me on the road; when I saw the last of them cross the hill, I gave myself up for lost; and cursed the ball that had not done its business completely, and rid me of a troublesome existence. But the kindness of the Spaniards supplied all my wants, and soon put me on my legs . . . I took a long round to avoid the enemy: and I shall never forget the excessive kindness of the Spaniards, who cleansed my wound, which had got into a very bad state, and supplied me with an ass to carry me from town to town: and upon entering a town, every hand was ready to relieve the poor Englishman some with bread, or meat or money; and by their active assistance I was enabled once more to join the corps that I have had the honour to be several times engaged with.[7]

Dutton was not the only soldier of the Buffs to have favourable memories of the kindness of Spanish civilians who provided generously for the escapees they encountered:

On the seventh evening I left them [his French captors] in open daylight and after getting two miles lay down. Shortly a piquet passed close by me but they did not see me. Soon after I arose, and though a mere skeleton, I rushed forward to a hill, crossed it, and entered a cornfield where I was again alarmed by the trampling of hooves. I immediately fell on my face; it again pleased heaven to save me, [and] they passed on and did not observe me. I again rose, and travelled over mountains, through vallies [*sic*] and rivers, till exhausted by excessive fatigue, I sat down and was unable to rise. Here a refreshing sleep allayed my hunger and recruited my exhausted nature. I arose and proceeded to a village where I was received according to the Scriptures; 'I was naked and they clothed me; hungry and they fed me.' Such treatment I never before

7. Corporal Dutton, Extract of a Letter, pp. 358–9.

experienced as going through this extensive country, every person outvying with each other to relieve the hardships I had endured. In sixteen days I reached Elvas and soon after joined my regiment.[8]

The circumstances of captured officers and other ranks could be very different because of the concept of 'parole'. Because all officers were deemed to be gentlemen, it was an almost universal custom to allow a captured officer significant relief from restrictions on his freedom in return for his word of honour not to attempt to escape, but the giving of parole could put an officer in an extreme dilemma. For instance, Major Brooke was happy to give his parole just after he was captured so that he could accept the hospitality of a Spanish family and find better treatment for his wounds. Unfortunately, when the major shortly thereafter found himself in a position to escape, he was honour-bound not to do so:

> Long before dawn I felt myself shaken, and was alarmed to find two men standing by my bed ... I was at first at a loss to comprehend their intentions, but they soon made me understand that their mission was to effect my escape ... As I did not speak Spanish sufficiently well to make myself clearly comprehended, I represented to him [the master of the house] in Italian, which he well under-stood, that my escaping might bring destruction on him and his family, that my own honour was pledged, and that, although the opportunity was so favourable to escape, I must decline to take advantage of it.[9]

Brooke was incapacitated by his wounds for many weeks at Seville, but after he recovered his strength he concluded that his parole had been effectively revoked when the French put him under close arrest in the same prison used for rank and file prisoners. The conditions of his confinement were ameliorated when a senior French officer discovered that Brooke was a fellow Freemason, but Brooke was nonetheless receptive when a friendly Spaniard offered to help him make his escape. He slipped out of prison on 27 July and, after an arduous journey, reached General Hill's headquarters in Portugal on 10 August.[10]

Not all of the escapees were able to return to duty. Major Brooke was so exhausted from his ordeal that he was sent off to England within two weeks of his return and never again saw active service. Corporal Dutton of the Buffs was also used up by his experiences, but he was lucky enough to have a family connection that brought his case to the attention of Warren Hastings, a former Governor General of India. Hastings wrote to his brother, Lieutenant General Sir Charles Hastings, for assistance in obtaining a discharge and a pension for Dutton:

> I shall be much obliged to you for your advice, how to proceed in order to obtain the discharge of a young man from the service in Portugal, a corporal of the Old Buffs. He was at the taking of Oporto, in the battle of Talavera, and in almost every action since the B[ritish] army has been in Spain. In the last, which was that of Albuera, he was badly wounded in the head, taken prisoner by the

8. Anonymous, 'Extract from a letter from a private of the Buffs'.
9. Brooke, 'Prisoner', p. 183.
10. Brooke, 'Prisoner', pp. 193–206. The news of Brooke's escape was reported in *The Times*, 7 October 1811, p. 3, col. D.

French, but made his escape, and [is] now (if living) in the hospital at Lisbon, troubled with fits from the effects of his wounds, or rather that in his skull, a fragment of which was extracted. My interest in this young man arises from my good housekeeper, who is his aunt. I suppose his discharge is not difficult to obtain, as he cannot be fit for service; but that he looks to obtain a provision with it.[11]

British prisoners who did not escape faced the very long ordeal of the journey from Seville back to France. The trip took many months due to the need to wait for convoys with sufficient escorts, and the interim stops were usually unpleasant and ill-equipped to handle additional mouths to feed. There was also real danger involved in cases where convoys were attacked from ambush by Spanish guerillas who might not be able to distinguish easily between friend and foe in such circumstances. At the end of the road for these journeys were the fortress prisons of northern France such as Verdun and Metz. Many of the officers taken at Albuera may have been exchanged or otherwise obtained their freedom in the next eighteen months, because there are very few Albuera prisoner names on a list of captive British officers in France compiled as of 1 January 1813.[12] There are no systematic records concerning the fate of rank and file Albuera prisoners, but details can occasionally be found in unit muster rolls. For instance, Private Nanty Barrett of the 66th Foot, who was a miner before he joined the army, turned up again in the regimental records listed as returned 'from French Prison' on 15 May 1814, nearly three years to the day after his capture.[13] He lived to collect his General Service Medal with clasps for 'Talavera', 'Busaco' and 'Albuhera'.[14]

Whether they were taken by the Spaniards or by the British and Portuguese, French soldiers being marched into captivity had no opportunity for escape because they were surrounded by a hostile civilian population. The unwounded ones in British custody were delivered to Lisbon, where they were kept under close confinement until transport could be found to an even more distant and secure destination. Transfer of prisoners to England had been halted by the British government in 1810 in the hope that some less financially burdensome alternative could be found, but the inability of the Portuguese government to pay for any of these forced the British to resume sending captured Frenchmen back to Great Britain just after Albuera. When the captured French soldiers arrived at their destinations (typically Plymouth or Portsmouth in the first instance), a detailed description of each man was meticulously recorded by the clerks of the Transport Board responsible for their care.[15] As a result, we know for instance that 34-year-old Pierre André l'Homme of the 12th Light, who had been wounded in the thigh at Albuera, was a 'stout' man 5 feet 6 inches tall, with dark hair and hazel eyes, an oval face and a sallow complexion. His comrade, 26-year-old Corporal François Hamapp, was a relatively gigantic 5 feet 9½ inches tall. He was also 'stout', but had blue eyes, light hair and a light complexion. Since there are few instances of multiple entries in the record books for the same regiment on the same

11. Dutton, Extract of Letter, p. 358.
12. John Bulloch, 'British Prisoners in France in 1813', *Journal of the Society for Army Historical Research*, Vol. 17, 1938, pp. 77–9.
13. NA/PRO WO 12/7534. These biographical details were generously provided by Mr Colin Message.
14. The medal was sold at auction by Glendining's in December 1950.
15. NA/PRO Series ADM 103/295 *et seq.*

day, it appears that the British made no effort to keep men from the same unit together for purposes of transport and confinement.

Ironically, wounded French prisoners had initially better prospects for rejoining their regiments since the British effectively ignored them for both medical and custodial purposes. As a result, many of the wounded Frenchmen who had been abandoned to the British when Soult retreated were liberated when the combined French armies advanced again into Extremadura in June:

> We went immediately to the convent where we had left our wounded twenty-eight days before. We found neither the surgeon nor the medic we left behind – the English had led them away as prisoners the night before along with many wounded men who were strong enough to travel. Of the 280 men we left behind, only 143 were left, and they were in a terrible state.[16]

The wounded men were elated to see their countrymen and they had one atrocity to relate – there was a Polish lancer among them who had been mistreated in revenge for the pitiless behaviour of the Poles on the day of battle. He was still dressed in the uniform he had worn on 16 May, had a broken leg and a gangrenous foot and was lying on a pallet of straw fouled with his own waste. The other wounded men explained: 'For 24 days, the English refused to treat his wounds or give him any food. He would have died of hunger if we had not taken turns feeding him.'[17] After his leg was amputated, he was evacuated to Seville.

French officer prisoners, of course, received better treatment than their men and were routinely offered the opportunity of parole. However, Wellington had become aware of a number of cases of parole violation and argued forcefully that the French should no longer be given that privilege:

> I am sorry to say that, under existing circumstances, no confidence can be placed in the parole of any French officer. I know many who have been allowed to quit England, on their parole not to serve till exchanged, who are now serving in the armies in Spain, although no British Officers, or others, have been sent from France in exchange for them.[18]

Fortunately for the French, Wellington's views did not lead to a change in government policy even though there were to be more high-profile instances of parole violation in the next few years. Parole was not routinely granted to French officers who were captured by the Spanish armies. Captain Martin Lacroix (b. 1768) of the 55th Line Regiment, who had been wounded in the head and left for dead on the field, was made prisoner on 18 May.[19] Since he was captured by Spanish forces, he was sent to the notorious prison camp on the Isle of Cabrera rather than to England. He did not survive his captivity.

French rank and file prisoners, like their British peers, have left a minimal imprint on history so we have only occasional glimpses of their individual fates after Albuera.

16. D'Héralde, *Mémoires*, p. 164
17. *Ibid.*
18. W. to Admiral Berkeley, 30 June 1811, *Dispatches*, Vol. 8, p. 62.
19. Lacroix's entry in Martinien's *Tableaux* actually says that he was captured by 'brigands' near Albuera, so it is possible he fell into the hands of guerilla troops rather than Spanish regulars. His biography can be found in Lievyns, *Fastes de la Légion d'Honneur*, Vol. 2, p. 47.

Napoleon never negotiated any formal convention for prisoner exchanges with the British, but nevertheless a total of twenty-two assorted French corporals and sergeants were exchanged in 1812 under an arrangement known as the 'James Cartel'.[20] Some soldiers sought a way out of captivity by enlisting in the army of their captors, as was the case with Corneille Jansens of the 64th Line, André Simone of the 9th Regiment of the Duchy of Warsaw and Jacques Coppreutz of the 12th Light, a native of Flanders, all of whom joined the King's German Legion in 1812.[21] The vast majority of these French prisoners, however, remained in captivity until the return of peace in 1814.

20. NA/PRO Series ADM 103/300. The course of prisoner exchange negotiations between France and Britain in 1810 and 1811 is summarised in Pierre Coquelle (trans. Gordon D. Knowle), *Napoleon & England, 1803–1813*, London, 1904.
21. NA/PRO Series ADM 103/295 and 299.

Chapter 14

The Dead of Albuera

Death is the constant companion of both victory and defeat and its effects are multiplied by the fact that each battlefield death also touches intimately the lives of the family members and friends of the man who died. The tremendous death toll of Albuera consequently caused repercussions throughout the Peninsula and Europe. These repercussions would be both emotional and economic.

The notification of next of kin is a sombre military ritual that has tempered the thrill of victory for battle survivors throughout the ages and, during the Napoleonic era, the ritual was observed in very different ways for enlisted men and officers. As befitted a society that held to the notion that all officers were gentlemen, the British casualty report for Albuera that was published in the *London Gazette* listed every officer killed or wounded by name, so the family of an officer would quickly learn if their loved one had been struck down. The younger brother of Second Lieutenant Hall of the 23rd Fusiliers remembered vividly the circumstances in which he learned of his brother's death:

> In Cork, it was known that a great battle had been fought, and the *Gazette* that gave the list of killed and wounded was eagerly and tremblingly looked for. A copy had been received at the post-office. My father went there to learn the news. Pale as death he returned to where we were all waiting together, and his words as he entered were, 'Let us pray.' Even the youngest of the group knew what the words meant.[1]

The Spanish and Portuguese Armies likewise published lists giving the name of every officer casualty, but the French, surprisingly, did not. The final French bulletin concerning Albuera published in the Paris newspapers did contain information about a number of specific dead and wounded officers, but only senior commanders and staff officers were mentioned.

The notification of rank and file deaths was far less systematic. The military bureaucracy of each of the armies involved in the battle was theoretically obligated to send a death notice and back pay to the family of each deceased soldier, but in practice such communications would come, if at all, only long after the event. In Britain, an anxious family would at least be able to draw some information from the published casualty report which, even though it did not identify any of the rank and

---

1. Hall, *Retrospect of a Long Life*, p. 589.

file by name, provided separate aggregate statistics of killed, wounded and missing for each rank in the military hierarchy. The casualty figures for Albuera were so gruesome that they were shocking to even casual readers of the press. Jane Austen had a reaction that was simultaneously both sensitive and somewhat callous: 'How horrible it is to have so many people killed! And what a blessing that one cares for none of them!'[2]

Another civilian back in Britain recognised that the large number of Albuera casualties masked an equivalent amount of personal tragedy: 'But amidst all this rejoicing [over the victory of Albuera], it is sad to reflect how many hearts must ache for the thousands who have fallen.'[3] However, one cynical officer expressed the belief that the public only respected a victory if it was purchased at a high cost in terms of casualties:

> I have learned one thing since I have been in this country [Spain], and that is how easily England is duped ... and how perfectly content she is [with any news of victory], so long as there is a long list of killed and wounded.[4]

The only cases in which notification to the relatives of deceased other ranks worked well were those in which the survivor was actually present in the theatre of operations. For instance, the casualty records of the 57th Foot indicate that ten of the soldiers killed in action or who died from wounds were survived by their respective wives, four of whom were with the regiment and one of whom was at Lisbon.[5] There were also other relationships which led to swift notification. For instance, Privates Edward Blunt and John Waters of the 57th were both survived by brothers in the regiment. More intriguingly, Privates James Seymour and Michael Walsh both listed Sergeant Egar of the 57th as their next of kin, perhaps as a result of some arrangement designed to provide an economic benefit to the survivor of the trio.

The situation of the French in regard to death notifications was far more challenging. Since the French forces were fighting in the hostile environment of southern Spain with only limited means of communication with home, it was difficult if not impossible to ensure that news reached the families of deceased soldiers back in France in any timely fashion, and letters of condolence from comrades were often lost to guerillas. The French Army bureaucracy thrived on paperwork, however, so much of this information eventually made its way to the Ministry of War, which is why there was raw material in personnel folders for Martinien to create his famous lists of officer casualties. Unfortunately, that information did not always make its way to the families of rank and file soldiers. The archives of the French War Ministry and of municipal and departmental governments are consequently also full of letters from citizens seeking information about missing loved ones and, in the aftermath of the wars, one enterprising publisher came out with a printed list of dead French soldiers just to help answer such inquiries.[6] The Spanish government had its own special

2. Jane Austen to Cassandra Austen, 31 May 1811, in R. W. Chapman (ed.), *Jane Austen's Letters*, London, 1969, No. 73, pp. 284–7, at 286.
3. Diary entry for 30 May 1811, in Jackson, *The Bath Archives*, Vol. 1, p. 256.
4. Mills, Letter to Mother, June 27, 1811, in *For King and Country*, pp. 45–9, at 46.
5. Casualty Returns of the 1st Battalion, 57th Regiment, NA/PRO WO 25/1893.
6. E. Mehlis, *Liste de Seize Mille Militaires Français ... qui sont morts en Russie ...* , Paris, 1826.

difficulties in notifying next of kin because so much of the country was occupied by enemy forces.

Often, comrades of the fallen would notify families of their loss by virtue of writing to them in an effort to ease their grief. There are many examples of such communications, including the one quoted earlier written to the guardians of Ensign Thomas of the 3rd by his company commander. One of the most moving letters of this sort comes (somewhat unexpectedly given his reputation for callousness towards his men) from the pen of the Duke of Wellington, who took time after the battle to convey his sympathies to the mother of Sir William Myers:

> I do not address your ladyship with the hope, that any thing I can write will have the immediate effect of alleviating your sorrow ... It must, however, be some consolation to you hereafter to know that your son fell in an action, in which, if possible, the British troops surpassed all their former deeds ... I could not deny myself the melancholy satisfaction of communicating to you my sense of your late son's merits, in the hopes that at some future period the occasion and mode of his death, as well as this evidence of my favourable opinion of him ... may alleviate your affliction.[7]

As Wellington's letter acknowledges, there is no good way to deliver news of bereavement, but in some cases other circumstances could make the death almost impossible for the survivor to bear. The most melancholy incident in this regard concerning Albuera relates to Lieutenant Colonel Duckworth of the 48th. He was only twenty-three at the time of his death, but he had married at an early age and already had a four-year-old child. The grief of his even younger widow, Penelope (aged twenty-two), must have been all the greater because, 'On the day the afflicting news of the Colonel's death arrived at Plymouth, their only son ... lay dead in the house, and was buried the following day.'[8] To make matters worse, the simultaneous deaths of her husband and son had a catastrophic effect on the economic well-being of Duckworth's widow: 'The admiral [Admiral Duckworth, the colonel's father] is at sea, and his infant son by his second wife, Miss Butler, will now be heir to the title and estate. Such are the changes and chances of life.'[9] Mrs Duckworth never remarried prior to her death almost forty-four years to the day after that of her husband.[10]

Battlefield deaths also had a variety of economic consequences other than the unusual loss of station that affected Mrs Duckworth. During the Napoleonic wars, surviving family members of officers and men killed in action did not have any automatic entitlement to compensation or death benefits, so anyone being supported by a soldier who was killed could be thrown into immediate financial difficulties. The most significant negative point for the families of British officers was that the value of a purchased commission died with its owner – there were no posthumous sales permitted. There were some pension and insurance schemes in place in Britain and France, but they tended to benefit wounded rather than deceased officers and men. In the event of cases of extreme hardship, some form of government assistance might

7. W. to Lady Myers, 20 May 1811, *The Royal Military Chronicle*, Vol. 2, 1812, p. 502.
8. Obituary of Colonel Duckworth, *Gentleman's Magazine*, 1811, p. 679.
9. Diary entry for 30 May 1811, in Jackson, *The Bath Archives*, Vol. 1, p. 258.
10. Obituary of Mrs Penelope Duckworth, *The Times*, 16 May, 1855, p. 1, col. A.

be made available, although this was very much a matter of whim rather than entitlement. For instance, sixteen years after the battle, the mothers of three British officers killed at Albuera (Lieutenant William Duguid of the 29th and Ensigns Thomas Rothwell of the 48th and George Walker of the 66th) were granted annual allowances from the 'Military Compassionate List'.[11]

Even if a soldier or officer possessed significant property, economic complications could ensue if he died without making a will. Captain MacDonald of the 23rd would have been in that position had he not survived his mortal wounds long enough to dictate deathbed instructions to a fellow officer, who subsequently described them to the captain's heir:

> He [Captain MacDonald] directed that his papers and effects (after paying ten pounds Sterling to the soldier who attended him for his care and attention) should be put into my hands to be remitted to you, to whom he has left the charge of dividing his whole property equally among his brothers and sisters excluding the Frazers from any share. The principal part of his property is a grant of land in Picton in Nova Scotia for which he might have got £500 ... There is £100 in the hands of a Mr. Harrington in London and nearly an equal sum due by different officers of the Reg't. which the Pay master will collect, and with the proceeds of his baggage which is ordered to be sold in Lisbon, will be delivered into my hands. I shall lose no time in remitting the whole, as well as the memorandum he dictated ... together with [such] papers of his I may find.[12]

As this passage reveals, there were often debts outstanding among officers, and it is uncertain whether all of them would have been paid in the event of the death of the debtor or the creditor.

One patriotic Spanish officer who did make a will before the battle used the occasion to set an example for his countrymen:

> I, Martin de Parraga y Pison, Second Adjutant of the General Staff of the 4th Army, declare, that, if by any accident I should lose my life, it is my will that all my property ... be sold, and the proceeds placed at the disposal of the lawful government of Spain (which is that which supports the cause of the liberty and independence of the nation), in order that it may promote the just cause which it supports against the unjust aggression of the tyrant of Europe, Napoleon.[13]

The clichéd sentiments of this document would seem unbelievable except for the fact that de Parraga did die in action at Albuera and his property did pass to the Spanish state as he desired.

Sales of the personal effects and baggage of deceased soldiers were an important means by which useful equipment was recycled to where it could do the most good. Hence one finds Captain Dickens of the 34th Foot, newly promoted as a result of the death of his company commander in the battle, noting in a letter home: 'I bought a few days ago, at a sale of the effects of the late Major Scott of the 37th [actually, the 57th] regt., a map of Spain and Portugal, on a very superior scale. I gave 21 dollars

11. *The Naval and Military Magazine*, Vol. 1, London, 1827, pp. 596–7.
12. MacDonell, Letter to Cousin, 23 May 1811.
13. 'Reports from Spanish Papers', *The Times*, 16 July 1811, p. 3, col. B.

for it.'[14] The proceeds of such sales would be sent to the family of the deceased, but it is a sad fact of Albuera that the market for used military goods was flooded with inventory in the weeks following the battle.

In an era before the establishment of government war graves commissions, the dead themselves were generally slighted by the living, and that was certainly the case with Albuera. In this instance, however, the careless disposal of bodies ironically gave the dead of Albuera a very high profile in the short run. During the manoeuvring of the French and allies in the middle of June, both sides spent some time at the old battlefield, and they were appalled at what they saw there. A private in the 71st Foot noted with disgust that 'The carcasses of both men and horses [had been] . . . dragged into heaps and burned.'[15] Surgeon d'Héralde also remarked on the burning of corpses when he visited the battlefield with General Girard shortly afterwards. With clinical detachment he noticed that this disposal method had one signal drawback: 'The English, according to their custom, burned all the bodies after the battle – the arms, legs and trunks were all consumed but the heads did not burn.'[16] Instead, the skulls had to be thrown into the mass graves.

Despite all these efforts, the battlefield clean-up was still far from comprehensive. When Captain Lapène returned to the site, he saw 'trenches full of bones many feet in depth dug at various points of the old line of battle, but most of all at the two extremities, near the village and near the far right [of the British position], where the fighting had been fiercest.'[17] He came across an even more gruesome sight when he discovered some bodies in the woods on the French side of the river. These men had died of their wounds and had simply been left unburied where they expired, thus leading to an unexpected result: 'The brilliant sun of June had shrunk, dried out and blackened the corpses without changing their features, so they looked exactly like Egyptian mummies.'[18] As if these sights alone were not bad enough, the entire area reeked with 'a heavy, nauseous smell . . . partly caused by the immense number of dead lying buried under the ground, and partly by the fleshy fuel of the fires.'[19]

The smell of decomposing corpses eventually dissipated, but grim reminders of the battle were still visible a year later. British troops occupying a defensive position at Albuera in 1812 easily identified the mass graves:

> On taking possession of the ridge of Albuera, we were a good deal astonished to find a trench, nearly forty yards in length, nearly half-filled with human skeletons, without so much as a handful of mould spread over them, to screen them from the eye of the eagle, the vulture or the carrion crow. 'Look!' cried the men, one to another, on first beholding the horrifying spectacle, 'behold our reward'.[20]

---

14. [Dickens], Letter, 24 May 1811, p. 293.
15. Anonymous, *Vicissitudes*, p. 172.
16. D'Héralde, *Mémoires*, p. 162.
17. Lapène, *Conquête*, p. 226.
18. Lapène, *Conquête*, p. 225.
19. Anonymous, *Vicissitudes*, p. 172.
20. Hope, *Military Memoirs*, p. 163. Lieutenant Ingilby of the Royal Horse Artillery also noticed that the bodies in the trenches 'had been left to decay without being covered up' when he visited the battlefield in 1812. 'Diary of Lieutenant Ingilby, R.A., in the Peninsular War', p. 252.

Another British soldier who also visited Albuera in 1812 saw similar sights and had a similar reaction:

> When I came upon the spot where the battle of Albuera had been fought I felt very sad; the whole ground was still covered with the wrecks of an army, bonnets, cartridge-boxes, pieces of belts, old clothes and shoes; the ground in numerous ridges, under which lay many a heap of mouldering bones. It was a melancholy sight; it made us all very dull for a short time.[21]

There was no formal memorial to the dead of Albuera until 1853. In that year, the Spanish government raised a massive monument in the centre of the village that, surprisingly, had as its only adornment a bust of General Castaños, although it is inscribed with the names of the most prominent British, Portuguese and Spanish commanders of the day. There was no other memorial on the battlefield until 1978, when the Spanish General Staff School put up a monument to Don Emetrio Velarde and Don Martin de Parraga, the two members of the General Staff who were killed in the battle. The only memorial added since then is one dedicated in 2001 by the Princess of Wales's Royal Regiment, the successor by way of consolidation and amalgamation to several of the British regiments that fought in the battle. There is still no memorial of any sort to the French soldiers who fought and died in the battle, although in 1812 they did have an appropriate epitaph scratched with charcoal on the wall of a chapel near the village: 'The war in Spain leads to fortunes for generals, boredom for officers and death for soldiers.'[22]

21. Anon., *A Soldier of the 71st*, London, 1975, p. 70.
22. Sherer, Recollections, p. 189.

Chapter 15

Controversy and Conclusions

The shocking details of the battle of Albuera engendered passionate controversy amongst the allies almost as soon as the French retreated. It started with Beresford's own ambivalence about the horrific human cost of the battle, as expressed in his letters to Wellington, and then spread as officers and men alike chimed in with their criticisms and opinions concerning the performance of their commander. The newly-arrived men of Kemmis's brigade found that as early as the 17th Beresford's men had already formed strong views about their experience: 'All the survivors with whom we conversed were heartless and discontented. They complained bitterly that the army had been sacrificed by a series of blunders . . .'[1] This grumbling in the ranks was bad enough, but the controversy swelled as officers felt free to express their opinions of events in uncensored letters to family, friends and patrons back in Britain. Wellington abhorred such behaviour:

> . . . as soon as an accident happens, every man that can write, and who has a friend that can read, sits down to write his account of what he does not know and his comments on what he does not understand; and these are diligently circulated and exaggerated by the idle and malicious, of whom there are plenty in all armies. The consequence is, that officers and whole regiments lose their reputation; a spirit of party, which is the bane of all armies, is engendered and fomented; a want of confidence ensues; and there is no character, however meritorious, and no action, however glorious, which can have justice done to it.[2]

These views help to explain why Wellington altered the marshal's original dispatch about the battle – he anticipated that his own officers might be critical of Beresford's performance at Albuera so he wanted public discussion to begin with as positive a story about the battle as possible. His machinations did not go entirely unnoticed. Edward Pakenham warned his relatives that the official report concerning the battle should be treated with scepticism, but he evidently did not realise that Wellington was responsible for much of its content:

---

1. Emerson, 'Recollections' in Maxwell, *Peninsular Sketches*, Vol. 2, pp. 235–6.
2. W. to General R. Craufurd, 23 July 1810, *Dispatches*, Vol. 6, pp. 286–7, at 287.

After all I told you of the Fusiliers' conduct you must have been surprised to peruse the dispatch of Beresford. In truth there never was an Official detail which more completely failed to put the Authorities, to whom so ever it might have been addressed, in possession of both the circumstance and fact of the Affair.

I dreadfully fear that Wellington may be implicated in the public mind, for bearing a Man through whom he must know has in many points deceived those to whom his report is intended to convey truths.[3]

Wellington also took some other practical steps to control the initial dissemination of information about the battle. First, he asked the British ambassador in Lisbon to embargo all communications out of Lisbon until Beresford's dispatch was ready:

I think it desirable that, if possible, no flying details of the battle of Albuera should go home till Sir William Beresford's report shall be sent. I conclude that the account that there had been a battle went by the mail yesterday, which is of no importance; but where there are many killed and wounded the first reports are not favourable; and it is not doing justice to the Marshal to allow them to circulate without his.[4]

Second, he called upon the Royal Navy to make sure that Colonel Arbuthnot arrived home with the official report of the battle safely and quickly: 'I shall be very much obliged to you if you will send a ship of war with him, as it is desirable that he should arrive as soon as possible.'[5]

Wellington's efforts to protect Beresford could, however, do no more than postpone the inevitable flood of commentary that followed because, as Wellington recognised, neither he nor 'any other Officer in command of a British army, can prevent the correspondence of the officers with their friends'.[6] The letters came from writers of all ranks and were addressed to a variety of recipients. For instance, one finds Fitzroy Somerset, Wellington's own military secretary, writing in the following vein to his brother, the Duke of Beaufort, shortly after he had visited the battlefield and spoken with the survivors: 'Beresford does not appear to have managed the battle with much skill or I think our loss would not have been so severe.'[7] A subaltern writing to his mother was far more blunt: 'Genl. Beresford is the most noted bungler that ever played the game of soldiers, and at Albuera he out-bungled himself.'[8]

The criticism of Beresford after Albuera had two main themes. First and foremost, Beresford was attacked for the way in which he took up the Albuera position and arrayed his forces along the ridge. In particular, the popular view was that he had improperly neglected to occupy the southern knoll and thereby put his army in jeopardy. General Long was predictably scathing in commenting on this point in a letter he sent to his friend, General Gaspard Le Marchant, the head of the Royal Military College:

3. EP to Tom, 5 June 1811 in Pakenham, *Letters*, pp. 100–1, at 100.
4. W. to Charles Stuart, 20 May 1811, *Dispatches*, Vol. 7, p. 579.
5. W. to Vice-Admiral George Berkeley, 22 May 1811, *Dispatches*, Vol. 7, p. 580.
6. W. to Liverpool, 16 March 1811, *Dispatches*, Vol. 7, pp. 368–9, at 369.
7. Somerset, Letter to the Duke of Beaufort, 23 May 1811.
8. Mills to Mother, 27 June 1811, in Mills, *For King and Country*, pp. 45–9, at 46.

Had I not been a personal witness of the fact, I never could have believed it possible for a human being with his eyes in his head (brains were not wanted) to make so egregious a mistake as was committed at Albuera in the distribution & arrangement of the troops.[9]

Long elaborated on this point in a letter to his brother:

Having taken up the position, I proceeded to reconnoitre the ground, & to my utter astonishment found that the heights that formed the key of the position were not intended to be occupied. All the forces were drawn up parallel to the Badajoz road, assuming that the enemy's attack would be directed on our left and not upon our right. A tyro in military matters ought to have seen otherwise . . . Be it observed that not a shot was fired on the ground selected and originally taken up by us for the field of battle, & that the whole contest was carried on upon the strong ground & heights which form the key to the position of Albuera, & which we had neglected to occupy.[10]

Edward Pakenham was another soldier who agreed with Long's assessment, although his comments seem to refer to the southern knoll:

The Right seems to have been the point of greatest importance, in as much as there was a very commanding Knoll from which our Line was nearly enfiladed. The enemy as soon as possessed of this height, according to custom loaded it with Artillery, the annoyance of which was so great, it was evident in seconds that the Height must be recovered, or the day Lost.[11]

The extreme version of the criticism of the way in which Beresford had the allies take up the Albuera position comes from a letter written by Charles Stewart (later Lord Londonderry), Wellington's adjutant-general, to an unidentified correspondent:

Beresford on the morning of the [16th] seems not to have attempted to take up the ground in the manner which might have rendered it very formidable but like a Spanish army and officers, as the high road led from Albuera to Badajoz, he placed his army across it as if this alone could stop the foe. From this period to the commencement of the action his right seems to have been placed where his left should have been & by the continued struggle to secure the high ground on the right which the enemy early avail'd themselves of, all of our calamitous loss was sustained whereas if the right hills had been strongly occupied, which (more especially as it was our line of communication with Valverde, the only way we had to retreat) became doubly necessary, the victory might have been gain'd with a very slight loss. In fact the right was the key of the position, & this does not seem to have been perceived until the enemy was actually in possession of it.[12]

This critique, from someone considered by Beresford to be a friend, gained wide circulation because of the appeal of the embedded quip that 'his right seems to have been placed where his left should have been'. In fact, that proposition is entirely

9. Long, Letter to Le Marchant, 5 June 1811.
10. Long, Letter to C. B. Long, 30 May 1811.
11. EP to Tom, 29 May 1811, in Pakenham, *Letters*, pp. 98–9, at 98.
12. Stewart, Letter to Unidentified Correspondent, 22 May 1811.

absurd. If Beresford's left had rested on either the northern or southern knoll from the outset, then he would have been abandoning the Royal Road to Badajoz, an even more unpalatable alternative. A more reasonable and constructive point is that made by Captain de Roverea – both knolls should have been fortified with field works to define and protect the allied right flank. That is precisely what General Rowland Hill did when he occupied the Albuera position in 1812.

The other favourite criticism of Beresford had to do with the possibility that he ordered a retreat during the course of the battle before he became aware of the success of Cole's advance:

> The other circumstance I omitted is that towards the latter part of the action it was at one moment intended to retreat. The Artillery at Albuera was ordered to move back by the Valverde Road and M. Gl. Alten was directed to withdraw his troops, which he had actually done, and the enemy had thrown forward some of their people into the village, when the retreat was countermanded in consequence of affairs turning out well upon the right.[13]

Wellington's brother, William Wellesley-Pole, reported that this was commonly believed to have been the case: '[T]here are so many letters from the army detailing particulars that everybody knows the whole story, even to the general's loss of head and ordering the retreat etc.'[14] This line of criticism was intolerable to Beresford because it was the one that went most centrally to his competence as a general. As discussed above, both Major Dickson and General Alten did receive orders late in the day to withdraw from their positions, but the preponderance of evidence does seem to suggest that this was a mere tactical re-positioning of those troops rather than the first step in an intentional abandonment of the field of battle to the enemy. Beresford was consequently zealous in asserting that he had never ordered a retreat in the classic sense of that word and he was seconded in his public relations efforts by D'Urban, who forcefully expressed the Beresford party line in a letter written to Colonel Sir Herbert Taylor, King George III's military secretary, in August 1811:

> It only remains for me to observe upon that part of your letter, by which I see that some misinformation had led you to suppose it was at one period of the day Sir William Beresford's intention to retreat. I am clear and positive, and I pledge myself that no such intention was ever formed, that no such order was ever given, or meditated.[15]

Despite such protestations, rumours to the effect that Beresford had lost his nerve and nearly lost the battle as a result proved remarkably resilient. They continued to weigh heavily on the marshal, who wrote letters to his brother, Sir John Beresford, in November 1811 and January 1812 complaining about such rumours and strongly denying their substance.[16]

---

13. Murray, Letter to Gordon, 22 May 1811.
14. Wellesley-Pole, Letter to W., 16 June 1811. William added the name Pole to his own as the result of an inheritance.
15. D'Urban, Letter to Sir Herbert Taylor, 29 August 1811. Colonel Taylor had also served as military secretary to the Duke of York.
16. Beresford-Peirse Family Papers, Fonds ZBA, North Yorkshire Records Office, Northallerton, United Kingdom.

Although the post-Albuera commentary was primarily unfavourable to Beresford, there was one recurring point that worked in his favour by suggesting that the appalling losses suffered by the British were caused, not by his failings as a general, but by the fact that the Spanish troops could not be efficiently utilised in the battle because they lacked the ability to manoeuvre in combat conditions. One source suggests that this view may have originated with Beresford himself:

> The Marshall [*sic*] mentions that if he had been capable of manoeuvring the Spaniards then nothing could have saved the French from being completely destroyed – or probably in other words he found it impossible to get them forward after having been driven from their position.[17]

However it originated, the point was immediately taken up by Wellington:

> The Spaniards, by all accounts, behaved remarkably well; but they were immoveable; and their want of discipline, and of the power of manoeuvring, appears to me to have created the necessity for using the British infantry in all parts of the field, and to have thrown upon us the great burden of the battle.[18]

He repeated the same thought in a number of letters, suggesting that he once again was making a conscious effort to mitigate the criticism being directed at Beresford:

> Beresford's was a terrible fight; but he would have succeeded without much loss, if the Spaniards could have moved; nevertheless there they stood like stocks, both parties firing upon them, and it was necessary to apply the British everywhere.[19]

> We had a very good position, and I think should have gained a complete victory in it, without any material loss, if the Spaniards could have manoeuvred; but unfortunately they cannot.[20]

It must have been very convenient and appealing for the British to blame the Spaniards instead of Beresford, but this criticism does not really hold up under scrutiny. The performance of the Spanish troops in changing front in response to the French flank attack, and then in changing places with Hoghton's brigade fully refutes the proposition. In fact, a large number of observers went out of their ways to comment favourably on the performance of the Spanish troops. A simpler and more likely explanation for Beresford's limited use of the large Spanish force available was that the marshal did not feel comfortable relying on his allies in a crisis situation. A combination of not-so-latent xenophobia and the unhappy past history of Anglo-Spanish military cooperation left him with a decided preference for using his own men wherever the fighting was most fierce.

Coincidentally, the Spaniards, too, were inclined to slight their allies in assigning credit for the victory. Major John Hope, one of General Graham's aides-de-camp, was significantly offended by the initial Spanish reports of the battle that circulated in Cadiz:

17. Hope, Letter to General Hope, 29 May 1811.
18. W. to Charles Stuart, 20 May 1811, *Dispatches*, Vol. 7, p. 579.
19. W. to E. Cooke, 23 May 1811, *Supp. Despatches*, Vol. 7, p. 135.
20. W. to General Sir Brent Spencer, 22 May 1811, *Dispatches*, Vol. 7, pp. 579–80, at 580.

We were for some days most anxious for Beresford's account. Those which were transmitted to the Spanish Gov't by Blake & Castaños and many other private descriptions of the action left some room to doubt whether the British had been much engaged or not. They of course ascribed the greater part of the merit to themselves ... General Beresford's dispatches only reached us yesterday [28 May], & in the course of today a fresh instance has occurred of the most ungrateful conduct & want of feeling on the part of the Spaniards. Instead of sympathising with us for the loss of so many brave men in fighting for their cause, many of the leading men have had the presumption to declare that Beresford's dispatch is a fabrication & and our own loss magnified & exaggerated to enhance our own merit & detract from theirs. It is currently asserted here that the brunt of the action fell upon them & that during the course of it, our men fired a volley upon their deliverers, which they term themselves upon this occasion ... From every account, we certainly should not have met with so great a loss had we been alone and unaided by them & it certainly is the most heartrending reflection to think, that so much of our blood & so many fine fellows have fallen in fighting for such a pack of ungrateful lying scoundrels.[21]

There were two points about the battle not related to Beresford upon which everyone was in agreement. The first was that human cost of the battle had been extraordinarily high: 'The gallantry of our troops never underwent such a severe trial. The loss of the British ... exceeds for the numbers engaged anything that was ever heard of.'[22] That sentiment is echoed in innumerable letters and reports, including one by General Long: 'The carnage at Albuera exceeded any thing I ever saw in my life in the same space of time & of ground. The theatre of action was a human slaughter house.'[23]

This extreme loss of human life in the battle inspired a number of different reactions. Some thought that a war of attrition in the Peninsula actually favoured the allies and therefore applauded the bloodbath:

> This victory of Marshal Beresford has made everybody wild with delight, for it is most glorious and most complete. And although it is, indeed, also a most bloody one, and has cost very dear, it is worth what it cost. A few such battles as that of Albuera will go further than anything else towards shortening the war.[24]

Others thought that the significance of the human costs could not be fully assessed until all the consequences of the battle had become clear and could be added into the calculation:

> Though this was certainly a glorious victory, there never has been one more dearly purchased & one is puzzled whether to rejoice or bewail at it – if the result is not equal to the price that we have paid for it, the latter feeling will always prevail.[25]

21. Hope, Letter to General Hope, 29 May 1811.
22. Stewart, Letter to Unidentified Correspondent, 22 May 1811.
23. Long, Letter to Le Marchant, 5 June 1811.
24. Diary entry for 2 June 1811, in Jackson, *Bath Archives*, Vol. 1, p. 263.
25. Hope, Letter to General Hope, 29 May 1811.

A final viewpoint was that the number of casualties was simply a function of the way the battle unfolded:

[I]n this terrible contest, error, confusion, and misfortune attended our first disposition. Victory had to be retrieved from a brave and experienced foe, under many untoward and disheartening circumstances, and it seems universally agreed that the annals of war scarcely afford an instance of so bloody a battle having ever been fought in proportion to the numbers engaged.[26]

The second point on which most commentators generally agreed was that the victory had been won by the tenacity and determination of the allied soldiers rather than as a result of brilliant work by their commander: 'Beresford's action is considered here as a proof of the astonishing bravery of the British troops, which appears to have saved him and his army.'[27] General Long had similar praise for the troops, concluding that Albuera was 'a battle which we should have lost but which the unconquerable spirit of the Troops secured to their fortunate commander'.[28] This fundamental truth was well-recognised, but there was no consensus as to exactly how that tenacity of purpose came to be. One battle survivor expressed the view that the allies simply willed themselves to victory:

On the other side the British troops seem to have been determined, to a man, never to come out of the action but with success. The persevering valour which they displayed is perhaps unparalleled, certainly it was never surpassed; and the French were at length wholly unable to maintain themselves any longer against the unceasing efforts of the remains of our gallant battalions.[29]

General Charles Stewart quickly concluded that there might not be any rational explanation for the battle's outcome:

The whole British force [was] either hors de combat or so diminished a Battn. could scarce be produced & the Portuguese and Spanish must have yielded to the general dismay that must have been the result. Providence, however, for the sake of mankind desired it otherwise… [and victory was] reap'd by the unextinguishable, unexampled & (I may say) incomprehensible valour of the British soldiers.[30]

Soult would probably have agreed whole-heartedly with Stewart's choice of adjectives if he had been aware of them, since the French marshal is reputed to have summarised the performance of the opposing army in the following ironic terms:

There is no beating these fellows, in spite of their Generals. I always thought them bad soldiers, and now I am sure of it; for I turned their right flank, penetrated their centre; they were completely beat and the day was mine, but yet they would not run.[31]

26. Leslie, *Military Journal*, p. 223.
27. Wellesley-Pole, Letter to W., 16 June 1811.
28. Long to Brother, 22 May 1811, McGuffie, *Peninsular General*, pp. 105–8, at 105.
29. Murray, Letter to Gordon, 22 May 1811.
30. Stewart, Letter to Unidentified Correspondent, 22 May 1811.
31. Tomkinson, *Diary of a Cavalry Officer*, pp. 108–9. No French source for this remark by Soult has ever been traced.

Marshal Soult had his own public relations issues as a result of Albuera, but they were simpler than Beresford's because he ultimately had to worry about only one person's opinion. Soult might have aggressively put forward a claim to victory because he did force the allies to abandon the siege of Badajoz and because he inflicted significant damage on the allied army, including the symbolically important capture of some British regimental colours. That he declined to do so speaks volumes for his own opinion about the battle. His inability to press on to Badajoz after Albuera must simply have been too obvious a proof of failure to explain away. As he admitted to Marshal Marmont in a letter dated 27 May: 'We would have considered Albuera a signal victory if the threat to Badajoz, the whole object of the battle, had been eliminated, but I was not able to achieve that.'[32] Soult instead contented himself with developing an honourable explanation for the battle's result. In his formal 18 May report to Berthier Soult mentions that he was surprised to find that Blake and his troops had already arrived on the scene, but he asserts that he would nevertheless 'infallibly have had a decisive success' but for 'a mistake' made at the crucial moment by his subordinates. He never gives the name of the person who made the mistake, but he does provide substantive details of what happened. After describing the destruction of Colborne's brigade, he goes on to say:

A general rout of the enemy would have followed this success if, immediately thereafter, our first line had been deployed so as to offer an equal front to that of the enemy, but there was hesitation and our men were forced to sustain an unequal fire-fight with the second line of English troops which moved forward and was able to fire into the flanks of our attack columns.[33]

The culprit in this version of events was obviously General Girard. It is unclear why Soult chose not to name him in the report since the marshal made no secret of his views in the Armée du Midi. When Captain Vigo-Roussillon, who had been captured at the Battle of Barrosa, was exchanged and returned to duty, he was asked by Soult how the British perceived his abilities. Vigo-Roussillon replied:

'The English regard you as one of foremost generals of Europe in choosing a position and organising an army ... but they do not think the same of your manner of conducting a battle.' Suddenly the marshal stopped me and spoke passionately: 'I know why, it's the battle of Albuera to which they refer. But it was that scoundrel Gérard [Girard] ... who lost the battle; against my orders he brought the columns of the second line [division] into the intervals between the columns of the first line [division].'[34]

When Girard was defeated later in the year at Arroyo de Molinos, he said he suspected that Soult would enjoy his failure because the marshal was still annoyed about the defeat at Albuera. Girard also had his own explanation for the French defeat:

Marshal Soult will be delighted to find me in trouble since he has already accused me of having manoeuvred badly at Albuera. If at that battle, like at ... Ocaña, I had overthrown the enemy, he would have taken the credit. And

32. Soult to Marmont, 27 May 1811, in Marmont, *Mémoires*, Vol. 4, pp. 93–5, at 95,
33. Soult, Unpublished Report.
34. Vigo-Roussillon, *Grenadier de l'Empire*, pp. 295–6.

we certainly would have been victorious at Albuera if he hadn't taken fright and had attacked the enemy boldly at the head of his reserves.[35]

In 1820, an important French history of the Napoleonic wars advanced the theory that the battle was actually lost by Godinot rather than Girard because he did not press his attack on the village of Albuera with sufficient vigour to divide the attention of the allies, but that view seems untenable given the fact that Godinot was significantly outnumbered by the British, Portuguese and KGL forces defending the village.[36]

Napoleon never communicated directly with Soult about the battle, but the emperor did express his views in two ways. First, he, like Wellington, edited the report of his commander to create a more acceptable narrative. Napoleon apparently thought that the admission of a mistake was not suitable for public consumption because the version of Soult's report to Berthier (now dated 21 May), that was published in *Le Moniteur* on 13 June 1811, makes no mention of errors and instead states that Soult was unable to take advantage of some early successes in the day because of the surprise arrival of Beresford's Spanish allies, which created such a disparity of numbers that he could not continue his attack.[37] In accordance with the accepted French narrative conventions of the day, Soult declared that his troops had 'covered themselves with glory', but the word 'victory' does not appear in the revised document.

Next, Napoleon dictated some specific criticisms of Soult's conduct that were delivered second-hand by Berthier in the middle of a long memorandum to Soult dealing with a variety of administrative matters:

> It seems to His Majesty that you would have prevailed in the battle of 16 May if you had merely held your ground; the London newspapers make it clear that the English really wanted to retreat. The Emperor thinks you did not assemble enough men for this battle and that you should have brought along 8,000–10,000 more ... When one decides to give battle, it is essential to use all the available troops. His Majesty is pained to see that this principle is not habitually put into practice.[38]

The only other time Napoleon is known to have spoken about Albuera was during his imprisonment on St Helena. The subject was raised by Barry O'Meara, one of his doctors, during a conversation he had with Napoleon on 4 September 1817:

> I observed that I had been told by some of the English officers who had been present at the battle of Albuera, that if Marshal Soult had advanced after the attack made by the lancers, he would have cut the English army to pieces. Napoleon acquiesced in this, and said he had censured Soult for having neglected to do so.[39]

35. D'Héralde, *Mémoires*, p. 174.
36. Beauvais de Préau, *Victoires et Conquêtes*, Vol. 20, pp. 240–1.
37. Soult, 'Rapport.'
38. Memo from Berthier to Soult, 21 July 1811, Document 5820 in Picard, Ernest, and Tuetey, Louis, eds., *Correspondance Inédite de Napoléon 1er Conservée aux Archives de Guerre*, 5 vols., Paris, 1912–25, Vol. 4, pp. 490–1.
39. O'Meara, *Napoleon in Exile*, Vol. 2, p. 194. The English officers mentioned by O'Meara were from the 66th Foot, which was in garrison at St Helena at that time.

When Soult sent Napoleon the colours that had been captured in the battle, the emperor had a bizarre reaction because of the identity of the officer who had been entrusted with the trophies. Captain Joseph-Pierre-Hippolyte de Lafitte was not actually a 'foreigner' as Napoleon complained, but certainly was an odd choice to convey the standards to Paris since he was an émigré Frenchman who had served in the Austrian and Portuguese Armies before becoming attached to Soult's headquarters in 1809. The marshal, however, esteemed him as an officer 'of great merit and great bravery', and Lafitte had distinguished himself at the siege of Badajoz, the Battle of the Gevora and Albuera, where he was severely wounded.[40] Nevertheless, when Lafitte arrived with the colours, Napoleon ignored the opportunity to publicise a humiliation of the forces of his arch-enemy and instead threw a tantrum because he felt insulted by Lafitte's presence:

> Express my displeasure to Marshal Soult for sending me the flags of Albuera by a foreigner. It appears this officer was in the Austrian service, and he must therefore have fought against us. It is ridiculous of Soult to send such a man. Let Captain —— [Lafitte] know that he is not to return to Spain and that I have given the order for him to be placed with his current rank in the 9th Light Horse Lancers.[41]

Soult was just as touchy as Beresford about any criticism of his performance at Albuera, but he faced less of it because events in Spain commanded relatively little attention in France. One relevant person who did have some unflattering things to say on that topic was Marshal Marmont. It is not clear how much of his views he might have communicated to Marshal Soult at the time, but in his memoirs he blasted his fellow marshal in no uncertain terms:

> His [Soult's] troops, arrayed in columns, forced back the first line [of the enemy] and occupied the high ground; but, having arrived there, and being exposed to lively enemy musket fire, should have responded by forming in line and maximising their own firepower. Soult, however, as was always his preference, was far away from where his troops were in action and could not order them to deploy. The generals on the scene were not smart enough to prescribe the correct formation and so, after suffering severe casualties, the troops retreated and the battle was lost when, under any other general, it would have been won.[42]

Given this level of animosity, it is remarkable that the two marshals were able to collaborate in June 1811 to lift the second siege of Badajoz.

For most soldiers who fought at Albuera, the controversies about the battle were of academic interest only. What mattered was whether the battle helped them receive promotion or some other tangible form of reward. As in any battle so bloody, the survivors found themselves with promotion opportunities galore, especially if they had the right patrons. Wellington himself took a personal interest in many promotion cases:

40. Gotteri, *Soult*, pp. 330 and 434.
41. N. to Berthier, 23 August 1811, *Correspondance*, No. 18076, Vol. 22, p. 436. See Appendix E for more information about the captured British colours.
42. Marmont, *Mémoires du Maréchal Marmont*, Vol. 4, p. 42.

I conceive that [Major Gregory] Way, having lost his arm in the late action, the Commander in Chief would be disposed to give him the vacant Lieut. Colonelcy of the 29th, for which I long ago recommended him ... there is one [other] officer, Major [Guy] L'Estrange, of the 31st, whom I must recommend in the strongest manner for promotion in some way or other. After the other parts of the same brigade were swept away by the cavalry, this little battalion alone held its ground against all the *colonnes en masse*![43]

It will come as no surprise that both of these officers ultimately reached the rank of major general. Officers who lacked prominent patrons faced greater challenges with respect to promotion and, indeed, it was felt by many that staff officers were promoted more frequently than line officers because they were 'more likely on occasions of promotion to come under notice, than regimental officers who ("out of sight out of mind") have their merits frequently overlooked.'[44] One case that seems to reflect that prejudice is that of Edward Hawkshaw, the commander of the 1st Battalion of the Lusitanian Legion who was seriously wounded during the battle:

This officer having then held only the rank of Major in the British army, and of the same standing as Sir Henry Hardinge, one would have imagined that he would have had at least the same pretensions to the British rank of Lieut.-Colonel, his name was nevertheless omitted from the list of promotions granted for that battle, while Hardinge was included in that list. Hawkshaw returned to England and retired in disgust from the service, like so many others, by the sale of his commission.[45]

There was also a view held by many that it was harder for subalterns (ensigns and lieutenants) in the British Army to gain promotion for merit than it was for officers with the rank of captain or higher. That does not seem to have been the case at Albuera, however, perhaps because the large number of officer casualties created a pressing need for immediate promotions. Others were commissioned without purchase. Thomas Servantes, a young man who had fought in the battle as a volunteer with the 66th Foot, was gazetted to an ensigncy in the 97th Foot while Sergeant William Gough of the 7th Fusiliers was given a commission as an ensign in the 2nd West India Regiment in recognition of his having recovered a colour of the Buffs. Sergeant William Grey of the Buffs was appointed ensign in the 58th Foot for an unspecified act of heroism.[46]

Senior British generals and staff and line officers were eligible for gold medals for specific actions, subject to the strict conditions that the action had to be one of importance and that the individual had to have distinguished himself in some way (although distinction was effectively presumed for anyone who commanded a unit in

43. W. to Torrens, 22 May 1811, *Dispatches*, Vol. 7, p. 584. Wellington was mistaken about Major Way's arm – it was saved by the prompt medical attention he received from Surgeon Guthrie.

44. Maxwell, *Impending Dangers*, p. 88.

45. *Ibid.*, p. 89. One frustrated ex-officer of the Lusitanian Legion expressed the extreme view that Hardinge's preferment was all the more inequitable because Portuguese staff officers at Albuera 'were, in point of fact, nonentities on the day of battle, having no responsibility whatever attached to them'. Lillie, Letter to the Editor.

46. For Servantes, see his entry in *Hart's Army List*, 1841, p. 188; for Gough and Grey, see Knight, *The Buffs*, p.353.

the battle that had exchanged musketry fire with the enemy). Wellington himself thought that 'officers of the British army don't require an honour of this description to stimulate their exertions, and that the grant of the medal is therefore useless,' but he was willing to go along with the scheme so long as the medals were truly awarded on the basis of merit and not merely on the basis of physical presence, as was the case with a similar medal for the Navy.[47] Based on the recommendations of Marshal Beresford, fifty-two gold medals were awarded for Albuera, with multiple medals going to many regiments because they were commanded by multiple officers during the day. The only other distinction an officer could obtain was a sword or other commemorative object awarded by private citizens. For instance, Captain Edward Fleming of the 31st was given a sword by Lloyd's Patriotic Fund in recognition of having lost an eye at the battle.[48] In 1816, surviving officers and men who had served at Albuera received prize-money payments from the sale of captured materials and stores. These payments ranged from over £134 for a general to just 7 shillings and 6 pence (£0.375) for a private.[49]

Aside from a unique medal later awarded to Lieutenant Latham of the Buffs (*see* Appendix F, pp. 307–9 below), there were no medals available to reward or commemorate extraordinary bravery or effort by individual British soldiers at Albuera. The need for such 'baubles' was the subject of periodic passionate debate in the British military and society as a whole, particularly after medals were awarded to all soldiers present at the Battle of Waterloo, but it was not until 1847 that Peninsular War veterans were awarded the Military General Service Medal with clasps for each significant action they survived. A rough count from the regimental lists used in validating medal entitlements indicates that just under 2,700 officers and men survived to collect MGS medals with clasps for 'Albuhera'.[50] Of these, perhaps the most special medal was that awarded to Private Daniel Loochstadt, a rifleman in the 5th/60th Foot. Not only did he receive clasps for a total of fifteen actions, a number equalled by only one other soldier, Corporal James Talbot of the 45th Foot, but Loochstadt is also one of only six individuals who received clasps for both the Battle of Fuentes de Oñoro (on 3–5 May 1811) and Albuera. The explanation for this last oddity was that he was a member of a small detachment (consisting mainly of artillerymen and commanded by Major John Galiffe of the 5th/60th) which was despatched from the battlefield of Fuentes de Oñoro in time to reach Albuera for the action on 16 May.[51]

The French, of course, did have a medal for valour, the famous 'cross' of the Legion of Honour, founded by Napoleon, and it was available to officers and private soldiers alike. The awards for Albuera appear to have been included in the nomination of 6 August 1811, when Napoleon, working from the recommendations of Marshal Soult, conferred the decoration on approximately eighty-eight officers and men from regiments which fought in the battle.[52] (Being recommended by Soult was not a

47. W. to Liverpool, 11 July 1811, *Dispatches*, Vol. 8, pp. 94–6 at 95.
48. Captain Fleming's sword is now in the NAM. Lloyd's Patriotic Fund was founded as a charitable organisation in 1803. L. R. Wriggett, 'Lloyd's Patriotic Fund', *Journal of the Society for Army Historical Research*, Vol. XXXIII (Spring 1955), p. 43.
49. Notice in the *London Gazette*, Issue No. 17103, 27 January 1816, p. 5
50. Mullen, *Military General Service Roll*.
51. Butler, *Annals of the Rifles*, Vol. 2, pp. 138–9.
52. The list of recipients on that date can be found in Lacepéde, *État Général*, Vol. 2, pp. 447–9.

guarantee of the requested reward. Napoleon deferred the cross for some of the proposed medal winners on the basis that they were *'trop jeune'* ('too young') and he also without explanation granted Colonel Lallemand a cash award of 2,000 francs instead of making him a commandant of the Legion of Honour and promoting him to the rank of brigade general.)[53] French veterans of Albuera who did not win the Legion of Honour had to wait even longer than their British peers for recognition – the Médaille de Sainte-Hélène, the decoration for men who served in the campaigns of the First Empire, was not issued until 1857 and, even then, it was not associated with specific actions. The Spaniards were the first and only nation to issue a medal specifically for all veterans of 'Albuhera', which they did in March 1815. The Portuguese did not have any single-action medals and even their general commemorative medal was issued in very limited numbers.

As Wellington famously said about the Battle of Albuera, 'It was a strange affair.' Beresford fought only reluctantly and Soult fought rashly, taking on an immensely superior enemy. The French executed a brilliant plan of attack, but the allies countered with a dogged determination and refusal to acknowledge defeat. There were consequently highlights and lowlights for each of the contending forces:

> It is difficult to say on which side the Victory lay; we had the honour of repulsing the Enemy in his attack, and frustrating his intention of relieving Badajoz; moreover all his wounded fell into our hands. On the other side, in a charge made by his Cavalry he succeeded in taking near a thousand of our Men Prisoners, besides the Colours of three Regiments and a Howitzer. Each Party will doubtless claim the Day, but the decision must be made by some who cannot be weighed in it by partiality.[54]

In the face of conflicting claims, however, it is important to remember that Albuera was a battle about Badajoz. The successful defence of that fortress through both the first and second sieges gives the French as much claim to a strategic triumph as the allies had to a tactical victory.

The most lasting impact of Albuera, however, was in the realm of morale, rather than of strategy or tactics, because it was a fight to remember for every army present on that rain- and blood-soaked field. For the Spaniards, it was a rare day of victory in a long war of defeats. For the Portuguese, it was a successful baptism of fire under extreme circumstances. For the French, it was sobering evidence that the spirit that had carried the imperial troops to victory at Austerlitz, Jena and Friedland might not suffice alone to conquer their determined Peninsular foes. For the British, it was the ultimate validation that their army, for all its regimental and administrative idiosyncrasies, was a fighting force second to none. This last view was best expressed by Lieutenant Sherer, the young officer whose memoirs reveal that he was as much a philosopher as a warrior:

> I have read the annals of modern warfare with some attention, and I know of little, which can compare with, nothing, which has surpassed, the enthousiastic

53. Soult, Statement on Solicited Promotions and Distinctions, 6 August 1811.
54. Boutflower, *Journal*, pp. 92–3.

[*sic*] and unyielding bravery, displayed by these [British] corps on the field of Albuera. Yet this dear-bought, and, let me add, not useless victory, won by unaided courage, graced with no trophies, and followed by no proportionate result, has almost sunk into oblivion, or is remembered only, and spoken of, as a day of doubtful success, if not positive disaster. It was certainly not useless, because the object of Marshal Soult, which was the relief of Badajos [*sic*], and the expulsion of our troops from Spanish Estremadura, was wholly defeated; but it had yet a higher, a nobler, a more undying use, it added one to the many bright examples of British heroism; it gave a terrible and long-remembered lesson to the haughty legions of France; and, when Soult rode by the side of his Imperial master on the field of Waterloo, as the cheering of the English soldiery struck upon his ear, Albuera was not forgotten, and he could have whispered to him, that they were men, who could only be defeated, by being utterly destroyed.[55]

55. Sherer, *Recollections*, pp. 157–8.

APPENDICES

Appendix A

Orders of Battle

All orders of battle use the following symbols: † = killed in action,
‡ = mortally wounded, * = wounded

Part 1: Anglo-Portuguese Army

Sources: D'Urban, *Report of Operations*; Challis; Gil; Lady Inglis; Nunes; Ward 1975

Commander-in-Chief	***Marshal Sir William Carr Beresford***
Military Secretary	*Lt. Col. Robert Arbuthnot*
Aide-de-Camp	*Captain Charles Malloy*
British Staff	
Assistant Adjutant-General	*Lt. Col. John Rooke (3rd Foot Guards)*
Deputy Assistant Adjutant-General	*?*
Assistant Quartermaster-General	*Lt. Col. Otto William Offeney (7th Line Btn., KGL)*
Deputy Assistant Quartermaster-General	*?*
Artillery Commander	*Major George Julius Hartmann (KGL)*
Engineer Commander	*Captain John Squire (Royal Engineers)*
Portuguese Staff	
Adjutant-General	*Brigadier General Manoel de Brito Mozinho*
Quartermaster-General	*Colonel Benjamin D'Urban*
Deputy Quartermaster-General	*Lieutenant Colonel Henry Hardinge*
Artillery Commander	*Major Alexander Dickson*
2nd Division	***Major General William Stewart****
	(vice Major General Rowland Hill)
Assistant Adjutant-General	*?*
Deputy Assistant Adjutant-General	*Lieutenant Charles Bayley (31st Foot)*
Assistant Quartermaster-General	*Captain Robert Waller* (103rd Foot)*
Deputy Assistant Quartermaster-Generals	*Captain Nathaniel Thorn (3rd Foot),*
	Lieutenant R. Heathcote (Royal Dragoons)
Aide-de-camp	*Captain Robert Gabriel (2nd Dragoon Guards)*

1st Brigade	***Lieutenant Colonel John Colborne (66th Foot)***
	(vice Major General William Stewart)
Brigade Major	*Captain William Dunbar (66th Foot)*
1st Battalion, 3rd Foot	*Lieutenant Colonel William Stewart*
2nd Battalion, 31st Foot	*Major Guy G. C. L'Estrange*
2nd Battalion, 48th Foot	*Major William Brooke**
2nd Battalion, 66th Foot	*Captain Conway Benning† (vice Lt. Col. Colborne)*
2nd Brigade	***Lt. Col. Alexander Abercromby (28th Foot)***
	(vice Major General Lumley)
Brigade Major	*Captain Johnson (58th Foot)*
2nd Battalion, 28th Foot	*Major Charles Patterson*
2nd Battalion, 34th Foot	*Lieutenant Colonel William Fenwick*
2nd Battalion, 39th Foot	*Major Patrick Lindsay*
3rd Brigade	***Major General Daniel Hoghton†***
Brigade Major	*Captain James Taylor (48th Foot)*
Aide-de-camp	*Captain George Ramsden (1st Foot Guards)*
29th Foot	*Lieutenant Colonel Daniel White**
1st Battalion, 48th Foot	*Lieutenant Colonel George Henry Duckworth†*
1st Battalion, 57th Foot	*Lieutenant Colonel William Inglis**

2nd Division Artillery

2nd Company, KGL Artillery	*Captain Andrew Cleves*
(5 x 6-pounder guns, 1 x 5½-inch howitzer)	
4th Company, Royal Artillery	*Captain J. Hawker*
(5 x 9-pounder guns, 1 x 5½-inch howitzer)	

2nd Division Light Troops	*Major John Galiffe (5th Battalion, 60th Foot)*
3 companies, 60th Rifles	*Captains MacMahon, Franchini and Blassiere*

4th Division	***Major General Sir Galbraith Lowry Cole****
Assistant Adjutant-General	*Lieutenant Colonel Thomas Reynell (71st Foot)*
Deputy Assistant Adjutant-General	*Captain Richard Egerton* (34th Foot)*
Assistant Quartermaster-General	*Major Charles Broke [Vere] (5th Foot)*
Deputy Assistant Quartermaster-General	*Captain Philip Bainbrigge (93rd Foot)*
Aides-de-camp	*Captain Alexander de Roverea* (Sicilian Regt.),*
	Captain Thomas Wade* (42nd Foot)

1st Brigade	***Brigadier James Kemmis (absent on 16 May)***
Light companies of the 2nd/27th, 1st/40th and 1st/97th Foot	
(All other units of the brigade were absent on 16 May 1811)	

2nd Brigade	***Lieutenant Colonel William J. Myers‡ (7th Foot)***
Brigade Major	*?*
1st Battalion, 7th Foot	*Major John Nooth*
2nd Battalion, 7th Foot	*Lieutenant Colonel Edward Blakeney**
1st Battalion, 23rd Foot	*Lieutenant Colonel Henry Ellis**

3rd Brigade (9th Portuguese Line Bde)   *Brigadier General William Harvey*

Brigade Major   *?*

11th Portuguese Line (1st & 2nd Btns.)   *Lieutenant Colonel Donald MacDonell*

23rd Portuguese Line (1st & 2nd Btns.)   *Lieutenant Colonel Thomas W. Stubbs*

Loyal Lusitanian Legion (1st Btn.)   *Lieutenant Colonel Edward Hawkshaw**

4th Division Artillery

4th Company, KGL Artillery   *Captain Frederick Sympher*

(5 x 6-pounder guns, 1 x 5½-inch howitzer)

4th Division Light Troops

1 company, Brunswick-Oels   *Captain L. Wachholtz*

Portuguese Division   ***Lieutenant General John Hamilton***

Assistant Adjutant-General   *?*

Assistant Quartermaster-General   *?*

Aide-de-Camp   *?*

1st Brigade (2nd Portuguese Line Brigade)   *Brigadier General Agostinho Luiz da Fonseca*

Brigade Major   *?*

2nd Portuguese Line (1st & 2nd Btns.)   *Colonel Antonio Hypolito da Costa*

14th Portuguese Line (1st & 2nd Btns.)   *Lieutenant Colonel James W. Oliver*

2nd Brigade (4th Portuguese Line Brigade)   *Brigadier General Archibald Campbell*

Brigade Major   *?*

4th Portuguese Line (1st & 2nd Btns.)   *Lieutenant Colonel Alan Campbell*

10th Portuguese Line (1st & 2nd Btns.)   *Col. Don Luiz Benedicto de Castro, Conde de Rezende*

Portuguese Division Artillery

Foot Battery, 1st Artillery Regiment   *Captain J. S. de Arriaga*

(5 x 6-pounder guns, 1 x 5½-inch howitzer)

Foot Battery, 2nd Artillery Regiment   *Captain William Braun*

(5 x 9-pounder guns, 1 x 5½-inch howitzer)

First Independent Brigade (KGL)   *Major General Charles Alten*

Brigade Major   *?*

Aide-de-camp   *Captain George Baring**

1st Light Battalion, KGL   *Lieutenant Colonel Ernest Leonhart*

2nd Light Battalion, KGL   *Lieutenant Colonel Colin Halkett*

Second Independent Brigade (Port.)   *Brigadier General Richard Collins**

Brigade Major   *?*

5th Portuguese Line (1st & 2nd Btns.)   *Lieutenant Colonel Francisco da Silva Pereira*

5th Caçadores (1st Btn.)   *Lieutenant Colonel Michael McCreagh*

Cavalry Division	*Major General William Lumley*
	superseding Brigadier Robert Long
Aide-de-camp	*Captain George Dean (Royal West India Rangers)*

Heavy Brigade	*Colonel George De Grey*
Brigade Major	*? Holmes*
3rd Dragoon Guards	*Lieutenant Colonel Sir Granby Calcroft*
4th Dragoons	*Major Burgh Leighton*
	(vice Lieutenant Colonel J. C. Dalbiac, sick at Elvas)

Unbrigaded Regiment	
13th Light Dragoons	*Colonel Michael Head*

1st Portuguese Cavalry Brigade	*Colonel Loftus Otway*
Brigade Major	*Capt. Bento Maria Lobo Pessanha (1st Portuguese Regt.)*
1st Portuguese Regiment	*Lieutenant Colonel Miguel Pais do Amaral*
7th Portuguese Regiment	*Lieutenant Colonel Henry Watson*

3rd Portuguese Cavalry Brigade	*Brigadier General George Madden (absent on 16 May)*
5th Portuguese Regiment (1 squadron)	*Captain Frederick Watson*
8th Portuguese Regiment (1 squadron)	*Captain Henry Wyndham*
[3rd Portuguese Regiment (2 squadrons)	*Major Pinto de Lacerda* (Regt. absent on 16 May 1811)]

Cavalry Division Artillery	
D Troop, Royal Horse Artillery	*Captain G. Lefebure*
(3 x 6-pounder guns, 1 x 5½-inch howitzer)	

Part 2: Combined Spanish Armies

Sources: Burriel, *Batalla de la Albuhera*; Spain, Sección de Historia Militar, *Estados*, No. 64.

4th (Andalucian) Army Expeditionary Corps

	Teniente General Don Joaquin Blake
Aides-de-camp	*Sebastian de Llano, Carlos Oppen, Pedro Muzo*
Chief of Staff	*Adjutant-General Antonio Burriel*
Staff Officers	*Antonio Ramón del Valle, Juan Blake,*
	Jose Sanchez Boado, Luis de Landaburu
Commander of Headquarters Guard	*Tomás Valiente*
Quartermaster-General	*Luis Elexaburu*
Artillery Commander	*Lieutenant Colonel José Savaria*
Engineer Commander	*Lieutenant Colonel Joaquin de Ribacoba*
Attached Officer	*Captain Francisco Remirez*

Vanguard Division — *Mariscal de Campo José de Lardizabal*

Staff Officer	*Lieutenant Colonel Marcos Nunez Abreu**
Murcia Regiment	*?*
Canarias Regiment	*?*
2o de León Regiment	*?*
Campo Mayor Regiment	*?*
Cazadores Reunidos	*Teniente Colonel Lorenzo Calvo*

Third Division — *Teniente General Francisco Ballasteros*

Aides-de-camp	*Captain Manuel Guerrero, Captain Rafael Soravia*
Staff Officers	*Adjutant-General Felipe Montes, Miguel Aulestia, First Adjutant Emeterio Velarde‡, Second Adjutant Martin de Parraga†, Antonio Arron, Geronimo Valdes, Manuel Granados, Juan Millana, Juan Manuel Peron, Miguel Aulestia**
1o Voluntarios de Cataluña	*Colonel Francisco Dionisio Vives*
Voluntarios de Barbastro	*Brigadier Francisco Merino*
Pravia Regiment	*Colonel Luis Diaz‡*
Lena Regiment	*Colonel Jayme Butler**
Castropol Regiment	*Colonel Pedro Gastelù*
Cangas de Tineo Regiment	*Colonel Guillermo Livezay*
Infiesto Regiment	*Colonel Diego Clark*

Fourth Division — *Mariscal de Campo José de Zayas*

Aide-de-camp	*Teniente Colonel Berthold von Schepeler*
Chief of Staff	*Marques de la Roca*
Staff Officers	*Captain Julian Zurita, Captain Juan de la Hera, Captain Ramón de Sentmanat*

First Section [Brigade] — *Brigadier Juan de la Cruz Mourgeon*

2o Reales Guardias Españolas	*Brigadier Juan Urbina**
4o Reales Guardias Españolas	*Colonel Diego Ulloa*
Irlanda Regiment	*Lieutenant Colonel Ramón Velasco*
Voluntarios de la Patria	*Colonel Fernando de Mazarredo*

Second Section [Brigade] — *Brigadier Ramón Polo*

Imperiales de Toledo Regiment	*?*
Legion Extrangera	*Colonel Juan Omlin*
Ciudad Rodrigo Regiment	*?*
Reales Guardias Walonas	*?*
Zapadores	*?*

Cavalry Division — *Brigadier Casimiro Loy*

Escuadrón de Granaderos	*?*
Escuadrón de Instrucción	*?*
Provisional de Santiago	*?*
Husares de Castilla	*?*

5th (Extremaduran) Army   *Capitán General de Ejército Don Francisco Xavier de Castaños*

Aides-de-camp   *?*
Chief of Staff   *Mariscal de Campo Martin de la Carrera*
   Staff Officers   *?*
Artillery Commander   *Brigadier José Garcia Paredes*
Engineer Commander   *Manuel Puella*

First Division   *Brigadier Carlos de España**
Staff Officers   *Adjutant-General Tulio O'Neill*, Colonel Estanislao Sanchez Salvador*

Zapadores (1 company)   *Captain Hermosilla*
Guias   *Lieutenant Clemente Grimas*
Rey Regiment   *?*
Zamora Regiment   *?*
Voluntarios de Navarra   *?*

Cavalry Division   *Brigadier Count Penne-Villemur*
Liaison Officer   *Lieutenant William Light (4th Dragoons)*

Carabineros Reales   *?*
Reina Regiment   *?*
Borbon Regiment   *?*
Lusitania Regiment   *?*
Algarve Regiment   *Lieutenant Colonel Antolin Riguilon*
Husares d'Extremadura   *?*
Cazadores de Sevilla   *?*

Artillery   *Colonel José Miranda*
   6 x 4-pounder guns

Part 3: French Expeditionary Force

Sources: 'Situation des Troupes composant l'Armée Impériale du Midi a l'époque du 1er Mai 1811', SHAT C⁸/356; Berthier, 'Report of Losses at Albuera'.

Commander-in-Chief   *Marshal Jean-de-Dieu Soult*
Aides-de-camp   *Colonel Hulot, Squadron Chief Tholosé*, Captains Ricard, Lecaron, Petiet*, Choiseul*
Attached Officers   *Battalion Chief Bedart, Captains Feres, Lafitte, Bory de St Vincent, Pressart, Destrabenrath, Dandlowe, Dezan, Denizot, Banch, Ingaldo, Chabourri*, Lieutenants Galabert*, Michel**
Chief of Staff   *Division General Gazan**
   Assistant Chief of Staff   *Adjutant-Commandant Moquery*
   Aides-de-camp   *Battalion Chief Darnaud, Captain d'Espérandieu**

Artillery Commander	*Brigade General Ruty*
Artillery Chief of Staff	*Colonel Berge**
Aides-de-camp	*Lieutenants Albrespil, Depresle*
Engineer Commander	*Division General Léry*
Aides-de-camp	*Lieutenants St Denis, Léry*
Intendant General	*Mathieu-Favier*
Gendarmerie (1 officer and 8 gendarmes)	*Colonel Mathis*
Baggagemaster	*Captain Porcher*
1st and 3rd Coys., 1st Baggage Train Btn.	*Lieutenant Aillor*

V Corps	***Division General Jean-Baptiste Girard****
Aides-de-camp	*Captain Duroc-Mesclops‡, Lieutenants Massot*,*
	*Barbeu-Dubourg**
Attached Officers	*Battalion Chief Valguarnera (Sp.)*,*
	Captains Romanski, Flocquerel, Lieutenant Urbanski**
Artillery Commander	*Brigade General Bourgeat*
Artillery Chief of Staff	*Colonel Bouchu*
Aide-de-camp	*Captain Pernet*
Engineer Commanders	*Battalion Chief Lamare, Battalion Chief Amillet*
Ordonnateur en Chef	*Bazire*
War Commissar	*Deseclin*
Assistant	*Garnier*
Attached Officers	*Battalion Chief Petitpierre, Captain Aserlin,*
	2nd Lieutenant Porzozowski

First Division	***Division General Girard***
	(also temporary commander of V Corps)
Chief of Staff	*Battalion Chief Hudry**
Aides-de-camp	*Captain Duroc-Mesclops‡, Lieutenants Massot*,*
	*Barbeu-Dubourg**
Attached Officer	*Battalion Chief Roubeau*
Artillery Commander	*Battalion Chief Lambert*
Attached Officer	*Captain Dubois*
Engineer Commander	*Captain Andoucaud‡*
War Commissar	*Mery*

First Brigade	***Brigade General Brayer***
Aides-de-camp	*Captain Carlier†, Captain Voirol*, Lieutenant Thevenin*
34th Line	*Colonel Remond*
1st Battalion (detachment)	*?*
2nd Battalion	*?*
3rd Battalion	*Battalion Chief Velten*
40th Line	*Colonel Chasseraux*
1st Battalion	*Battalion Chief Woirol**
2nd Battalion	*Battalion Chief Gaspard-Bonnot‡*
3rd Battalion (detachment)	*Battalion Chief Supersac‡*

Second Brigade	*Brigade General Veilande*
64th Line	*Battalion Chief Astruc[†]*
1st Battalion (detachment)	*Battalion Chief Henry**
2nd Battalion	*Battalion Chief Pichard**
3rd Battalion	*[Battalion Chief Astruc[†]]*
88th Line	*Colonel Letourneur**
1st Battalion (detachment)	*Battalion Chief Marguet*
2nd Battalion	*Battalion Chief Dubarry**
3rd Battalion	*Battalion Chief Monnet*

Divisional Artillery

19th Company, 6th Foot Artillery Regiment	*Captain Quirot**
11th Company (part), 6th Foot Artillery Regt.	*?*
8th Company (part), 5th (Bis) Train Btn.	*Sous Lieutenant Tournaflotte*

Second Division	***Brigade General Pépin[‡]***
Chief of Staff	*Adjutant Commandant Forestier*
Aides-de-camp	*Captains Coffe, Vattier*
Artillery Commander	*Battalion Chief Colin*
Engineer Commander	*Captain Faivre*
War Commissar	*Chrétien*

First Brigade	***Brigade General Pépin[‡]***
	(also temporary commander of Second Division)
21st Light	*Colonel Lagarde*
2nd Battalion	*Battalion Chief Broudel*
3rd Battalion	*Battalion Chief Bigot[†]*
100th Line	*Colonel Quiot**
1st Battalion	*Battalion Chief Gaud**
2nd Battalion	*Battalion Chief Amadieu*

Second Brigade	***Brigade General Maransin****
Aide-de-camp	*Captain Philippon**
28th Light	*Colonel Praefke[‡]*
1st Battalion	*Battalion Chief Camus[†]*
2nd Battalion	*Battalion Chief Gerrain[‡]*
3rd Battalion	*Battalion Chief Dedoual*
103rd Line	*Colonel Rignoux*
1st Battalion	*Battalion Chief Lapierre[‡]*
2nd Battalion	*Battalion Chief Huguet**
3rd Battalion	*Battalion Chief Livrat*

Divisional Artillery

| 4th Company, 6th Foot Artillery Regiment | *Captain Petitdidier* |
| 2nd Company, 5th (Bis) Artillery Train Btn. | *Sous-Lieutenant Dellin* |

Corps Artillery Park

Artillery

11th Company, 6th Foot Artillery	*Captain Maurice*
4th Company (part), 6th Horse Artillery	*?*
4th Company (detachment), Artillery Workers	
5th (Bis) Artillery Train Battalion	*Captain Chrisnard*

Engineers

2nd Company, 1st Miner Battalion	*Captain Gillet*
1st Company, 2nd Sapper Battalion	*Captain Martin*
5th Company, 2nd Sapper Battalion	*Captain Coste*

Baggage Train

4th Company, 8th Baggage Train Battalion	*? vice 2nd Lieutenant Dujat*

First Independent Brigade	*Brigade General Werlé†*
Aide-de-camp	*2nd Lieutenant Fabreguettes**
12th Light	*Colonel Dulong**
1st Battalion	*Battalion Chief Louis**
2nd Battalion	*Battalion Chief Bernard**
3rd Battalion	*Battalion Chief Armand**
58th Line	*Colonel Legrand**
1st Battalion	*Battalion Chief Fourcade†*
2nd Battalion	*Battalion Chief Tracy**
3rd Battalion	*Battalion Chief Berlancourt*
4th Battalion	*Battalion Chief Bayle-Doguet*

Second Independent Brigade	*Division General Godinot*
Aide-de-camp	*Captain Vidal*
16th Light	*?*
1st Battalion	*Battalion Chief Ghenezer**
2nd Battalion	*Battalion Chief Rubellin*
3rd Battalion	*Battalion Chief Ruffat*
51st Line	*Battalion Chief Bisot*
1st Battalion	*[Battalion Chief Bisot]*
55th Line	*Colonel Schwitter**
1st Battalion	*Battalion Chief Petreil*
2nd Battalion	*Battalion Chief Gauthier*
3rd Battalion	*Battalion Chief Gaudener*
Combined Grenadiers	*Colonel Varé (45th Line)*

Grenadier Companies of 8th (2 coys.), 45th, 63rd and 95th Line, 4th Poles and several other regts.

Reserve Cavalry **Division General Latour-Maubourg**
Aides-de-camp *Battalion Chief Dutas, Captains Matarel, de Nadaillac*, Kierzkowski*

Light Cavalry Brigade *Brigade General Briche*
Aides-de-camp *Captain Gigogne, Lieutenant Sahustron*

2nd Hussars *Colonel Vinot*
1st Squadron *Squadron Chief Boyer*
2nd Squadron *Squadron Chief Braun*
3rd Squadron *?*

10th Hussars *Colonel Laval*
1st Squadron *Squadron Chief Desmarets*
2nd Squadron *Squadron Chief Bosse*
3rd Squadron *?*

21st Mounted Chasseurs *Major Gaydon*
1st Squadron *Squadron Chief Muller*
2nd Squadron *Squadron Chief Piola*
3rd Squadron *?*

1st Dragoon Brigade *Brigade General Bron*
Aide-de-camp *Lieutenant Cassalet*

4th Dragoons *Colonel Farine*
1st Squadron *Squadron Chief Baillot**
2nd Squadron *Squadron Chief Caron*

20th Dragoons *Major Dejean*
1st Squadron *Squadron Chief Coulon*
2nd Squadron *Squadron Chief Doldenel**
3rd Squadron *Squadron Chief Lejeune*
4th Squadron *?*

26th Dragoons *Squadron Chief Laffitte*
1st Squadron *[Squadron Chief Lafitte]*
2nd Squadron *Squadron Chief Parrin*

2nd Dragoon Brigade *Brigade General Bouvier des Eclats*
14th Dragoons *Squadron Chief Hardy*
1st Squadron *?*
2nd Squadron *Squadron Chief Salmon*

17th Dragoons *Major Daubessard*
1st Squadron *Squadron Chief Leopold*
2nd Squadron *Squadron Chief Colombel*
3rd Squadron *?*
4th Squadron *?*

27th Dragoons	*Colonel Lallemand*
1st Squadron	*Squadron Chief Duguai*
2nd Squadron	*?*
3rd Squadron	*?*
4th Squadron	*?*

Independent Cavalry Units

1st Vistula Lancers	*Colonel Konopka*
1st Squadron	*Squadron Chief Duffie*
2nd Squadron	*Squadron Chief Kostowiecki*
3rd Squadron	*Squadron Chief Huppet**
4th Squadron	*?*
27th Mounted Chasseurs	*Colonel Arenberg*
1st Squadron	*Squadron Chief Moteau*
2nd Squadron	*?*
3rd Squadron	*?*
4th Spanish Chasseurs	*Major Forest*
1st Squadron	*?*
2nd Squadron	*?*

Reserve Cavalry Artillery

4th Company, 6th Horse Artillery	*Lieutenant Bellencontre‡*
1st Company, 5th (Bis) Artillery Train Btn.	*Lieutenant Derozier*

Reserve Artillery Park

Artillery

12th Company 1st Foot Artillery	*Captain Claudin*
8th Company, 7th Foot Artillery	*Captain Poinsot*
2nd Company, 2nd Horse Artillery	*Captain Lebeau*
2nd and 3rd Companies, 3rd Horse Artillery	*Captain Michel*
7th Company, 4th Horse Artillery	*Captain Paetz*

Artillery Train

2nd & 5th Companies, 2nd Art. Train Btn.	*2nd Lieutenant Marechal*
3rd & 4th Companies, 8th Art. Train Btn.	*2nd Lieutenant Fernand*
3rd Company, 11th Art. Train Battalion (detachment)	
1st Company, 12th Art. Train Battalion	?
2nd Company, 6th (Bis) Art. Train Btn.	*Lieutenant Scernica*
3rd, 5th & 6th Coys. (part), 10th (Bis) Train Btn.	
	Lieutenant Perrier
4th Company (detachment), Artillery Workers	?

Appendix B

Unit Strengths and Casualties

Part 1: Anglo-Portuguese Forces

"Present" = Information from Oman, *History*, Vol. 4, App. XV, pp. 631–4.
"Casualties" = Information from Londonderry, *Narrative*, Vol. 2, App. XXXIX.
K, W, M = Killed, Wounded, Missing

British and Portuguese General Staff

	Officers			NCOs and soldiers			Total
Present	>50			>6			>56
Casualties (K, W, M)	2	8	0	?	?	?	10
Survivors							>46

British Infantry
1st Battalion, 3rd Foot

	Officers			Serg'ts & drummers			Rank and file			Total
Present	27				728					755
Casualties (K, W, M)	4	14	2	4	12	16	208	222	161	643 (85%)
Survivors										112

1st Battalion, 7th Foot

	Officers			Serg'ts & drummers			Rank and file			Total
Present	27				687					714
Casualties (K, W, M)	0	15	0	2	14	0	63	263	0	357 (50%)
Survivors										357

2nd Battalion, 7th Foot

	Officers			Serg'ts & drummers			Rank and file			Total
Present	28				540					568
Casualties (K, W, M)	2	14	0	1	17	0	46	269	0	349 (61%)
Survivors										219

1st Battalion, 23rd Foot

	Officers			Serg'ts & drummers			Rank and file			Total
Present	41				692					733
Casualties (K, W, M)	2	12	0	1	13	1	73	232	5	339 (46%)
Survivors										394

2nd Battalion, 27th Foot

	Officers			Serg'ts & drummers			Rank and file			Total
Present	?					?				1 coy. (60?)
Casualties (K, W, M)	0	0	0	0	0	0	3	5	0	8
Survivors										?

2nd Battalion, 28th Foot

	Officers			Serg'ts & drummers			Rank and file			Total
Present	28					491				519
Casualties (K, W, M)	0	6	0	1	8	0	26	123	0	164 (32%)
Survivors										355

29th Foot

	Officers			Serg'ts & drummers			Rank and file			Total
Present	31					476				507
Casualties (K, W, M)	5	13	0	2	12	0	73	220	11	336 (66%)
Survivors										171

2nd Battalion, 31st Foot

	Officers			Serg'ts & drummers			Rank and file			Total
Present	20					398				418
Casualties (K, W, M)	0	7	0	3	4	0	26	115	0	155 (37%)
Survivors										263

2nd Battalion, 34th Foot

	Officers			Serg'ts & drummers			Rank and file			Total
Present	28					568				596
Casualties (K, W, M)	3	4	0	3	6	0	27	85	0	128 (21%)
Survivors										468

2nd Battalion, 39th Foot

	Officers			Serg'ts & drummers			Rank and file			Total
Present	33					449				482
Casualties (K, W, M)	1	4	0	0	4	0	14	72	2	97 (20%)
Survivors										385

1st Battalion, 40th Foot

	Officers			Serg'ts & drummers			Rank and file			Total
Present	?					?				1 coy. (60?)
Casualties (K, W, M)	0	0	0	0	0	0	3	8	0	11
Survivors										?

1st Battalion, 48th Foot

	Officers			Serg'ts & drummers			Rank and file			Total
Present	33					464				497
Casualties (K, W, M)	3	14	0	6	10	0	58	185	6	282 (57%)
Survivors										215

2nd Battalion, 48th Foot

	Officers			Serg'ts & drummers			Rank and file			Total
Present	29					423				452
Casualties (K, W, M)	4	10	9	4	4	15	40	82	175	343 (76%)
Survivors										109

1st Battalion, 57th Foot

	Officers			Serg'ts & drummers			Rank and file			Total
Present		31			616					647
Casualties (K, W, M)	2	21	0	4	14	0	83	304	0	428 (66%)
Survivors										219

5th Battalion, 60th Foot

	Officers			Serg'ts & drummers			Rank and file			Total
Present		4			142					146 (3 coys.)
Casualties (K, W, M)	0	1	0	1	2	0	1	16	0	21 (14%)
Survivors										125

2nd Battalion, 66th Foot

	Officers			Serg'ts & drummers			Rank and file			Total
Present		24			417					441
Casualties (K, W, M)	3	12	0	2	13	5	50	91	96	272 (62%)
Survivors										169

1st Battalion, 97th Foot

	Officers			Serg'ts & drummers			Rank and file			Total
Present		?			?					1 coy. (60?)
Casualties (K, W, M)	0	0	0	0	0	0	0	1	0	1
Survivors										?

1st Light Battalion, KGL

	Officers			Serg'ts & drummers			Rank and file			Total
Present		23			565					588
Casualties (K, W, M)	0	5	0	0	3	0	4	55	2	69 (12%)
Survivors										519

2nd Light Battalion, KGL

	Officers			Serg'ts & drummers			Rank and file			Total
Present		19			491					510
Casualties (K, W, M)	1	1	0	0	3	0	3	28	1	37 (7%)
Survivors										473

Brunswick-Oels

	Officers			Serg'ts & drummers			Rank and file			Total
Present		3			80					83
Casualties (K, W, M)	?	?	?	?	?	?	?	?	?	?
Survivors										?

Portuguese Infantry

2nd Portuguese Line – 2 battalions

	Officers			NCOs and soldiers			Total
Present		?			?		1,225
Casualties (K, W, M)	0	0	0	3	5	0	8 (<1%)
Survivors							1,217

4th Portuguese Line – 2 battalions

	Officers			NCOs and soldiers			Total
Present		?			?		1,271
Casualties (K, W, M)	0	1	0	9	50	0	60 (5%)
Survivors							1,211

5th Portuguese Line – 2 battalions

	Officers			NCOs and soldiers			Total
Present		?			?		985
Casualties (K, W, M)	0	4	0	10	36	10	60 (6%)
Survivors							925

10th Portuguese Line – 2 battalions

	Officers			NCOs and soldiers			Total
Present		?			?		1,119
Casualties (K, W, M)	0	0	0	0	11	0	11 (<1%)
Survivors							1,108

11th Portuguese Line – 2 battalions

	Officers			NCOs and soldiers			Total
Present		?			?		1,154
Casualties (K, W, M)	0	2	0	2	4	5	13 (1%)
Survivors							1,141

14th Portuguese Line – 2 battalions

	Officers			NCOs and soldiers			Total
Present		?			?		1,204
Casualties (K, W, M)	0	0	0	2	0	0	2 (<1%)
Survivors							1,202

23rd Portuguese Line – 2 battalions

	Officers			NCOs and soldiers			Total
Present		?			?		1,201
Casualties (K, W, M)	1	1	0	3	14	0	19 (2%)
Survivors							1,182

Loyal Lusitanian Legion – 1 battalion

	Officers			NCOs and soldiers			Total
Present		?			?		572
Casualties (K, W, M)	0	6	0	66	89	10	171 (30%)
Survivors							401

5th Caçadores – 1 battalion

	Officers			NCOs and soldiers			Total
Present		?			?		400
Casualties (K, W, M)	0	0	0	5	25	1	31 (8%)
Survivors							369

British Cavalry

3rd Dragoon Guards

	Officers			Serg'ts & trumpets			Rank and file			Total
Present		23			351			374		
Casualties (K, W, M)	1	0	0	0	0	0	9	9	1	20 (5%)
Survivors										364

4th Dragoons

	Officers			Serg'ts & trumpets			Rank and file			Total
Present		30			357			387		
Casualties (K, W, M)	0	2	2	1	3	0	2	15	2	27 (7%)
Survivors										360

13th Light Dragoons

	Officers			Serg'ts & trumpets			Rank and file			Total
Present	23						380			403
Casualties (K, W, M)	0	0	0	0	0	0	0	1	0	1
Survivors										402

Portuguese Cavalry
1st Portuguese Cavalry

	Officers			NCOs and soldiers			Total
Present	?			?			327
Casualties (K, W, M)	0	0	0	0	0	0	0
Survivors							327

5th Portuguese Cavalry – 1 squadron

	Officers			NCOs and soldiers			Total
Present	?			?			104
Casualties (K, W, M)	0	0	0	0	0	0	0
Survivors							104

7th Portuguese Cavalry

	Officers			NCOs and soldiers			Total
Present	?			?			314
Casualties (K, W, M)	0	0	0	0	2	0	2
Survivors							312

8th Portuguese Cavalry – 1 squadron

	Officers			NCOs and soldiers			Total
Present	?			?			104
Casualties (K, W, M)	0	0	0	0	0	0	0
Survivors							104

Artillery
British Artillery – 2 companies

	Officers			Serg'ts & trumpets			Rank and file			Total
Present	9						246			255
Casualties (K, W, M)	0	1	0	0	0	0	3	10	1	15 (6%)
Survivors										240

KGL Artillery – 2 companies

	Officers			Serg'ts & trumpets			Rank and file			Total
Present	10						282			292
Casualties (K, W, M)	0	1	0	0	0	1	0	17	29	48 (16%)
Survivors										243

Portuguese Artillery – 2 companies

	Officers			NCOs and soldiers			Total
Present	?			?			221
Casualties (K, W, M)	0	0	0	2	8	0	10 (5%)
Survivors							211

Part 2: Spanish Forces

'Present' = Information from Spain, Sección de Historia Militar, *Estados*, No. 64.
'Casualties' = Information from Burriel, *Batalla de la Albuhera*, Chart of Casualties.

Spanish General Staff

		Officers		NCOs and soldiers			Total
Present		>30			>6		>36
Casualties (K, W, M)	3	7	0	?	?	?	10
Survivors							>26

Spanish Infantry

Murcia

		Officers		NCOs and soldiers			Total
Present		49			657		706
Casualties (K, W, M)	2	5	0	26	58	0	91 (13%)
Survivors							615

Canarias

		Officers		NCOs and soldiers			Total
Present		13			420		433
Casualties (K, W, M)	2	4	0	16	64	0	86 (20%)
Survivors							347

2o León

		Officers		NCOs and soldiers			Total
Present		19			567		586
Casualties (K, W, M)	0	0	0	11	47	0	58 (10%)
Survivors							528

Campo Mayor

		Officers		NCOs and soldiers			Total
Present		26			647		673
Casualties (K, W, M)	0	4	0	5	36	0	45 (7%)
Survivors							628

Vanguard – Cazadores Reunidos

		Officers		NCOs and soldiers			Total
Present		Included in strengths of constituent regiments					
Casualties (K, W, M)	0	1	0	1	10	0	12

Barbastro

		Officers		NCOs and soldiers			Total
Present		17			546		563
Casualties (K, W, M)	0	2	0	5	23	0	30 (5%)
Survivors							533

Pravia

		Officers		NCOs and soldiers			Total
Present		31			542		573
Casualties (K, W, M)	0	3	0	19	36	0	58 (10%)
Survivors							515

Lena

	Officers			NCOs and soldiers			Total
Present		28			499		527
Casualties (K, W, M)	1	4	0	12	25	0	42 (8%)
Survivors							485

Castropol

	Officers			NCOs and soldiers			Total
Present		26			562		588
Casualties (K, W, M)	0	2	0	3	30	0	35 (6%)
Survivors							553

Cangas de Tineo

	Officers			NCOs and soldiers			Total
Present		21			559		580
Casualties (K, W, M)	0	1	0	3	16	0	20 (3%)
Survivors							560

Infiesto

	Officers			NCOs and soldiers			Total
Present		20			447		467
Casualties (K, W, M)	2	1	0	8	16	0	27 (6%)
Survivors							440

Zapadores/Gastadores

	Officers			NCOs and soldiers			Total
Present		?			40		>40
Casualties (K, W, M)	0	0	0	2	11	0	13 (33%)
Survivors							>27

2o Bat. de Reales Guardias Españolas

	Officers			NCOs and soldiers			Total
Present		24			606		630
Casualties (K, W, M)	0	10	0	25	139	0	174 (28%)
Survivors							463

4o Bat. de Reales Guardias Españolas

	Officers			NCOs and soldiers			Total
Present		19			628		647
Casualties (K, W, M)	0	2	0	37	130	0	169 (26%)
Survivors							478

Irlanda

	Officers			NCOs and soldiers			Total
Present		41			708		749
Casualties (K, W, M)	0	13	0	36	223	0	272 (36%)
Survivors							477

Voluntarios de la Patria[1]

	Officers			NCOs and soldiers			Total
Present		28			566		594
Casualties (K, W, M)	0	0	0	1	2	0	3 (<1%)
Survivors							591

1. The commander of the Voluntarios de la Patria later stated that his unit in fact lost 150 killed and wounded at Albuera, which suggests that Spanish casualty figures may also have been under-reported. F. Mazarredo to Duke of Sussex, 24 June 1812, reproduced in *Supp. Despatches*, Vol. 7, pp. 349–50.

Imperiales de Toledo

	Officers			NCOs and soldiers			Total
Present		32			545		577
Casualties (K, W, M)	0	1	0	4	16	0	21 (4%)
Survivors							556

Legion Extrangera

	Officers			NCOs and soldiers			Total
Present		19			528		547
Casualties (K, W, M)	0	0	0	0	19	0	19 (3%)
Survivors							528

Ciudad Rodrigo

	Officers			NCOs and soldiers			Total
Present		22			423		445
Casualties (K, W, M)	0	0	0	0	13	0	13 (3%)
Survivors							432

Reales Guardias Walonas

	Officers			NCOs and soldiers			Total
Present		12			621		633
Casualties (K, W, M)	0	0	0	0	8	0	8 (1%)
Survivors							645

5th Army Zapadores and Guias

	Officers			NCOs and soldiers			Total
Present		4			66		70
Casualties (K, W, M)	0	0	0	0	0	0	0
Survivors							70

Rey

	Officers			NCOs and soldiers			Total
Present		28			474		502
Casualties (K, W, M)	0	2	0	0	6	0	8 (2%)
Survivors							494

Zamora

	Officers			NCOs and soldiers			Total
Present		14			330		344
Casualties (K, W, M)	0	0	0	0	3	0	3 (<1%)
Survivors							341

Voluntarios de Navarra

	Officers			NCOs and soldiers			Total
Present		10			851		861
Casualties (K, W, M)	0	1	0	0	18	0	19 (2%)
Survivors							842

1o Voluntarios de Cataluña

	Officers			NCOs and soldiers			Total
Present		11			216		227
Casualties (K, W, M)	0	1	0	14	47	0	62 (27%)
Survivors							165

Spanish Cavalry

Escuadrón de Granaderos

	Officers			NCOs and soldiers			Total
Present	24			260			284
Casualties (K, W, M)	0	0	0	1	16	0	17 (6%)
Survivors							267

Escuadrón de Instrucción

	Officers			NCOs and soldiers			Total
Present	12			120			132
Casualties (K, W, M)	0	2	0	1	10	0	13 (10%)
Survivors							119

Provisional de Santiago

	Officers			NCOs and soldiers			Total
Present	30			308			338
Casualties (K, W, M)	0	0	0	3	4	0	7 (2%)
Survivors							331

Husares de Castilla

	Officers			NCOs and soldiers			Total
Present	27			384			411
Casualties (K, W, M)	0	0	0	2	1	0	3 (<1%)
Survivors							408

Carabineros Reales

	Officers			NCOs and soldiers			Total
Present	4			43			47
Casualties (K, W, M)	0	0	0	0	0	0	0
Survivors							47

Reina

	Officers			NCOs and soldiers			Total
Present	20			118			138
Casualties (K, W, M)	0	1	0	5	7	0	13 (9%)
Survivors							125

Borbon

	Officers			NCOs and soldiers			Total
Present	24			111			135
Casualties (K, W, M)	0	0	0	0	0	0	0
Survivors							135

Lusitania

	Officers			NCOs and soldiers			Total
Present	13			73			86
Casualties (K, W, M)	0	0	0	0	0	0	0
Survivors							86

Algarve

	Officers			NCOs and soldiers			Total
Present	13			88			101
Casualties (K, W, M)	0	2	0	3	4	0	9 (9%)
Survivors							101

Husares de Extremadura

	Officers			NCOs and soldiers			Total
Present	12			80			92
Casualties (K, W, M)	0	0	0	3	3	0	6 (7%)
Survivors							86

Cazadores de Sevilla

	Officers			NCOs and soldiers			Total
Present	1			121			122
Casualties (K, W, M)	0	0	0	0	0	0	0
Survivors							122

Spanish Artillery
4o Regimiento Artilleria del 5o Ejército

	Officers			NCOs and soldiers			Total
Present	4			58			62
Casualties (K, W, M)	0	0	0	2	7	0	9 (15%)
Survivors							53

Estados No. 64 indicates that the 4th Army had an artillery contingent of 7 officers and 96 men but Burriel's report is clear that no artillery from the 4th Army was present at Albuera.

Spanish Engineers
Ingenieros

	Officers			NCOs and soldiers			Total
Present	6			0			6
Casualties (K, W, M)	0	0	0	0	0	0	0
Survivors							6

Part 3: French Forces

"Present" = Information from return dated 1 May 1811.
"Casualties" = Information from official casualty return dated 19 July 1811.
"Per Martinien" = Information from Martinien's *Tableaux* plus *Supplement* (1899) and *Supplemental Part* (1909).

Generals and Staff

	Officers			NCOs and soldiers			Total
Present[1]	>88			>8			>96
Casualties (K, W, M)	4	9	0	?	?	?	13
Per Martinien	4	23	0	*Survivors*			>83

French Infantry
34th Line – 2 battalions

	Officers			NCOs and soldiers			Total
Present	23			930			953
Casualties (K, W, M)[2]	4	13	0	104	298	0	419 (44%)
Per Martinien	7	8	0	*Survivors*			534

1. No information in 1 May return.   2. Men missing were possibly reported as killed.

40th Line – 2 battalions

	Officers			NCOs and soldiers			Total
Present	35			778			813
Casualties (K, W, M)	4	9	1	35	226	73	348 (43%)
Per Martinien	10	13	0	*Survivors*			465

51st Line – 1 battalion

	Officers			NCOs and soldiers			Total
Present	22?			729?			751?
Casualties (K, W, M)	0	0	0	2	1	0	3 (<1%)
Per Martinien	0	0	0	*Survivors*			748 (?)

55th Line – 3 battalions

	Officers			NCOs and soldiers			Total
Present	58			1,757			1,815
Casualties (K, W, M)	4	6	0	68	235	38	351 (19%)
Per Martinien	4	10	0	*Survivors*			1,464

58th Line – 3 battalions

	Officers			NCOs and soldiers			Total
Present	55			1,587			1,642
Casualties (K, W, M)	6	15	2	23	258	24	328 (20%)
Per Martinien	4	20	0	*Survivors*			1,314

64th Line – 3 battalions

	Officers			NCOs and soldiers			Total
Present	50			1,539			1,589
Casualties (K, W, M)	5	18	0	99	361	168	651 (41%)
Per Martinien	5	21	0	*Survivors*			938

88th Line – 2 battalions

	Officers			NCOs and soldiers			Total
Present	21			878			899
Casualties (K, W, M)[1]	0	5	6	0	253	141	405 (45%)
Per Martinien	7	5	–	*Survivors*			494

100th Line – 2 battalions

	Officers			NCOs and soldiers			Total
Present	33			705			738
Casualties (K, W, M)	4	8	2	50	152	51	267 (36%)
Per Martinien	4	16	0	*Survivors*			471

103rd Line – 3 battalions

	Officers			NCOs and soldiers			Total
Present	38			1,252			1,290
Casualties (K, W, M)	4	10	3	48	148	74	287 (22%)
Per Martinien	7	11	0	*Survivors*			1,003

Combined Grenadiers – 2 battalions

	Officers			NCOs and soldiers			Total
Present	33			1,000			1,033
Casualties (K, W, M)	–	10 total	–	–	362 total	–	372 (36%)
Per Martinien	5	8	0	*Survivors*			661

1. Men killed were probably reported as missing.

12th Light – 3 battalions

		Officers		NCOs and soldiers			Total
Present		62			2,102		2,164
Casualties (K, W, M)	3	14	1	108	511	132	769 (36%)
Per Martinien	6	23	0	Survivors			1,395

16th Light – 3 battalions

		Officers		NCOs and soldiers			Total
Present		49			1,624		1,673
Casualties (K, W, M)	2	7	0	39	321	12	381 (23%)
Per Martinien	2	15	0	Survivors			1,292

21st Light – 2 battalions

		Officers		NCOs and soldiers			Total
Present		43			745		788
Casualties (K, W, M)	3	11	2	61	154	24	255 (32%)
Per Martinien	5	8	0	Survivors			533

28th Light – 3 battalions

		Officers		NCOs and soldiers			Total
Present		62			1,305		1,367
Casualties (K, W, M)	7	10	1	53	313	112	496 (36%)
Per Martinien	10	20	0	Survivors			871

French Cavalry

4th Dragoons – 2 squadrons

		Officers		NCOs and soldiers			Total
Present		21			385		406
Casualties (K, W, M)	3	1	0	27	38	1	70 (17%)
Per Martinien	2	9	0	Survivors			336

14th Dragoons – 2 squadrons

		Officers		NCOs and soldiers			Total
Present		17			299		316
Casualties (K, W, M)	0	1	0	6	17	0	24 (8%)
Per Martinien	0	1	0	Survivors			292

17th Dragoons – 4 squadrons

		Officers		NCOs and soldiers			Total
Present		17			297		314
Casualties (K, W, M)	0	3	0	12	29	1	45 (14%)
Per Martinien	1	5	0	Survivors			269

20th Dragoons – 4 squadrons

		Officers		NCOs and soldiers			Total
Present		22			244		266
Casualties (K, W, M)	1	3	1	6	10	4	25 (9%)
Per Martinien	4	8	0	Survivors			241

26th Dragoons – 2 squadrons

		Officers		NCOs and soldiers			Total
Present		27			394		421
Casualties (K, W, M)	1	2	0	5	12	1	21 (5%)
Per Martinien	1	2	0	Survivors			400

27th Dragoons – 4 squadrons

	Officers			NCOs and soldiers			Total
Present		14			235		249
Casualties (K, W, M)	0	3	0	2	11	3	19 (8%)
Per Martinien	0	5	0	Survivors			230

21st Chasseurs – 3 squadrons

	Officers			NCOs and soldiers			Total
Present		21			235		256
Casualties (K, W, M)	0	3	0	3	19	0	25 (10%)
Per Martinien	0	5	0	Survivors			231

27th Chasseurs – 3 squadrons

	Officers			NCOs and soldiers			Total
Present		22			409		431
Casualties (K, W, M)	0	2	1	7	11	5	26 (6%)
Per Martinien	0	3	1	Survivors			405

2nd Hussars – 3 squadrons

	Officers			NCOs and soldiers			Total
Present		23			282		305
Casualties (K, W, M)	1	3	0	4	57	8	73 (24%)
Per Martinien	2	3	0	Survivors			232

10th Hussars – 3 squadrons

	Officers			NCOs and soldiers			Total
Present		24			238		262
Casualties (K, W, M)	1	4	0	3	21	3	32 (12%)
Per Martinien	1	6	0	Survivors			230

4th Spanish Chasseurs – 2 squadrons

	Officers			NCOs and soldiers			Total
Present		14			181		195
Casualties (K, W, M)	0	0	0	2	4	0	6 (3%)
Per Martinien	0	1	0	Survivors			189

Vistula Lancers – 4 squadrons

	Officers			NCOs and soldiers			Total
Present		28			563		591
Casualties (K, W, M)	1	9	1	41	78	0	130 (22%)
Per Martinien	3	11	0	Survivors			461

French Artillery

V Corps Artillery

	Officers			NCOs and soldiers			Total
Present		18			590		608
Casualties (K, W, M)	1	3	0	19	72	0	95 (16%)
Per Martinien	1	4	0	Survivors			513

Other Artillery and Miscellaneous

	Officers			NCOs and soldiers			Total
Present		25			600		625
Casualties (K, W, M)[1]	?	?	?	?	?	?	?
Per Martinien	?	?	?	Survivors			?

1. No information in 19 July return.

Part 4: Strength and Casualty Totals

British Army[1]

		Officers			NCOs and soldiers			Total
Present		565				10,038		10,603
Casualties (K, W, M)	33	165	13	850	2,570		530	4,161 (39%)

Portuguese Army

		Officers			NCOs and soldiers			Total
Present		?				?		10,201
Casualties (K, W, M)	1	14	0	102	244		26	387 (4%)

Spanish Armies

		Officers			NCOs and soldiers			Total
Present		734				13,818		14,552
Casualties (K, W, M)	10	69	0	248	1,048		0	1,375 (9.5%)[2]

All Allied Armies

		Officers			NCOs and soldiers			Total
Present		?				?		35,356
Casualties (K, W, M)	44	252	13	1,197	3,853		556	5,915 (17%)

French Army[3]

		Officers			NCOs and soldiers			Total
Present		965				21,891		22,856
Casualties (K, W, M)	59	182	21	827	3,972		875	5,936 (26%)

1. British Army figures include KGL and Brunswickers. All British and Portuguese General Staff listed in the first entry in Part 1 of this appendix have been assumed to be British for the purposes of this table. Similarly the three single companies from 2nd Brigade, 4th Division, have been assumed each to be composed of 57 other ranks and 3 officers. All other unknown figures for units in the British and other armies are assumed to be nil.

2. The official return incorrectly gives the total Spanish casualties as 1,365 officers and men.

3. French Army figures include allied Spanish troops. Casualties shown above for the Combined Grenadier battalions are not separated into the three categories of killed, wounded and missing; for the purposes of this calculation all have been assumed to be wounded.

Appendix C

Albuera Uniforms

Part 1: **British and Portuguese Uniforms**

Sources: René Chartrand, *The Portuguese Army of the Napoleonic Wars*, London, 2000–1; Ian Fletcher, *Napoleonic Wars – Wellington's Army*, London, 1996; Manuel A. Ribeiro Rodrigues, *Guerra Peninsular (1) – Infantaria 1806–1815*, Lisbon, 2000.

British and Portuguese Infantry and Other Troops

Regiment	Headwear	Jacket	Collar	Cuffs	Turnbacks	Lace	Overalls
3rd Foot	Shako	Red	Buff	Buff	White	Square Pairs	White
7th Foot	Shako	Red	Blue	Blue	White	Square Single	White
23rd Foot	Shako	Red	Blue	Blue	White	Bastion Single	White
27th Foot	Shako	Red	Buff	Buff	White	Square Single	White
28th Foot	Shako	Red	Yellow	Yellow	White	Square Pairs	White
29th Foot	Shako	Red	Yellow	Yellow	White	Square Pairs	White
31st Foot	Shako	Red	Buff	Buff	White	Square Single	White
34th Foot	Shako	Red	Yellow	Yellow	White	Square Pairs	White
39th Foot	Shako	Red	Pea Green	Pea Green	White	Square Pairs	White
40th Foot	Shako	Red	Buff	Buff	White	Square Pairs	White
48th Foot	Shako	Red	Buff	Buff	White	Square Pairs	White
57th Foot	Shako	Red	Yellow	Yellow	White	Square Pairs	White
5th/60th Foot	Shako	Green	Red	Red	Green	None	Blue
66th Foot	Shako	Red	Gosling Green	Gosling Green	White	Square Single	White
97th Foot	Shako	Red	Blue	Blue	White	Square Pairs	White
1st KGL Light	Shako	Green	Black	Black	Green	None	White
2nd KGL Light	Shako	Green	Black	Black	Green	None	White
Brunswick Jaegers	Shako	Green	Lt. Blue	Lt. Blue	Lt. Blue	n/a	Grey

Regiment	Headwear	Jacket	Collar	Cuffs	Turnbacks	Lace	Overalls
2nd Portuguese	Shako	Blue	Blue	White	White	None	White
4th Portuguese	Shako	Blue	Blue	Red	White	None	White
5th Portuguese	Shako	Blue	Blue	Red	Red	None	White
10th Portuguese	Shako	Blue	Blue	Light Blue	White	None	White
11th Portuguese	Shako	Blue	Blue	Light Blue	Red	None	White
14th Portuguese	Shako	Blue	White	White	Red	None	White
23rd Portuguese	Shako	Blue	Light Blue	Light Blue	Red	None	White
5th Caçadores	Shako	Brown	Scarlet	Scarlet	Brown	Black braid across chest	Brown
1st Loyal Lusitanian Legion	Shako	Green	Green	Green	Green	White braid across chest	Green
All Foot Artillery	Shako	Blue	Red with yellow trim	Red with yellow trim	White	Yellow Bastion Single	Grey

British and Portuguese Cavalry

Regiment	Headwear	Jacket	Collar	Cuffs	Turnbacks	Lace	Overalls
3rd Dragoon Guards	Bicorne hat	Red	White	White	White	Yellow	White
4th Dragoons	Bicorne hat	Red	Green	Green	Green	White	White
13th Light Dragoons	Helmet	Blue	Buff	Buff	None	Yellow braid across chest	White
1st Portuguese	Helmet	Blue	White	White	Scarlet	None	White
5th Portuguese	Helmet	Blue	Scarlet	Scarlet	Scarlet	None	White
7th Portuguese	Helmet	Blue	Yellow	Yellow	White	None	White
8th Portuguese	Helmet	Blue	Yellow	Yellow	Scarlet	None	White
Horse Artillery	Helmet	Blue	Red with yellow trim	Red with yellow trim	None	Yellow braid across chest	Grey

Part 2: Spanish Uniforms

Sources: José Maria Bueno Carrera, *Uniformes Españoles de la Guerra de Independencia*, nl, 1989; José Maria Bueno Carrera, *El Ejército y la Armada en 1808*, Malaga, 1982; René Chartrand, *The Spanish Army of the Napoleonic Wars*, London, 1998–9; Lt. Col. John Colquitt, 'Watercolour of Spanish Uniforms and Rank Distinctions 1811', Royal Collection, Windsor; Antonio Manzano Lahoz & Luis Gravalos Gonzalez, *Los Uniformes del Estado Militar de España del Año 1815*, nl, nd.

Spanish Infantry and Other Troops

Regiment	Headwear	Jacket	Lapels	Collar	Cuffs	Turnbacks	Overalls
Campo Mayor	Shako	Blue	N/A	Red	Red	Red	White
Canarias	Shako	White/Brown on campaign	Green	Red	Red	White	White
Cangas de Tineo	Shako	Brown	Green	Yellow	Green	White	Brown
Castropol	Shako	White	N/A	Red	Red	White	White
Ciudad Real	Shako	White	White	Red	Red	White	White
2o Guardias Reales	Shako	Blue	Red	Red	Red	Red	Blue
4o Guardias Reales	Shako	Blue	Red	Red	Red	Red	Blue
Guardias Walonas	Bicorne	Blue	Red with White Lace	Blue	Red	Red	Blue
Imperial de Toledo	Shako	Brown	Yellow	Yellow	Yellow	Yellow	White
Infiesto	?	?	?	?	?	?	?
Irlanda	Shako	Red	?	?	Blue	?	Red
Legion Extrangera	?	?	?	?	?	?	?
Lena	Shako	Brown	Blue	Red	Blue	Brown	Brown
2o León	Shako	White	Red	Red	Red	Red	White
Murcia	Bicorne	White	N/A	White	Light Blue	White	White
Voluntarios de la Patria	Shako	Green	Green	Red	Red	Red	White
Pravia	Shako	Blue	N/A	Red	Red	Red	Blue
Rey	?	Blue	?	?	Red	?	White
Voluntarios de Barbastro	Shako	Blue	White	Blue	Red	White	Blue
1o Voluntarios de Cataluna	Shako	Blue	Red	Red	Red	Red	White
Voluntarios de Navarra	Shako	Blue	N/A	Blue	Green	Green	White

Regiment	Headwear	Jacket	Lapels	Collar	Cuffs	Turnbacks	Overalls
Zamora	Bicorne	White	Black	Black	Black	Black	White
Zapadores	Helmet	Blue	Black with White Lace	Red	Red	Red	Blue
Artilleria	Bicorne	Blue	Blue	Red	Red	Red	Blue

Spanish Cavalry (other than Hussars)

Regiment	Headwear	Jacket	Lapels	Collar	Cuffs	Turnbacks	Trim	Overalls
Algarve	Bicorne	Scarlet	Buff	Buff	Buff	?	Yellow	Buff
Borbon	Bicorne	Blue	Scarlet	Scarlet	Scarlet	?	Yellow	Buff
Cazadores de Sevilla (ex-Tercio de Tejas)	Bicorne	Blue	Red	Blue	Red	Red	Yellow	Blue
Carabineros Reales	Bicorne	Blue	Red	Red	Red	Red	White	Blue
Lusitania	Bicorne	Yellow	Black	Yellow	Black	Black	White	Yellow
Escuadrón de Instrucción	?	?	?	?	?	?	?	?
Reina	Bicorne	Red	?	?	Blue	?	?	?
Provisional de Santiago	Bicorne	Blue	Scarlet	Scarlet	Scarlet	?	?	Buff

Spanish Hussars

Regiment	Headwear	Dolman	Collar	Cuffs	Pelisse	Lace	Overalls
Escuadrón de Granaderos	Busby ?	Blue	Red	Red	?	Yellow	?
Husares de Castilla	?	?	?	?	?	?	?
Husares de Extremadura	Shako	Sky Blue	Sky Blue	Sky Blue	Scarlet	White	Scarlet

Part 3: French Uniforms

Sources: René Chartrand, *Napoleonic Wars – Napoleon's Army*, London, 1996.

French Infantry and Other Troops

Type	Headwear	Jacket	Epaulettes	Lapels	Collar	Cuffs	Turnbacks	Overalls
Line Infantry Grenadier	Shako	Blue	Red	White	Red	Red	White	White
Line Infantry Voltigeur	Shako	Blue	Green	White	Yellow	Red	White	White
Line Infantry Fusilier	Shako	Blue	N/A	White	Red	Red	White	White
Light Infantry Carabinier	Shako	Blue	Red	Blue	Red	Blue	Blue	Blue
Light Infantry Voltigeur	Shako	Blue	Green	Blue	Yellow	Blue	Blue	Blue
Light Infantry Chasseur	Shako	Blue	N/A	Blue	Blue	Blue	Blue	Blue
Artillery	Shako	Blue	Red	Blue	Red	Red	White	White

French Cavalry (other than Hussars)

Regiment	Headwear	Jacket	Epaulettes	Lapels & Turnbacks	Collar	Cuffs	Cuff Flaps	Pockets	Overalls
Vistula Legion Lancers	Czapska	Blue	Yellow	Yellow	Yellow	Yellow	N/A	Vertical	Blue
21st Chasseurs	Shako	Green	Red[1]	N/A	Light Orange	Light Orange	N/A	Vertical	Green
27th Chasseurs	Shako	Green	Red[1]	N/A	Amaranth	Amaranth	N/A	Vertical	Green
4th Spanish Chasseurs	Shako	Green	Crimson[1]	N/A	Crimson	Crimson	N/A	Vertical(?)	Green
4th Dragoons	Helmet	Green	White[1]	Scarlet	Scarlet	Scarlet	Scarlet	Vertical	White
14th Dragoons	Helmet	Green	White[1]	Pink	Green	Pink	Green	Horizontal	White
17th Dragoons	Helmet	Green	White[1]	Pink	Green	Pink	Green	Vertical	White
20th Dragoons	Helmet	Green	White[1]	Yellow	Green	Yellow	Green	Horizontal	White
26th Dragoons	Helmet	Green	White[1]	Light Orange	Light Orange	Light Orange	Green	Horizontal	White
27th Dragoons	Helmet	Green	White[1]	Light Orange	Light Orange	Light Orange	Light Orange	Horizontal	White

French Hussars

Regiment	Headwear	Dolman	Collar	Cuffs	Pelisse	Cords	Overalls
2nd Hussars	Shako/Busby[1]	Brown	Brown	Sky Blue	Brown	Whites	Sky Blue
10th Hussars	Shako/Busby[1]	Sky Blue	Red	Red	Sky Blue	White	Sky Blue

1. *Worn by Elite Company only.*

Appendix D

How the 'Die Hards' Got Their Name

Readers familiar with British military history may be surprised that this book does not include an account of Lieutenant Colonel William Inglis of the 57th Regiment urging his men to 'Die hard!', thus giving rise to one of the best-known nicknames in British Army annals. After all, the 57th certainly became the 'Die Hards' as a result of the conduct of its soldiers at Albuera and the Inglis story adds a dramatic touch to any narrative about the battle. There are in fact two good reasons for this omission. The first reason is that there is absolutely no direct evidence that Colonel Inglis actually uttered that famous exhortation. The second reason is that, even if he did so, the incident probably took place in circumstances much different from those traditionally described.

The exact date that the nickname was first applied to the regiment is not known, but within a year of the battle it was already in common use. Lieutenant William Swabey, a Royal Horse Artillery officer who did not arrive in the Peninsula until the late summer of 1811, noted in his diary for 16 May 1812:

> This day was the anniversary of Albuera, and all the regiments here, viz., the 57th, or 'Die-hards', 31st, or young Buffs [fn omitted], 3rd, or old Buffs, etc., paid due honour to the occasion by getting what they term Royal rental [fn omitted] of their different exploits.[1]

All previous historians of the battle appear to have accepted that the verifiable existence of the nickname 'proves' that the Inglis story is true and they go on to present it as fact without supporting evidence. Take, for instance, the description of Albuera in the most comprehensive regimental history of the 57th, which refers to Colonel Inglis's conduct in two places. The first statement is that:

> Colonel Inglis ... was severely wounded ... but, refusing all offers to carry him to the rear, he remained where he had fallen, in front of the colours of his regiment, urging his men to keep up a steady fire and die hard.

---

1. Swabey, *Diary*, p. 99. Colonel F. A. Whinyates, the editor of the diary, did not recognise the term 'Royal rental', but concluded in a footnote that it meant 'they all got excessively drunk, as was usual on similar occasions.'

The history then goes on to mention that:

> The conduct of the regiment in the battle was highly praised and commended
> by all, and Colonel Inglis' words, 'Die hard, 57th', bestowed on it a sobriquet
> never to be forgotten.[2]

The imagery of these words is powerful, but upon reflection one must question
how credible this version of the Inglis story really is. First, upon the death of General
Hoghton, Colonel Inglis succeeded to command of the whole brigade and it is
unlikely he remained exclusively with his regiment thereafter. Second, the best
available evidence indicates that Inglis was only wounded 'near the close of the action'
when there would have been very few of his men left to encourage.[3] Thirdly, the ball
that wounded him made 'a deep incision in his neck a little above his collar bone',
and the effects of such an injury are likely to have made it difficult for him to move
his head and jaw enough to speak at all, to say nothing of shouting loud enough to
make himself heard above the din of battle.[4] Finally, and most importantly, this story
does not identify any member of the regiment who was an eye- or ear-witness to the
scene.

The regimental history should not be singled out for particular criticism for its lack
of attention to sources, however, because there is no other work that does any better
job in this regard, those of Fortescue and Oman included. The words ascribed to
Inglis sometimes vary (see, for example, the version of Inglis's words provided by
E. Cobham Brewer in his *Dictionary of Phrase and Fable* (London, 1898): 'Die hard,
my lads; die hard!') and they are sometimes placed in the mouth of a mortally
wounded Inglis instead of one who survives the battle, but they are never missing
from any story about Albuera and they are never supported by a source citation to
first-hand testimony concerning the events reported.

The possibility that all prior histories of Albuera are wrong about this point initially
seemed far-fetched, but the more research I have conducted, the more I have come
to the conclusion that this odd possibility is actually the right one. I have not found
any contemporary letter, newspaper article, commentary or book that specifically
attributes this phrase to Colonel Inglis. There is no reference to such an utterance by
Inglis in Ensign Hobhouse's letter, in Beresford's dispatch or in the colonel's own
description of Albuera in the *United Service Journal* in 1832, nor is it attributed to him
in his formal obituary or in the papers Lady Inglis collected to record her husband's
military service.[5] As discussed in the main text of this book (*see page 150*), there was
a newspaper account published on 6 June that describes a wounded officer refusing
aid and encouraging his men, but that officer was only a captain (probably Ralph

2. Woollright, *History of the Fifty-Seventh*, pp. 165 and 168.
3. Statement of W. Inglis Jr. in Warre, *Historical Records of the Fifty-Seventh*, p. 246; see also Lady
   Inglis, Services of Major General William Inglis.
4. At Bussaco, Colonel Wallace of the 88th Regiment ended his pre-battle speech to his men with the
   following statement that supports the conclusion that it would be difficult to hear even a strong
   voice above the normal noise of a Napoleonic battlefield: 'I have nothing more to say, and if I had
   it would be of no use, for in a minit [*sic*] or two there'll be such an infernal noise about your ears
   that you won't be able to hear yourselves'. Grattan, *Adventures with the Connaught Rangers*, p. 33.
5. Obituary of Lieutenant General Sir William Inglis, *The Annual Biography and Obituary: 1837*,
   Vol. XXI, London, 1837; Ms. History of the Services of Major General William Inglis, compiled by
   Lady Inglis 1828 (?), Archive Item 6504-52/33, NAM.

Fawcett), not Colonel Inglis. Napier (writing in 1832) makes no mention of either Inglis or the anonymous captain in his history. There is even an element of regimental tradition that clearly indicates that the regimental nickname came from Marshal Beresford rather than Colonel Inglis. That view is expressed in the last line of the second verse of 'The Jolly Die Hards', a regimental march written in the late 1860s:

> Our regiment has conquered, but never in vain,
> Bear witness those hills and the mountains through Spain,
> Bear witness the shades of those hundreds who fell
> At red Albuera, and our victory can tell
> How Soult and his Frenchmen were beaten and sank,
> As we fell on them fiercely, rank after rank,
> Invincible seemed those brave children of Mars,
> When Lord Beresford styled us the 'Gallant Die Hards'.[6]

I did eventually find three pieces of evidence that lend some support to the Inglis story, but they do not, individually or in combination, constitute definitive proof that Inglis said the words attributed to him. The first piece of evidence is a letter in the *United Service Journal* for 1829 from an anonymous correspondent who signed himself as 'A Die Hard'. The author claims to have been present at Albuera, but the fact that he is slightly off in the location of Inglis's wound (neck, not chest) detracts somewhat from the credibility of that claim. Assuming nevertheless that he was a participant, his description of the actions of Colonel Inglis superficially seems to validate the tale recounted in the regimental history and other secondary sources:

> When subsequently struck down by a grape-shot, which had perforated his left breast and lodged in his back, he [Colonel Inglis] lay on the ground close to the regiment, refusing all offers to be carried to the rear, and determined to share the fate of his 'die-hards', whom he continued to cheer to steadiness and exertion; and who, encouraged by the voice of their brave commander, continued to close in on their tattered and staff-broken colours, as their comrades fell in the line in which he had formed them.[7]

Two points undermine much of the credibility of this statement written eighteen years after the battle. The similarities between this story and the story of the heroic captain of the 57th reported in *The Times* on 6 June 1811 are obvious enough to raise the question as to whether there were two such incidents or only one involving a captain that was later mistakenly described as having involved Inglis. Even if one accepts that both officers acted in similar fashion, the author of the above passage manages to use the key phrase without putting it explicitly in the mouth of Colonel Inglis, so it does not constitute a direct attribution of the words to Inglis.

The second piece of evidence is a newspaper account of an Albuera Day commemoration held by the 57th Regiment in 1852. The story contains the following

6. L. Winstock, *Songs and Music of the Red Coats 1642–1902*, London, 1970, p. 230. The tune of this march was literally lost when the ship carrying the captured regimental band and its music from Hong Kong to Japan in 1942 was torpedoed by an Allied submarine, causing a loss of all the documents. Efforts to rediscover the tune after the Second World War proved fruitless. (I am indebted to Philip Haythornthwaite for bringing this source to my attention.)
7. A Die Hard, 'Letter from "A Die Hard"', pp 106–7.

statement attributed to a 'Major General M'Donald, C.B.', who is described as one of two veterans attending the dinner who had actually been present at Albuera (the other being George Browne, who had been a lieutenant in the 23rd in 1811):

> He [M'Donald] added that when the [57th] regiment had sustained a loss of two-thirds of its numbers the lieutenant colonel [Inglis] called out in a loud voice, 'Close your ranks, 57th – die hard', which expression was the origin of the name by which the corps is still called.[8]

This statement seems to provide a definitive answer to the question of what Inglis did or did not say and it seems all the more plausible because it does not involve Inglis using the phrase *after* he was wounded. Unfortunately, the article seems to have been wrong about one key fact and that error detracts significantly from the reliability of the statement reported. General M'Donald could not have been an eyewitness to any incidents involving Inglis and the 57th. There were two officers with the surname M'Donald on the rolls of the 57th in 1811 (Lieutenant Colonel Duncan M'Donald and Lieutenant Angus M'Donald), but neither lived long enough to receive the Military General Service Medal in 1847, so neither could be the officer referred to in the article. In fact, the only officer in the *Army List* for 1852 who fits the description from the article is Major General John M'Donald, who served at Albuera as a major in the 14th Portuguese Line, which never left the allied left flank.[9] So instead of being definitive evidence, the words of M'Donald quoted in the story in *The Times* appear to be simply a recounting of a popular version of the Die Hard story as it was understood by a particular aged Peninsular veteran, albeit one who had been present at the battle.

The last piece of evidence is found in a two-page biography of Inglis written by his son that appears as an appendix in the regimental history published in 1878. Major General William Inglis, Jr., did not fight in the Peninsula but he served in the 57th for many years and so what he knew about the battle must have come from information provided by his father and other Albuera veterans. His version of the story is significantly different from the traditional version: '. . . this Regiment obtained the appellation of the "Die Hards", from words spoken by their Colonel to his men while standing with ordered arms under a heavy fire.'[10] This source, however, also falls short of providing definitive proof of the Inglis story given that it was written long after the event and it does not quote actual words spoken by the author's father. Furthermore, the text of the regimental history to which this biography is appended concludes that the 57th earned 'the *Sobriquet* of the "Die Hards"', not because the words were said by Colonel Inglis, but because of 'the many instances of personal gallantry that distinguished the troops at Albuhera', including that of Captain Fawcett.[11] At the same time, this statement provides the strongest evidence available that even if Colonel

---

8. *The Times*, 22 May 1852, p. 5, col. C. The decorations for the dinner included a portion of the colours of the 57th carried at Albuera and the diners at the commemorative meal included Captain William Inglis, Jr., who had followed his father into the regiment, and Major Shadforth, whose father was a captain in the 57th who lost a leg in the battle. The newspaper account ends with the information that 'the party did not break up until long after the midnight hour, having passed a most convivial evening, which will be long remembered by those who partook of the festivity.'

9. Challis, 'British Officers', p. 57.

10. Statement of W. Inglis Jr., in Warre, *Historical Records of the Fifty-Seventh*, p. 246.

11. *Ibid.*, p. 53.

Inglis did utter the phrase 'Die hard!', he did so before, not after, he was wounded and that the traditional version of the Inglis story mistakenly incorporates heroic details that properly belong to the story of Captain Fawcett.

In the end, of course, it does not actually make any difference how the 57th got its proud and honourable nickname, since there is no doubt that it was fairly won as a result of the exemplary conduct of the regiment at Albuera. As Beresford himself stated in his official report concerning the battle:

> And it was observed that our dead, particularly the Fifty-seventh Regiment, were lying as they fought in ranks and every wound was in front ... and nothing could exceed the conduct and gallantry of Colonel Inglis at the head of his Regiment.[12]

For the purposes of this book, however, the story of this famous phrase cannot be sufficiently proven to be stated as fact. Needless to say, I would be pleased to hear from any reader who can provide additional primary-source information bearing on this issue.

It is worth noting for all of those who believe that surfing the Internet is exactly the same as conducting serious research that I once did find what appeared to be the definitive basis for the Inglis story on the website of the Princess of Wales's Royal Regiment, a successor unit to the 57th by way of amalgamation and consolidation. In 2003 that site had a page (since taken down) devoted to Albuera that contained the following quote from the recollections of one Corporal Nicholas Reid of the 57th: 'Through all this we could hear the voice of our commanding officer, Colonel Inglis, calmly repeating "Die hard, 57th, die hard."' You can imagine my excitement at this discovery, but you can also imagine my frustration and dismay when, in response to a request for more information about Corporal Reid, the regimental museum sent a reply that revealed that Corporal Reid '... is fictitious and he and other made up characters are used to convey personal accounts of the various Battles fought by our seven forebear regiments'.[13]

12. Beresford, Official Report to W., 18 May 1811.
13. Letter to the author from Major (retd.) J. C. Rogerson, 12 September 2000.

Appendix E

British Colours Captured at Albuera

There has historically been a great deal of confusion about the number of British colours lost at the Battle of Albuera. Soult claimed that his army captured a total of six colours during the battle, but British sources admit the loss of no more than four colours.[1] The definitive answer is that the British force lost five colours in all – the king's colour and the regimental colour of both the 2nd Battalion of the 48th Foot and the 2nd Battalion of the 66th Foot and the regimental colour of the 3rd Foot (or Buffs). However, the last of these was recovered on the battlefield by a soldier from another regiment, which left a total of four colours in French hands. The claim by the French that they captured more than four colours is, however, quite understandable since the French did temporarily capture one other colour intact and ultimately managed to carry off the flagstaffs of both colours of the Buffs. Nevertheless, that claim can be legitimately disputed by the Buffs since they retained large portions of the colours themselves after they had been ripped from their staffs.

The eyewitness evidence concerning the loss of the four British colours is quite straightforward. Lieutenant Edward Close of the 2nd/48th is definitive on the loss of both colours by his own battalion, while Lieutenants George Crompton and Robert Dobbin each confirm that their regiment also lost both of its colours.[2] Some commentators believe that another eyewitness, Lieutenant John Clarke of the 66th Foot, said that one of the colours of the 66th was saved, but that suggestion is based on a misreading of the following passage from his post-battle recollections: 'When I got close to the 7th regiment, they knelt to receive cavalry, and I threw myself down to avoid their fire, I got up, and passing through the regiment met Lieutenant Anderson carrying a colour.'[3] Since there was no Lieutenant Anderson in the 66th, but there was a Lieutenant James Anderson in the 7th Foot, this is really just a reference to the latter officer carrying one of the colours of his own regiment. The final tally of four lost colours is also given by Fitzroy Somerset: 'The Polish cavalry literally swept the first three regiments away and carried with them the colours of the 48th and the 66th.'[4]

1. Soult, Unpublished Report.
2. Close, *Diary*, p. 32; see above, Chapter 7, pp. 135–6 for the statements of Crompton and Dobbin.
3. Clarke, Narrative in Groves, *History of the 66th*, p. 54.
4. Somerset, Letter to the Duke of Beaufort, 23 May 1811.

The situation concerning the colours of the 3rd Foot, or Buffs, is more complicated even though many British survivors definitely thought they had been lost: 'The 3rd . . . are nearly destroyed and lost their Colours.'[5] The first point of confusion is that the regimental colour of the Buffs was definitely captured outright, staff and all, from Ensign Thomas, but it was subsequently recovered (apparently without the staff) by Sergeant William Gough of the 1st Battalion, 7th Fusiliers. The colour was immediately returned to the Buffs, but the sensitivity concerning the fact that it had been lost in the first place is clear from the following letter sent to General Stewart by Major John Nooth, the commanding officer of Gough's battalion:

> Sir,
>
> When the . . . Fusiliers under my command drove the enemy from the heights . . . the guns which our artillery on the left had been obliged to abandon, together with **the regimental colour** [emphasis added] of the Buffs, which fell into our hands, Sergeant Gough got possession of the colour, and I am requested by the regiment to say, if this is meant to be the subject of an official report to Field Marshal Beresford, that they do not wish to obtain, and will willingly forgo any credit to be acquired at the expense of the brave soldiers who discharged their duty to the utmost.[6]

This offered cover-up did not take place, however, because Stewart duly reported to Beresford: 'The Second Division is indebted to the 7th Fusiliers for the recapture . . . of the Regimental Colour of the 3rd or Buffs.'[7]

The second point of confusion resulted from the actions taken by Lieutenant Latham while defending the king's colour of the regiment. In the French Army, the cloth standard attached to the pole bearing a regiment's eagle was never as important as the eagle itself, but in the British Army the opposite view prevailed – the silk colour, not the flagstaff to which it was attached, was the important item. As a result, when Latham felt his colour was threatened with imminent capture, his last resort was to tear the colour from its staff and stuff the silk banner into his jacket. (Ensign Vance of the 29th did the same thing with the regimental colour of that battalion for the same reason.) The king's colour was consequently never lost to the French, but it was missing for some period of time until it was discovered under Latham's apparently lifeless body. The circumstances of that discovery were never recorded. Some sources, however, have incorrectly (although perhaps understandably) melded the two stories of the Buffs' colours into one and concluded that colour recovered by Fusilier Sergeant Gough must have been the one hidden under Latham, but that is patently not the case.

In the case of each of the colours of the Buffs, however, the staff was lost. That point is not made explicitly in any direct testimony, but it is the clear implication of the eyewitness statement of Captain Arthur Gordon of the 3rd Foot about how the colours of his regiment appeared at the end of the battle: 'Our colours were taken and retaken three times, and are now in our possession, fixed on two halberts.'[8] If the

---

5. Harrison, Letter to Mother, 18 May 1811, quoted in Glover, 'The Royal Welch Fusiliers', p. 147.
6. Nooth to Stewart, 18 May 1811, quoted in Knight, *Historical Records of the Buffs*, pp. 352–3.
7. Stewart to Beresford, 26 May 1811, Inglis Papers, Ms. No. 6504-52/16, NAM.
8. Gordon, 'Extract from a Letter from a Captain of the Buffs'. As matter of precise nomenclature, British sergeants were armed after 1792 with 'pikes' instead of 'halberts' (or, more correctly, 'halberds'), but the latter term was still used colloquially.

flagstaffs had been recovered, there would have been no need to use pikes/halberds as substitutes. It is consequently reasonable to assume that the staffs themselves fell into French hands, perhaps with shreds, or even larger pieces, of the colours still attached, and they would certainly have been considered as trophies by their captors. Lieutenant Close was one British officer who believed that the Buffs did in fact engage in a form of cover-up with respect to the status of their colours playing off the amount of cloth retained:

> There was much effort made to prove that the Buffs had not lost their colours; but they were seen, along with the others, in the hands of the enemy after the battle. A piece of one of the Buff's [sic] colours was preserved in an officer's pocket, it was said; and again, that Colonel Stuart [sic] ordered a sergeant to put by a scrap in his pack. One of the Buffs' standards was afterwards retaken by the Fusiliers, and returned to the regiment.[9]

Surprisingly, Napoleon did not make any propaganda use of the captured colours at the time they were presented to him, perhaps because he felt that the less said about Albuera, the better for all concerned, since it was, after all, a defeat for his forces. He changed his mind on that score in November 1813, however, in the aftermath of his defeat at Leipzig when he concluded that the French nation needed as much good news as he could muster. He consequently decided to include the Albuera colours as part of the arrangements for the sixteen flags captured at Wachau, Leipzig and Hanau, which he wanted presented to Empress Marie-Louise in a public ceremony and then transported to the Hôtel des Invalides:

> I also want you to deliver [to Les Invalides] a hundred or so of the flags which have been captured in Spain, of which six are English. Don't make a fuss about them except for the six English flags captured at the battle of Albufera [sic], which must be deposited with great pomp ... You have known for a long time what I think about such ceremonies, but under current circumstances I think this will be useful. I don't need to tell you that each flag should be carried by a mounted officer and they should march in a great procession.[10]

The number of flags referred to in this letter suggests that the French at that point still had the two flagstaffs of the Buffs.

The fate of the physical remains of the captured Albuera colours is hard to trace thereafter with certainty. According to one French source, all of them (except for one of the staffs of the Buffs) were placed on display at the Museum of Artillery in Paris starting in 1827 and one of these, the king's colour of the 2nd/66th Foot, was stolen when a mob looted the museum in 1830.[11] The four remaining colours were then transferred to the chapel of the Hôtel des Invalides in 1831 where they remained until they were damaged beyond repair by a fire that broke out during the funeral of Marshal Sebastiani in 1851. The only surviving remnant of these colours is the central

---

9. Close, *Diary*, pp. 32–3.
10. N. to General Clarke, Minister of War, 3 November 1813, Napoleon, *Correspondance*, No. 20854, Vol. 26, pp. 404–5.
11. Major A. F. Flatow, 'British Colours in Les Invalides', *Journal of the Society for Army Historical Research*, Vol. 27, 1949, pp. 138–9, citing Commandant Verillon, *Les Trophées de la France*, Paris, 1907.

escutcheon of one of the colours of the 2nd/48th (which was on public display at the French Museum of the Army in Paris as recently as 2002). It takes the shape of an embroidered crown above a red shield outlined in gold bearing the legend 'XLVIII Reg't'.[12] The stolen king's colour of the 2nd/66th turned up again as part of a collection of ten flags donated to Les Invalides on 26 February 1865 by General Duffourc d'Antist.[13] Jean Regnault, the one French vexilologist who has written on the subject, admits he is mystified as to how the flag came into that general's possession, but he mentions, without recognising its possible significance, the fact that Duffourc d'Antist served as a captain of mounted chasseurs in King Joseph's Spanish Army. If he was assigned to the 4th Spanish Chasseurs, he might have been present at Albuera and might have had a personal interest in recovering this banner. In 1934, this colour was described by the curator of the French Army Museum in the following terms:

> Silk Colour, blue ground, double English cross in red silk with large white borders; in the centre, embroidered in coloured silk, an escutcheon bearing the inscription 'LXVI Regt.' This escutcheon is surrounded with branches of roses and thistles also embroidered in silk and surmounted by a royal crown in gold and silver.[14]

This colour is still in the chapel of Les Invalides and, despite the fact that it is in very poor repair, it can still be identified.[15]

The last controversy about British colours at Albuera was brought on by a blatant mistake made by Lord Londonderry in his *Narrative of the Peninsular War* published in 1828. In enumerating the losses from Albuera, Londonderry declared that the British lost 'eight stand of colours, belonging to the Buffs, the 66th, the 48th, and 57th regiments.'[16] Colonel Inglis of the 57th, by then a lieutenant general, fired off a quick note to Londonderry pointing out that the Albuera colours of the 57th had never been captured and were still in his possession. Londonderry immediately agreed to correct his error and, although he failed to do make good on his promise in the second edition, such a correction did appear in the third edition.[17]

12. Illustrated in Paul Willing, *Napoléon et ses Soldats de Wagram à Waterloo 1809–1815*, Paris, 1987, p. 95.
13. Regnault, 'Les Drapeaux anglais d'Albufera [*sic*]', p. 29, n. 1.
14. Lieutenant Colonel R. J. T. Hills, 'British Colours in Les Invalides', *Journal of the Society for Army Historical Research*, Vol. 29, No. 118, Summer 1951, p. 90.
15. A photograph of this colour can be seen online in Luis Sorando Muzás's very helpful article, 'The Trophies of Albuera'.
16. Londonderry, *Narrative*, Vol. 2, p. 135.
17. The relevant correspondence is reproduced in Warre, *Historical Records of the Fifty-Seventh*, pp. 301–4.

Appendix F

After Albuera

Albuera touched many lives, some profoundly, some incidentally, some for good and some for bad. The paragraphs below recount the post-Albuera lives of some of the survivors of the battle and of some of the family members of those who died.

Beresford

Beresford was traumatised by his experiences at Albuera. As he explained to his friend, Charles Stewart, he was 'very much out of spirits from the conviction of having acted unwisely' and the great loss suffered by his army 'much weighed upon' his mind.[1] When he was relieved of his command, at the beginning of June, his physical health broke down as well and he required a period of complete rest: 'The Marshal is, I am happy to observe, somewhat better, though he will require some time of quiet of body and mind to put him quite right again.'[2] This period proved longer than anyone expected, however, since in October he was still unwell, suffering from 'a low fever and great debility, which has been hanging about him for some months, and, though it sometimes leaves him for a few days, has never given him time to gain strength.'[3] It was commonly understood that these physical ills were directly connected to the negative stories circulating about his performance at Albuera:

> The Marshal is confined to his bed by a *severe fever* – poor man he has not philosophy to bear up against the Buffets of Military Critics who attack on all quarters – You know not the severity with which he is treated.[4]

With the support of Wellington, Beresford eventually recovered from this post-Albuera depression and played a distinguished part in the remaining campaigns of the Peninsular War, suffering a serious wound at the Battle of Salamanca. However, he never again had a significant independent field command. Beresford also retained command of the Portuguese Army and had an important role in Portuguese politics until he was forced out of office and the country in 1820, whereupon he returned to England to hold various civil and military posts.[5] In 1832, at the age of sixty-four, he

1. Beresford, Letter to Stewart, 25 May 1811
2. Warre to Father, 20 June 1811, in Warre, *Letters*, p. 185.
3. Warre to Father, 17 October 1811, in Warre, *Letters*, p. 206.
4. Colonel Loftus Otway to Unidentified Correspondent, 4 October 1811, Archive Item No. 1968-07-414, Otway Papers, NAM, quoted in Uffindell, *The National Army Museum Book of Wellington's Armies*, p. 106.

married his cousin, Louisa Beresford Hope, and thereafter he lived a mainly peaceful life, disturbed only by his pamphlet wars (discussed in Appendix G) with Colonel Napier and General Long's nephew and by the death of his wife in 1851. Even a partial listing of the various titles and honours he held at his death in 1854 confirms that his career had been eminently successful despite the controversies over Albuera: William Beresford, Viscount Beresford of Beresford Hall (1823), Baron Beresford of Albuera and Dungarvon (1814); Duke of Elvas, Marquess of Campo Mayor and Count of Trancoso in Portugal; Privy Councillor; Knight Grand Cross of the Bath; and General in England, Marshal General in Portugal and Captain General in Spain.[6]

Benning

Conway Benning, the senior officer of the 66th Foot killed in the battle, was a young man from County Antrim, Ireland. Despite the fact that his father was a minister, he left for the Peninsula without marrying the woman who was then carrying his child, although he did give her:

> ... the only things he possessed – a charming miniature of himself, and his very large and handsome gold watch. The girl cut out a piece of paper which exactly fitted inside the cover of the watch, and on it she pricked with a pin:– 'For Love and Conway Benning'.[7]

When Benning's father received the gold medal awarded posthumously to his son for having commanded the 66th in the action, he made the extraordinarily gracious gesture of sending it on to the mother of the daughter his son had never seen. (Remarkably, both Captain Benning's medal and his watch (minus the paper insert) turned up in an auction at Christie's in London on 19 July 1988.) Records reveal that a death benefit of £150 was paid to Benning's daughter, Eliza, by Lloyd's Patriotic Fund on 28 October 1812 and she was also awarded a pension of £43 from the government in 1838, when she was identified as the 27-year-old unmarried 'orphan' of Captain Benning.[8]

Clarke

Lieutenant John Clarke of the 66th fought in five other major actions after Albuera and ultimately received the Military General Service Medal with eight clasps. He rose to the rank of lieutenant colonel in his regiment and had the unique experience of being in command when the 1st Battalion of his regiment was posted to the island of St Helena to guard Napoleon. He was apparently more gracious in victory than Napoleon's other jailor, Sir Hudson Lowe, since an obituary for Clarke notes that

> ... he was one of the officers who frequently had the surveillance of that great and extraordinary man; and he happily united in no ordinary degree firm fidelity to the important trust reposed in him with the kindness, courtesy, and

---

5. Beresford's post-war career in Portugal is covered in 'King Beresford: Este Britanico Odioso', in Rose Macaulay, *They Went to Portugal Too*, Manchester, 1990. Two later brief attempts to re-establish his power in Portugal were unsuccessful,

6. Cole, *Memoirs of British Generals*, pp. 215–16,

7. Brooke, *The Brimming River*, pp. 72–3.

8. Patriotic Fund Records, Archive Item No. 8504-32, NAM. The pension information (and the first name of Benning's daughter) come from a pension report in *The Times*, 25 August 1838, p.2, col. E.

humane consideration due to fallen majesty. He was alike the officer, the gentleman and the Christian.[9]

Close

Lieutenant Edward Close, the officer of 48th Regiment who had his sabre broken on the field of battle, was at one point so worried about his prospects for survival in the tumult of the French cavalry charge that he vowed to himself that he would build a church if his life was spared. After the Napoleonic Wars, he and his regiment were posted to Australia. He eventually settled there and became the owner of extensive land holdings in New South Wales. On 2 January 1837, he laid the cornerstone for St James's Church in the town of Morpeth, New South Wales. The church, completed in 1840, still stands today.[10]

Drummond

Sergeant Duncan Drummond (b. 1776) of the 66th Foot, a weaver by trade, joined the army in 1804 because he needed the enlistment bounty to pay off a debt he had incurred by guaranteeing a loan to a friend. When he went overseas, he left behind a wife, Elizabeth, and some young sons who were taken in by her father when his wife died early in 1811. He had the good fortune to survive the battle unscathed, a fact he announced to his father-in-law in very restrained terms: 'This will inform you that I am in good health, trusting to find you in the same. I hope my children are well and as good boys are obedient, diligent and careful with you.'[11] Unfortunately, his luck did not last the full year and he died of unspecified causes on 11 December 1811. The money produced by the sale of his effects was sent on to his children.

De España

This French émigré turned Spaniard was one of the few Spanish generals who was respected by Wellington, so he continued to command significant forces during the remainder of the Peninsular War. Those commands were not always successful, however, and his failure to block the bridges at Alba de Tormes after the Battle of Salamanca saved the French from an even worse defeat. He was a loyal supporter of Ferdinand VII when that monarch returned to his throne and was responsible for brutal repression of a rebellion in Catalonia in 1826. During the last years of his life he was involved in a multitude of exiles and other adventures. In 1839, he was arrested by command of a *junta* he had been serving and, for reasons that remain obscure, the soldiers guarding him strangled him and dumped his body in the River Segre on 2 November that year.[12]

D'Espérandieu

The military career of Captain Antoine d'Espérandieu is less brilliant than many from the period, but it epitomises the experience of an entire generation since he enlisted

9. Excerpt from an 1859 obituary of Clarke graciously communicated by Jann Gallen of Australia, the current owner of the family papers of Colonel Clarke's son.
10. Description of Morpeth in *Walkabout Australian Travel Guide* read on 30 March 2003 at <www.walkabout.com.au>.
11. Drummond to Archibald Shettleton, 28 May 1811, in Drummond, Documents.
12. Oleza, *España*, pp. 253–60; *Nouvelle Biographie Universelle*, Vol. 16, Col. 401.

in the French Army in 1791 at the age of only sixteen and was not discharged until 1815 when he was retired on half-pay with the rank of major. Along the way, this stolid veteran was besieged in Malta, imprisoned for several years in a British prison hulk and fought with the Grand Army from 1806 to 1809 and again at Leipzig and Waterloo. At Albuera, d'Espérandieu was officially just an ADC to General Gazan, but he also had a connection with General Pépin since he was a suitor for the hand of the general's daughter, Christine, and so he hurried to attend the general when he was wounded. The staff officer had first broached the subject of marriage in 1809, but Pépin insisted that the lovers take things slowly: 'The interested parties must get to know themselves and each other and mutually study their characters and if they are compatible the rest will come easily.' In the succeeding years, Pépin himself came to appreciate that d'Espérandieu 'although not a handsome man, is a good one and has an excellent heart'. As he lay dying, the general made sure he gave a final blessing to the match. D'Espérandieu did in fact marry Christine Pépin and on his death in 1854 was survived by his widow, a son named Théodore and a daughter named Paméla.[13]

Fendall

William Fendall was merely a very young subaltern officer of the 4th Dragoons at the time of the battle and he is not known to have distinguished himself in the action. He did, however, gain a peculiar Albuera distinction many years later. At the time of his death in January 1888 at the age of ninety-two, he was probably the last survivor of the battle. His Military General Service Medal with four clasps for Talavera, Albuhera, Vitoria and Toulouse was recently sold at auction.[14]

Fincke, Bussmann, Grass and Hebecker

Corporal Heinrich Fincke, one of the quick-witted NCOs who saved two of the guns from Captain Cleeves's battery, had the extraordinary good fortune after the battle to be singled out for praise by Wellington himself, who gave the corporal 'a handsome present of 100 Spanish dollars'.[15] This caused no little resentment among the others – although there is no information as to why Wilhelm Hebecker was not similarly rewarded, Friedrich Bussmann and Friedrich Grass appear to have missed out simply because they had been wounded and captured and were therefore absent from their unit when Wellington reviewed the KGL troops after the battle (although both escaped and ultimately returned to their battery). A similar arbitrariness cropped up in respect of the awards for bravery given out by the government of Hanover to KGL veterans. Bussmann received one of these so-called Guelphic Medals in 1818 (with a citation referring to his conduct at both Albuera and Waterloo), while Hebecker was similarly

13. Aineville, 'Deux Portraits', p. 64.
14. Obituary of Thomas Fendall, *The Times*, 19 January 1888, p. 6, col. G. The obituary does not state that he was the oldest survivor, but his age at the time of death and his age at the time of the battle (nineteen) make this a likely possibility. One source states without supporting details that the final survivor was a man named Holloway who was eleven years old when he served at Albuera as a drummer boy in the 57th Foot.
15. Beamish, *History of the KGL*, Vol. 1, p. 339 n. According to Surgeon Boutflower of the 40th Foot, Fincke was also recommended for promotion: 'Lord Wellington with a liberality worthy [of] his great mind has given him a hundred Dollars, & directed him to be promoted on the first vacancy.' Boutflower, *Journal*, p. 95.

honoured in 1821. Although the particulars of Fincke's conduct at Albuera and the nature of the reward he received are recorded in the Guelphic archives, it appears, however, that neither he nor Grass ever received that medal.[16] Bussman was apparently the only one of the four who survived to receive a Military General Service Medal when that decoration was awarded in 1848.

Gazan

General Honoré-Theodore-Maxime Gazan recovered from his Albuera wounds and remained in the position of chief of staff of the Army of the South. When Soult was summoned to Germany early in 1813, Gazan was promoted to command that army and he led it in the Battle of Vitoria. In the ensuing rout, his wife Marie was captured by the British and his two children went missing. One child was found the same day, but the general and his wife had to spend an agonising week before they learned that their young son was also safe, having been cared for during that time by a British cavalryman.[17] Gazan rallied to Napoleon only reluctantly during the Hundred Days, but that choice was enough to deprive him of any meaningful military command from 1815 until his death in 1845.

Girard

Though none questioned the courage of General Jean-Baptiste Girard in the aftermath of Albuera, some did question his choice of formation for V Corps and many in addition to Soult placed the blame for the loss of the battle squarely on his performance. His reputation suffered a further blow in October 1811 when his division was surprised and routed by General Rowland Hill at Arroyo de Molinos, after which he was recalled to France in disgrace. He held active but minor commands in Russia in 1812 and Germany in 1813 and ended up as a member of the blockaded garrison of Magdeburg in 1814. He was given a significant command when he rallied to Napoleon in 1815 and had a leading role in the Battle of Ligny on 16 June in which he was severely wounded. Family tradition holds that he was named 'Duke of Ligny' by order of Napoleon six days before he succumbed to his wounds on 27 June, but the title was never formally recognised.[18]

Godinot

General Baron Godinot, who had first served with Soult in 1799, was praised by the marshal in his report of the battle and promoted, but criticised by others for not doing a better job of pressing his attack against the village of Albuera.[19] In October 1811, he was involved in an operation against a Spanish expedition led by Ballasteros near Gibraltar in which he botched a chance to capture all the baggage and artillery of the enemy. His 'unpardonable ineptitude' on that occasion led to further murmuring against him and even caused Marshal Soult to deliver a personal rebuke.[20] Upset by these developments and by distressing family news from home, Godinot went to his

16. Vigors, *The Hanoverian Guelphic Medal*, entries 610 and 627.
17. Griffon de Pleineville, 'Fighting for Napoleon'; Browne, *Journal*, pp. 218–19.
18. Valynseele, *Princes et Ducs*, pp. 100–1.
19. Lapène, *Conquête*, p. 158.
20. Bouillé, *Souvenirs*, Vol. 3, pp. 439–40; the altercation with Soult is mentioned in Beauvais, *Victoires et Conquêtes*, Vol. 20, p. 272.

quarters on 27 October, borrowed a musket from one of the guards on duty and committed suicide by putting a bullet through his head.[21]

Gougeat

Louis-Antoine Gougeat (b. 1788) continued to serve his master, Captain de Marcy (b. 1785) for another sixteen years after Albuera. Having survived the Napoleonic wars, they carried their relationship into civilian life in 1814, when the captain, by then promoted to squadron commander, retired on half-pay. After de Marcy's death in 1827, Gougeat moved to the town of Marcy where he lived until his death in 1865 'loved by the de Marcy family and esteemed by the townspeople, who elected him their mayor several times'.[22]

Hardinge

Henry Hardinge's career subsequent to Albuera took him to the kind of prominence that his early conduct had led people to expect.[23] He continued as a valued member of Beresford's military family throughout the Peninsular War, rising to command a Portuguese brigade in 1814. He was part of the British delegation to the Congress of Vienna and then served as Wellington's liaison to Blucher at the start of the Waterloo campaign. His conduct was again exemplary, but he lost his left hand to a cannon ball at the Battle of Ligny and so missed the final engagement of Waterloo. In the aftermath of the Napoleonic wars, he held a number of important domestic political positions, but his involvement in military matters waned except for an acrimonious correspondence with Lowry Cole that sprang up because Hardinge failed to contradict statements in Napier's history to the effect that Hardinge had 'ordered' Cole to launch the attack of the 4th Division (*see* Appendix G).[24] Hardinge's position in this controversy seemed more than a shade opportunistic given that he had already conceded the key point in dispute in a letter written to Cole immediately following the battle: '[Y]our movement on the left flank of the enemy unquestionably saved the day and decided the victory.'[25]

Hardinge's military career was re-invigorated when he became Governor-General of India in 1844 and he provided inspired leadership during the First Sikh War. He succeeded Wellington as Commander-in-Chief of the British Army in 1852, thus becoming responsible for much of the conduct of the Crimean War, and was elevated to the rank of field marshal in 1855.[26]

---

21. Lapène, pp. 267–8 n. 15.
22. Gougeat, 'Mémoires d'un Cavalier', p. 322.
23. See generally, Haythornthwaite, 'Henry Hardinge'.
24. The correspondence began with a letter from Thomas Wade, one of Cole's former ADCs, published in the *United Service Magazine* in 1840 and grew to include letters to and from Wade, Cole, Napier and Hardinge. The letters were collected and reprinted in 1841 in Cole, *Correspondence*. The controversy flared up again after Hardinge's death when *The Times* repeated Napier's statements in Hardinge's obituary and received a passionate rebuttal in the form of a letter to the editor from J. S. Lillie, who had fought with the Loyal Lusitanian Legion. *The Times*, 26 September 1856, p. 8, col. A.
25. Hardinge to Cole, 24 May 1811, quoted in Cole, *Memoirs*, pp. 77–8.
26. For Hardinge's later career, see Hardinge, *Rulers of India*.

Harris

When old soldiers do not fade away, they face the problems of failing health in old age and governmental neglect. Albuera veteran Samuel Harris of the 66th Foot was wounded three times in action (at Talavera, Albuera and Vitoria), but he never applied for a pension until he became unable to work in 1849. His petition was rejected, however, based on a hard-hearted rationale expressed by the Duke of Wellington himself:

> This soldier ought undoubtedly to have been pensioned. His own neglect was evidently the cause that he was not. The Commander-in-chief has no power or authority in the case.[27]

Fortunately for Harris, a local gentleman stepped forward and provided a private pension to the old soldier.

Harrison

Lieutenant John Christopher Harrison recovered from his Albuera wound and went on to have a long and successful military career in the Royal Welch Fusiliers. He is particularly remembered for his actions in preserving two unique traditions of his regiment against assault by an unfeeling military bureaucracy.[28] Starting in 1808, every officer of the 23rd Regiment was accustomed to wear a set of five overlapping black ribbons, or 'flash', on the back of his collar. This distinction was not sanctioned by any regulation and in 1834 a dyspeptic inspector summarily ordered an end to the practice. Harrison, at that time a lieutenant colonel of the regiment, launched a successful appeal of the order that went all the way to William IV. At the same time, Harrison also obtained official sanction for the practice of keeping a goat as the regimental mascot.

Privates Heines, O'Harran and Royston

One unique outcome of the Battle of Albuera is that it actually saved the lives of three men – Privates Patrick Heines, Dennis O'Harran and James Royston of the 57th Regiment. They had been charged with robbing the house of J. E. R. Sylveira at Elvas at the end of March and a court martial held on 9 July 1811 found them guilty and sentenced them to be hung. Wellington chose to be merciful, however, and pardoned the men, in part because they had made restitution of the property stolen and in part because he wished to render a special honour to the 57th:

> The conduct of the 57th Regiment ... in the battle of Albuera ... has likewise rendered the Commander of the Forces anxious to be able to pardon these men, in order that the regiment might avoid the disgrace of their public execution.[29]

The same order also extended clemency to five other men of the regiment (one sergeant, one drummer and three privates) who had been charged with lesser crimes in connection with plundering at Elvas.

---

27. 'Old Peninsular Soldiers', in *The Times*, 2 June 1853, p. 6, col. B.
28. Browne, *Journal*, p. 28
29. G.O. for 27 July 1811 in Wellington, *General Orders*, Vol. 3, 1811, p. 155

Hicks

Private John Hicks also encountered an unyielding military bureaucracy in a similar (if not even more compelling) case to that of Samuel Harris. Hicks enlisted in the 48th Foot in 1808 and was 'severely wounded at Albuera by a gun-shot through his lungs, for which wound he was discharged in 1814, with a pension of 9d. [4p.] per day'. In 1815, however, the proud soldier found himself much improved in health. He thereupon ceased to draw his pension and instead lived by his own exertions until 1849. Afflicted by illness in that year, he applied to the government to reclaim his pension, only to find that he was disqualified on a technicality and, further, had no claim for back amounts.[30] Some retired officers took up his cause and publicised his case in local newspapers. It is not known, however, whether the power of the media had the desired effect in this case of either causing the government to change its stance or bringing forward some private benefactor to make up for the government's miserliness.

Hilton

Private James Hilton of the 48th Foot had been twenty years old when he joined his regiment in 1803. He fought at Talavera and Bussaco, survived Albuera and went on to fight in every subsequent significant action of the war from the sieges of Ciudad Rodrigo and Badajoz through to the Battle of Toulouse. As a result, the Military General Service Medal he received had a total of ten clasps. When he died in Lancashire on 24 February 1871, 'aged 87 years and 354 days', he was buried alongside his wife Anne, who had died in 1869. An elaborate memorial card produced by his family recalled his service with the following verses:

> The tired soldier, bold and brave,
> Now rests his weary feet;
> And to the shelter of the grave
> Has made a safe retreat.
> To him the trumpeter's piercing breath
> To arms shall call in vain;
> He's quartered now in the arms of death,
> He'll never march again.[31]

Latham

Given the magnitude of his injuries, it seemed doubtful that Lieutenant Matthew Latham of the Buffs would ever again be able to serve in the army, so in 1812 he was awarded two disability pensions totalling £170 per year.[32] Nevertheless, after a nearly two-year absence from the army to recuperate from his wounds, Latham was promoted to the rank of captain and posted to the Canadian Fencibles Regiment in February 1813. Before he was due to leave for Canada, however, he was able to return to his

30. 'A Neglected Veteran', in Official Appointments and Notices, *The Times*, 27 April 1850, p. 8, col. A.
31. The memorial card was sold on eBay in July 2006.
32. Palmerston, *Return of Names*, pp. 4–5.
33. Robert Henderson, 'Captains of the Canadian Fencibles in 1812', posted at <www3.sympatico.ca/dis.general/capt_cf.htm> on 6 April 1999, at p. 6.

old regiment by effecting an exchange with Captain Josias Taylor of the 2nd Battalion.[33] He was enthusiastically welcomed back and on 12 August 1813, Latham was presented by brother officers with a unique gold medal in honour of his gallant conduct at Albuera.[34] The sentiments of the regiment on this occasion were expressed in a letter from Lieutenant Colonel William Stewart, who was still in command at that time:

> In my absence, (which I regret on this occasion) Major Morris, in command of the 2d Batt., will present you with the Gold Medal which accompanies this, and which you already know, has long since been so cordially voted you by the unanimous voice of the whole body of your brother officers, as a lasting testimonial of the high sense they entertain of your distinguished conduct at the battle of Albuera.[35]

Latham's warm feelings about this honour shone through even the clichéd sentiments of his formal letter of reply:

> Suffer me to assure you and them [his fellow officers] that no circumstance can afford to me more heartfelt satisfaction than that my conduct met with your and their approbation, thus conveyed to me in a manner so highly flattering to my feelings, that it can never be erased from my memory. It shall be my greatest pride to wear this distinguished token of my brother officers' regards, and which has been so graciously sanctioned by our illustrious Commander-in-Chief.[36]

The Prince of Wales gave Latham a more practical form of compensation for his gallant conduct. On 20 January 1815, the Prince Regent referred Latham to the care of Joseph Carpue (1764–1846), a noted surgeon of the time, who had just re-discovered a forgotten surgical technique for using skin grafts to repair drastic nasal damage. Over the course of three procedures during the next year (all performed at the expense of the Prince Regent), Carpue created a new nose for Latham by cutting a flap of skin from his forehead and grafting it to the remains of his old proboscis. The result was not flawless, but it at least relieved Latham from the embarrassment and constant colds and sinus inflammations that had been his lot since the battle.[37] The technique used on Latham is still known to this day as Carpue's Operation or Carpue's Rhinoplasty.[38]

At least one other Albuera survivor, a lieutenant of the 7th Fusiliers, came to the perverse conclusion that, all told, Latham's fate was one to be relatively envied. As the fusilier lieutenant explained to another officer:

34. This unique medal for gallantry had to be specifically authorised by the Commander-in-Chief. See, Letter of Colonel Torrens to General Leigh, 4 January 1813, conveying the approval of the Duke of York, *The Royal Military Panorama or Officer's Companion*, Vol. III, October 1813, p. 43. The medal, which was worn on a red ribbon bordered with yellow stripes, featured an engraved representation of the fight for the colours and the words 'I will surrender it only with my life!' on the obverse. Jocelyn, Arthur, *Awards of Honour*, London, 1956.
35. Stewart to Latham, 2 August 1813, *The Royal Military Panorama or Officer's Companion*, Vol. III, October 1813, p. 44.
36. Latham to Stewart, 12 August 1813, *The Royal Military Panorama or Officer's Companion*, Vol. III, October 1813, p. 45.
37. Latham's treatment is described in detail in Carpue, *Account*, at pp. 91–7. Carpue was unable to do anything for the side of Latham's face, where the muscles and part of the cheek bone had been cut away. The scar over the affected area remained 'extraordinarily irritable' and frequently became 'broken out'.
38. See the related entries in *Dorland's Medical Dictionary*.

'I have only, you see, lost a leg, when that poor devil of the Buffs [undoubtedly Latham, despite some inaccurate details that follow] lost his two legs, an arm, and his nose, besides having the honour of a Lancer poking his spear right through his body twice.'

I stared at this: 'May I ask you if he is still alive?'

'Aye, and well. I wish I had half his luck!'

'Why, my dear friend, I think you are most unfortunate to lose one leg.'

'Agreed; it is too much. But what value is life now to me? Had I lost my legs, my arms, and nose, I would have been known and brought into notice. The Buffs have it all their own way; the Prince Regent has sent for him. What a lucky rascal he is!' [he said] with a loud burst of laughter.[39]

Latham did not rejoin his regiment on active service until 1816 when it was part of the allied occupation force in France after Waterloo. In one of the more astonishing ironies related to the Battle of Albuera, Captain Latham married a French woman in that same year and, after he retired from the army in 1820, he spent the rest of his life in a village in northern France.[40] (One can only imagine the conversations he might have had with French Army veterans at his local café.) He died in 1865 and a monument was erected over his grave by the Buffs. His gold medal remained in his family until it was presented to the Buffs Museum in 1974 by his lineal descendant, Madame Greithelf.[41]

Latour-Maubourg

Latour-Maubourg's success at Albuera led to a recall from Spain in 1812 and command of one of the magnificent Reserve Cavalry Corps of the Grand Army during the invasion of Russia. He played a similar role in 1813, which ended for him at Leipzig when one of his legs was cut off at the thigh by a cannonball. This wound earned him a place in the annals of black humour when he rebuked his valet, who was visibly distressed at the sight of his master's grievous injury, with the remark: 'What have you got to cry about – you have only one boot to polish from now on.'[42] Latour-Maubourg welcomed the return of the Bourbons and even voted for the death penalty in the trial of Marshal Ney after Waterloo. His loyalty was rewarded with many honours and positions during the Restoration, including a stint in 1819 as the French ambassador to the Court of St James during which he undoubtedly came into contact with many of his former Peninsular foes.

Long

Albuera marked the end of General Long's tenure as the commander of all of Beresford's cavalry, but he did retain command of a single light brigade for the next few years. He harboured a grudge over the way he had been treated by Beresford and was particularly upset by the fact that Beresford did not nominate him for a gold

39. Fyans, *Memoirs*, p. 29. Fyans joined the 48th Regiment in the Peninsula after Albuera and recorded that this conversation took place in a hospital in Lisbon. Fyans says the wounded officer was 'an old school friend' who served in the '9th' Fusiliers, but that designation is certainly wrong given the context and the substance of the conversation.
40. Hall, *Biographical Dictionary*, p. 335; Knight, *Historical Records*, Vol. 2, p. 428 n. 1.
41. Clipping from *The Daily Telegraph*, 1974, Archive Item No. 2001-07-567:14, NAM.
42. Pigeard, *Les Étoiles de Napoléon*, p. 581.

medal for Albuera even though he was one of the six officers mentioned by name in the 'Thanks' given by Parliament after the battle and had been mentioned positively by Beresford in his dispatch (along with General Lumley, who did receive a medal). Long's resentment boiled over after Vitoria, when he was awarded a gold cross for that battle. In order to publicise his view that he was unfairly deprived of the medal for Albuera, he took the extraordinarily perverse step of writing to the Horse Guards to propose that he should give back the Vitoria medal since he had done nothing more at Vitoria than he had at Albuera, and if he was not given a medal for Albuera, he consequently did not deserve one for the other battle.[43] When the authorities called his bluff and asked him to return the Vitoria medal, he grudgingly accepted it. His nephew, C. E. Long took up his uncle's cause in 1834 and petitioned for a posthumous award of a gold medal for Albuera to his relative. The petition was denied.[44]

Maransin

Many of the French doctors believed that the musket ball that traversed General Maransin's lower abdomen had caused a mortal wound and he even became the subject of premature death notices that appeared in newspapers as far away as the United States.[45] He nevertheless recovered after a three-month convalescence under the care of Chief Surgeon Chappe and Chief Physician Brassier, although he was obliged to wear a bandage wrapped around his waist every day of his life thereafter. He was wounded at Cartama in early 1812, but survived again to fight in many more campaigns before the fall of the Empire. His Albuera wound affected his lung capacity and he was never again able to play his favourite musical instrument, the clarinet. He also declared late in his life that '... my wounds [and] the feeble state of my health ... have condemned me to a life of celibacy'.[46]

McGowan

Grenadier Corporal Owen McGowan of the 57th Foot was one of the lucky few Albuera veterans who obtained a place as a pensioner residing in Chelsea Hospital when his fighting days were over. In his retirement, he was inspired to write a poem about Albuera which began with the following rousing stanza:

> Brave Britons attend to these verses
> When read you will find they are true
> How oft times the French were repulsed
> And left Marshal Soult in a stew.
> Lord Beresford was our commander
> Whose troops were in marshal [sic] array,
> Determined on glory or conquest
> Were the British on the 16th of May.[47]

43. Long to Torrens, quoted in C. E. Long, *Reply to Further Strictures*, pp. 139–40.
44. Long, *The Albuera Medal*.
45. See, e.g., the Providence, Rhode Island *Gazette*, 12 October 1811, p. 3.
46. Cambon, *Maransin*, pp. 85, 92, 113 and 192.
47. 'Lines pen'd in verse descriptive of the memorable and eventful Battle on Albuera's plains in Spain on the 16th of May 1811', Archive Item No. 65004-52-20, Inglis Papers, NAM.

Morisset

James Morisset of the 48th Foot, whose face was disfigured at the battle, continued to serve in the army and had a particularly notable career in the administration of Australia. One can only speculate about the psychological effect his injury may have had on Morisset, but it is a matter of record that the Australian penal colony on Norfolk Island gained an horrific reputation for inhuman treatment of prisoners under his command. Despite his disfigurement, he did marry and father ten children before his death in 1859.[48]

Pernet

French artillery Captain Jean-Étienne Pernet and his general were transferred to IV Corps after Albuera and then, at the end of the year, they were both recalled from Spain to play a role in the planned invasion of Russia. Unfortunately, they were part of the convoy that was famously ambushed in the Gorge of Salinas on 9 April 1812 by Spanish guerilla forces under the command of General Mina. Pernet was wounded twice in the fighting and, although he survived his injuries, his right arm was disabled and he was forced to retire from the army, the only home he had known since he had enlisted in 1791 at the age of nineteen.[49] He lived long enough to collect the Médaille de Sainte-Hélène awarded to French veterans in 1857.

De Roverea

After recovering from his Albuera wound, Captain de Roverea continued to serve with General Cole and even earned promotion to the rank of major. The two enjoyed such a close friendship that Cole was reduced to tears when his 'dear and inestimable friend' was killed in action on 28 July 1813. The general then wrote the following lines to de Roverea's father:

> Accustomed as I am in this profession to regularly losing my best friends, never before have I experienced a loss so cruel and, even though he lost his life in a brilliant affair . . . I cannot at this hour cope with it.[50]

Von Schepeler

This intrepid officer was taken prisoner at Valencia in 1812 along with many other Spanish Army veterans of Albuera, but his situation was more dangerous than that of most officers because, as a subject of the Kingdom of Westphalia, he was technically guilty of treason by virtue of his service in the Spanish armed forces. Fortunately, he managed to pass himself off as an Austrian and then make his escape altogether, so he was still in action at Burgos and Vitoria. He remained in Spain until 1823 as an army officer and then as the Prussian chargé d'affaires in Madrid. When he retired, he decided to write a history of the war in the Peninsula that would provide the Spanish version of events. His finished work was first published in German in 1826–7.

48. Champion, 'James T. Morisset', p. 225.
49. The action at Salinas is related in Pernet, 'Journal', pp. 105–7.
50. F. de Roverea, *Mémoires*, Vol. 4, pp. 114 and 116.

St George

Lieutenant Stepney St George, the young subaltern of the 66th who was wounded and almost carried off by a Polish lancer, recovered and served in the provisional battalion formed from the units that had suffered most at Albuera. Since he was a man of considerable financial means and, therefore, always well-mounted, he often served as an aide-de-camp to senior officers in significant engagements. Serving in such a capacity in one battle in the Pyrenees in 1813, he was riding up an extremely steep slope when he was hit in the arm and knocked from his horse. Unfortunately, he fell backwards and his head was pierced by the bayonet of one of his own soldiers coming up the slope behind him.[51] He nevertheless survived this extraordinary wound (and the trepanning operation that followed). St George later married a niece of Major Guy L'Estrange, the officer who commanded the 31st Foot at Albuera, and fathered a large family.

Soult

Soult was the 'Teflon' marshal of his day, since he was constantly embroiled in controversy (including a serious feud with King Joseph) but never fell into disgrace with Napoleon, though he did come close on occasion. His vigorous leadership forced the retreat of the British back to Portugal in the autumn of 1812, although he declined to engage Wellington's battered army in a battle that might have changed the course of the war. Soult was recalled to serve in the Grand Army in 1813, so he missed the disastrous French defeat at Vitoria, but he was then sent back to Spain by the emperor to defend the frontiers of France for the last eight months of Napoleon's reign. Under the First Restoration, he became the Minister of War, but he rallied to Napoleon in 1815 and served as Napoleon's chief of staff in the Waterloo campaign. He was consequently sentenced to death and forced into exile, but he was allowed to return to France in 1819, comforted in his retirement by the vast treasure of money and artwork he had amassed during his independent command in Andalucia. After the Revolution of 1830, he once again displayed his remarkable political resilience by serving as the Minister of War 1830–4 and again 1840–4. He was also ambassador extraordinary to the coronation of Queen Victoria and Minister for Foreign Affairs in 1839. He died in 1851.

Unknown Fusilier Officer

When the future Field Marshal Sir Evelyn Wood was an officer with the 90th Light Infantry in Scotland in 1872, he was called upon to attend a civic ceremony at Perth. He noticed in attendance a distinguished-looking old gentleman with a white beard who was described as being 'of no importance – only an old Peninsula soldier'. Sir Evelyn thought otherwise and, after discovering that the man had been present with the fusiliers at Albuera, he decided to show the old man greater respect. When Sir Evelyn was called upon to deliver a speech at a subsequent ceremony at which the gentleman was present, he explained to the audience that they were in the presence of a true hero. Wood proceeded to recite Napier's famous description of the charge of the fusiliers at Albuera and he then said: 'I call on Lieutenant —— [blank in original] of the Fusiliers to answer for the Army.' The old man, 'rising slowly and with difficulty,

---

51. L'Estrange, *Recollections*, pp. 161–2.

for he was more than eighty years of age, . . . doddered over to the table, and leaning heavily upon it said, simply "Let me greit [cry]!"' The old lieutenant eventually brushed away his tears and explained that he was overcome with emotion because no one had ever spoken to him about the Battle of Albuera: 'but now, when I have one foot in the grave, I see before me officers in the same coloured coats, and . . . they recount in wonderful language the crowning scene of my Military life.' Sinking back into a chair, he pronounced 'I shall die happy.'[52]

Vacher

Simon Vacher is another Frenchman whose experiences epitomise those of an entire generation. Born in 1780, he was a carpenter by trade until he was conscripted into the army.[53] He had worked his way up to the rank of corporal by 1809 and proved himself to be tough as well as diligent by surviving a wound in his left thigh at Albuera. He was consequently a trusted veteran when he was transferred to the Imperial Guard Grenadiers in February 1813 as part of the effort to recover from the horrendous losses from the Russian campaign. He received the cross of the Legion of Honour in the nomination of 17 May of the same year and went on to fight in many of the major battles of the last year of Napoleon's reign. He received the Médaille de Sainte-Hélène in 1857 and died in 1858.

Wade

Thomas Wade, General Cole's aide-de-camp, continued on active service, carrying within him the musket ball he had acquired at Albuera. He found himself drawn back to consideration of Albuera by the brief controversy which flared up around Colonel Napier's characterisation of General Cole's role in the battle, with Wade called upon as one of the key witnesses in support of his old commander's assertion that he alone had made the decision to attack. In the summer of 1846, thirty-five years after it was inflicted, Wade's old wound flared up and, remarkably, he found himself once again under the care of Surgeon Guthrie. When Guthrie examined his old patient, he concluded that the musket ball had moved to a spot where it could finally be removed. Surgery was scheduled, but Wade died from other natural causes before it could be performed.[54]

Woods

After his experiences at Albuera, Lieutenant William Woods of the 2nd/48th concluded he had had enough of life in the infantry and exchanged into a cavalry regiment. After the war, he was stationed in Newcastle, where he met and married the daughter of a local businessman. Soon thereafter, he resigned his commission and embarked on a commercial career. By the time of his death in 1864 at the age of seventy-seven, he had become one of the most successful bankers in the history of the city of Newcastle.[55]

---

52. Wood, *Midshipman to Field Marshal*, Vol. 1, pp. 250–1.
53. Labadie, *Dictionnaire*, p. 134.
54. Guthrie, *Commentaries*, p. 542.
55. Welford, *Men of Mark*, pp. 670–2.

The Napier–Beresford Pamphlet Wars

Despite the fact that he was not present at the battle, Sir William Napier has been part of the Albuera story since the publication of the third volume of his *History of the Peninsular War* in 1831 because of the immense popularity of his dramatic description of the charge of the fusilier brigade. It is almost impossible to find any nineteenth-century work describing the battle that does not include extensive quotations from Napier's narrative up to and including the most famous sentence in his entire work: 'The rain flowed after in streams discoloured with blood, and fifteen hundred unwounded men, the remnant of six thousand unconquerable British soldiers, stood triumphant on that fatal hill!'[1] The fact that Napier's vivid prose fails almost entirely to delineate the events that took place at the crucial phase of the battle has been brilliantly demonstrated by John Keegan, but that failing went unnoticed by Napier's original audience (and many subsequent generations of readers).[2] What was noticed, however, was Napier's highly opinionated and negative assessment of Beresford's performance as the Allied commander, and those opinions touched off a passionate brawl of letters and pamphlets that was ultimately to involve Beresford, Napier, Cole, Hardinge, General Long's nephew and numerous Albuera veterans and gave rise to hundreds of pages of opinions, analysis and information about Albuera. Although some of this material is clearly unreliable because it was the product of conscious or unconscious bias or because it was produced over two decades after the events in question, these documents do contain numerous items of helpful or unique information about the battle, so it is worth describing this series of paper feuds in some detail.

There was no history of animosity between Beresford and Napier prior to the start of the feud, but Napier's private correspondence reveals that, even as he was writing his history, he was aware that the parts of his narrative dealing with Beresford would not be flattering: 'Beresford I have not any high opinion of and I shall show that in the work without any particular notice of him.'[3] Beresford appears only briefly in

---

1. W. Napier, *History*, Vol. 3, p. 547.
2. John Keegan, *The Face of Battle*, New York, 1976, pp. 36–41.
3. Napier to Colborne, 23 June 1824, quoted in 'Letters from Colonel William Napier to Sir John Colborne', *English Historical Review*, Vol. 18, 1903, pp. 725–40 at 735.

Napier's first volume as a subordinate commander in Sir John Moore's army, but he is a more prominent figure in the second volume (published in 1829) and, as a result, Napier's attitude towards him became much more evident. Indeed, one anonymous supporter of Beresford was so incensed by what he viewed as Napier's unjustified criticisms of the marshal that he took to print to refute them in an 1831 pamphlet:

> I determined to enter into a minute examination of those passages in Lieutenant Colonel Napier's work, which appear to me to bear unfairly on the professional character of Lord Beresford, and to meet them with a plain, clear, and unornamented counter-statement of facts.[4]

Napier was extremely offended by what he viewed as slurs against his reputation as an historian and was convinced that Beresford was behind the document:

> Although anonymous attacks should be disregarded, I notice this pamphlet, written in defence of Lord Beresford, because the writer would have it understood, either that he is Lord Beresford, or that he writes from his Lordship's dictation.[5]

Because of this background, the publication of Napier's third volume created an immediate furore because the author's bias against Beresford was now frequently and obviously on display. Imagine, if you will, how Beresford must have felt when he opened that book to read about his career-defining victory at Albuera and found his performance blasted in the following derogatory terms:

> ... in this dreadful crisis, Beresford wavered. Destruction stared him in the face, his personal resources were exhausted, and the unhappy thought of a retreat rose in his agitated mind ... But while the marshal was thus preparing to resign the contest, Colonel Hardinge boldly ordered General Cole to advance with the 4th Division.[6]

Beresford's anonymous defender took up his pen again to present *Further Strictures* against Napier's work,[7] but when Napier had the temerity to defend himself in print rather than acknowledging the validity of the criticism and, furthermore, heaped additional abuse on the marshal via *New and Curious Facts Relative to the Battle of Albuera*, Beresford finally joined the pamphlet wars under his own name with his *Refutation of Colonel's Napier's Justification of His Third Volume* (London, 1834). The feud was then carried to its logical extreme conclusion when Napier published a final salvo in the form of a document with the marvellously self-descriptive title, *A Letter to General Lord Beresford, Being an Answer to his Lordship's Assumed Refutation of Colonel Napier's Justification of his Third Volume* (London, 1834).[8] By this point, all pretence of civility had disappeared. Beresford effectively

---

4. Anonymous, *Strictures*, pp. 2–3.
5. William Napier, *Reply to the Strictures upon Colonel Napier's History of the Peninsular War*, London, 1832, p. 1.
6. W. Napier, *History*, Vol. 3, p. 545.
7. Although the *Strictures* and *Further Strictures* works were first published separately, they were also later published in a combined edition under the first title.
8. Mark Thompson, 11 Friarsfield Close, Chapelgarth, Sunderland SR3 2RZ, UK, has assisted Peninsular War researchers by publishing reprints of all of these works.

accused Napier of lying, while Napier resorted to words and phrases such as 'scurrility', 'bad taste' and 'mortified vanity' in describing Beresford's remarks. No one could ever be deemed a 'winner' of a feud that had fallen to such a low level of discourse and, indeed, Moyle Sherer wrote to Napier to express the view that there was fault on both sides on the controversy:

> Your treatment of Marshal Beresford in your history I have always thought hard. His difficulties and perplexities and manifest inability to sustain them, demanded at your hands more allowance than you were willing to make. In controversy he has invited and therefore merited hard measure.[9]

Any reader of the pamphlets can easily detect an irrational level of passion on both sides of the debate, but the source of the passion for Napier was different than it was for Beresford. The driver for the marshal was righteous indignation about slurs cast on his military reputation. In the case of Napier, the driver was the obsession that he was correct and an unwillingness to admit any mistakes. There is an intriguing possibility that the irrational element in Napier's defence of his masterpiece may have been the result of physical as much as psychological factors:

> It must, however, be mentioned in extenuation of some of his [Napier's] most outrageous misstatements that, while writing the last volumes of his history [and his pamphlets], he was in such a state of irritation through pain and disease as to be hardly sane. For this reason, many people who were in a position to correct his inaccuracies abstained through sheer compassion from doing so.[10]

The controversy over Albuera was not restricted to Beresford and Napier alone, however. The first off-shoot was a battle between Beresford and Charles Edward Long, the nephew of General Long, who felt duty-bound to object to aspersions cast on his dead uncle's name during Beresford's defence of his own reputation. This side-bar consisted of five separate publications, three by Long (all containing extensive extracts from the general's correspondence) and two by Beresford. Long certainly did no favours to his uncle's memory by inspiring Beresford to repeat publicly all the private criticisms he had directed towards General Long at the time.

The other off-shoot was a spirited exchange of letters about the advance of the 4th Division that played out primarily in the pages of the *United Service Journal*, a periodical founded in 1828 for a military audience. The spark for this controversy was the statement by Napier (quoted above) that Hardinge 'ordered' the attack of General Cole's division, but it did not cause a conflagration until 1840, when Colonel Wade, one of Cole's ADCs at the battle, belatedly challenged the statement on its merits. Napier and Hardinge both responded and Napier in particular suggested that Cole must have agreed with the description because Cole had never uttered a word of contradiction about the text even though he had met with Napier several times after the passage was published. That suggestion finally brought Cole into the fray despite his reluctance to become part of a public spectacle, a reluctance that had 'not been

---

9. M. Sherer to Napier, 7 November 1834, quoted in Bruce, *Life of Napier*, pp. 413–14.
10. Fortescue, *History*, Vol. IX, p. 260, n. 1. Fortescue explains in his note that this information was brought to his attention by 'some letters among the Gurwood papers owned by Lord Esher' that are now with the Wellington Papers at the University of Southampton.

lessened by the bitterness of the controversy' between Napier and Beresford.[11] It turned out that Cole had hoped that Hardinge would clarify what happened on his own initiative and eliminate the need for him to do so and Cole was clearly disappointed that Hardinge instead continued to foster the popular notion that he alone had saved the day at Albuera. Once Cole made his points in writing, however, Napier conceded that his choice of words might have been unfortunate and in later editions he modified his text and said only that Hardinge 'urged' Cole to attack. Napier nevertheless persisted in asserting that the victory was due primarily to Hardinge's actions:

> Still, the masterly conception of changing the order of battle from a defensive one to an offensive one at a moment when all appeared desperate, was, I still think so, due to Sir Henry Hardinge. For, be it remembered, the attack of the Fusiliers would have been only a half measure, perhaps an unsuccessful one, if Abercrombie's [sic] brigade had not assailed the French right at the same time.[12]

11. Cole, *Correspondence*, p. 20.
12. *Ibid.*, p. 29.

Bibliography

A Die Hard, 'Letter from "A Die Hard"', *United Service Journal*, 1829, Part 2, pp. 106–7

Aineville, Charles Marie-Blanche d' & Espérandieu, Antoine d', 'Autour de Deux Portraits de Famille: Le Général Baron Joseph Pépin', *Revue de l'Institut Napoléon*, No. 142, 1984, pp. 57–66

Aitchison, John, *An Ensign in the Peninsular War*, London, 1981

Alten, Charles von, 'Narrative of General Count Alten, October 1833', H.N. Estrangeiros Caixa 205, Maço 166 (2), Arquivos Nacionais/Torre do Tombo, Lisbon, Portugal

An Eyewitness, 'The Attack Upon Soult's Rear-Guard at Seville in August 1812', *United Service Journal*, Vol. 51, 1846, Part 2, pp. 87–91

An Old Soldier, 'Albuera', *United Service Journal*, 1840, Part 3, pp. 107–8

An Old Soldier, 'Battle of Albuera', *United Service Journal*, 1835, Part 3, pp. 535–6

Anonymous, *Army Officers Awards, Napoleonic Period*, London, 1853, reprinted London, 1969

——, 'Bataille d'Albuera', File C⁸ 72, SHAT, Château de Vincennes, Paris

——, 'The Battle of Albuhera', *Regimental Journal of the Worcestershire & Sherwood Foresters Regiment*, April 1931, pp. 7–18

——, 'Biographical Sketch of G. J. Guthrie, Esq., F.R.S.', *The Lancet*, 1850, pp. 726–36

——, 'Diario do Segundo Sitio . . . de Badajoz [Diary of the Second Siege . . . of Badajoz]', in Chaby, *Excerptos Historicos*, p. 375, n. 2

——, (Private, 3rd Foot), 'Extract from a letter from a private of the 3rd Regiment of Foot, or Buffs, who was taken prisoner and effected his escape from the enemy', *The Soldier's Companion; or, Martial Recorder, Consisting of Biography, Anecdotes, Poetry, and Miscellaneous Information Peculiarly Interesting to Those Connected with the Military Profession*, London, 1824

——, 'Extract from a Letter dated Lisbon, 24 May 1811', *The Times*, 6 June 1811, p. 3, col. A

——, *Further Strictures on Those Parts of Col. Napier's History of the Peninsular War Which Relate to the Military Opinions and Conduct of General Lord Viscount Beresford*, London, 1832, reprinted Sunderland, 1995

——, (Officer, 2nd KGL Light Battalion), Letter from a KGL Officer, 27 May 1811, posted March 2007, www.napoleon-series.org/military/battles/albuera/c_kglalbuera.html

——, (Officer, 1st/48th Foot), 'Letter from an Officer, 19 May 1811', *Evening Star*, 5 June 1811, p. 3, col. D

——, 'Life of Sir William Myers', *The Royal Military Chronicle*, October 1811, pp. 469–74

——, 'Memoir on the Province of Andalusia', *The Royal Military Chronicle*, November 1812, pp. 9–20

——, 'The Regimental Museum', *Regimental Journal of the Worcestershire & Sherwood Foresters Regiment*, October 1937, pp. 307–8

——, *Strictures on Certain Passages of Lieut.-Col. Napier's History of the Peninsular War Which Relate to the Military Opinions and Conduct of General Lord Viscount Beresford*, London, 1831, reprinted Sunderland, 1995

——, 'The 29th at Albuhera', *Regimental Journal of the Worcestershire & Sherwood Foresters Regiment*, April 1931, pp. 19–25

——, *Vicissitudes in the Life of a Scottish Soldier*, London, 1827

Arnold, James, 'A Reappraisal of Column Versus Line in the Peninsular War', *Journal of Military History*, Vol. 68, No. 2, 2004, p. 547

Atkinson, C. T., 'The Composition and Organisation of the British Forces in the Peninsula, 1808–1814', *English Historical Review*, Vol. 17, No. 65, 1902, p. 110–33

——, 'A Swiss Officer in Wellington's Army', *Journal of the Society for Army Historical Research*, Vol. 35, 1957, pp. 71–8

——, *The Dorsetshire Regiment – Vol. 1, The 39th Foot*, Oxford, 1947

Austin, Thomas, *'Old Stick-Leg' – Extracts from the Diaries of Major Thomas Austin*, London, 1906

Ayres de Magalhães Sepúlveda, Christiovam, *Historia Organica e Politico do Exército Portuguez*, 12 vols., Coimbra 1902–17; Volume 11, 1916, deals with Albuera

Bakewell, Robert (Ensign, 27th Foot), Transcript of Bakewell Diaries (3 Vols.), Archive Item No. 7509-75, National Army Museum, London

Barrès, Jean-Baptiste (Bernard Miall, tr.), *Memoirs of a Napoleonic Officer*, London, 1925

Barrett, C. R. B., *History of the XIII Hussars*, 2 vols., London, 1911

Bayley, Charles (Lieutenant, 31st Foot), Letter to Miss Sally Smith, 'Camp near Albuera, 18 May 1811, 10 O'Clock Morning', Private Collection

Beamish, N. Ludlow, *History of the King's German Legion*, 2 vols., London, reprinted 1993

Beauvais de Préau, G. T. (ed.), *Victoires, Conquêtes, Désastres, Revers et Guerres Civiles des Français de 1792 à 1815*, 27 vols., Paris 1817–21; Volume 20 (1820) deals with Albuera

Benavides Moro, Nicolas & Yaque Laurel, José A., *El Capitán-General Don Joaquín Blake y Joyes, regente del Reino, Fundador del Cuerpo de Estado Mayor*, nl [Madrid], nd [1960]

Belmas, J., *Journaux des Sièges Faits ou Soutenus par les Français dans la Péninsule, de 1807 à 1814*, 5 vols., Paris, 1836–7

Bennett, Thomas (Sergeant, 13th Light Dragoons), 'Memoirs of a Saddler Sergeant', in Fortescue, *Following the Drum*, pp. 81–103

Beresford, William C., Letter to Sir Charles Stewart, 25 May 1811, Letters of Lord Londonderry, Durham Records Office, D/LO/C —18/63I, Durham, England

——, *A Second Letter to Charles Edward Long, Esq.*, London, 1843

——, *Letter to Charles Edward Long, Esq., on the Extracts Recently Published from the Manuscript Journal and Private Correspondence of the Late Lieutenant General R. B. Long*, London, 1833

——, *Refutation of Colonel Napier's Justification of his Third Volume*, London, 1834

——, Official Report to Wellington, 18 May 1811, *London Gazette Extraordinary*, 4 June 1811; this report is reproduced in many other sources including *The Times*, 4 June 1811, p. 2, and *Dispatches*, Vol. 7, pp. 588–93

Berthier, Louis Alexandre, Report of French Losses at Albuera, AF IV 1630, Plaq 1(iv), Archives Nationales de France, Paris

Blanco, Letter to the Editor, November 1834, *United Service Journal*, 1834, Part 3, p. 546

Bonaparte, Joseph (A. Du Casse, ed.), *Mémoires et Correspondance Politique et Militaire du Roi Joseph*, 10 vols., Paris, 1854–5

Boothby, Charles, *A Prisoner of France. The Memoirs, Diary, and Correspondence of Charles Boothby, Captain Royal Engineers, during his last Campaign*, London, 1900

Bouillé, J. de, *Souvenirs et Fragments*, 3 vols., Paris, 1911

Boutflower, C., *The Journal of an Army Surgeon during the Peninsular War*, nl, nd [1912]

Bouvier, J.-B., *Historique de 96e Régiment (ex-21e Léger)*, Lyon, 1892

Brasier de Thiry, ?, *Historique du 103e Régiment d'Infanterie*, Mamers, 1886

Bremond d'Ars, A. de, *Historique du 21e Régiment de Chasseurs à Cheval 1792–1814*, Paris, 1903

Brice, Raoul & Bottet, M., *Le Corps de Santé Militaire en France*, Paris, 1907

Bridgeman, George, *Letters from Portugal, Spain, Sicily and Malta in 1812, 1813 and 1814*, London, 1875

Brooke, Raymond F., *The Brimming River*, Dublin, 1961

Brooke, William (Major, 2nd/48th Foot), 'A Prisoner of Albuera', in Oman, *Studies in the Napoleonic Wars*

Brotherton, Thomas (Bryan Perrett, ed.), *A Hawk at War: The Peninsular Reminiscences of General Sir Thomas Brotherton, CB*, Chippenham, England, 1986

Browne, Thomas (Roger N. Buckley, ed.), *The Napoleonic War Journal of Captain Thomas Henry Browne 1807–1816*, London, 1987

Bruce, Henry Austin, *The Life of Sir William Napier*, 2 vols., London, 1864

Burriel, Antonio (Chief of Staff, 4th Army), *Batalla de la Albuhera*, Cadiz, 1811

Butler, Lewis, *Annals of the King's Royal Rifle Corps*, 6 vols., London, 1913

Cadell, Charles, *Narrative of the Campaigns of the 28th Regiment*, London, 1835

Calvo Perez, Juan Luis, *El Regimiento de Infanteria de Linea de Castropol*, Madrid, 1996

Cambon, Jean, *Jean-Pierre Maransin, Général de Division, Baron d'Empire, 1770–1828*, Tarbes, France, 1991

Cannon, Richard, 'Memorandum Relating to the Preservation of the Colour of the Third Regiment of Foot ... at the Battle of Albuhera', Horse Guards, London, 1 October 1841; the text was published on 24 November 1877 in *Notes and Queries*, Fifth Series, Vol. 8, July–December 1877, pp. 402–4

Cantlie, Neil, *A History of the Army Medical Department*, 2 vols., London, 1974

Carter, Thomas, *War Medals of the British Army and How They Were Won*, London, 1893

Carpue, Joseph C., *An Account of Two Successful Operations for Restoring a Lost Nose From the Integuments of the Forehead*, London, 1816, reprinted Birmingham, Alabama, 1981

Cienfuego Linares, Julio, *La Albuera – Memorial de la Batalla (16 Mayo 1811)*, Badajoz, Spain, 1992

Chaby, Claudio de, *Excerptos Historicos e Collecçâo de Documentos Relativos a Guerra Denominada da Peninsula – Parte Terceira: Guerra da Peninsular*, Lisbon, 1863

Challis, Lionel S., 'British Officers Serving in the Portuguese Army, 1809–1814', *Journal of the Society for Army Historical Research*, Vol. 27, 1949, pp. 50–60

Champion, B. W., 'James T. Morisset of the 48th Regiment', *Royal Australian Historical Society Journal and Proceedings*, Vol. XX, Part IV, 1934, pp. 209–26

Charrié, Pierre, 'Les Trophées de la Guerre d'Espagne 1807–1814', *Carnet de la Sabretache*, No. 79, 1985, pp. 95–100, and No. 81, 1985, pp. 5–10.

Chevillet, Jacques, *Ma Vie Militaire 1800–1810*, Paris, 1906

Clarke, ?, *The Georgian Era: Memoirs of the Most Eminent Persons, Who have Flourished in Great Britain, from the Accession of George the First ...*, 4 vols., London, 1832–4

Close, Edward Charles (Lieutenant, 2nd/48th Foot), *Diary of E. C. Close*, London, nd

Cobbold, Richard, *Mary Anne Wellington, the Soldier's Daughter, Wife and Widow*, 3 vols., London, 1846

Colborne, John (Lt. Col., 66th Foot), Letter to Rev. Duke Yonge, 18 May 1811, in Smith, *Life of Lord Seaton*, pp. 160–1

Colchester, Charles Abbot, *The Diary and Correspondence of Charles Abbott, Lord Colchester, Speaker of the House of Commons, 1802–1817*, 3 vols., London, 1861

Cole, Galbraith Lowry, *The Correspondence of Colonel Wade, Colonel Napier, Major General Sir H. Hardinge and General the Hon. Sir Lowry G. Cole, Relating to the Battle of Albuera*, London, 1841

——, (Maude Cole and Stephen Gwynn, eds), *Memoirs of Sir Lowry Cole*, London, 1934

Cole, John William, *Memoirs of British Generals Distinguished During the Peninsular War*, 2 vols., London, 1856

Combermere, Viscountess Mary & Knollys, W., *Memoirs and Correspondence of Field Marshal Viscount Combermere*, 2 vols., London, 1866

Conrady, G. von, *Leben und Wirken des ... Carl von Grolman*, 3 vols., Berlin 1894–6

Cooke, John, *Memoirs of the Late War, Comprising the Personal Narrative of Captain Cooke, of the 43rd Regiment Light Infantry*, 2 vols., London, 1831

Cooper, John Spencer (Sergeant, 7th Foot), *Rough Notes of Seven Campaigns*, London, 1869

Correia de Mello, José, Journal Excerpts, in Chaby, *Excerptos Historicos*, pp. 396–7

Creevey, Thomas, *The Creevey Papers*, 2 vols., London, 1903

Cross, Edward J., 'The British Soldier in the Peninsular War: The Acquisition of an Unjust Reputation', *Proceedings of the Annual Meeting of the Western Society for French History*, 1991, Vol. 18, pp. 243–51

Crossard, Baron, *Mémoires Militaires et Historiques*, 6 vols., Paris, 1827

Crompton, George (Lieutenant, 66th Foot), Letter to Mother, 18 May 1811, *Journal of the Society for Army Historical Research*, Vol. I, 1921–2, p. 130

Daly, Gavin, 'Napoleon's Lost Legions: French Prisoners of War in Britain 1803–1914', *History*, Vol. 89, no. 295, 2004, pp. 361–80

Daniell, D. Scott, *4th Hussars 1685–1958*, London, 1959

Davies, Huw, 'Secret Intelligence in the Peninsular War: The Case Study of El Bodon, 25 September 1811', *Archives: The Journal of the British Records Association*, Vol. XXXI, No. 112, 2005

Delavoye, A. M., *Life of Thomas Graham, Lord Lynedoch*, London, 1880

Dessirier, ? (ed.), *Historique de 34e Régiment d'Infanterie*, Mont-de-Maisan, France, 1894

D'Héralde, Jean Baptiste (Surgeon, 88th Line), *Mémoires d'un Chirurgien de la Grande Armée*, Paris, 2002

[Dickens, S. R.] (Lieutenant, 34th Foot), Letter to Unidentified Correspondent, 24 May 1811, *Report on the Manuscripts of the Late Reginald Rawdon Hastings, Esq., of the Manor House, Ashby de la Zouch*, London, 1934, Vol. 3, pp. 289–93

Dickson, Alexander, *The Dickson Manuscripts*, 5 vols., Woolwich 1908 (reprinted Cambridge 1987–91); Volume 3 deals with Albuera

——, Letter to Beresford, 25 July 1833, Ministério dos Negócios Estrangeiros, Caixa 208, Maço 168 (1), Arquivos Nacionais/Torre do Tombo, Lisbon

Dilley, James (Private, 40th Foot), Letter to his 'Honoured Parents', 5 November 1811, Archive Item No. W 1/5508, Bedfordshire Record Office, Bedfordshire, England

Dobbin, Robert Brown (Lieutenant, 66th Foot), Letter to Uncle, 23 May 1811, Regimental Archives of The Duke of Edinburgh's Royal Regiment, Salisbury, England

Drummond, Duncan (Sergeant, 66th Foot), Documents Concerning Duncan Drummond, Archive Item No. 2003-12-9:47, Drummond Papers, National Army Museum, London

Du Casse, Robert, *Le Volontaire de 1793; Général du Premier Empire – Jean-Baptiste Girard*, Paris, nd [1880]

Duncan, Francis, *History of the Royal Regiment of Artillery*, 2 vols., London, 1879

D'Urban, Benjamin (Portuguese Quartermaster-General), Memorandum for Colonel Colborne, 29 April 1811, Private Collection

——, Letter to H. Taylor, August 29, 1811, Private Collection; previously on loan as Archive Item No. 7805-46-143, NAM

——, *The Peninsular Journal of Major General Sir Benjamin D'Urban, 1808–1817*, London, 1930

——, *Report of the Operations in the Alemtejo and Spanish Estremadura, During the Campaign of 1811*, London, 1817, reprinted 1832

Dutton, Corporal (3rd Foot), 'Extract of a letter from Corporal Dutton', *Historical Manuscripts Commission Report on the Manuscripts of Reginald Rawdon Hastings*, London, 1934

Dutton, Geoffrey, *Founder of a City – The Life of Colonel William Light*, Adelaide, 1984

E. M., 'Albuera, etc.', *United Service Journal*, 1835, Part. 2, p. 536

Eeckhoudt, Guy Van, *Les Chevau-Légers Belges du Duc d'Arenberg*, Paris, 2002

Ellis, J. D., 'Drummers for the Devil? The Black Soldiers of the 29th (Worcestershire) Regiment of Foot, 1759–1843', *Journal of the Society for Army Historical Research*, Vol. 80, No. 323, Autumn 2002, pp. 186–201.

Emerson, J., 'Recollections of the Late War in Spain and Portugal', in W. H. Maxwell, *Peninsular Sketches*, Vol. 2, pp. 205–42.

Esdaile, Charles J., *The Peninsular War*, London, 2003

——, *The Spanish Army in the Peninsular War*, Manchester, 1988

Espinchal, Hippolyte d', *Souvenirs Militaires, 1792–1814*, 2 vols., Paris, 1901

Everard, H., *History of Thos. Farrington's Regiment Subsequently Designated the 29th (Worcestershire) Foot 1694 to 1891*, Worcester, 1891

[Farmer, George] (Private, 11th Light Dragoons), (G. R. Gleig, ed.), *The Light Dragoon*, London, 1850, reprinted, nd [2004]

Fitz-Clarence, George, *A Hussar's Life on Service in Four Letters*, London, nd

Fletcher, Ian, *Bloody Albuera: The 1811 Campaign in the Peninsula*, Ramsbury, UK, 2000

——, *Galloping at Everything – The British Cavalry in the Peninsular War and at Waterloo 1808–1815*, Staplehurst, Kent, 1999

Fortescue, John W., *A History of the British Army*, 20 vols., London, 1899–1930; Volume 8 (text) and Volume 8 (maps), 1917, deal with Albuera

——, *Following the Drum*, London, 1931

Fraser, Edward, *The Soldiers Whom Wellington Led – Deeds of Daring, Chivalry and Renown*, London, 1913

Fryer, Mary B., *'Our Young Soldier': Lieutenant Francis Simcoe, 6 June 1791 – 6 April 1812*, Toronto, 1996

Fyans, Foster, *Memoirs Recorded at Geelong, Victoria, Australia by Captain Foster Fyans (1790–1870)*, Geelong, 1986

Gazan, Honoré-Théodore-Maxime, Letter to Berthier, 19 May 1811, AF IV 1630, Plaq 1(111), Archives Nationales, Paris

Gell, Thomas (Captain, 29th Foot), Letter to Father [Philip Gell], 17 May 1811, Papers of the Gell Family of Hopton, Ms. D3287/28/20/1, Derbyshire Record Office, Derbyshire, England

Gil, Ferreira, *A Infantaria Portuguese na Guerra da Peninsula – Segunda Parte*, Lisbon, 1913

Gil, J., 'O Centenario d'Albuera', *Revista Militar*, 1911, pp. 210–22

Girard, Jean Baptiste (French General), Report to Marshal Soult, 16 May 1811, excerpted in Sainsbury, *The Napoleon Museum*, p. 481

Girault, Philippe-René, *Les Campagnes d'un Musicien d'État-Major Pendant la Republique et l'Empire 1791–1810*, Paris, 1901

Gleig, George Robert, *The Subaltern*, London, nd (Everyman's Library edition)

Glover, Michael, 'Beresford and His Fighting Cocks', *History Today*, Vol. XVIII, No. 4, April 1968, pp. 262–8

——, 'The Royal Welch Fusiliers at Albuera', *Journal Of the Society for Army Historical Research*, Vol. LXVI, No. 267, Autumn 1988, pp. 146–54

Gómez de Arteche y Moro, José, *Guerra de la Independencia – Historia Militar de España de 1808 á 1814*, 14 vols., Madrid, 1868–1903; Volume 10 deals with Albuera

Gómez Ruiz, Manuel, *El Ejército de los Borbones Pt. V – Reinado de Fernando VII*, Vol. 1, Madrid, 1999

Gordon, Arthur (Capt., 3rd Foot), 'Extract of a Letter from a Captain of the Buffs, who was wounded in the action at Albuera, to His Brother Officer in England, 20 May 1811', *The Star*, 8 June 1811, p. 4, col. 1

Gotteri, Nicole, *Le Maréchal Soult*, Paris 2000

——, (Jaques-Olivier Bourdon, ed.), 'L'Entourage Militaire du Maréchal Soult', *Armée, Guerre et Societé à l'Époque Napoléonienne*, Paris, 2004

Gougeat, Louis-Antoine (Trooper, 20th Dragoons), 'Mémoires d'un Cavalier d'Ordonnance de 20e Dragons (1804–1814)', *Carnet de la Sabretache*, Vol. 9, 1902, pp. 331–44 and 400–22.

Grattan, William, *Adventures with the Connaught Rangers 1809–1814*, London, 1902

Graves, Donald E., *Fix Bayonets! A Royal Welch Fusilier at War, 1796–1815*, Toronto, 2006

Green, John, *The Vicissitudes of a Soldier's Life*, London, 1827, reprinted Cambridge, England, 1996

Green, William (John and Dorothea Teague, eds.), *Where Duty Calls Me – The Experiences of William Green of Lutterworth in the Napoleonic Wars*, nl, 1975

Griffon de Pleineville, Natalie, 'Fighting for Napoleon: General Gazan de la Peyriere', *History Today*, 1 April 2003

Groves, J. Percy, *Some Notable Generals and Their Notable Battles*, London, nd

——, *The 66th Berkshire Regiment*, London, 1887

Gurney, Russell, *History of the Northamptonshire Regiment 1742–1934*, Aldershot, 1935

Guthrie, George J., *Commentaries on the Surgery of War in Portugal, Spain, France, and the Netherlands, From the Battle of Rolica, in 1808, to that of Waterloo, in 1815*, London, 1853

——, *On Gunshot Wounds of the Extremities*, London, 1815

Hall, C. D. (ed.), 'Albuera and Vittoria: Letters From Lieutenant Col. J. Hill', *Journal of the Society for Army Historical Research*, Vol. LXVI, No. 268, Winter 1988, pp. 193–8

Hall, John A., *The Biographical Dictionary of British Officers Killed and Wounded, 1808–1814*, London, 1998

Hall, Samuel C., *Retrospect of a Long Life*, New York, 1883

Halliday, Andrew, *Observations on the Present State of the Portuguese Army*, London, 1811

Hanger, George, *A Letter to the Right Hon. Lord Castlereagh*, London, 1808

Hansard, T. C., *Parliamentary Debates*, Vol. XX, 13 May–24 June 1811

Hardinge, Charles, Viscount, *Rulers of India – Viscount Hardinge*, Oxford, 1891

Harris, R. G., 'Two Military Miniatures', *Journal of the Society for Army Historical Research*, Vol. LXIII, No. 254, Summer 1985, pp. 99–103

Harrison, John (Lieutenant, 23rd Foot), Letter to Father, Lisbon, 22 June 1811, Royal Welch Fusiliers Archives, Caernarfon Castle, Gwynedd

——, Letter to Mother, Elvas, 18 May 1811, *ibid.*; reproduced in Glover, 'Royal Welch Fusiliers', pp. 146–7

——, Letter to Mother, Elvas, 24 May 1811, *ibid.*; reproduced in Glover, 'Royal Welch Fusiliers', pp. 149–54

Hartmann, Sir Julius von, 'Beitrage zur Geschichte des Krieges auf der Pyrenaischen Halbinsel in den Jahren 1809 bis 1813', *Hannoversches Militairisches Journal*, Vol. 2, 1831, pp. 91–126

Hartmann, Major von, *Der Königlich Hannoversche General Sir Julius von Hartmann – Eine Lebenskizze*, Hannover, 1858

Hay, Andrew Leith, *A Narrative of the Peninsular War*, London, 1830

Hayman, Peter, *Soult – Napoleon's Maligned Marshal*, London, 1990

Haythornthwaite, Philip, *The Armies of Wellington*, London, 1994

——, *Die Hard! Dramatic Actions from the Napoleonic Wars*, London, 1996

——, 'Henry Hardinge', *Military Illustrated*, No. 25, June 1990, pp. 49–50

Hill, John (Capt., 23rd Foot), Letter to Mother, 18 May 1811, Royal Welch Fusiliers Archives, Caernarfon Castle, Gwynedd; reproduced in C. D. Hall, 'Albuera and Vittoria', p. 193

Hill, John, Letter to Mother, 22 May 1811, *ibid.*; reproduced in Hall, 'Albuera and Vittoria', pp. 194–5

Hobhouse, Benjamin (Ensign, 57th Foot), Letter to 'My Dear Father', 17 May 1811, *The Times*, 25 February 1915, p. 9, col. B

Holme, Norman & Kirby, E. L., *Medal Rolls: 23rd Foot – Royal Welch Fusiliers, Napoleonic Period*, London, 1978

[Hope, James Archibald], *Military Memoirs of an Infantry Officer*, Edinburgh, 1833

Hope, John M. (Major, ADC to General Graham), Letter to General Sir John Hope, 29 May 1811, Hopetoun Papers, Vol. 177, pp. 55–62, Scottish Record Office, Edinburgh

Horward, Donald D., *Napoleon and Iberia: The Twin Sieges of Ciudad Rodrigo and Almeida, 1810*, Tallahassee, FL, 1984

Hugo, Abel, *France Militaire: Histoire Militaire des Armées Françaises de Terre et de Mer de 1792 à 1837*, 4 vols., Paris, 1838

Ingilby, Lieutenant, 'Diary of Lieutenant Ingilby, R.A., in the Peninsular War', *Minutes of Proceedings of the Royal Artillery Institution*, Vol. 20, 1893, p. 252.

Inglis, Lady, Manuscript History of the Services of Major General William Inglis, compiled by Lady Inglis 1828 (?), Archive Item No. 6504-52/33, Inglis Papers, NAM

Inglis, William, Letter to the Editor, *United Service Journal*, 1832, Part 2, pp. 241–2

J. L., 'Captain Gibbons of His Majesty's Thirty-Fourth Foot', *The Royal Military Chronicle*, April 1812, pp. 431–2

Jackson, Lady (ed.), *The Bath Archives – A Further Selection From the Diaries and Letters of Sir George Jackson, K.C.H., From 1809 to 1816*, 2 vols., London, 1873

James, John Haddy (Jane Vansittart, ed.), *Surgeon James's Journal 1815*, London, 1964

Jomini, Antoine (Ferdinand Lecomte, ed.), *Guerre d'Espagne Extrait des Souvenirs Inédit du Général Jomini (1808–1814)*, Paris, 1892

Jones, John T., *Journals of Sieges Carried on by the Army under the Duke of Wellington in Spain, During the Years 1811 to 1814*, 3 vols., London, 1846

Jones, Rice (British Engineer Officer), *An Engineer Officer Under Wellington in the Peninsula*, reprinted Cambridge, 1986

Juretschke, Hans, 'El Coronel von Schepeler – Caracter y Valor Informativo de su Obra Historiografica Sobre el Reinado de Fernando VII', *Revista de Estudios Politicos*, No. 126, 1962, pp. 229–49

Kelly, Jack, *Gunpowder*, New York, 2004

Kirkor, Stanislaw, *Legia Nadwislanska 1808–1814*, London, 1981

Knight, C. R. B., *Historical Records of the Buffs East Kent Regiment (3rd Foot) 1704–1914, Part 1: 1704–1814*, London, 1953

Kujawski, Marian, *Z Bojow Polskich w Wojnach Napoleonskich: Maida–Somosierra–Fuengirola–Albuera*, nl [London], 1967

Lacepéde, Count de, *État Général de la Légion d'Honneur*, 2 vols., Paris, 1814

Labadie, Jean-Yves, *Dictionnaire des Médaillés de Ste Hélène dans l'Eure*, Paris [2003]

Lamare, Jean-Baptiste (French Engineer Officer), *Relation des Sièges et Défenses d'Olivença, de Badajoz et de Campo-Mayor en 1811 et 1812*, Paris, 1837

Lamarque, Maximien, *Mémoires et Souvenirs du Général Maximien Lamarque*, 3 vols., Paris, 1835–6

Lamathière, Théophile, *Pantheon de la Légion d'Honneur*, 17 vols., 1875–1911

Landmann, George, *Recollections of My Military Life*, 2 vols., London, 1854

Lapène, Édouard (Artillery Officer, V Corps), *Conquête de l'Andalousie – Campagne de 1810 et 1811 dans le Midi de l'Espagne*, Paris, 1823

Latour-Maubourg, Count V. de, Report to Marshal Soult, Usagre, 27 May 1811, Add. Ms. 37425, ff. 65–9, British Library, London

Lauzun, Ph., 'Épisodes de la Guerre d'Espagne et de la Retraite de France (1809–1814) d'après de Nouvelles Lettres de Bory de Saint Vincent', *Revue de l'Agenais*, Vol. 37, 1910, pp. 421–557

Lavaux, François (Alfred Darmon, ed.), *Mémoires de François Lavaux, Sergent au 103e de Ligne (1793–1814)*, Paris. nd

Lemaitre, L., *Historique du 4e Régiment de Dragons (1672–1894)*, Paris, 1894

Leslie, Charles (Lieutenant, 29th Foot), *Military Journal of Colonel Leslie, K.H., of Balquhain*, Aberdeen, 1887

Leslie, J. H., 'Medals Which Were Awarded to Officers of the Royal Regiment of Artillery ... ', *Journal of the Royal Artillery*, Vol. LI, No. 6, pp. 403–9

L'Estrange, George B., *Recollections*, London, nd [1874]

Lievyns, A., *Fastes de la Légion d'Honneur – Biographie de tous les Décorés accompagnée de l'Histoire législative et réglementaire de l'Ordre*, 5 vols., Paris, 1842–7

Lillie, John Scott (Lieutenant, Lusitanian Legion), Letter to the Editor, *The Times*, 26 September 1856, p. 8, col. A

Lindau, Freidrich (Rifleman, 1st KGL Light Battalion), *Erinnerungen Eines Soldaten aus den Feldzügen der Königlich, Deutschen Legion*, Hameln, 1846

Lloyd, E. M., 'The Battle of Albuera', *Journal of the Royal United Service Institution*, Vol. 39, No. 21, Sept. 1895, pp. 903–11 plus map

Londonderry, Charles William Vane, Marquess of, *Narrative of the Peninsular War from 1808 to 1813*, 2 vols., London, 1829

Long, Charles Edward, *A Reply to the Misrepresentations and Aspersions on the Military Reputation of the Late Lieutenant General R. B. Long Contained in a Work Entitled 'Further Strictures ... ' Accompanied by Extracts From the Manuscript Journal and Private Correspondence of that Officer, and Corroborated by the Further Testimony of Living Witnesses*, London, 1832

——, *The Albuera Medal*, London, nd [1838]

——, *Letter to General Viscount Beresford, GCB in Reply to his Lordship's Letter to the Author Relative to the Conduct of the Late Lieutenant General R. B. Long in the Campaign of 1811*, London, 1833

——, *Reply to Lord Beresford's Second Letter to the Author Relative to the Campaign of 1811 and the Conduct of the Late Lieutenant General Long, then Commanding the Allied Cavalry*, London, 1835

Long, Robert Ballard, Letter to C. B. Long, 30 May 1811, printed in C. E. Long, *A Reply to ... a Work Entitled 'Further Strictures ... '*, London, 1832

——, Letter to Le Marchant, 5 June 1811, Le Marchant Papers, Packet 13a, Item 8, p. 4, Royal Military Academy, Sandhurst

Loureiro, José Jorgé, Letter to Father, 20 May 1811, *Revista Militar*, Vol. 55, 1903, pp. 364–6

Luz Soriano, Simão José da, *Historia da Guerra . . . em Portugal . . . desde 1777 até 1834 – Guerra de Peninsula*, Vol. 3: *(1809–1811)*, Lisbon, 1874

MacDonnell, Donald (Lt. Col., 11th Portuguese Regiment), Letter to his Cousin [Archibald MacDonald], 23 May 1811, Royal Welch Fusilier Archives, Caernarfon Castle, Gwynedd

Madden, Charles Dudley (Lieutenant 4th Dragoons), 'The Diary of Charles Dudley Madden, Lieutenant 4th Dragoons, Peninsular War 1809–1811', *Royal United Services Institution Journal*, Vol. 58, 1914, pp. 334–49 and 501–26.

Madden, George (Portuguese General), 'Narrative of the Operations of the 5th, or Spanish Estremaduran Army', *Royal Military Calendar*, 5 vols., London, 1820, Vol. 4, pp. 66–93.

——, Letter to D'Urban, 18 May 1811, Arquivos Nacionais/Torre do Tombo, Lisbon

Malaguti, Captain, *Historique du 87e Régiment d'Infanterie de Ligne (ex-12e Léger) 1690–1892*, Paris, 1892

Marmont, Marshal, *Mémoires du Maréchal Marmont, Duc de Raguse, de 1792 à 1814*, 9 vols., Paris, 1857

Marshal-Cornwall, James, *Marshal Masséna*, London, 1965

Martin, E., *Le 55e Régiment d'Infanterie*, Avignon, 1888

Martinien, A., *Tableaux par Corps et par Batailles des Officiers Tués et Blessés Pendant les Guerres de l'Empire (1805–1815)*, Paris, 1899, reprinted nl, nd [1980?]

——, *Tableaux par Corps et par Batailles des Officiers Tués et Blessés Pendant les Guerres de l'Empire (1805–1815) (Partie Supplementaire)*, Paris, 1909, reprinted San Diego, 2000

Masséna, André (General Koch, ed.), *Mémoires d'André Masséna, Duc de Rivoli, Prince d'Essling, Maréchal d'Empire*, 8 vols., reprinted Paris, 1966

Matthews, Elizabeth, Letter to Londonderry, 14 September 1828, in Appendix of Correspondence, in Londonderry, *Narrative*, Vol. 2, pp. 317–19

Maxwell, W. H. (ed.), *Peninsular Sketches by Actors on the Scene*, 2 vols., London, 1845

Maxwell, W. M., *Impending Dangers of England and Evils of our Naval and Military Organisation*, London, 1859

Mayne, Richard, *A Narrative of the Campaigns of the Loyal Lusitanian Legion*, London, 1812, reprinted Cambridge, 1986

McGuffie, T. H. (ed.), *Peninsular Cavalry General 1811–1813: The Correspondence of Lieutenant General Robert Ballard Long*, London, 1951

Menuau, Maurice L., *Historique du 14e Régiment de Dragons*, Paris, 1887

Message, Colin, 'Dying Hard – Military General Service Medals for the Battle of Albuera', *Medal News*, April 2000, pp. 26–7

Millevile, Henry J.-G. de, *Armorial Historique de la Noblesse de France*, Paris, 1845

Mills, John (Ian Fletcher, ed.), *For King and Country: The Letters and Diaries of John Mills, Coldstream Guards, 1811–1814*, Staplehurst, Kent, 1995

Moorsom, W. C., *History of the Fifty-Second Regiment 1755–1816*, London, 1860

Morillon, M., 'L'Artillerie de Montagne Sous le Premier Empire', *Soldats Napoléoniens*, No. 9, March 2006, pp. 27–36

Muir, Rory, *Tactics and the Experience of Battle in the Age of Napoleon*, New Haven, 1998

Mullen, A. L. T., *The Military General Service Roll 1793–1814*, London, 1990

[Murray, George] (Wellington's Quartermaster-General), Manuscript Account of the Battle of Albuera, Papers of Alexander Gordon, Ref. GD 364, Item 1216, Hope-Lufness Papers, Scottish Record Office, Edinburgh

——, Letter to Alexander Gordon, 22 May 1811, Item 1217, *Ibid.*

Murray, John (Surgeon, 66th Foot), Letter to his Father, Lisbon, 29 June 1811, Ms. RAMC 830, Wellcome Library, London

Myers, Sir William (Colonel, 23rd Foot), 'Life of Sir William Myers', *The Royal Military Chronicle*, October 1811, pp. 469–74

Nadaillac, Colonel de, 'Lettres et Notes du Sigismond de Pouget, Marquis de Nadaillac (1787–1837)', *Carnet de la Sabretache*, Vol. 19, 1911, p. 473

Napier, George (W. C. E. Napier, ed.), *The Early Military Life of General Sir George T. Napier K.C.B.*, London, 1886

Napier, William F. P., *A Letter to General Lord Viscount Beresford Being an Answer to his Lordship's Assumed Refutation of Colonel Napier's Justification of his Third Volume*, London, 1834

——, *Colonel Napier's Justification of his Third Volume; Forming a Sequel to his Reply to Various Opponents, and Containing Some New and Curious Facts Relative to the Battle of Albuera*, London, 1833

——, French Peninsular War Documents sent to Napier, Archive Item No. 6807/98, NAM

——, *History of the War in the Peninsula and in the South of France from the Year 1807 to the Year 1814*, 6 vols., London, 1828–40; Volume 3 deals with Albuera.

——, *The Life and Opinions of General Sir Charles James Napier G.C.B.*, London, 1857

Nafziger, George F., *The Armies of Spain and Portugal 1808–1814*, nl [privately printed], 1992

Napoléon 1, *The Confidential Correspondence of Napoleon Bonaparte with his Brother Joseph*, 2 vols., New York, 1856

Napoléon I, *Correspondance de Napoléon Ier (Publiée par l'ordre de l'Empereur Napoléon III)*, 32 vols., Paris, 1858–69

Nettleship, Andrew, *That Astonishing Infantry – A History of the 7th Foot (Royal Fusiliers) in the Peninsular War 1809–1814*, Chippenham, England, 1989

Norris, A. H. & Bremner, R. W., *The Lines of Torres Vedras*, Lisbon, 1980

Norton, John (Lieutenant, 34th Foot), *A List of Captain Norton's Projectiles, and His Other Naval and Military Inventions*, London, 1860

Nunes, J. Lucio, *As Brigadas da Cavalaria Portuguesa Na Guerra Peninsular*, Lisbon, 1954

Oatts, Lewis Balfour, *I Serve: A Regimental History of the 3rd Carabiniers (Prince of Wales's Dragoon Guards)*, Chester, 1966

Oleza, José de, *El Primer Conde de España, sus Proezas y su Asesinato*, Madrid, 1944

Oman, Sir Charles W., *A History of the Peninsular War*, 7 vols., Oxford, 1902–30; Volume 4, 1911, deals with Albuera

——, 'Albuera (A Lecture Delivered at the Royal Artillery Institution, Thursday, 7th January, 1909)', *The Journal of the Royal Artillery*, Vol. XXXVI, 1909–10, pp. 49–69.

——, 'Albuera Once More', *The Army Quarterly*, July 1932, pp. 337–42

——, *Studies in the Napoleonic Wars*, London, 1929

O'Meara, Barry, *Napoleon in Exile or, A Voice from St. Helena*, 2 vols., New York, 1853

Painvin, Achille Paul Arsène, *Historique de 51e Régiment d'Infanterie*, Paris, 1891

Pakenham, Edward (British Colonel), *Pakenham Letters, 1800–1815*, nl, 1914

Palmerston, Lord, *Return of the Names of the Officers in the Army, Who receive Pensions for the Loss of Limbs, or for Wounds*, London, 1818

Pattison, Frederick Hope, *Personal Recollections of the Waterloo Campaign*, Glasgow, 1873, reprinted 1992

Peacocke, Thomas (Capt., 23rd Portuguese Infantry), *Memoirs of Major General Thomas Peacocke*, Tours, 1855; microfilm copy at NAM

Pearse, Hugh W., *History of the 31st Foot, Huntingdonshire Regt., and 70th Foot, Surrey Regt., Subsequently the 1st and 2nd Battalions of the East Surrey Regiment*, 2 vols., London, 1916

Pearson, Andrew, *The Soldier Who Walked Away – Autobiography of Andrew Pearson, a Peninsular War Veteran*, London, 1987

Pelet, Jean Jacques, *The French Campaign in Portugal*, Minneapolis, MN, 1973

——, *Mémoires sur ma Campagne de Portugal (1810–1811)*, Paris, 2003

Pépin de Bonnerive, ?, 'Un Soldat de l'Empire: Le Général Pépin (1765–1811)', *Carnet de la Sabretache*, 1932, pp. 62–91, 189–217, 274–89 and 354–77.

Pernet, Captain Étienne (Capt., 5th Horse Artillery), 'Journal', in Rey & Remy, *Général Bourgeat*

Perrin-Solliers, ? (Sous-Lieutenant, 21st Light), [Review of *Examen Raisonné* by Okouneff] *Le Spectateur Militaire*, No. 13, 1832, pp. 353–78

Petiet, Auguste (ADC to Soult) (N. Gotteri, ed.), *Souvenirs Historiques, Militaires et Particuliers 1784–1815*, Paris, 1996

Philipps, Grismond (Lieutenant, 23rd Foot), 'Letters Home', *The Waterloo Journal*, Vol. 20, No. 2, August 1999, pp. 20–6.

Pigeard, Alain, *Les Étoiles de Napoléon*, Paris, 1996

Priego Lopez, Juan, *Guerra de la Independencia, 1808–1814: Volumen 6, La Campaña de 1811 (Primer Periodo)*, Madrid, 1992

Prieto Llovera, Patricio, *El Grande de España Capitán General Castaños, Primer Duque de Bailén y Primer Marques de Portugalete (1758–1852)*, Madrid, 1958

Quintin, Bernard and Danielle, *Dictionnaire des Colonels de Napoléon*, Paris, 1966

Regnault, Jean Charles Louis, 'Les Drapeaux anglais d'Albufera et de Berg-op-Zoom au Musée de l'Armée', *Revue de la Societé des Amis de la Musée de l'Armée*, No. 69, 1965, pp. 26–32

Rey, Jules & Remy, Emile, *Le Général Baron Bourgeat 1760–1827 d'après sa Correspondance et des Documents Inédits*, Grenoble, 1898

Robinson, Thomas Gerald, *Los Sitios de Badajoz y La Batalla de la Albuera*, Badajoz, nd

Ross-Lewin, Harry, *With the 'Thirty-Second' in the Peninsula*, Dublin, 1904

Roverea, Alexander de (Captain, ADC to General Cole), Letter to Father, (?) October 1811, in F. de Roverea, *Mémoires*, Vol. 4, pp. 27–45

Roverea, Ferdinand de, *Mémoires de F. de Roverea*, 4 vols., Paris, 1848

Sainsbury, John, *The Napoleon Museum*, London, 1845

Saint-Chamans, Alfred-Armand-Robert (ADC to Soult), *Mémoires du Général Comte de Saint-Chamans, Ancien Aide de Camp du Maréchal Soult 1802–1832*, Paris, 1896

Sañudo Bayón, Juan José, *La Albuera 1811 – Gloriosa Campo de Sufrimiento!*, Madrid, 2006

Scharnhorst. Gerhard von, *Uber die Wirkung des Feuergewehrs*, Berlin, 1813; translated by Bill Leeson as *Results of Artillery and Infantry Gun Trials*, Hemel Hempstead, UK, 1992

Schepeler, Andreas Daniel Berthold von (Spanish Staff Officer), *Histoire de la Révolution d'Espagne et de Portugal*, 5 vols., Liége, 1831

Scovell, George, Diary, Vol. 2 (1810–11), Public Records Office, WO 37/7(a), Kew

Severn, John Kenneth, *A Wellesley Affair – Richard Marquess Wellesley and the Conduct of Anglo-Spanish Diplomacy, 1809–1812*, Tallahassee, FL, 1981

Sherer, Moyle (Lieutenant, 34th Foot), 'Kit Wallace – A Recollection', *The Museum of Foreign Literature, Science and Art*, January 1829, pp. 7–9

——, *Recollections of the Peninsula*, London, 1824, reprinted 1996

Six, Georges, *Dictionnaire Biographique des Généraux at Amiraux Français de la Révolution et de l'Empire*, 2 vols., Paris, 1934

Smith, G. C. Moore, *The Life of John Colborne, Field Marshal Lord Seaton*, London, 1903

Smith, Harry, *The Autobiography of Lieutenant General Sir Harry Smith*, 2 vols., London, 1902

Smythies, R. H. Raymond, *Historical Records of the 40th (2nd Somersetshire) Regiment*, Devonport, 1894

Société d'Hommes de Lettres et de Militaires, *Les Fastes de la Gloire ou les Braves Recommandés à la Postérité*, 5 vols., Paris, 1817–22

Somerset, Fitzroy, Letter to Duke of Beaufort [his brother], 23 May 1811, Manuscript Fm M 4/1/6(13), Badminton Archives, Badminton, England

Sorando Muzás, Luis, 'The Trophies of Albuera', posted on www.napoleon-series.org.

Soriano, S. J. L. da, *Historia da Guerra Civil e do Estabelecimento do Governo Parlamentar em Portugal*, 15 vols., Lisbon, 1866–92

Soult, Jean de Dieu, Letter to Berthier, 4 June 1811, excerpted in Sainsbury, *The Napoleon Museum*, p. 483

——, (Louis & Antoinette de Saint-Pierre, eds.), *Mémoires du Maréchal Soult – Espagne et Portugal*, Paris, 1955

——, 'Rapport de S. Exc. Le maréchal duc de Dalmatie à S. A. S. le prince de Neufchâtel, major général', 21 May 1811, *Le Moniteur Universel*, [Paris] 13 June 1811; this report is reproduced in a number of other different sources including *Supplementary Despatches*, Vol. 13, pp. 651–3; an English translation appeared in *The Times*, 21 June 1811, p. 3, col. D

——, Statement on Solicited Promotions and Distinctions, 6 August 1811, excerpted in Sainsbury, *The Napoleon Museum*, p. 485

——, Unpublished Report to 'Prince de Wagram', 18 May 1811, File C8* 147*, pp. 196–203, SHAT, Château de Vincennes, Paris

Spain, Escuela Superior del Ejército, 'La Batalla de Albuera – Un Ejemplo de Coordinación Hispano-Portuguesa (16 de Mayo de 1811)', Conferencia Pronunciada en el Instituto de Altos Estudios Militares (Portugal), Lisbon, 1983

Spain, Sección de Historia Militar, *Estados de la Organización y Fuerza, de los Ejércitos Españoles Beligerantes en la Peninsula, Durante la Guerra de España Contra Bonaparte*, Barcelona, 1822

Squire, John (Captain, Royal Engineers), Letters, Add. Ms. 63106, ff. 28–40, British Library, London

Stampa Piñeiro, Leopold, 'La Batalla de Albuera, 16 de Mayo de 1811', *Dragona*, Vol. 3, No. 6, March 1995, pp. 45–9

Stanhope, Philip Henry, Earl, *Notes of Conversations with the Duke of Wellington, 1831–1851*, London, 1938

Stewart, General Sir Charles (Wellington's Adjutant-General), Letter to Unidentified Colonel, 22 May 1811, Letters of Lord Londonderry, Durham Records Office D/LO/C —18/62, Durham, England

——, Letter to Lord Londonderry, 30 May 1811, *ibid.*, D/LO/C —18/63

Stewart, Sir William, *Cumloden Papers*, Edinburgh, 1871

Swabey, Lieutenant, *Diary of Campaigns in the Peninsula for the Year 1811, 1812 and 1813*, London, 1895, reprinted Cambridge, 1984

Thompson, Mark S., *The Fatal Hill: The Allied Campaign under Beresford in Southern Spain in 1811*, Chapelgarth, England, 2002

Thoumas, Charles Antoine, *Les Grands Cavaliers du Premier Empire: Notices Biographiques*, 3 vols., Paris, 1890–1909

Titeux, Eugene, 'Le Général Dulong de Rosnay', *Carnet de la Sabretache*, 1901, pp. 3–15.

Tomkinson, William, *The Diary of a Cavalry Officer in the Peninsular War and Waterloo Campaign 1809–1815*, London, 1895

Tone, William Theobald Wolfe, 'Narrative of My Services and Campaigns in the French Army', Appendix – Part III to *Life of Theobald Wolfe Tone . . . Edited by his Son, William Theobald Wolfe Tone*, 2 Vols., Washington, D.C., 1826

Toreno, José M. Q. de L. R. de S. Count of, *Histoire de Soulèvement, de la Guerre et de la Révolution d'Espagne*, 4 vols., Paris, 1836; Volume 4 deals with Albuera

Unger, L.-A., *Histoire Critique des Exploits et Vicissitudes de la Cavalerie pendant les Guerres de la Révolution et de l'Empire*, Paris, 1848

Unger, William (Lieutenant, KGL Artillery), 'Description to the Plan of the Battle of Albuera . . . 24 May 1811', *Journal of the Royal Artillery*, Vol. XIII, 1885, pp. 126–7

Valynseele, Joseph, *Les Princes et Ducs du Premier Empire*, Paris, nd

Vere, Charles Broke (Assistant Quartermaster-General), *Marches, Movements, and Operations of the 4th Division of the Allied Army, in Spain and Portugal in the Years 1810, 1811 & 1812*, Ipswich, 1841

Verner, Willoughby, *History and Campaigns of the Rifle Brigade 1800–1813*, reprinted London, 1995

Vichness, Samuel E., 'Marshal of Portugal: The Military Career of William Carr Beresford, 1785–1814', Ph.D. dissertation, Florida State University, 1976

Vigo-Roussillon, François, *Grenadier de l'Empire*, Paris, 1981

Vigors, Desmond D., *The Hanoverian Guelphic Medal of 1815 – A Record of Hanoverian Bravery During the Napoleonic Wars*, privately printed, 1981

W. T., 'Battle of Albuera', *United Service Journal*, 1836, Part 3, pp. 401–2

Wachholtz, H. C. von, ed. 'Auf der Peninsula 1810 bis 1813. Kriegstagebuch des Generals Friedrich Ludwig v. Wachholtz', *Beihefte zum Militär-Wochenblatt*, 1907, pp. 259–326

Ward, S. G. P., 'The Portuguese Infantry Brigades, 1809–1814', *Journal of the Society for Army Historical Research*, Vol. LIII, No. 214, Summer 1975, pp. 103–12

——, 'The Quartermaster-General's Department in the Peninsula, 1809–1814', *Journal of the Society for Army Historical Research*, Vol. XXIII, 1945, pp. 133–54

Warre, H. J., *Historical Records of the Fifty-Seventh, or, West Middlesex Regiment of Foot*, London, 1878

Warre, William (Staff Officer, Portuguese Army), *Letters from the Peninsula*, London, 1909

Welford, Richard, *Men of Mark 'Twixt Tyne and Tweed*, London, 1895

Wellesley-Pole, William, Letter to Wellington, 16 June 1811, Wellington – Ms. Letter No. 114, Raglan Papers, Gwent County Record Office, Cwmbran, Wales

Wellington, Duke of (J. Gurwood, ed.), *The Dispatches of Field Marshal The Duke of Wellington During His Various Campaigns in India, Denmark, Portugal, Spain, The Low Countries and France*, 13 vols., London, 1838

——, *General Orders for Spain and Portugal*, 6 vols., London, 1809–14

——, *The General Orders of . . . Wellington . . . Compiled Alphabetically*, London, 1838

——, *Supplementary Despatches, Correspondence, and Memoranda of Field Marshal Arthur Duke of Wellington K.G.*, 15 vols., London, 1858–72

Westmoreland, John Fane, Earl of, *Correspondence of Lord Burghersh, afterwards eleventh Earl of Westmoreland, 1808–1840*, London, 1912

Wheeler, William, *The Letters of Private Wheeler*, Boston 1951

Whinyates, Edward C. (Lieutenant, Royal Horse Artillery), Letter to his Sisters, 30 May 1811, in F. Whinyates, *Whinyates Family Records*, Vol. 2, pp. 233–4

——, Letter to his Uncle, 20 and 22 May 1811, *Ibid.*, pp. 230–3

Whinyates, Frederick T. (Comp.), *Whinyates Family Records*, 3 vols., Cheltenham, England, 1894

Wilson, Sir James (Major, 1st/48th Foot), Manuscript Journal of Sir James Wilson 1810–1812, The Newberry Library, Chicago, Illinois

Wojciechowski, Kajetan (Lieutenant, Vistula Legion Lancers), *Pamietniki Moje W Hiszpanii*, reprinted Warsaw, 1978

Wood, Evelyn, *From Midshipman to Field Marshal*, 2 vols., New York 1906

Woods, William (Lieutenant, 2nd/48th Foot) (Timothy Cooke, ed.), 'A Second Prisoner of Albuera: A Letter from Lieutenant William Woods of the 48th Foot 29 May 1811', *The Waterloo Journal*, Vol. 26, No. 3, Winter 2004, pp. 3–10

Woolgar, C. M., 'Writing the Dispatch: Wellington and Official Communication', *Wellington Studies II*, Southampton, 1999, pp. 1–25

Woollwright, H. H., 'Albuera, 16th May 1811', *United Service Magazine*, Vol. 82, June 1911, pp. 306–18

——, *History of the Fifty-Seventh (West Middlesex) Regiment of Foot 1755–1881*, London, 1893

Wyld, James, *Maps and Plans, Showing the Principal Movements, Battles & Sieges in which the British Army was Engaged during the War from 1808 to 1814, in the Spanish Peninsula and the South of France*, London, [1840]; maps principally drawn by Thomas L. Mitchell

Index